Edited by John Lloyd and John Mitchinson

Art Direction by David Costa

ff

faber and faber

Other books from QI

The Book of General Ignorance
The Book of Animal Ignorance
Advanced Banter: The QI Book of Quotations
The Sound of General Ignorance
The QI Book of the Dead
The Second Book of General Ignorance
The QI H Annual

This omnibus first published in 2010
by Faber and Faber Limited
Bloomsbury House, 74–77 Great Russell Street, London, WC1B 3DA

Printed and bound in Great Britain by Butler, Tanner & Dennis, Frome, Somerset

A CIP record for this book
is available from the British Library

ISBN 978–0–571–27098–9

2 4 6 8 10 9 7 5 3 1

Escherichia coli (or *E. coli*) were discovered in 1885 by the German paediatrician and bacteriologist Theodor **Escherich** (1857–1911) and named a him in 1919. Human beings **excrete** between 100 billion and 10 trillion *E. coli* bacteria a day. Thomas Cowperthwait **Eakins** (1844–1916) is one America's few indisputably great painters. **Eckhart** von Hochheim, known as Meister **Eckhart**, was one of the greatest mystical Christian theologian all time. He was born in about 1260 and became a Dominican monk at **Erfurt**, the same town where Martin Luther, as a young university student, struck by lightning in 1505 and vowed to become a monk if he recovered. Francis Henry **Egerton**, 8th **Earl** of Bridgewater, gave dinner parties for d in Paris. He wore each pair of shoes only once, after which he arranged them in rows so that he could measure the passing of time. A short-sighted keen sportsman, he had the wings of all the partridges on his **estate** clipped so he could still shoot them. **Eccles cakes** are small, flat puff pastries of raisins, sometimes called 'dead fly pies'. They were first sold from James Birch's shop on the corner of Vicarage Road, **Eccles**, in 1793. 25% of Russian **economy** is owned by just 36 men. The annual income of the US shopping chain Wal-Mart is larger than that of three-quarters of the wor **economies**. J. G. Becanus (1518–1572) claimed that German was superior to all other languages, because it was the language spoken by Adam in Garden of **Eden**. The Swedish writer Andreas Kempe (1622–1689) asserted on the contrary that Adam in fact spoke Danish, God spoke Swedish and serpent spoke French. According to Persian legend, the serpent spoke Arabic (the most persuasive language in the world), Adam and Eve spoke Pers (the most poetic) and the Angel Gabriel spoke Turkish (the most menacing). The word *eden* is Hebrew for 'pleasure' or 'delight'. So The Garden of E literally means 'pleasure garden'. Some theological authorities believe that the Forbidden Fruit (which is not specifically named in the Bible) was in a banana. Michael Faraday, who invented the **electric motor** and the **electric generator**, learned to read and write but otherwise was not educate all. Benjamin Franklin left school at 10. George Stephenson, inventor of the passenger railway, did not learn to read and write until he was 20. He lear maths from doing his son's homework with him. The American astronomer **Edward Emerson Barnard** discovered Amalthea, one of Jupiter's innermost moons, in 1892. It was the first of Jupiter's moons found since Galileo's discovery of the original four in 1610, and the last moon in the s system to be discovered by direct visual observation. 'Duke' **Ellington's** real name was **Edward Kennedy Ellington** (1899–1974). **Edward Gibb** (1737–1794), author of *The History of the Decline and Fall of the Roman Empire* (1776–1788), was the **eldest** and only survivor of seven children: all rest died in infancy. Sickly and diminutive, he almost died more than once during his childhood. His mother neglected him and then died when he was and his aunt took care of him. With the onset of puberty at 14, his health suddenly took an inexplicable turn for the better and remained **excellent** the rest of his life, though he never became strong, tall or attractive, and in later life got extremely fat. Until the 1860s, gentlemen in **England** wal through woods and shot pheasants as they flew away. Thereafter, it was the **estate workers** who did the walking, driving the pheasants towards gentlemen, who stood still and shot them as they flew by. **Edwardian** shoots were so expensive that they caused the bankruptcies of Maharajah Dul Singh and Lord Walsingham. The 5th Lord Walsingham shot all the hummingbirds in London's Natural History Museum. **Eileen Regina Edwards** is be known as Shania Twain. She lives outside Montreux, Switzerland, in the manor of La Tour-de-Peliz and she is married to her producer, Mutt Lange. began singing in old people's homes at the age of 8. She was brought up by her stepfather, Jerry, an Ojibwa Indian with whom she went moose-hunt **Edwin Beard Budding** (1795–1846) of Stroud, Gloucestershire, invented the lawnmower (1831) and the adjustable spanner. **Eggplants** are among most popular vegetables in the world. Botanically speaking, however, they are fruits and are classified as berries. Turkey produces more **eggplants** t the whole of **Europe**. There are only seven basic smells, one of which is the smell of rotten **eggs**. The African **egg-eating snake** can swallow an twice as big as its own head. The largest **egg** relative to the size of the bird is a kiwi's. A kiwi's **egg** can be 20% of the mother's own weight. commonest **elbow injury** is lateral **epicondylitis**, or 'tennis elbow': it is not usually caused by playing tennis. The 'funny bone' is neither funny n bone. The unpleasant and peculiar sensation caused by banging your **elbow** comes from the ulnar nerve that runs around the tip of the **elbow**. The lar billed reed-warbler (*Acrocephalus orinus*) is the world's most **elusive** bird. For 140 years, just one specimen was known, collected in India in 1867 March 2007, another was found in a drawer at an outpost of the Natural History Museum in Tring, Hertfordshire, and the first known live example captu in Thailand. An **elver-cake** is a cake made from young eels. An **elvet** is a tiny **elf**. The *Dictionary* (1538) of Sir Thomas **Elyot** (c.1490–1546) was the f **English dictionary** to bear the name. **Elyot** also wrote *The Boke named the Gouvenour* (1531), *The Image of Gouvernance* (1540), *The Castel of H* (c.1536) and *The Doctrinall of Princis* (c.1533), translated from Isocrates. His translations popularised the classics in **English**. He was the ancestor of poet T. S. **Eliot**. **Emetophobia** is the irrational fear of vomiting. According to the International **Emetophobia Society**, it is the fifth most comr phobia. Googling 'fear of being sick' produces 29 million hits. An **emmet** is another name for an ant. The Wood Ant (*Formica rufa*) is sometimes kno as the Horse-**Emmet**. More than a third of Roman **Emperors** were assassinated. The **Emperor Augustus** wore platform shoes. For many years a his death, an unknown person placed flowers on the grave of the **Emperor Nero** on his birthday. The **Emperor Hadrian** was the first Roman emp to be bearded. Maximilian, a Hapsburg made **Emperor of Mexico** by Napoleon III, arrived in the country in 1862 knowing nothing about it, hav gained most of his information from a book on court **etiquette**. His wife **Empress Carlota** died insane in Belgium in 1927. The **emperor** himself v shot by firing squad in 1867. **Energy** is **everywhere** and **everything** is made of energy. Einstein's formula E=mc² states that matter is **energy** **energy** is matter. A tiny amount of matter is equivalent to an immense amount of **energy**. If 1 gram of matter could be totally converted into ener it would be enough to: lift 15 million people to the top of Mount **Everest**; boil 55 million gallons of water; or supply a town of 15,000 people v **electricity** for a year. If sound waves could be converted into **electricity**, 100,000,000,000,000,000 mosquito buzzes would be enough to powe reading lamp. The **English Civil War** killed a higher proportion of the British population than any other. In the seven years between 1642 and 1649 amazing one in 10 of the adult male population died: more than three times the proportion that died in World War One and five times the proporti that died in World War Two. The three letters E, T, and A account for well over a quarter of all letters used in **English**. A quarter of all words use **English** are the nine words: THE, OF, AND, TO, IT, YOU, BE, HAVE, WILL. **Entomology** is the study of insects. There are 900,000 known species, **estimates** of the number of unknown species range from 2 to 30 million. There are thought to be some 10 quintillion (10,000,000,000,000,000,0 individual insects alive at any one time. There may be as many as 200 million insects for every human on the planet, and the total weight of inse outweighs that of humans by 300 to 1. The **Ephori** were powerful magistrates at Sparta in ancient Greece. There were five of them, each serving one year, and they were equivalent to the tribunes of ancient Rome, created to defend civil liberties. They could both convene and dissolve the pop assemblies, including the Greater Assembly (the 9,000 citizens of the city of Sparta) and the Lesser Assembly (the 33,000 Lacedaemonians inhabi the outlying towns and villages). The **Ephori** had power over the kings and could imprison them if guilty of irregularities. In one of their most dracor judgements, according to Theophrastus, they fined King Archidamus for 'marrying a woman of short stature' – on the grounds that she would sup Sparta with kinglets not with kings. In due course, the couple did indeed give birth to the small, lame, but irrepressibly cheerful, brave and pop Agesilaus, who grew up to be a tiny little King of Sparta. An **erg** is a unit of **energy**. The word comes from the Greek *ergon*, 'work'. An **erg** is defi as the amount of **energy** needed to move 1 gram through 1 cm with an acceleration of 1 cm per second per second. This is approximately the amo of energy used when a mosquito takes off, a flea hops, or a single human nerve cell fires. If the **entire population of the world** queued at the bott of the nearest **escalator**, they would all reach the top in less than four days. There are no **escalators** in Uganda. Ludovic Lazarus Zamen (1859–1917) devised **Esperanto**. While at first sight **Esperanto** looks a bit like Central **European gobbledegook** from some long-forgotten P Ustinov comedy, in fact it is beguilingly neat, clever and simple. For an **English-speaker**, **Esperanto** is reckoned to be five times as easy to learn Spanish or French, 10 times as easy as Russian and 20 times as easy as Arabic or Chinese. More or less anyone can learn to speak it in about an h **Esperanto** is probably the only language in the world with no irregular verbs: French, by comparison, has 2,238; Spanish and German about 700 ea The first film to be made entirely in **Esperanto** was *Incubus* (1965) starring William Shatner. A duck wishing to be understood in **Esperanto** would h to say 'gik-gak'. There are about 15,000 living Old **Etonians**, 18 of whom have been Prime Minister of Great Britain and one of whom has been Pr Minister of Northern Ireland. Fictional old **Etonians** include James Bond, Captain Hook, Tarzan, Bertie Wooster, John Steed from *The Avengers* Darcy from *Bridget Jones's Diary*. James Hogg (1770–1835), aka **The Ettrick Shepherd**, was a poet and novelist and friend of Sir Walter Scott. B at **Ettrick Hall**, at the top of the **Ettrick Valley**, he left school after six months and started work as a cowherd aged seven. His maternal grandfat Will O'Phaup, was said to have been the last man to converse with the fairies. The word **Eucharist** (the sacrament of the Lord's Supper or Commun means 'thanksgiving'. It comes from the ancient Greek *eucharistia*, as does the modern Greek word for 'thank you', *efcharistó*. Horses have **eyebrows**: except in the animated film *Spirit: Stallion of the Cimarron* from DreamWorks SKG. Animators couldn't get the facial **expressions** r without adding them to the faces of Spirit, his girlfriend Rain and other horses in the movie. Dinosaurs had no **eyelashes**: only mammals have which includes **eyelashes**. Birds, reptiles and fish don't have **eyelashes** either. The **escapologist** Harry Houdini could pick up pins with his **eyelash**

elongate

SQUEEZE

ELECTRICITY

eye

EARWIG

peel

EDISON

EVAPORATION

helix

EJECT

ETUDE

escape

EBB

ELEGANT

EDIFICE

bumblebee

EGG

EARTH BRA

EMPTY

enroll

effervescence

eel

ENCOMPASSING

EDIBLE

elevate

& pea

POWER

EXPERIMENT

elastic

Erotica

KEY "EFFORT"

E·C·C·L·E·S·I·A·S·T·I·C·A·L

First published in 2007
by Faber and Faber Limited
3 Queen Square London WC1N 3AU

Printed in the United Kingdom by Butler Tanner and Dennis Ltd

A CIP record for this book
is available from the British Library

ISBN 978–0–571–23779–1

2 4 6 8 10 9 7 5 3 1

This book
belongs to:

....

'E'

*e*dit

Edited by John Lloyd

Art Direction by David Costa

ff

faber and faber

Stephen here!

Ee, ye be reet well and cheerly greeted, deer reeder t't letter E. The clever elves tell me, the endless need...

No, no, no. This just isn't going to work. I had planned to write an introduction containing only our hero letter, 'E', but aside from the level of difficulty, I suddenly realised, with a stab of wonder and joy, that I couldn't be sedding, beggering ersed.

For a nation, many of whom who grew up on the *Blue Peter Annual*, the arrival of the *QI Annual* must surely be a cause of nothing but rapture and enchantment of the highest, giddiest kind. If we are to enter a new Age of Annuals then perhaps all is not quite lost with our vulgar, etiolated and degraded culture? V-necked and sandalled, lying on our tummies, felt-pens or wax crayons at the ready, we leaf through the big pages not daring to take everything in at once, for the pleasures and secret corners of each page must be saved to the end like the fruity veins of a raspberry ripple. Hurrah for annuals, hurrah for puzzles and facts and drawings. Hurrah for... oh Lord, I think I've polluted myself.

Look, the point is that this is sent to you in love and friendship from all at QI, who have no higher aim, and no lower, than to please.

QI – changing the world one letter at a time.

Stephen Fry.

A message from the Editor

Hi there Fact Nuts,

Welcome to the QI 'E' Annual!

We think this one is even better than the 'A', 'B', 'C' and 'D' Annuals. You may have missed those. We certainly did.

Most people felt they were a bit on the 'blank' side – or 'non-existent', as one bookworm put it.

Hopefully, we have put all that to rights in this super E edition. It's packed with E-type information – plus, there are cartoons, games and quizzes; loads of articles by your favourite QI celebs; and a chance to win £1,000 in cash!

We hope this will be the first of many QI Annuals, so please write to us and tell us what you think – what you liked and what you didn't like – so that we can make it even better next year. And let us know which letter is your favourite: 'R' perhaps, or maybe 'Y'.

Mr Fry's QI Elves are online round-the-clock, slaving away in the QI nugget mines on your behalf. Drop in for a chinwag at www.qi.com/E

See you there! Your chum,

'JumpingJack' Lloyd

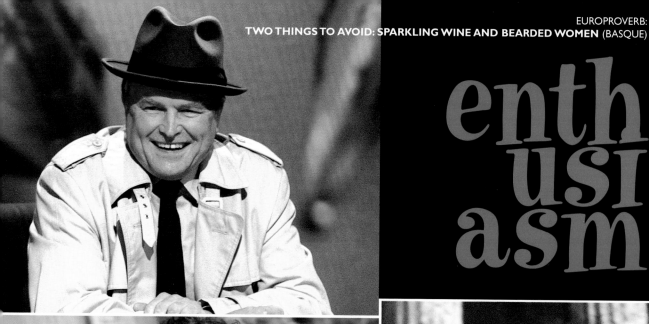

enth
usi
asm

Eric comes from the Old Norse name *Eirikr*, meaning 'ever ruler'. Notorious Viking **ERIC BLOODAXE** was the son of the far more genteel sounding King Harold Finehair of Norway. Bloodaxe was referred to in one Latin text as *Fratris Interfector*, or 'brother killer'. He is thought to have earned his gory nickname not through the everyday axework associated with rape and pillage, but rather by having craftily murdered anything up to nineteen of his own blood brothers in order to guarantee his succession to the throne.

The world's wealthiest Eric is **ERIC SCHMIDT**, chairman and CEO of Google Inc. In 2007 'Forbes' magazine ranked him the 116th richest man in the world, with an estimated $6.2 billion. He is also a director of Apple Inc.

Another Viking, **ERIC THE RED,** took his name from his ginger hair, and not from the mists that often enveloped him. His boisterous behaviour saw him evicted first from Norway, then from Iceland. Ironically, Eric the Red is credited with discovering Greenland, which he named after the colour of the vegetation thereon, as opposed to the colour of his beard. Eric the Red was the father of Leifr Eiriksson, the first European to have landed in North America (as opposed to Leif Erickson the American actor who played Big John Cannon in the popular 1960s televison series *The High Chaparral*).

ERICS
through the ages

Throughout history people called Eric have played a major role in shaping the world in which we live. Here is just a small selection of exceptional yet often unsung Erics.

The 1930s truly were the 'golden age' of Erics in English football. Only four Erics have ever worn the famous Three Lions jersey, and three of them did so during that decade. One was **ERIC BROOK** of Manchester City, whose goals helped England win the 1934 World Cup. Having declined an invitation to compete in that year's competition (on the grounds that they would win it too easily) the English FA then challenged the eventual winners, Italy, to an 'unofficial' final at Highbury stadium. The game became known as the Battle of Highbury. The Italians were up for it, Mussolini having promised every player an Alfa Romeo sports car if they beat England. The shit hit the fan in the second minute when the Italian centre-half was stretchered off with a broken leg, and the game rapidly descended into a brawl. England won 3-2, thanks to Eric Brook, who ended the game with a brace of goals, plus a broken arm for his troubles.

English sculptor **ERIC GILL** created the iconic Gill Sans typeface in 1928. For many years it was the standard type used on all Penguin book jackets, as well as on railway signs and posters. Gill also designed postage stamps for the Royal Coronation in 1937. His erotic engraving 'Eve', featuring a naked bird and a snake, is regarded by many as his most important work. Gill was obsessed with the erotic, often requiring life models to perform sex while he sculpted. He was also a big fan of cocks. One of his lesser known works, 'Studies of Parts', is a sketch book containing dozens of detailed drawings of male members belonging to himself and his friends. For all his artistic ability, Gill appears to have been, even by modern-day standards, a raving pervert. His diaries reveal that he had regular sex with his sister Gladys, he sodomised his daughters, and according to his own notes, on December 8th 1929 he successfully concluded a sexual experiment with his dog.

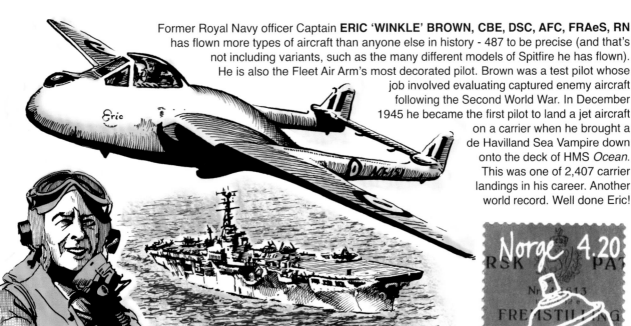

Former Royal Navy officer Captain **ERIC 'WINKLE' BROWN, CBE, DSC, AFC, FRAeS, RN** has flown more types of aircraft than anyone else in history - 487 to be precise (and that's not including variants, such as the many different models of Spitfire he has flown). He is also the Fleet Air Arm's most decorated pilot. Brown was a test pilot whose job involved evaluating captured enemy aircraft following the Second World War. In December 1945 he became the first pilot to land a jet aircraft on a carrier when he brought a de Havilland Sea Vampire down onto the deck of HMS *Ocean*. This was one of 2,407 carrier landings in his career. Another world record. Well done Eric!

Bingo boss **ERIC MORLEY** was the man who put the glitterballs into British TV. The Dunkirk veteran kicked-off his kitsch campaign in 1949 when he launched *Come Dancing*, and two years later he brought the infamous Miss World TV beauty pageant into our living rooms. Morley also stood as Tory candidate for Dulwich in the 1979 general election. When the results were announced (in reverse order of course), Eric had lost by a mere 122 votes. That was one rare occasion when Morley declined to kiss the winner.

Thanks to spray paint, colourfully applying your name to the side of a train or a subway wall only takes seconds. But if it wasn't for Norwegian **ERIC ROTHEIM** young graffiti artists would be labouring away for hours with tins of paint and a brush. Scientist Eric patented his design for the first aerosol spray can in 1928. And in 1998, Norway, a nation not over-burdened with national heroes, issued a special postage stamp to celebrate their ingenious Eric's achievement.

The man responsible for Big Brother was an Eric. In George Orwell's novel, Big Brother was the dictator of a totalitarian state in which the entire population was under constant surveillance. The book's title was to have been *1980*, and then *1982*, but its publication was delayed due to Orwell's poor health. When it was eventually published in 1949 it was called *1984*. Orwell was not the author's original name either. It was the pen name chosen by **ERIC ARTHUR BLAIR**. Eric chose his new moniker from a shortlist of four, the runners-up being being Kenneth Miles, H. Lewis Allways and P.S. Burton. Orwell died from tuberculosis in January 1949, shortly after the book was published. And so, mercifully, he never got to see the television series his classic work inspired.

His moustache may not be familiar to you, but actor **ERIC THOMPSON**'s voice would be. When asked to narrate an English translation of the French TV series *Le Manège Enchanté*, Eric ignored the original scripts. Instead he watched the French programmes without the soundtrack, then made up his own stories to match the action. Thus *The Magic Round-about* was born. A *Playschool* presenter in the 1960s, Eric was an accomplished thespian but seldom performed on TV. One of his rare television drama appearances came in 1966 when he played a Huguenot in a Dalek-free episode of *Dr Who* set in 16th-century Paris. Sadly Eric died in 1982. Actresses Emma and Sophie Thompson are his daughters.

German-born psychologist, psycho-analyst and philosopher **ERICH FROMM** used the biblical story of Adam and Eve as an allegorical explanation for human biological evolution and existential angst. He is associated with the Frankfurt School of critical theory. Eric's best-selling book *The Art of Loving*, published in 1956, should not be confused with *The Art of Loving* by Salgado Herrera, published in 1998, which is a glorified Spanish jazz mag featuring lots of dirty pictures.

EIGHT

There are eight protons in an oxygen atom; eight pinches in
a teaspoon; eight quavers in a note; and eighty-eight notes on a piano.
Wagner said that the first eight notes of 'Rule Britannia' summed up the whole of
the British character. Eight days is the amount of time needed to get used to glasses that
turn the images on your retina upside down. When you take them off, it takes less than eight
hours for everything to return to normal. The Irish playwright Brendan Behan became an alcoholic at
the age of eight. On her eighth birthday, Shirley Temple got 135,000 birthday presents. Eight was the
average age for choirboys to be castrated in 17th-century Italy. Unsupported breasts move in a figure-of-
eight motion when running. Both male and female ferrets have eight nipples. Quolls are carnivorous marsupials
native to Australia and Papua New Guinea that copulate continuously for eight hours. The first of the world's first
surviving octuplets was born in Houston, Texas, on December 8th, 1998. The rest were born by Caesarean section
on December 20th. The amount of cloud in the sky is measured in oktas. Eight oktas means the sky is totally
overcast. In 2001, the Ministry of Defence spent £260 million on eight Chinook helicopters. They couldn't be flown
because the MOD didn't have the software codes, and the US wouldn't release them for security purposes. The
House of Commons Public Accounts Committee described the purchase as 'one of the worst acquisitions' it had
ever seen. Cows are descended from extinct wild oxen called aurochs, a word that is both singular and plural.
An aurochs bull stood eight feet tall. In *The Gallic Wars*, Julius Caesar described it as only slightly smaller
than an elephant. The last recorded aurochs was killed in a Polish forest in 1627. The Spanish dollar or
peso was common currency in the US well into the 19th century. It was often cut into eight pieces
for small change – hence the term 'pieces of eight'. Two-eighths make a quarter, so a quarter
dollar (25 cents) is known as 'two bits'. There are eight bits in a byte; eight furlongs in a
mile; eight tablespoons in a gill and eight fluid ounces in a cup. There are eight
Lords a-leaping. Coca-Cola was invented in 1888. In the first eight
months of his new business, John Stith Pemberton
managed to sell less than half a dozen drinks a
day, despite the fact that he claimed it would cure morphine
addiction, indigestion, headache, neurasthenia and impotence. On his death
in Atlanta, Georgia, later the same year, no Coca-Cola at all was sold throughout the
city as a mark of respect. According to the Harvard Education School, there are eight kinds of
intelligence: Linguistic, Logical, Musical, Bodily, Spatial, Interpersonal, Intrapersonal and Naturalist.
Charles Darwin spent eight years studying barnacles before he wrote *The Origin of the Species*. The poet
Samuel Taylor Coleridge went for eight years without seeing his children. The philosopher Kierkegaard studied
theology at university for eight years without ever taking an exam. In 1890, Frenchman Clément Ader achieved the first
powered take-off in a steam-powered aircraft. It reached an altitude of eight inches. Italian anatomist Gabriello Fallopio,
after whom Fallopian tubes are named, designed a condom made from linen that was tied on with a pink ribbon. It was eight
inches long. Leeches and Hercules beetles can both grow to eight inches long. Mammoths' penises were eight inches in
diameter. The Republic of Maldives is in the *Guinness Book of Records* as The World's Flattest Country. There are more than
thousand islands in the Republic, 80% of which are less than a metre above sea level and none of which attains a height of m
than eight feet. Eight is a lucky number in Japanese. Toyota is named after the company's founder, Sakichi Toyoda, who chang
his name to Toyota because in Japanese it is written in eight characters. The first box of Crayola (sold for 5 cents in 1903) ha
the same eight colours found in the box today: red, blue, yellow, green, violet, orange, black and brown. The 1960s cartoo
superhero 'The Eighth Man' increased his strength by smoking cigarettes. The average Greek smokes eight cigarettes a day.
Octopus is Greek for eight feet. The giant Brazilian otter can be eight feet long. Britons use eight billion plastic bags a year.
In the 11th century there were eight vineyards in Essex. Sweden was a good place to be eight in 1994. At the beginning
of the year, there were 112,521 eight-year-old girls; by the end of the year, every single one of them was still alive.
Eight US publishers rejected George Orwell's *Animal Farm*. One of them kindly explained: 'We are not doing
animal books this year.' According to the World Conservation Union, one in eight bird species is at risk of
extinction. The last execution in the Tower of London took place on Thursday, August 14th, 1941,
when Josef Jakobs, a German spy, was shot by an eight-man firing squad. Subatomic
particles are classified by means of the Eightfold Way. The way to enlightenment is
via the eight steps of Buddhism's Noble Eightfold Path. An eight on its
side represents infinity and there are

888 words on this page.

NINE 'E' THINGS THAT COME IN BATCHES OF NINE

1. EXTRA TERRESTRIALS The first flying saucers were a group of nine unidentified objects spotted by travelling salesman Kenneth Arnold from his private plane on June 24th, 1947. He described them as moving at 1,200 mph like 'pie plates skipping over the water'. A newspaper coined the phrase 'flying saucer' and within weeks there were hundreds of such sightings. The likeliest explanation is that they were a mirage, the reflection of the nine snow-capped peaks of the Cascade Mountains in Washington, some sixty miles away. **2. ELMS** Nine Elms in Vauxhall, London, is home to New Covent Garden Market, the capital's wholesale fruit and veg hub, relocated in 1974 from Covent Garden, where it had stood for more than 400 years. Battersea Power Station and Battersea Dogs Home are also in Nine Elms. To be 'battersea'd' was 18th-century slang for being treated for venereal disease. Herbs used to cure the condition were sold in Battersea Market. *3. ELLICE ISLANDS* The South Pacific island group formerly known as the Ellice Islands comprises the world's fourth smallest country, now known as Tuvalu. The name means 'cluster of eight' in Tuvaluan though there are actually nine islands. Eight of these – Nanumaga, Niutao, Nanumea, Nukulaelae, Nui, Nukufetau, Vaitupu and Funafuti – have lagoons in the middle. The ninth and most southerly island – Niulakita – only has a swamp. Nobody lives there so it's not counted. **4. ECUADOREAN VOLCANOES** Nine volcanoes surround Quito, the capital of Ecuador, which lies in the Avenue of Volcanoes, a 325 km valley between two massive ranges of the Andes. In Ecuador as a whole, there are 39 volcanoes, including Chimborazo (the world's highest inactive volcano) and Cotopaxi (the world's highest active one) but since records began with the Spanish invasion in 1534, only nine of them have erupted. The famous Galapagos Islands, an offshore province of Ecuador, are themselves the tops of huge underwater volcanoes. *5. EVILS* In Bhutan, The Meeting of Nine Evils, or Ngenpa Guzom, is a public holiday. The Bhutanese believe nothing good can be achieved on this day. There is no merit in performing good deeds, and bad deeds produce really bad karma, so people minimise the risk by doing as little as they conceivably can. They stay indoors, if possible, eating and drinking. If they do go out, they never travel anywhere, but may indulge in a little light archery – Bhutan's national sport. In Dante's The Divine Comedy there were nine levels of Hell. **6. EGYPTIAN AND ETRUSCAN GODS** The nine main gods of ancient Egypt were known as the Ennead, Greek for nine. Nun (water) had always existed. Then Atum (the sun) condensed out of the mist and sneezed, giving birth to Shu (air) and Tefnut (moisture). Tefnut and Shu gave birth to Geb (earth) and Nut (sky). The Etruscans (forerunners of the Romans) also had nine gods – Juno, Minerva, Tinia, Vulcan, Mars, Saturn, Hercules, Summanus and Vedius, immortalised in Macaulay's poem 'Horatius' (1842): 'Lars Porsena of Clusium, by the nine gods he swore...' *7. ENDINGS* On the death of a pope, the cardinals celebrate a series of funeral masses for nine days. They are known as the 'Novemdiales.' The Aztecs believed that there were nine stages of the afterlife. Thomas Edison's favourite piece of poetry was the ninth verse of Thomas Gray's 'Elegy in a Country Churchyard'. He would recite it all the time: 'The boast of heraldry, the pomp of power, And all that beauty, all that wealth e'er gave, Awaits alike the inevitable hour: The paths of glory lead but to the grave.' **8. ENIGMA VARIATIONS** Edward Elgar's *Enigma Variations* are said each to relate to how one of his friends would have played the music. The ninth, and perhaps most famous, variation, is called 'Nimrod', after the Old Testament patriarch described in the Bible as 'a mighty hunter'. It was named punningly for Elgar's best friend Augustus J. Jaeger, whose surname means 'hunter' in German. 'Nimrod' is always played at the Cenotaph in London on Remembrance Sunday. *9. EXTRAS* The largest egg ever laid was by the extinct Great Elephant Bird (Aepyornis maximus). It had a volume of nine litres, equivalent to 15 dozen hen's eggs. Bodhidharma, the founder of Zen Buddhism, found enlightenment by sitting facing a wall on Mount Songshan in northern China for nine years. E999 is an extract from the bark of a South American tree. It is used as a foaming agent in ginger beer and cream soda, and by Andean Indians as cough mixture because it softens phlegm.

QI ANNUAL PUZZLE PAGE

1. Stare at the cross in the middle for about fifteen seconds, without looking away. Then, while continuing to stare at the cross, move your head towards and away from the page.

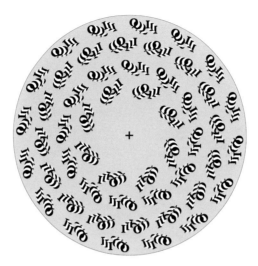

2. Stare at the three dots in the middle of this image for a full thirty seconds – don't let your eyes wander. Then look away at a bright surface, and keep watching for ten seconds. Don't worry – the ghostly image should go away sometime before you try to go to sleep...

3. Stare at the white dot in the middle of the first image for thirty seconds. No cheating or looking away. After the full thirty seconds, quickly move your focus to the same white dot in the middle of the second, black-and-white picture. It appears colourful until you move your focus even slightly.

eleven elevens

I've dealt with numbers all my life, of course, and after a while you begin to feel that each number has a personality of its own… Eleven is tough, an outdoorsman who likes tramping through woods and scaling mountains.

PAUL AUSTER
'The Music of Chance'

11 comes from the Old English word *endleofan*, which means 'one left'. When counting manually, it's what's left once you've used up all your fingers and thumbs. Twelve comes from *twelf*, meaning 'two left'. If the Inuit need to count to more than eleven, they have to do it in Danish.

11 is the maximum number of times you can fold a piece of paper – not seven as popular wisdom has it. This was nailed early in 2007 by a team from the US TV show *Mythbusters*. They used a NASA hangar to make up a huge single sheet by sticking 17 rolls of paper together – the final dimensions were 170 x 220 feet. This was folded and folded, until it got stuck at 11 folds.

11+2 and 'eleven plus two' are both anagrams of 12 + 1 and 'twelve plus one'.

It's **11** million years since the relatives of the Laotian stone rat (*Laonastes aenigmamus* or 'enigmatic stone-dwelling mouse') wandered the earth. A specimen discovered hanging in a Laotian butchers in 1996 was subsequently confirmed, not only as a new species but the only living member of a rodent family that had been assumed extinct for aeons. The stone rat is easily mistaken for a grey squirrel, except for its limp tail and waddling, duck-like walk.

The German for **11** is *Elf*. So, in German-speaking Austria, ELF – the French brand of petrol – is called is ELAN. *Elan* is French for 'elk'.

Plovdiv, the second city of Bulgaria, has been renamed **11** times. The city has existed for 9,000 years, making it as old as Troy – and older than Athens or Rome. Its first name, whose origin is lost in the mists of history, was Kendros. The Thracians renamed it Eumolpias. It then became Philippopolis (Greek); Pulpudeva (Thracian again); Trimontium (Roman); Ulpia Thrimonzium (Roman again); Pulden, Populdin, Ploudin (all Slavic); and Filibe (Turkish). It finally became Plovdiv after Bulgaria gained independence from Turkey in 1878. After which, the mainly Muslim population was subject to brutal ethnic cleansing. The remaining few, like the city itself, had to take Slavic names.

The deepest patch of sea is the Marianas Trench in the Pacific, off the coast of Guam. It is **11** kilometres (6.8 miles) deep. A coin dropped into it would take more than an hour to reach the bottom.

11 days were lost when the Gregorian calendar was introduced into Britain in 1752. People went to bed on September 2nd and woke up on September 14th. This caused havoc. Contracts (and people's wages) were due to start on days that no longer existed.

General Antonio López de Santa Ana was President of Mexico **11** times between 1833 and 1855, during which he managed to lose more than half of the country's territory. Vain, corrupt and ruthless, he styled himself the 'Napoleon of the West', 'President for Life' and 'Serene Highness'. But he was a shrewd political operator and a great showman. In 1842, he had the leg he'd lost in a battle four years earlier dug up and paraded around Mexico City before mounting it in a shrine as testament to his heroism and courage.

Marilyn Monroe didn't have **11** toes. The rumour stems from a single photo taken on a beach in 1946 when she was still Norma Jean Dougherty. The 'extra toe' was just a lump of wet sand sticking to her foot. The photographer, Joseph Jasgur, invented the story as a publicity ruse for his 1991 book *The Birth of Marilyn: The Lost Photographs of Norma Jean*. He had noticed the 'extra toe' while preparing the original proofs over 40 years.

THE FIRST WORLD WAR ENDED AT THE **11TH** HOUR ON THE **11TH** DAY OF THE **11TH** MONTH OF 1918. NUMEROLOGISTS BELIEVE THAT EVENTS OCCUR AT **11:11** MORE REGULARLY THAN THEY SHOULD BY CHANCE ALONE. SINCE 9/11, THEY'VE BEEN WORKING OVERTIME. THE TWIN TOWERS FORMED AN '**11**' AND TOOK **11** YEARS TO BUILD; THE FIRST PLANE TO HIT WAS FLIGHT **11**; 9+1+1 = **11**; AND 'GEORGE W BUSH', 'MOHAMMED ATTA', 'NEW YORK CITY', 'THE PENTAGON' AND 'WAR DECLARED' ARE EACH FORMED FROM **11** LETTERS.

Spooky eh? But then, the same goes for Jesus Christ, Harry Potter and Bart Simpson.

ENGLAND

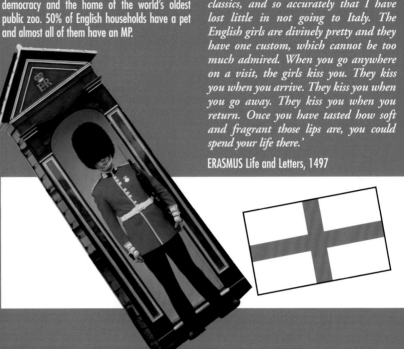

'There are many things in life more worthwhile than money. One is to be brought up in this our England, which is still the envy of less happy lands.'

LORD DENNING Observer, 1968

England is about the same size as New York State – 74 times smaller than the USA, 59 times smaller than Australia and 3 times smaller than Japan. More than 83% of the people in the UK live in England, where the population density is 4 times that of France and more than 10 times that of the USA. More languages are spoken in England than in any other country in Europe. Over 300 different languages are spoken by London schoolchildren. From 1066 to 1362, the official language of England was French. England and Wales have the worst crime rate in the Western world. Every year, about 100 children in England and Wales are killed by their parents. The English consume a third of the world's tea exports. They drink more TEA than anyone else in the world: 2 ½ times as much as the Japanese and 22 times as much as the Americans or French. England is the world's oldest parliamentary democracy and the home of the world's oldest public zoo. 50% of English households have a pet and almost all of them have an MP.

'The air is soft and delicious. The men are sensible and intelligent. Many of them are learned. They know their classics, and so accurately that I have lost little in not going to Italy. The English girls are divinely pretty and they have one custom, which cannot be too much admired. When you go anywhere on a visit, the girls kiss you. They kiss you when you arrive. They kiss you when you go away. They kiss you when you return. Once you have tasted how soft and fragrant those lips are, you could spend your life there.'

ERASMUS Life and Letters, 1497

ECUADOR

Ecuador is the world's largest exporter of bananas, the world's largest exporter of the anti-malarial drug quinine and the world's largest source of balsa wood for model aircraft. Its next most important exports are oil, cut flowers and prawns. Panama hats all come from Ecuador. They were originally produced for export to workers on the Panama Canal. A good Panama hat can be rolled up, passed through a napkin ring and then reshaped perfectly, but locals turn their noses up at them, saying they are only for gringos: they prefer the classier Montecristo hat. Ecuador means 'equator' in Spanish. Ecuador's highest mountain, Chimborazo, was for a long time mistakenly believed to be the highest mountain in the Andes, which is strange, because at least 20 Andean peaks are taller.

On the other hand, because of the country's geographical position, even the beaches of Ecuador are further from the centre of the earth than the top of Mount Everest. Ecuador was originally called Quito, the name of its capital, the oldest in South America and the world's cheapest city to live in. It is said to have the best climate in the world. Quito is Spanish for 'I'm going' but it's actually named after the local Quitu indians.

Quito's proper name is San Francisco. Its full title is Villa de San Francisco de Quito ('the town of St Francis in Quito'). The state airline of Ecuador is called TAME. There are at least 1,500 different species of bird in Ecuador, including the oilbird, the world's only nocturnal fruit-eating bird, once melted down by the natives to make cooking oil. Over a million people in Ecuador speak Quechua, the language of the Incas, from which we get the words alpaca, coca, condor, guano, jerky, llama, pampas, puma and vicuna. George Lucas used it as the basis for Huttese, the language of Jabba the Hutt in Return of the Jedi.

EL SALVADOR

El Salvador is Spanish for 'The Saviour' and is named after Jesus Christ. It is the smallest country in Central America. It's also the most densely populated country on the mainland of either North or South America.

The most famous son of El Salvador was the Roman Catholic Archbishop Óscar Romero (1917–1980), revered locally as 'San Romero', the country's unofficial patron saint. In 1980, he spoke out in a sermon against the government, calling on soldiers to disobey orders that violated basic human rights.

Moments later, he was assassinated at the altar, his blood spilling into the communion wine. El Salvador's longest-serving president was General Maximiliano Hernández Martínez (1882–1966), the first of many such military men. He clung to power for 13 years. A keen spiritualist, he liked to say, 'It is a greater crime to kill an ant than a man,' on the grounds that human beings are reincarnated but an ant dies forever. No doubt he felt this justified massacring 40,000 peasants in an anti-Communist purge in 1932. Although an admirer of Hitler, he joined the Allies in World War Two and saved 40,000 Hungarian Jews by issuing passports to make them Salvadorean citizens. This meant they were not legal enemies of the Third Reich, entitling them to protection by the International Red Cross. El Salvador was the only country in the world to do this and never received (nor asked for) anything in return. Martinez was ousted from power in 1994, by which time Hungary had more Salvadorean citizens than all their other foreign nationals combined, though hardly any of them spoke Spanish or could point out El Salvador on a map. It is also the only Latin American nation to have sent troops into Iraq since the US-led invasion of 2003. At home, though, politics are more complicated. In the 1984 elections, a US $10 million computerised register was used – the old one had to be scrapped after it was found to contain 92,000 errors.

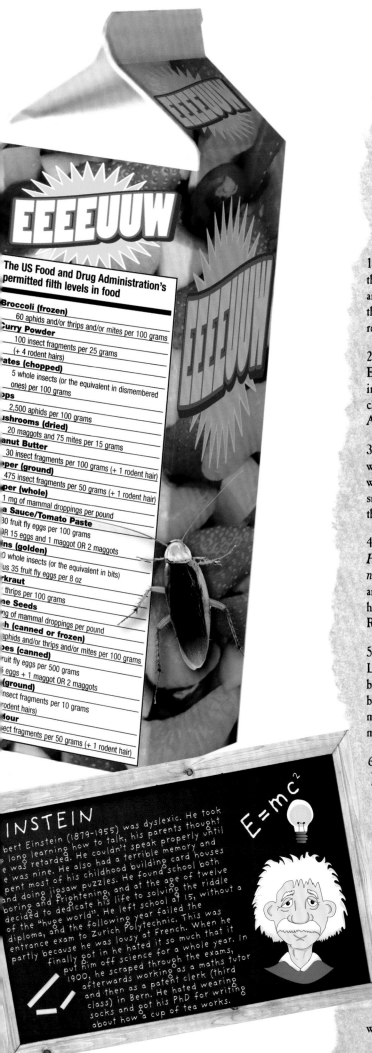

EEEEUUW

The US Food and Drug Administration's permitted filth levels in food

Broccoli (frozen)
  60 aphids and/or thrips and/or mites per 100 grams
Curry Powder
  100 insect fragments per 25 grams
  (+ 4 rodent hairs)
...ates (chopped)
  5 whole insects (or the equivalent in dismembered
  ...ones) per 100 grams
...ps
  2,500 aphids per 100 grams
...shrooms (dried)
  20 maggots and 75 mites per 15 grams
...anut Butter
  30 insect fragments per 100 grams (+ 1 rodent hair)
...per (ground)
  475 insect fragments per 50 grams (+ 1 rodent hair)
...per (whole)
  1 mg of mammal droppings per pound
...a Sauce/Tomato Paste
  ...30 fruit fly eggs per 100 grams
  OR 15 eggs and 1 maggot OR 2 maggots
...ins (golden)
  ...0 whole insects (or the equivalent in bits)
  ...us 35 fruit fly eggs per 8 oz
...rkraut
  ...thrips per 100 grams
...ne Seeds
  ...ng of mammal droppings per pound
...h (canned or frozen)
  ...aphids and/or thrips and/or mites per 100 grams
...es (canned)
  ...ruit fly eggs per 500 grams
  ...5 eggs + 1 maggot OR 2 maggots
...(ground)
  ...nsect fragments per 10 grams
  ...rodent hairs)
...lour
  ...ect fragments per 50 grams (+ 1 rodent hair)

EINSTEIN

...bert Einstein (1879–1955) was dyslexic. He took
...o long learning how to talk, his parents thought
...e was retarded. He couldn't speak properly until
...e was nine. He also had a terrible memory and
...pent most of his childhood building card houses
...and doing jigsaw puzzles. He found school both
...boring and frightening, and at the age of twelve
...decided to dedicate his life to solving the riddle
...of the "huge world". He left school at 15, without a
...diploma, and the following year failed the
...entrance exam to Zurich Polytechnic. This was
...partly because he was lousy at French. When he
...finally got in he hated it so much that it
...put him off science for a whole year. In
...1900, he scraped through the exams,
...afterwards working as a maths tutor
...and then as a patent clerk (third
...class) in Bern. He hated wearing
...socks and got his PhD for writing
...about how a cup of tea works.

$E = mc^2$

PIECES OF EIGHT
— OR —
A Pirate's Life For Me
BY CAPT^N VIC REEVES

1. When Julius Caesar was captured by pirates, he treated them with utter contempt, told them to double his ransom and swore he would crucify them when they let him go. They thought he was joking. A few days after his release, he returned and kept his promise.

2. The pirate William Dampier (1652–1715) was the first European to see a kangaroo. He introduced many new words into English, including avocado, breadfruit, caress, cashew, chopsticks, petrel, posse, snug and barbecue (from the Arawak Indian word, *barbacoa*).

3. The French version of *barbacoa* was *boucan*, from which we get the word 'buccaneer'. French settlers on Hispaniola were called *boucaniers* because they lived by hunting and smoking pigs – until the Spaniards drove them out and forced them to take up piracy.

4. The Jolly Roger is first mentioned in *A General History of the Robberies and Murders of the most notorious Pyrates* (1724). It didn't always carry a skull and crossbones – Blackbeard's had a skeleton and a bleeding heart. Even more feared than the Jolly Roger was the 'Bloody Red', which signified that no life would be spared.

5. Most supposed pirate terms are pure fiction. Robert Louis Stevenson's *Treasure Island* (1883) introduced the black spot, the pirate map (with X marks the spot) and buried treasure. Even walking the plank seems to have been a myth: the only recorded case happened in 1829, well after most piracy had ceased.

6. Pirates didn't go 'Arrr!' Robert Newton, who played Long John Silver in the 1950 film of *Treasure Island*, started it. It wasn't even in the script, although 'avast', 'shiver my timbers!', 'yo-ho-ho' and 'matey' were.

7. The unique rongorongo script of Easter Island was the only written language to have existed in the whole of the Pacific before the 20th century. Only the island's chiefs could read it. In 1862, they were all kidnapped by Peruvian pirates and perished in Chilean guano mines, along with a third of the island's population and, of course, the language.

8. Blackbeard (Bristol-born Edward Teach) 'liked to put cannon fuses in his hair and beard and light them so that he looked like the devil'. The Chinese female pirate Ching Shih commanded 70,000 buccaneers on over 400 ships. But the most ruthless pirate of all was the Frenchman François l'Ollonais (see over).

Bill Bailey's Embarrassingly Named Composers

THE BLESSED ST NOTKER BABULUS ('ST NOTKER THE IDIOT') WAS A SWISS MONK WHO WAS ONE OF THE PIONEERS OF THE GREGORIAN CHANT AND A FRIEND OF THE HOLY ROMAN EMPEROR CHARLES THE FAT, KNOWN IN GERMAN BY THE EVEN MORE EMBARRASSING NAME OF KARL DER DICKE.

Notker was born in about AD 840 and died on April 6th 912. He stuttered so much that the other monks named him Babulus ('The Stammerer'). Rather embarrassingly, this also means 'fool' in Latin. By way of apology, Pope Julius made him a saint 900 years after his death.

V. G. BACKFART (1507–1576) was born in Transylvania. Mrs and Mrs Backfart doubtless toyed with naming their son 'Very Good', but settled on Valentinus Graevius for obvious reasons. Backfart was a Polish-Hungarian composer who tried to wriggle out of his name by variously spelling it Bakfart, Bakfark, Bakfare, Backfarckh and Bekwark. He died of the plague in Padua in 1576.

PHILIP GREELEY CLAPP (1888–1954). The American composer Clapp was strongly influenced by Muck. Dr Karl Muck was conductor of the Boston Symphony Orchestra. Probably too embarrassed to carry on, he allowed Clapp to have a go.

ANDREAS CRAPPIUS (1542–1623). The talented son of Johannes Krapp, he disguised his name by translating it into Latin. His uncle Philipp (1497–1560) also changed his name – from Schwarzerd (the faintly lavatorial 'Black-soil') to its Greek equivalent, Melanchthon.

DR WILLIAM CROTCH (1775–1847) started playing with his father's organ at the age of two. His painting *View From Hurley Bottom* (1806, on paper) is in the Tate Gallery. He penned 'Lo, star-led chiefs Assyrian odours bring'. Theorists pore over his 'Experiment in Motivic Saturation'. There is a picture of him wearing a dress in the National Portrait Gallery.* He was a musical genius who played before the King and Queen at Buckingham Palace at 4, was Organist of Christ Church at 15, Oxford Professor of Music at 22 and the first President of the Royal Academy of Music (1822–1832). He wrote the chimes of Big Ben. (The original 'hour bell' is named after Benjamin Caunt, a 17-stone boxer. It weighed nearly 17 tonnes. The present one weighs 13 tonnes and has an 11-inch crack.)

STOTEN

FERENC FARKAS (1905–2000) was a distinguished Hungarian composer whose works include 60 songs under the collective title 'Play Up, Gipsy!'

J.J. FUX (1160–1741). Born into an obscure peasant family, Johann Joseph Fux rose to become Music Director at the Imperial Court of Emperor Leopold I, the highest musical position in Europe.
This meant that absolutely everybody knew his name. To make matters worse, Austria issued a Fux postage stamp in 1985.

An embarrassing composer   *Aged 3.

BRIAN HAVERGAL (1876–1972) lived to be 96, and wrote 32 symphonies.

THOMAS-ANTOINE KUNTZ (1756–1830) invented the orchestrion, a forerunner of the harmonium, in 1791. He was born Thomas Anton Kunz, but cleverly altered his name slightly so that no one would find it childishly amusing.

LUIGI NONO (1924–1990). The Italian Marxist composer Luigi Nono struggled on with the name he was born with, despite the fact that it allowed music critics to review every example of his work as 'another Nono'. Not known for easy listening, he set *The Communist Manifesto* and Viet Cong press releases to music and married Schoenberg's daughter Nuria. It's a pity he never wrote a nonet (a piece for nine players). If he had, it would have been known as a Nono Nonet.

HEINRICH POOS (1928–) is a contemporary German composer of Dutch descent. The name Poos is not embarrassing. It's Dutch for 'interval'.

EDMUND RUBBRA (1901–1986) was a working-class Buddhist from Northampton who was taught music by Gustav Holst. During the Second World War he formed a piano trio with two other spelling mistakes, Norbert Brainin and William Pleeth. He wrote 162 works, including 11 symphonies.

PETER SCHAT (1935–2003) of Utrecht was subject to the unwelcome attentions of Professor Fokker. Schat was an avant-garde composer. Fokker had a low opinion of his work, or Schit, as he called it. Stop tittering at the back, there. Schat is Dutch for 'sweetie-pie'.

LUDVIG THEODORE SCHYTTE (1848–1909). The Danish composer Schytte was born in Aarhus. He wrote '24 Little Fantasies'.

VLADISLAV SHOOT (1941–) narrowly avoided having an embarrassing name by being born in Vosnesensk in the Ukraine. He studied composition at the Gnesin Institute in Moscow and was music editor of *Sovetsky Kompositor* (1967–82). He now lives in Devon.

The composer and violinist JOSEPH SUK (1874–1935) was both the pupil and the son-in-law of Dvořák.

ANTON TITZ (1742–1810) was a German violinist and composer resident in Russia.

The Austrian composer HERBERT WILLI (b.1946) plays the Fagott.**

This is a faggott

You may also be unfamiliar with the oeuvres of ELSE AAS, JIRI BENDA, ROBERTA BITGOOD, LEO BLECH, DICK BOLKS, BENEDICTUS BUNS (1642–1716), POMPEYO CAMPS, ELI COFF, JEAN CRASS, ERIC FUNK, JESTER HAIRSTON, OSWALD JOOS, CYRILLIUS KREEK, CONRAD MAXIMILIEN KUNZ, JOHANN LICKL, WOUTER PAAP, GIUSEPPE MARIA PO, NICOLAS PONCE, HERMAN PYS, SAMUEL SCHEIDT, CORNELIUS SCHUYT, TIBOR SERLY, FERNANDO SOR and JOHANNES WORP.

Pronunciation guide: Fux is pronounced Fooks; Kuntz and Kunz as Koonts; Suk is Sook. Manuel and Juan Ponce, being Spanish, are both pronounced Ponthay; Jose Pons, a Spaniard in Italy, is Ponz; the Swiss-Dutch composer Luctor Ponse (b.1914) is (tee hee) Ponce.

**It's not what you think. Fagott is German for bassoon.*

Two young composers with names so embarrassing they can't be mentioned

EUROPEAN LANGUAGES
No. 1: Turkish

The Turkish language can be conveniently (if fruitlessly) laid out in the following manner:

1. Turkish words that look like English but mean something entirely different

arse	violin bow
bap	chapter
basin	the press
batman	thrust (as in a jet engine)
bay	gentleman
ben	I, myself. Also, a mole or beauty spot
bender	commercial port
berk	hard, firm, solid, strong, rugged
bet	face. Also, bad, ugly
bilge	learned, wise
bin	thousand; son of
bint	daughter; girl
bit	louse
bite	bollard
biz	we
bot	dinghy
bum	bang
fart	talking nonsense
zip	suddenly
zip!	pop!
zit	the opposite

2. Turkish words that look quite like English but mean something entirely different

bastarda	flagship
bok	shit
cok	many
erk	power, energy
kunt	thick
zonk zonk zonk	throbbing

3. Turkish words that look like Belgian but mean something entirely different

belge	document

4. Turkish words that look like a Belgian speaking English but aren't

zat	person, essence, substance, individual
zem	blame

5. Very Turkish-sounding Turkish words

zamazingo	mistress
zamir	inner consciousness
zulmen	cruelty

6. Concepts uniquely expressible in a single word in Turkish

bender	a fortress controlling the sea
bibi	a paternal aunt
bidik	short and plump
bingil bingil	quivering like a jelly (i.e. enormously fat)
bizbiz	a left-hand drumstick
sule	the blue part of a candle flame
yakmoez	the effect of moonlight sparkling on water
zebella	a huge, thickset man
zibidi	weirdly dressed
zilli	with bells on
zula	a secret store for smugglers or thieves

7. Colourful idiomatic Turkish phrases

zemzem kuyusana isemek
to do something revolting just to get famous. Literally, 'to seek glory by urinating in the sacred well of Mecca'

EIGHTEENTH-CENTURY CRIMINALS

The criminal classes in 18th-century England produced a vast array of specialist rogues.

RUFFLERS
WERE ARMED ROBBERS DISGUISED AS OUT-OF-WORK SOLDIERS.

PRIGGERS
WERE EITHER MEMBERS OF A THREE-MAN SHOPLIFTING TEAM OR HORSE-THIEVES.

SWADDLERS
NOT ONLY STOLE FROM THEIR VICTIMS BUT BEAT THEM UP AS WELL,
SOMETIMES MURDERING THEM INTO THE BARGAIN.

SWIG-MEN
COVERED THEIR ROGUERY BY PRETENDING TO BE ITINERANT HABERDASHERS.

STROWLERS
WERE CON MEN WHO CONVINCED COUNTRY GENTLEMEN TO 'LEND' THEM MONEY
SO THEY COULD GO TO LONDON.

DOMMERERS
WERE BEGGARS POSING AS ESCAPED SLAVES WHO HAD HAD THEIR TONGUES CUT OUT BY THE TURKS
FOR REFUSING TO ACCEPT ISLAM.

GLIMMERERS
WERE WOMEN WHO WENT AROUND IN FLOODS OF TEARS CLAIMING THAT THEIR HOUSES HAD BEEN BURNED DOWN.
ALTERNATIVELY, THEY SET OTHER PEOPLE'S HOUSES ON FIRE, IN ORDER TO LOOT THEM IN THE CONFUSION.

BAWDY-BASKETS
WERE WOMEN POSING AS SELLERS OF PINS AND NEEDLES OR PORNOGRAPHIC BOOKS TO DISGUISE THEIR REAL GAME,
WHICH WAS STEALING LINEN CLOTHES OFF HEDGES.

BULLY-HUFFS
HUNG ROUND BROTHELS, SURPRISING AND THREATENING THE CUSTOMERS BY CLAIMING
THAT THE WOMAN THEY WERE IN BED WITH WAS THEIR WIFE. IN BETWEEN TIMES, THEY INTERCEPTED LUCKY GAMBLERS
AS THEY LEFT THE CASINO TO RELIEVE THEM OF THEIR WINNINGS.

BUFFER-NABBERS
WERE PROFESSIONAL DOG-THIEVES WHO KILLED THE ANIMAL TO SELL ITS SKIN.

RUM-BUBBERS
SPECIALISED IN STEALING SILVER TANKARDS FROM TAVERNS
(not to be confused with rum-dubbers, who were run-of-the-mill lock-pickers).

BUNG-NIPPERS
STOLE THE GOLD BUTTONS FROM CLOAKS AND THE SILVER TASSELS FROM HATBANDS.

MUMPERS
WERE GENTEEL BEGGARS.

CLAPPERDOGEONS
WERE PROFESSIONAL VAGABONDS, VARLETS WHO WORE PATCHED CLOAKS AND THREE HATS, ONE ON TOP OF THE OTHER.

TATMONGERS
WERE CARD-SHARPS.

Exclusive Clubs of the Eighteenth Century

1. Name: The Farting Club, Cripplegate
Members: Flatulent
Activities: Meeting once a week 'to poison the neighbourhood, and with their noisy crepitations attempt to outfart one another'.

2. Name: The Everlasting Club
Members: Bores
Activities: Sitting in a drinking session for twenty-four hours a day, 'no person presuming to rise until he was relieved by his appointed successor'.

3. Name: The Humdrum Club
Members: 'Gentlemen of peaceable dispositions'
Activities: 'Meet at a tavern, smoke pipes and say nothing till midnight'.

4. Name: The Surly Club, Billingsgate
Members: Tradesmen
Activities: 'To sharpen the practice of contradiction and of foul language'.

5. Name: Beefsteak Club
Members: Politicians and wits
Activities: 'Devoted to drinking and wit interspersed with snatches of song and much personal abuse'.
(Rivals: The Sublime Society of Steaks)

6. Name: Kit-Kat Club, Shire Lane
Members: Leading Whigs
Activities: Toasting beautiful women and eating pies.

7. Name: Twopenny Club
Members: Poor men
Activities: 'If any neighbour swears or curses, his neighbour may give him a kick upon the shin'.

8. Name: The No-Nose Club
Members: Unknown
Activities: Unknown.

9. Name: The Club of Broken Shopkeepers, Southwark
Members: Bankrupts
Activities: Cheap drinking.

10. Name: The Man-Killing Club, St Clement Danes
Members: Anonymous
Activities: Membership barred to anyone 'who had not killed his man'.

11. Name: The Mock Heroes Club
Members: Fantasists
Activities: 'Each member would assume the name of a defunct hero'.

12. Name: The Lying Club, Westminster
Members: Wags
Activities: 'Members were banned from uttering any true word'.

13. Name: The Golden Fleece
Members: Amusing drunks
Activities: Inventing names such as Sir Boozy Prate-All, Sir Whore-Hunter and Sir Ollie-Mollie.

DARA O'BRIAIN'S EIRE

AS IRISH AMBASSADOR TO QI, here's a golden opportunity to bore you senseless with some stuff about our Nobel Laureates. We get them so often I'm tempted to bang this piece through the spell-checker and send it to Stockholm just in case it's my turn. Four for Literature alone: Britain, with 15 times the population, only has six. We've even won a couple of Peace Prizes, which is quality since it was our war in the first place.

We've not won for Medicine, mind you – the forgotten Nobel, I always feel, especially in pub quizzes, much like Aston Villa winning the European Cup – despite some quite astonishing contributions to the world of health.

Irish Pioneers of Medicine, I salute you!

Typhoid Mary – *Now wash your hands*

Born Mary Mallon in Ireland in September 1869, and moving to New York at 15, The Typher was a domestic cook with a poor head for spotting co-incidences. **'Wow,'** she would never say, **'All these people have caught typhoid! That's just what happened in my last five jobs! I really am unlucky in my choice of employers. Better get that CV out again.'** Over the course of her career she managed to infect 53 people with typhoid, all but the first batch of whom should probably have been a bit more thorough on the old **'And why did you leave your last job?'** question.

Her first job lasted only two weeks before typhoid struck. Her next gig led to fevers, diarrhoea and the laundress dying. She then went to work for a lawyer and gave seven of the eight members of the household the disease. Moving to a job in Long Island, within the fortnight, six more were laid up. Three more households were to become infected before fingers finally began to point.

And did she not like being accused of spreading disease! Jesus, she did not. She got quite tetchy about it. Even when she had been written up in the *Journal of the American Medical Association* she still wouldn't play ball. After all, she hadn't ever even had typhoid!

Mary had not suffered herself as she was an 'asymptomatic' carrier of the disease, possibly from before birth, and this all occurred during that awkward time in history, before we knew what an asymptomatic carrier of a disease is, and how they should be quarantined, but after the time where we happily burned people for being witches just because their last five jobs ended in houses filled with wheezing, dying people. And either of those solutions would have been better from a public health viewpoint than just sending Madge back to the temping agency for another go.

She was sent into compulsory quarantine twice; the second time for life. Which seems harsh, but she was only released from the first quarantine under strict instructions that she never work with food again. Our heroine then changed her name to Mary Brown and got a job in New York's Sloan Hospital, working in (surprise, surprise) the kitchens. Man, that Mary just loves to cook. 25 more people were infected.

She lived out the rest of her days on North Brother Island on the East River and became something of a celebrity at the time, regularly interviewed by journalists. These days she'd probably bring out a celebrity diet cookbook and get sworn at by Gordon Ramsay.

She died of pneumonia in 1938, and an autopsy found typhoid bacteria in her gallbladder. They cremated her. Twice, probably.

Burke and Hare – *If I said you had a beautiful body, would you sell it to me for £15?*

The history of effective medicine is surprisingly short. Only 300 years ago it was still blood-letting, leeches and homeopathy. Luckily, none of that nonsense remains today.

Surgeons began as barbers (this is the reason qualified surgeons are still called Mr rather than Dr in deference to their lowly beginnings)

and medicine only started coming on in leaps and bounds when they stopped thinking it was all about imbalances in your bile and phlegm and started cutting people up and having a look. But where to get the bodies? Well, if it's 1827 and you're Edinburgh anatomist Prof. Robert Knox you naturally pay two Irish lads when they turn up at your doorstep with the corpse of a man who owed one of them £4 rent. And you don't ask questions, neither. You just hand over £7 and start slicing. For Burke and Hare this was a clear £3 profit. And in such moments are great entrepreneurs born.

The following 11 months led to 16 further instances of supply and demand, where the two lads delivered to Knox sickly tenants, prostitutes, beggars, acquaintances and a mother and daughter two-for-one.

In at least two of these instances, the medical students recognised the bodies placed before them for dissection but clearly Knox was quite the talker. Plus, it's said that he took the precaution of dissecting the face first. There's a good reason CSI isn't set in Edinburgh in 1827: **'We can't recognise the face.' 'Well, then you're free to go sir. Sorry for wasting your time. Oh and don't forget to take the rest of your cadaver with you on the way out. After all, it's probably worth a few quid.'**

The business language I'm using here is not inappropriate: Knox paid more for fresher corpses. And the boys further boosted their profits by killing most of their victims by strangulation, in an effort to present the most usable body.

Burke and Hare were finally caught out when two other tenants in Hare's boarding house found a tiny fragment of incriminating evidence: a freshly killed body hidden under one of the beds. Even so, between alerting the police and the fuzz arriving to search the house, B&H still managed to sell the body to Knox yet again.

They later broke under questioning though, the body was identified and they were brought to trial. There was a final twist however. Without sufficient evidence to prosecute them, Hare was offered immunity to testify against Burke. His testimony led to Burke's hanging in 1829.

That's not the twist though, this is the twist…

Burke's body was then used by Edinburgh medical students for anatomy lessons. What a quality twist! What a dazzling irony! What a brilliant final shot!

We start on the dead face of Burke, the hangman's rope barely eased… and the camera pulls out. We see the scalpel lowered to his chest as a voice calmly says, **'If we make our initial incision here…'** and as the camera continues to pull out we see a professor surrounded by white coated students… as the blade makes contact and the skin is opened, the students lean in, obscuring the view of the body. The camera continues to pull out over the class room, up and out through the bright windows, into the bright Edinburgh streets and out across the city. The End. Roll credits. The audience stumble out into the streets, frightened certainly, but still, reassured by such top-quality screenwriting.

Hare doesn't feature in the ending, by the way, because after he was released, he disappeared, his last known sighting being in Carlisle.

Prof. Knox was never found guilty of any crime, but his career understandably stalled in Edinburgh and he later moved to the London Cancer Hospital.

In 1832, the Anatomy Act was passed to supply cadavers legally for medical education about which *The Lancet* wrote, 'Burke and Hare… are the real authors of the measure.'

And Burke can still be seen, partly. After the dissection of his body, his skin was used to create the binding of a book, still on view in the excellent, and intermittently gruesome, museum at the Royal College of Surgeons of Edinburgh.

I've seen it. Disappointingly, it just looks like a book. It hasn't got an ear on the cover or anything.

EUROPEAN LANGUAGES
No. 2: Irish

My one claim to originality amongst Irishmen is that I have never made a speech.
GEORGE MOORE (1852–1933)

Dublin is Irish for Blackpool.

In Irish, fear means man and bean means woman. Fear used as a noun means 'man'; used as a verb it means to 'wage' (as in war). From bean we get the word banshee (bean sí : 'woman of the fairies'). The literal translation of the Irish word for jellyfish is 'seal-snot'.

Irish, also known as Gaelic, has the oldest literature in Europe apart from Latin or Greek.

Irish has been compulsory in schools in the Republic since independence in 1922. In surveys, between 1,000,000 and 500,000 people claim to speak it. They're lying. Out of a total population of 3.5 million, only about 50, 000 people speak Irish with any degree of fluency, and less than 20,000 speak it like a native. There is only one weekly newspaper in Irish. It's called *Anois* and has a circulation of 5,000. Compare this to Wales where 10 times as many people speak Welsh. There are 500,000 fluent Welsh speakers out of a population of 2.9 million.

In Ireland, it is your legal right to have a speeding ticket served on you in Irish. To avoid being fined, speak nothing but Irish to the policeman. The chances are he won't be able to remember enough schoolboy Irish to complete the procedure.

It's often said that if the Irish government really wanted to have Irish widely spoken in Ireland, they should have forbidden it.

IRISH DICTIONARY: SOME INTERESTING SUB-DIVISIONS OF THE IRISH LANGUAGE ARE:

1. Irish words that look exactly like English words but aren't

ball	member
bang	swimming stroke
beach	bee
bean	woman
biog	chirp
bob	trick
bod	penis
bog	to move
both	hut
brá	hostage
bran	raven, bream, bran
brat	cloak
bun	bottom
cab	gob
cabhailt	torso
cad?	what?
can	to sing or speak
cart	to scrape clean
clip	tease, torment
clog	clock, blister
corn	cup
corn	to coil
cos	foot, leg
crap	to shrink
go	to, that, until, well, and
gó	undoubtedly
gob	a bird's beak
mac	son
sin	that

2. Irish words that look like English names but aren't

beith	being, entity, birch
bri	meaning, significance
cath	battle
gus	courage

3. Irish words that look like French but aren't

bac	hindrance
bain	remove
bás	death
bis	vice
bord	table
cas	twist
col	aversion

4. Irish words that look like French and are

banc	bank

5. Irish words that look like Italian but aren't

bâsta	waist

6. Irish words that look like German but aren't

bonn	sole of shoe, coin

7. Irish words that look like Spanish but aren't

cáca	cake

8. Irish words that look like Icelandic but aren't

brillin	clitoris

9. Irish words that look like Finnish but aren't

clapsholas	twilight

10. Ludicrously long Irish words with impossibly complicated spelling

caoinfhulangach	tolerant
cnuasainmneacha	collective nouns
comhaimsearthacht	contemporaneity
comhbhráithreachas	confraternity
comhchoibhneasach	correlative
réamhchoinníôllacha	precondition

11. Irish words that look disgusting or sinister but turn out not to be

bangharda	policewoman
bothóg	shanty, cabin
bumbóg	bumblebee
cathair	city
deathoil	goodwill
fear gorm	black man
gorm	blue (or black when referring to skin)

CLARKSON'S
edible environment

SOMETIMES, AS I TRAVEL THE WORLD IN MY ENORMOUS CAR, I GLIMPSE NATURE THROUGH THE WINDSCREEN. THIS MAKES ME FEEL PECKISH. IF NO DECENT RESTAURANT IS AVAILABLE, I TEND TO LUNCH OFF THE LAND. HERE ARE SOME FAVOURITES.

Alligators The edible bit is the tail, roasted or fried. The meat is flaky and tastes like chicken. Or veal. Or crocodile.

Ants Bit fiddly if you're in a hurry. Can be mashed to a pulp then dried and used to thicken soup. Dried, powdered ant keeps for ages. Roasted leafcutter ant abdomens are sold in cinemas in South America instead of popcorn. In Mexico, *escamoles* (ant pupae) are on the menu in the finest restaurants, fried in butter, or with onions and garlic. Ants should be cooked for at least 6 minutes to remove formic acid.

Something from my glove compartment

Badgers are related to skunks and polecats, but young badger tastes like pork. In the 18th century, salted spit-roasted badger was a treat for peasants.

Barnacles are chewed with pleasure in Portugal, Spain and Chile and by American Indians of the Pacific Northwest.

Bats should be disembowelled, then skinned like a rabbit after removing their wings and legs. Catch them by knocking them off their roosts with a stick while asleep during the day. The tastiest are plump fruit bats.

Beavers secrete aspirin through their skin, so may be good for headaches or stomach pains: especially those caused by eating bats. The best part of a beaver to eat is its scaly, paddle-like tail.

Bees are edible at all stages in their life cycle – pupa, larva and adult. Remove legs, wings and stings before roasting or boiling.

Bird's dribble is the sole ingredient of Chinese bird's nest soup, which is made entirely from the spittle of the Asian cave swift.

Caterpillars Over 30 species are eaten in the Democratic Republic of the Congo. You can get tinned caterpillars in Botswana and South Africa.

Cats Domestic cats are perfectly edible. Lions and tigers too, provided they don't eat you first. A bit on the stringy side, though. Stew thoroughly.

On the stringy side

Cicadas were a favourite of the ancient Greeks. Aristotle recommended fried pregnant cicadas as a particular titbit.

Cockroaches are a perennial treat in Belize, where roasted mashed roaches make up *cena molida* ('crushed supper' in Spanish).

Dogs are a delicacy in Korea, but also, as is less well known, in Switzerland. Wild dogs, foxes and wolves are impossible to stalk, but you may be able to lure them towards you by going about on all fours so that they think they're stalking you. Meat can be gristly. Remove anal glands.

Dormice fattened up by feeding them nuts and cooked in honey were a favourite of the ancient Romans.

Dragonflies are a popular dainty in Laos, Japan, Korea and Bali with coconut milk, ginger, garlic or shallots. Or try them plain-grilled and crispy.

Grasshoppers may be roasted or sautéed. Remove the wings and legs and season with onion, garlic, cayenne, chilli peppers or soy sauce. Candied grasshoppers, or *inago*, are a favourite cocktail appetiser in Japan.

Guinea pigs are enjoyed all over Peru and make good eating. In the cathedral at Cuzco, there is a painting of the Last Supper where Christ and his disciples are shown tucking into roast guinea pig.

Hornets are absolutely wolfed down in the remote mountain villages of Japan, where the giant variety are part of the staple diet. They are eaten deep-fried, or raw, as hornet sashimi. There are two main types: nocturnal and diurnal. Day hornets should be collected at night. Night hornets (which are collected by day) have a sting that has been likened to a white-hot rivet being driven into the body. They usually attack the face. *Bon appétit!*

Hyenas in ancient Egypt were fattened for the dinner table, but nobody enjoyed them much. Boil thoroughly to remove parasites.

Insects are more nutritious than vegetables – rich in fat, carbohydrates and protein – especially their succulent grubs. Beetle grubs can be larger than sausages, up to 7 inches long. Most insects are better for you if eaten raw, but taste better if cooked. Boiling is best, but roasting is easier. If you haven't got a saucepan, place them on hot stones or the embers of a fire. To eat a hairy caterpillar, squeeze it to remove its innards. Don't eat the skin. Nasty.

Congolese rat recipe. Soak 12 small smoked field-rats in water for 30 minutes. Cook tomato, onion, pimento and palm oil in a large pan. Drain rats and skin. Remove any other inedible parts (your choice). Fry for 20 minutes, turning occasionally. Eat piping hot, bones and all. Serve as hors d'oeuvres.

Owls are a protected species, and both the Bible and the Koran forbid eating them. But folk wisdom says that if a woman feeds her husband roast owl, he will become subservient to her every wish. No doubt this is why owl is all the rage in China. Chan Chen Hei, 52, a top Cantonese chef in Singapore, says owl is the best meat in the world to make soup with – better than chicken, pork, snake or turtle – but the smell can permeate the entire restaurant. He advises sealing the gap under the kitchen door with wet towels to prevent the stench escaping. Few people other than the Chinese, the Eskimos and the good folk of Louisiana eat owls for pleasure, but they've often been used for medicinal reasons. In medieval England, owl broth was given for whooping cough. The Romans thought it cured epilepsy whereas in India it was only good for rheumatism. For epilepsy, stewed owls' eyeballs were the thing. Mixed with owls' brains, they were also said to reduce labour pains. In 16th-century Switzerland, jellied owl brains in seawater were recommended for constipation. They weren't eaten, though, because that would have been silly. They were popped up the bottom.

Pigs' milk is twice as rich as cows' milk, but difficult to get hold of. Cows produce milk for ten minutes at a time but pigs can only manage it for 15 seconds. Pigs have 14 small nipples all down their belly, whereas cows have four huge nipples conveniently clumped together. No one has so far devised a successful pig-milking machine. But perhaps their heart wasn't in it.

Porcupines are a delicacy in Gabon, Sudan, Nigeria, Ghana, Cameroon and in India, where they are compared to (and preferred to) pork. Malaysian porcupine curry is rather good. In Thailand, porcupine is barbecued with garlic, pepper and salt. It tastes like duck, only crunchier.

Rabbits Young rabbits often lie quite still and can be harvested simply by picking them up. Watch it, though: their flesh lacks fat and vitamins. Trappers in Canada literally ate themselves to death this way. The body uses its own

CLARKSON'S CHOICE!

Earthworms are extremely nutritious, very low in fat and 60 – 70% top-quality protein. Eating worms is a key survival skill for soldiers trapped in enemy territory. If forced to eat them raw, they should be starved for a day and then squeezed to remove any grit or poo. Raw, untreated worms taste like dirt. After starving and squeezing they taste like worm. This is barely an improvement.

If not a soldier in enemy territory but an ordinary, worm-eating civilian, purge your earthworms by soaking them in water overnight. This causes them to defecate. You may need to squeeze them to help the process along. Next wipe their bottoms and wash them in cold water. Plunge the live worms into boiling water and cook for 15 minutes. Drain. Boil again in fresh water at least once more, to remove all the mucus from their bodies.

After boiling they can be chopped and used in casseroles instead of chicken or beef. For oven-baked worms, freeze them to death. This stops them from wriggling off the baking tray. Defrost thoroughly, and bake in the oven at 200 degrees F for 30 minutes. The dried worms can be ground into a protein-rich meal and used instead of flour to make bread or cakes. Dried chopped worms can also be used instead of raisins or nuts. Mmmm.

The gourmet worm-fan will want The Worm Book by Loren Nancarrow and Janet Taylor. Try Worm 'N' Apple Cake, Apricot-Earthworm Balls and Oatmeal Earthworm-Raisin Muffins. NB Many of these contain eggs and cheese (as well as earthworms), so are not suitable for vegans.

vitamins and minerals digesting rabbit, which are then excreted in the faeces. The more rabbit is eaten, the worse the deficiency becomes. People who eat nothing but rabbit will starve to death. Eating vegetation of any kind would have allowed the trappers to survive, but it was all buried under the snow.

Don't eat insects that are sick or dead; that smell bad; that feed on carrion or dung; that produce a skin rash when handled; or that are brightly coloured. Everything else is yummy.

Rats Live rats in the Guangxi Zhuang region of China cost 50 cents a pound, almost as much as chicken. Marinated rat steak from Fujian is said to be the best in the world. When gutting a rat be careful not to split its innards.

Scorpions In southern China, scorpions are reared in 'ranches' in people's homes, then sold in the markets. They have a woody taste and are eaten whole, except for the tail. Obviously. Scorpion soup, with pork, dates and berries, is nicer than toilet water from a motorway service station. In my view.

Seagulls Well, why not? First trap your seagull by wrapping food round a stone and throwing it in the air. The gull swallows the bait while still in flight, but the weight of the stone causes it to crash-land. It should be despatched as soon as you catch it in case it learns to take off with the new payload aboard. This method is best used over land. At sea, if you have a fishing rod handy, the ability of gulls to catch food in mid-air can be even more easily exploited by baiting a hook and casting it into the sky. Reel in and despatch by hand.

Puddings are for girls

Slugs are just snails covered with mucus instead of a shell. What's not to like? Try them seethed in milk, Italian-style. *The Best Washington State Slug Recipes* by Frank Howard is the 3,156,355th best-selling book on Amazon.

> *Porcupines are the most delicious and tender of all game animals. Do not skin them: the skin is the best part (rather like crackling). Pluck out the large quills then drop the animal into boiling water. Scrape the remaining feathery quills off. It will now look like a suckling pig with feet closely resembling a human hand. Set the feet aside. Remove entrails, head and anal scent glands, stuff with rice and dried fruit and leave in fridge overnight. Grease skin. Bake in oven until golden brown. When your guests ask what they're eating, produce one of the 'hands' and watch the reaction!*

Snakes Human beings all over the world eat snakes wherever they are found. I know I do. They are quite safe as long as you don't eat the head. Grass snakes in France are known as *anguilles de haie* ('hedge-eels'); the Japanese prefer sea snakes. In Oxfordshire, we make vipers into soup.

Spiders Large, tarantula-like varieties are particularly sought after in northern Cambodia and New Guinea. They taste like peanut butter. The Indians of French Guiana grill giant bird-eating spiders after plunging them in boiling water to remove the hairs. To make spider egg omelette, squeeze eggs out of spider onto a leaf and then smoke. Eat with tiny, tiny chips.

Termites can be boiled, fried or roasted, but are better for you if eaten raw. Termite meat has twice the protein of sirloin steak. They are widely eaten in Africa where they are lured by candlelight. Break the wings off before frying – delicious! The enormous termite queens are a special treat and are often reserved for children or grandparents, unless I can get there first.

Warthogs have been described as 'hideously grotesque long-legged pigs'. Their heads are covered with long blunt warts strengthened by gristle and they can be cooked in any of the ways suitable for cooking pork. But they don't taste like pork. Oh no. The chefs on South African Airlines recommend warthog terrine. Very smooth yet delightfully warty.

Wasps Most normal people (like me) remove legs, wings and sting before roasting or boiling, but canned whole wasps, wings and all, are sold in Japan. Wasp pupae are enjoyed in the inland region of Nagano as a substitute for fish. Rice cooked with wasps was a favourite dish of the Emperor Hirohito.

Whale was served for school lunches in Japan between 1945 and 1962, but most young people there have never tasted it. Traditionally eaten only in coastal whaling towns (and by gourmets in cities), after WWII food shortages led to the occupying US forces allowing the Japanese to hunt whales. By the early sixties, they had done this so effectively that there were very few whales left in the seas around Japan and consumption declined. Whale milk is as thick as cottage cheese, so it doesn't dissolve in water if it gets spilt. In the 19th century, the Tillamook Indians of Oregon ate blubber from whales washed ashore in Tillamook Bay. Their legends say that, in olden times, the whales cruised into the bay to be milked. It's thought that waxy lumps found along the shore may be petrified whale-milk cheese.

Witchetty grubs Large, white, wood-boring larvae of various moths are a popular snack in Australia. Skilled hunters can pluck the grub from its hole without 'spilling the gravy'. Eaten raw or roasted, they have a rich, nutty flavour, mainly because they are full of half-digested sawdust.

I've seen more meat on a butcher's biro.

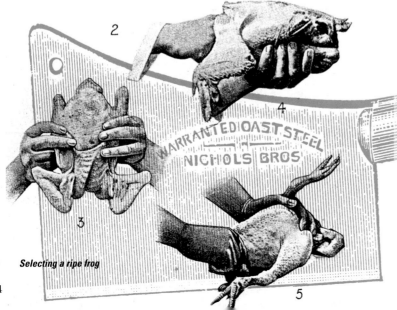

Selecting a ripe frog

ANSWERS TO THE ENGLISH VILLAGE GAME

The first (a-l) list are all English villages except for (h) Spero Dedes, who is a Greek-American US sportscaster. The second (a-l) list are all American commentators except for except for (f) Bentley Pauncefoot, which is in Worcestershire. Of the pictures of the personalities, Harley Brinsfield is the only genuine name of a commentator although he actually presents jazz on the radio, not basketball on TV. All the rest are actually Testcone Delamere (Herefordshire) really is a village, the others are all names of US TV and radio personalities.

Big Phill's ENGLISH VILLAGE Game

It's often struck me that the average English village sounds more like an American sports commentator or news anchor than a place.

Driving through this green and pleasant land, I find myself barking out lines like 'This is Fenny Bentley and Brant Broughton with *The News at Nine*' or 'This has been *Volleyball Tonight* – I'm Betton Strange' or '*Good Morning Albuquerque*, with Mansell Grange, Hoo Meavy, Nelson Rotman, Roseberry Topping, Toller Whelme, Rumbles Moor, Stanley Pontlarge and Scott Willoughby'.

See if you can tell which of these villages is actually a famous US TV personality, and which gritty-sounding bloke is really a sweet little English village.

| Danby Wiske | Verne Langdon | Marston Thrussell | Tedstone Delamere | Yardley Hastings | Gideon Yago | Harley Brinsfield | Nelson Burton |

Which of these is a famous American TV personality?

(a) Devin Scillian
(b) Regis Cordic
(c) Cawood Ledford
(d) George Nympton
(e) Sway Calloway
(f) Mort Crim
(g) Brant Hansen
(h) Spero Dedes
(i) Bucky Waters
(j) Neda Ulaby
(k) Hilliard Gates
(l) Nachum Segal

And can you spot the English Village?

(a) Patrick Brompton
(b) Shudy Camps
(c) Chaldon Herring
(d) Cary Lytes
(e) Charley Knoll
(f) Bentley Pauncefoot
(g) Bradford Bryan
(h) Clifford Chambers
(i) Newbold Saucy
(j) Curry Load
(k) Kex Beck
(l) Kirk Hallam

(Answers opposite)

ANGER

FEAR

GRIEF

LOVE

JEALOUSY

Emotions

Given the daily range, variety and power of human emotional experience, there has been surprisingly little research into the subject.

According to ancient Chinese philosophy there are only five basic emotions: ANGER, FEAR, GRIEF, LOVE AND JEALOUSY. These are subtly demonstrated on the left.

Paul Ekman, who studied the remote, Stone-Age Fore tribe of Papua New Guinea, also concluded that there are only five, but came up with a different list: ANGER, FEAR, SADNESS, HAPPINESS AND DISGUST.

One of the most influential people in the field is Robert Plutchnik, who identifies eight primary human emotions: ANGER, FEAR, SADNESS, DISGUST, SURPRISE, CURIOSITY, ACCEPTANCE AND JOY.

At QI, however, we think there are a lot more emotions than eight, including:

ANGUISH	LAZINESS
ANXIETY	LONELINESS
BAFFLEMENT	LUST
BITTERNESS	MISCHIEVOUSNESS
CERTAINTY	MISERY
CHAGRIN	NARCISSISM
CHEERFULNESS	NONCHALANCE
COMPASSION	OBSEQUIOUSNESS
CONTEMPT	PANIC
CONTENTMENT	PETULANCE
CRUELTY	PLAYFULNESS
CURMUDGEONLINESS	POIGNANCY
CYNICISM	RELIEF
DELIGHT	REMORSE
DETERMINATION	SCHADENFREUDE
DISCOMFITURE	SELF-CONFIDENCE
DISTRUST	SELF-SATISFACTION
DOUBT	SHAME
EMPATHY	SHOCK
EXCITEMENT	STINGINESS
FOREBODING	STUBBORNNESS
FORGIVENESS	SUSPICION
FRUSTRATION	SYMPATHY
GLOOM	TENDERNESS
HARD-HEARTEDNESS	TORPOR
HATRED	VANITY
HOMESICKNESS	VEHEMENCE
HORROR	VENERATION
HUBRIS	VENGEFULNESS
INDECISION	WARINESS
INDIFFERENCE	WARMTH
INDIGNATION	WISTFULNESS
IRRITABILITY	WORLD-WEARINESS
JOLLITY	and WORRY

PLUS twenty more lavishly exemplified on the right.

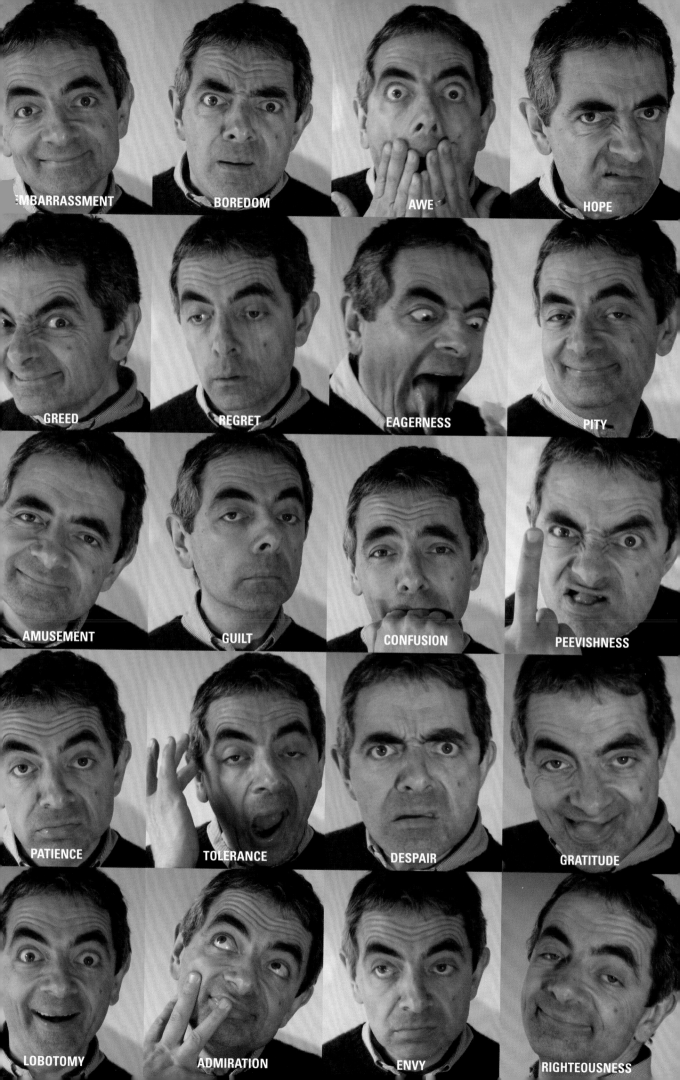

Words With No
English Equivalents

Would you care for jam Sir?

Kouloúra
(Greek: a ring shaped loaf of
bread or a lavatory seat)

Manjan
(Malay: to rove in
quest of girls)

EXCLUSIVE
CLUB

Sorry, you can't come in
here, you're not wearing a dog

Ikkuserpok
(Inuit: to tie one leg
of a dog to one's neck)

Song!
Song!

Song
(Malay: call to an elephant
to lift one leg)

An amusingly horrid little
wine don't you think?

Dreimannerwein
(German: a wine so disgusting
it takes three men to
make you drink it)

Age-Otori
(Japanese: looking less attractive after a hair-do)

Mamihlapinatapei
(Tierra Del Fuego: looking into each others eyes, each hoping the other person will make the first move)

Raphanidóo
(Ancient Greek: to thrust a radish up someone's fundament)

Atiqtuq
(Inuit: bears going down to the sea)

THE ENGLISH ELM by CLIVE ANDERSON

SINCE BOTH WORDS BEGIN WITH E, ENGLISH ELMS ARE A PERFECT SUBJECT FOR THIS BOOK. PERFECT FOR ME, CERTAINLY, AS I'M PRESIDENT OF THE WOODLAND TRUST, A CHARITY WHOSE AIM IS TO PRESERVE ANCIENT WOODLAND AND PLANT MORE NATIVE BRITISH TREES (POSSIBLE MOTTO: 'BRING BACK THE BIRCH').

TREES ARE US
Europe as a whole has about 250 native tree species, which makes Britain's 30-something look very puny. Even 250 is nothing when compared to the tree-rich rain forests of the tropics where hundreds of species grow in a single acre – assuming, that is, they haven't all been chopped down by the time you read this.

THE 'ENGLISH' ELM
Ulmus procera (Latin for 'foremost elm') has been known as the 'English Elm' for centuries. This doesn't necessarily mean anything. There are no lions running around Britain, but that hasn't stopped them being adopted as our national symbol – the result, perhaps, of Scottish lions rampant getting into bed with English lions couchant. And, in fact, it seems that, though English Elms have been living – and dying – in our woods and hedgerows for centuries, most experts agree they did not grow in this country until they were brought here from continental Europe. Just when that happened is not clear, but it seems certain that the English Elm is not, in fact, English.

THERE'LL ALWAYS BE AN ENGLAND
Several tree species are called 'English', notably the English Oak *(Quercus robur)*. It's one of only two species of oak (of which there are hundreds worldwide) native to Britain. Also snappily known as the pedunculate oak, it's common to many parts of Europe. But, in some corner of a foreign field, it is forever English to us. Much the same is true of the English Yew. The Scots Pine *(Pinus sylvestris scotia)* has a far greater claim to Scottishness. It's unique to the Scottish Highlands.

RETURN OF THE NATIVE
What is a native British tree species anyway? There certainly aren't very many of them. When the last (or at any rate the latest) Ice Age finished about 12,000 years ago, there were no trees in Britain at all. The cold and the glaciers had wiped them all out. Between the time things warmed up enough for trees and the English Channel was formed about 6,000 years later, Britain was connected to Europe and trees were able to spread north. Only 30 or so species made it before the water closed behind them.

BEATING ABOUT THE BUSH
I say '30 or so' because not everyone agrees which woody plants are big enough to count as trees and are not merely bushes or shrubs. Something woody that grows to 6 metres high is generally entitled to be called a tree. Though not the thing bananas grow on. A banana plant may look like a tree and be as tall as a tree and many people may call it a tree but, strictly speaking, it's just a herb with attitude.

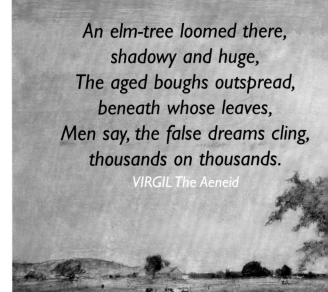

An elm-tree loomed there, shadowy and huge, The aged boughs outspread, beneath whose leaves, Men say, the false dreams cling, thousands on thousands.

VIRGIL *The Aeneid*

BORN TO BE WILDWOOD
Are British woodlands made up of only about 30 tree species? Well, no. As in other parts of the world, the tree population has been much affected by humans – chopping them down in huge numbers but also taking and planting new species outside their natural range.

GOING NATIVE
In Britain, many familiar trees thrive in local conditions once they've been given a helping hand to get here. They are not native but have *gone* native. Sycamores and Horse Chestnuts, for example, fall into this category. Human action in such cases has completed the distribution of trees otherwise prevented by accidents of geography.

TREE MUSEUM
Trees of foreign origin have been cultivated in Britain for ages. Apple, cherry, pear – most fruit trees in our orchards were imported from other parts of the world. In our parks, estates and gardens there are dozens of types of trees not native to Britain. The London Plane, for example, is not a Londoner. It's a Spanish hybrid of the

TRUE BRITS
Many authorities have settled on 33 as the number of truly British native trees. They are: Alder, Ash, Aspen, Bay Willow, Beech, Bird Cherry, Black Poplar, Box, Common Oak, Crab Apple, Crack Willow, Downy Birch, Field Maple, Goat Willow, Hawthorn, Hazel, Holly, Hornbeam, Juniper, Large Leaved Lime, Midland Thorn, Rowan, Scots Pine, Sessile Oak, Silver Birch, Small Leaved Lime, Strawberry Tree, White Willow, Whitebeam, Wild Cherry, Wild Service Tree, Wych Elm and Yew.

Oriental and American Plane. But it thrives in polluted streets and may be the tree most often seen by British city dwellers.

TREE FARMS

In the 20th century, vast areas of this country were planted with fast-growing conifers to produce industrial quantities of timber. Not usually aesthetically pleasing or adding much to biodiversity, such trees now probably outnumber native species in upland Britain.

WHEN? WHO? WYCH?

Until recently, most experts believed the 'English Elm' arrived in Britain in Neolithic times, brought by migrant humans from Europe. But it's now thought it was the Romans who first planted them, some three thousand years later. This seems like a big margin of error, but ancient pollen

samples are difficult to analyse, being easily confused with those of the Wych Elm (Ulmus glabra), which is a native species.

BACK TO NATURE

One of the greatest living experts on British trees, Oliver Rackham, always doubted the theory that Neolithic settlers brought the English Elm to England. No other examples of this sort of long-range tree planting are known until Roman times. According to recent Spanish research published in Nature, DNA evidence shows that elms planted by the Romans in Italian and Spanish vineyards (where they were used to support grape vines) are identical with the English Elm. When I contacted Dr Rackham to tell him this, I assumed he would be impressed. But no, he is sceptical of this theory as well. Even if the DNA is identical (which he doubts) it proves nothing. Spanish and Italian elms could equally well have been taken there from England. For that matter, he does not accept the notion that elms were used to provide support for vines. His view is that a prehistoric introduction of English Elms into England is very unlikely and, though the Romans may have been responsible, it's not yet proven.

MY OLD DUTCH

However they got here, English Elms flourished in Britain until they were destroyed in their millions by Dutch Elm Disease in the 1970s. Once a defining characteristic of the English landscape, the mature English Elm is magnificent – a straight trunk supporting a series of domes like a giant pear with its fat end upwards. Even people who don't get out much are likely to have seen in them the landscapes of Constable. Not so long ago, it would have been hard to imagine an England without her elms. That is, until it all went pear-shaped.

NIGHTMARE ON ELM STREET

Dutch Elm Disease is caused by fungus spread by beetles that live in the elms' bark. It killed 90% of England's English Elms, perhaps 25 million trees in total. The disease is not really Dutch either. Early in the 20th century, research on the disease was first carried out by Dutch scientists (most of them women) and the name stuck.

NO SEX PLEASE WE'RE ENGLISH

What made Dutch Elm Disease so deadly is that the English Elm doesn't reproduce sexually. Maybe this is what makes it so English. English Elms almost never grow from seeds: they spread by suckering. This means that the trees are genetic carbon copies of each other, which makes them particularly vulnerable. If a tree is susceptible to an infection, all of its suckers are too. So there have been many earlier instances of fatal elm disease: in the 20th and 19th centuries, and way back to the Neolithic era, when elms all over Europe were apparently hit by a huge decline.

TREES ARE US

There are still English Elms around. If you happen to be in New York there's a famous English Elm in Washington Square. It is known as the Hangman's Elm because executions used to take place there. Nearer to home, Brighton managed to keep Dutch Elm disease at bay and has a few left, and there are a few more in Edinburgh. But if you really want to see English Elms in all their glory you need to go to Australia. Geographical isolation and stringent quarantine regulations mean Dutch Elm disease never got there. There are estimated to be 70,000 mature English Elms in the State of Victoria alone. You can find still small English Elms in English hedges because the suckers keep growing back. But as soon as they grow tall enough, Dutch Elm Disease kills them all off again.

THE END OF THE ENGLISH ELM

So there you have it. The English Elm is probably not English. Stone Age Europeans may have planted it, or the Romans, or possibly neither of them. Either way it was in England before the English. And now there are hardly any left. This is because of Dutch Elm Disease, which is not Dutch. Quite interesting. Or, at any rate, quite complicated.

ELM FACTS
- *Elm trees can live for 300 years.*
- *Elm wood keeps its strength even when permanently wet, so it was used for keels and bilge planks; cart wheels; naval blocks and pulleys; wheelbarrows and coffins. Before cast iron, hollowed elm trunks were used as water pipes.*
- *According to Giraldus Cambrensis (Gerald of Wales), writing in the 12th century, English longbows were made of yew, but Welsh bows of elm.*
- *There are approximately 40 species of non-English Elm. They are found throughout the Northern Hemisphere from Siberia to Indonesia and from Mexico to Japan. The greatest diversity is in China.*
- *'Elm Street' is the 15th commonest road name in the US.*
- *In the US, the value of a mature elm for insurance purposes is US $2,500.*
- *The 7,700,000 elms in North American towns are worth over US $19 billion.*
- *The cooling effect of one elm tree is equivalent to five air-conditioning units.*

Gainful EMPLOYMENT

Why Not Become Pope?

THERE WAS A TIME when every boy wanted to be a train driver or a coal miner, but these days there's a whole new world of possibilities open for a young lad with the right attitude towards hard work and an ambiguous attitude towards women.

My advice to chaps has always been 'aim high', so for those of you thinking of going into the Church isn't it about time you said to yourself, 'Could I be the next Pope?' And just look at the benefits! Your own state (with you as supreme autocratic ruler), a job for life, infallibility (terms and conditions apply) and free access to nuns (no touching). I know it all sounds rather daunting at first, doesn't it, but then being a professional clog dancer is no picnic either. In both cases it pays for a lad to sit down with a piece of paper and a nice sharp pencil and draw up a list of requirements to see if the cap fits.

Mr J. D. 'Bo'sun' Pollard, MA (Cantab.)

So what does it take to become Pope?

1. Sex:
Traditionally Popes have been men, with the exception of Pope Joan who lived in the ninth century and was entirely fictional. According to the legend she gave birth during a papal procession which rather compromised her position. The crowd, full of righteous Christian indignation, then quite correctly beat her and her child to death. So this is strictly a game for boys!

2. Sex:
Although frowned upon in the modern Church, plenty of Popes have mired themselves in the loathsome but strangely compelling sins of the flesh. During the eleventh century, the almost complete control over the papacy held by a group of papal mothers, lovers and prostitutes led to the period becoming known as the 'pornocracy'. Your Greek master can explain this word to you.

3. Age:
You don't have to be old to be Pope – far from it. The Church needs spunky young men to inject some fresh blood into its age-old institutions. Benedict IX allegedly became Pope when just eleven although, as we have no idea when he was born, the calculation is perhaps a touch shaky. John XII was certainly only eighteen when he became Pope, although he only survived nine years before being murdered by the irate husband of one of his lovers (see *'Sex'* above).

4. Life:
The best Popes have all been alive, but this is not an absolute requirement. Pope Formosus was exhumed, dressed in his papal robes and tried for sins against the Church when he was very much dead. Then they threw him in the Tiber.

5. Belief:
Believing in God is at least a nominal requirement for the job, but frankly this can hold you back in your pursuit of worldly self-interest. Over a dozen Popes have been charged with Satanism, which demonstrates a sort of belief. John XXII believed in magic. Boniface VIII believed Christianity was an invented religion and that Mary was as much a virgin as his own mother. Benedict IX simply believed the papacy was a good way to make money, selling the job to his godfather for 650 kg of gold.

6. Goodness:
Goodness me, what a sweet thought! There's nothing in the job description that requires a Pope to be good. Alexander was a married, philandering, nepotistic murderer (and a Borgia to boot) and he still got the top job. The Anti-Pope John XXIII was a pirate.

Now before we get too excited and start filling in application forms willy-nilly you probably have some questions.

Don't I need to be a cardinal?
Mais non! Urban VII wasn't a cardinal, although his election did start the Western Schism. It does help, however, and it can be easier than it looks. Leo X was made a cardinal at just fourteen and Cesare Borgia at eighteen – by his father who happened to be Pope *(Thanks Dad!)*.

Don't I need the other cardinals all to vote for me?
Now there's no need for such negative talk. There are 185 cardinals, but Innocent VII was elected by just eight. This is less than the number of cardinals you need to collect for your Boy Scouts 'Divinity' badge.

Don't I have to be celibate?
Frankly you're too young to know what that means, but if you'd care to remove your hand from your trousers, young man, I'll explain. Whilst celibacy is supposedly de rigueur for Popes, discretion is just as good, although some Popes haven't really bothered with this either. At least thirteen Popes have had illegitimate children, not always before they became Pope. Some of these have also been accused of bestiality, incest, fornication, adultery and rape. John XII was said to have turned the Lateran basilica into a brothel.

So there we are.

Has this inspired you to become Christ's only vicar on Earth? If so, it's time to put away beastly thoughts of self-abuse, put down your penis and pick up a pen to apply. But before you ask the current Pope to move over and make way for some young blood there's one last thing to check. Is he dead? Unless you want to become an Anti-Pope or can persuade the living Pope to resign (and why should he?), this is a requirement. Traditionally the way to tell is to ask the Cardinal Camerlengo to hit the previous incumbent three times on the head with a silver mallet whilst shouting his baptismal name. If he's just having a nap this should wake him up. If he's dead it probably won't.

Good luck chaps – or should I say, 'Your Holiness'!!!

NEXT WEEK – HOW TO BECOME A BANK ROBBER.

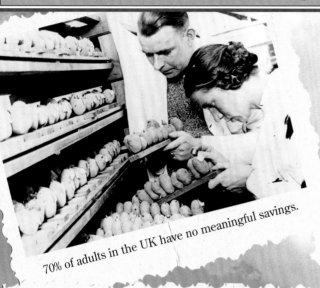

70% of adults in the UK have no meaningful savings.

When Liverpool's Ian Rush was signed to Juventus for a year and asked how he found living in Italy, he said it was 'like being in a foreign country'.

Around 210,000 people are reported missing in Britain every year.

According to a *Which?* survey in 2005, 93% of the nutritional information on food labels is inaccurate.

Delays on British railways in 2001 resulted in a total of 3,500 years of wasted time.

Many young people in the UK think that the Battle of Britain took place in 1066.

33

65% of British schoolchildren cannot name a single composer and 69% don't know what a cello is.

Britain is the windiest country in Europe.

There are 3,600 static and 460 mobile libraries in Britain, between them holding about 87 million books.

The amount of road space in Britain has grown by 25% since 1950, but the number of cars has increased by 700%.

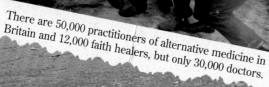

There are 50,000 practitioners of alternative medicine in Britain and 12,000 faith healers, but only 30,000 doctors.

23% of Britain's wealth is owned by 1% of the population.

There are at least 280,000 heroin and crack addicts in Britain who between them cost the British taxpayer £19 billion a year.

...re are about 80,000 prostitutes working in the UK.

Ministries of the British Government currently employ more than 25,000 public relations officers.

Royal Mail staff steal about 200,000 letters and parcels every year and deliver 22 million letters to dead people.

In the UK's 2001 Official Census, 390,000 people entered their religion as 'Jedi'.

82% of Britons are surprised by their bank balance at the end of the month.

EIGHTH-CENTURY EXAMINATION

QI 700 (JP)

Welcome to the eighth century. Before taking up residence you are required to pass a 'Life in the Eighth Century Test' which shows you understand the basics of Anglo-Saxon citizenship. Before taking this test you should read the 'Life in Anglo-Saxon England: A Journey to Ceorldom' handbook available from your local ealdorman.

QUESTION 1
Is the statement below TRUE or FALSE?
Children under 10 shouldn't be hanged.
- ☐ TRUE
- ☐ FALSE

QUESTION 2
Where does the King live?
- ☐ Westminster
- ☐ Winchester
- ☐ Wilton
- ☐ No fixed abode

QUESTION 3
Is the statement below TRUE or FALSE?
Women can own things.
- ☐ TRUE
- ☐ FALSE

QUESTION 4
What is the main disadvantage of becoming a monk?
- ☐ The bad haircut
- ☐ The lack of sex
- ☐ The early mornings
- ☐ Having to learn to read
- ☐ Being hacked to death by marauding Vikings

QUESTION 5
Which of these statements is correct?
- ☐ There's no time for poetry in our kin-based warrior society
- ☐ Hwæt! We Gardena in geardagum
  þeodcyninga þrym gefrunon
  hu ða æþelingas ellen fremedon

QUESTION 6
Which of these are NOT kingdoms in the heptarchy?
- ☐ Wessex ☐ Northumbria ☐ Sussex
- ☐ Essex ☐ Southumbria ☐ Isle of Man
- ☐ East Anglia ☐ Mercia ☐ Runnymede
- ☐ Ford Anglia ☐ Kent

QUESTION 7
The City of London is mainly inhabited by:
- ☐ Rapists and pillagers
- ☐ Bankers and property speculators
- ☐ Rats, vermin and other creepy-crawlies
- ☐ Ghouls and denizens of hell

QUESTION 8
Someone cuts off your finger in a fight. In retaliation you cut off two of his toes. Who is worse off?
- ☐ He is – he can barely walk
- ☐ I am – I'll never play the harp again
- ☐ I'd call it even-stevens

QUESTION 9
According to the laws of Wessex, fire is:
- ☐ A boon
- ☐ A beggar
- ☐ A thief
- ☐ A useful way of getting Vikings out of your house

QUESTION 10
Is the statement below TRUE or FALSE?
Life expectancy in the eighth century is shorter than under the Romans.
- ☐ TRUE
- ☐ FALSE

Please tick boxes as appropriate

THE ANSWERS

Q1 TRUE – Laws vary from kingdom to kingdom but generally children under 10 (12 in some areas) are not considered responsible in law.

Q2 No fixed abode – Eighth-century kings are peripatetic. Although they have palaces (in the broadest sense) the lack of an efficient administration means they have constantly to travel around their kingdom to prevent it all falling apart.

Q3 TRUE – Women are individuals under Saxon law – unlike under Norman law where they are the possessions of their husbands or fathers.

Q4 Since their first appearance at Lindisfarne in 793, being hacked to death by Vikings is certainly the most depressing drawback to a life in holy orders. Early mornings, on the other hand, are a way of life in Anglo-Saxon society, as are bad haircuts. Learning to read is a rare privilege, so that's nothing to complain about, and recent scandals suggest there is still an opportunity for sex in at least some Saxon monasteries, particularly the mixed ones.

Q5 'Hwæt! We Gardena in geardagum, þeodcyninga þrym gefrunon, hu ða æþelingas ellen fremedon.' As these lovely opening lines from the epic poem *Beowulf* (probably written in the late eighth century) show, there is plenty of time in Anglo-Saxon England for poetry.

Q6 Ford Anglia, Southumbria, Isle of Man and Runnymede are not kingdoms of the heptarchy.

Q7 It's full of ghosts. Many of the old Roman cities of Britain lie in ruins and are a focus for superstitions. With little understanding of what once happened in them (and no need for them) they are left abandoned and considered to be the realm of spirits.

Q8 Even-stevens it is. Anglo-Saxon laws work on a compensation basis. Every person and every part of a person has a value that must be paid if an individual is deprived of it. A Welsh slave's life is worth half as much as a Welsh peasant's, and a member of the King's household is worth ten times that. Every body part also has a value, and a finger is worth two toes. So you're quits.

Q9 According to the laws of King Ine of Wessex (688–726), fire is a thief for it can burn down trees in a forest. The axe used to fell a tree is considered an 'informer', however, not a thief.

Q10 FALSE – Despite everyone going on about what the Romans did for us, life expectancy has increased for ordinary people since the collapse of Roman rule.

HOW DID YOU DO?

0–3 Are you a Viking by any chance?
4–8 Perhaps you should try the eighteenth century.
9–10 You've passed! Welcome to the eighth century. Pull up a parasitic infestation and join us at the mead bench.

Matt's English Proverbs

Everything must have a beginning

Help me to salt, help me to sorrow

He who lies down with dogs will rise with fleas

Happy is the country that has no history

Don't halloo 'til you're out of the wood

Keep a thing seven years and you'll find a use for it

It will all be the same a hundred years hence

Cards are the devil's books

My idea of exercise is a good, brisk sit. PHYLLIS DILLER
EXERCISE
EIGHTEEN EX-OLYMPIC EVENTS
(AND THE YEARS IN WHICH THEY WERE INCLUDED)

Club Swinging (1904, 1932)
At the 1932 Games during the Depression, unemployed American George Roth won gold. After being awarded his medal in front of 60,000 spectators, he walked out of the stadium in Los Angeles and hitchhiked home.

George Roth hits the road again

Cricket (1900)
Great Britain (actually Devon & Somerset Wanderers CC) beat 'France' (a team from the British Embassy in Paris). The French team was almost entirely made up of Englishmen.

Croquet (1900)
Held at the Paris Olympics, France won all the medals in all the categories, as only French competitors took part.

Duelling (1906)
Contestants didn't shoot at each other but at dummies in frock coats with a bulls-eye embroidered on the chest.

Golf (1900, 1904)
Golf has only been an Olympic sport twice for men, and only once for women (in 1900). The USA took 9 of the 12 medals. All the female medallists were American – including Margaret Abbott, the first woman to win an Olympic gold. In 1904, Canadian silver medallist George Lyon accepted his trophy after walking to the podium on his hands.

Lacrosse (1904, 1908)
Lacrosse was only held twice and it was a men's event. The bronze medallists in 1904 were a team of Mohawk Indians whose members included Rain-in-Face, Snake Eater and Man Afraid Soap.

... and last but certainly not least...
... mr man afraid soap

1904 OLYMPICS

I am pushing sixty. That is enough exercise for me.
MARK TWAIN

Long Jump for Horses (1900)

A horse called Extra Dry won the only example of this event at the Paris Olympics with a jump of 20 feet and a quarter of an inch. It was a pretty poor effort – 2.63 metres short of the current world record for humans.

Motor Boating (1908)

The 1908 Games were meant to be in Rome, but the Italians panicked after the eruption of Mount Vesuvius and London stepped in at the last minute. Since it was their Games, they added Motor Boating to the list of events. This was a disaster. The speed of the boats rarely exceeded a pedestrian 19 mph; six of the nine races were cancelled due to bad weather; and the three that were held were too far off shore to be seen by anyone.

Obstacle Race (1900)

Competitors had to climb over a pole, scramble over a row of boats then swim under another row of boats. No Olympic swimming events were held in a pool until 1908. Before that they were in the river Seine (1900), a lake in St Louis, USA (1904), and, in 1896, in the sea. Gold medallist Alfred Guttmann commented: 'My greatest struggle was against the towering 12-foot waves and the terribly cold water.'

One-Handed Weightlifting (1896, 1904, 1906)

Pigeon Shooting (1900)

The Pigeon Shooting event was the only time in Olympic history when animals were deliberately killed. The birds were released in front of the competitors and the winner was the one who shot the most.

Polo (1900, 1908, 1920, 1924, 1936)

At the 1908 London Olympics, Britain won all three medals. Teams from Roehampton and Hurlingham came first and second, and Ireland (then still part of Great Britain) took the bronze. The captain of the Irish team was John Hardress Lloyd, the great-uncle of the producer of *QI*.

Real Tennis (1900)

Although held at the Paris Olympics and billed under its French name of Jeu de Paume, the US and Britain took all the medals.

Rope Climbing (1896, 1904, 1906, 1924, 1932)

The object of the event was to shin up to the top of a rope. At the 1896 Olympics, only two competitors managed it. Over the years, they kept changing the length of the rope to try to get it right.

Solo Synchronised Swimming (1984, 1988)

This contradiction in terms was thrown out as an official event in 1992. Supporters argued that the swimming was 'synchronised' to the music rather than to the other people in the team, but to no avail.

Tug-of-War (1900, 1904, 1906, 1908, 1912, 1920)

Tug-of-War first became an Olympic event in 500 BC. In 1908, all the medallists were British police teams. The City of London Police took gold, Liverpool Police silver and the Metropolitan Police bronze. The USA, who were beaten in moments, accused the British of cheating – claiming their spiked boots gave them an illegal advantage. The British offered a rematch in their socks... and still beat the Americans.

Tumbling (1932)

Introduced by the US at the Los Angeles Games and won by an American, Rowland 'Flip' Wolfe, using his revolutionary back-flip with double twist.

Underwater Swimming (1900)

Competitors were awarded two points for each metre swum, and one point for each second that they stayed under water.

I believe that the Good Lord gave us a finite number of heartbeats and I'm damned if I'm going to use up mine running up and down a street.

NEIL ARMSTRONG

Arthur Smith's... Edinburgh

The Insider's Guide to the Edinburgh Festival

HOW TO GET...

1. FREE ACCOMMODATION.

Hang around the streets two days before the Festival until you see a van disgorge some young people in identical T-shirts. Observe which flat they go into and report there an hour later with your bags saying you are the lighting technician for 'the other show' and it's all been arranged with Murray. You will be given a room (sharing with nine others).

2. INTO EVERY SHOW WITHOUT PAYING.

Write PRESS in large red letters on an old train ticket. Adopt a look of extreme self-importance as you present it.

3. MONEY FOR NOTHING.

Look for a miserable man in the Assembly Rooms bar. Be sympathetic and earnest until he gives you money to help publicise his failing show. Take cash and dump leaflets in a bin.

4. FAMOUS.

Identify the hot new comedian and proposition him after his show. Unless you are physically repulsive and smell he will say yes. Use your phone to take pictures and ring papers the next day. Suggested angle:

FUNNY MAN'S FUNNY WILLY

T.V. EXEC

This could make a great show on Channel 4

5. YOUR OWN TV SERIES.

During the Edinburgh Television Festival run naked into the George Hotel, shit on the bar and shout that you are the new Messiah.

Spice up your conversation with this selection of thought-provoking spontaneous remarks

Epigrams

1. Tuesdays and Fridays are rubbish days.

2. If at first you don't succeed then skydiving is not for you.

3. You know what they say so there's no point in them saying it.

4. Maybe the hokey cokey IS what it's all about.

Embroidery Tips

Life's too Short For embroid...

Experimental Art Works

'Oil on canvas' (oil on canvas)

The Moving Finger writes; and, having writ, Moves on: nor all your Piety nor Wit Shall lure it back to cancel half a Line, Nor all your Tears wash out a single wo

"According to the philosopher Epictetus (AD 55–135)," piped young Stephen, "we have two ears and one mouth so that we can listen twice as much as we speak." "What?" said the man.

"I say," exclaimed Stephen, "this puts me in mind of Epimetheus who foolishly opened Pandora's Box, thus releasing all manner of evil on the human race. And an anteater's cock, apparently!"

"If you're trying to measure the circumference of the earth, or the tilt of its axis," called Stephen from the boat, "you're wasting your time! It's already been done by Eratosthenes of Cyrene (276–194 BC)!"

"Very little is known of Euclid's life," said Stephen urgently, "but he may have been a pupil of Plato in Athens. Though he was not the greatest mathematician Greece produced (compared to, say, Archimedes), his *Elements* is one of the most influential books in the history of the world. Have one – it's a cracking read!"

"The principal doctrines of Epicurus", suggested Stephen, "were (1) That the highest good is pleasure and (2) That the gods do not concern themselves at all with human behaviour."
"Get off me before I break your arm," said Polkinghorne Minor.

"Good gracious!" whispered Stephen. "We've caught Erichthonius, fourth King of Athens, red-handed, right here under the tuck-shop, inventing the chariot!"

"Don't be a fool!" cried Stephen. "In the words of Euripides (480–406 BC), 'Whom the gods wish to destroy, they first make mad.'" "Wasn't he the author of 95 plays?" grunted the Mountie. "Wrong!" parried Stephen, brilliantly. "Four of them were almost certainly by Critias!"

From outside the gunroom, came a mysterious voice. "Epicharmus (540–450 BC)", it intoned, "is said to have added the letters theta (θ) and chi (χ) to the Greek alphabet, invented comedy and been the first to use plots in drama." "Who on earth could that be at this time of night?" muttered the Brigadier.

Dr Huby burst into the room, angrily balancing a book on his ear. "Give me the dates of Epiphanius, Bishop of Salamis!" he demanded. "Circa AD 315–403," said Stephen, without looking up.

"The ancient Greek philosopher Empedocles (490–430 BC) killed himself by jumping into a volcano," insinuated Stephen pointedly.

"Who's this poor devil?" enquired Lady Hore-Glossop. "Epimenides of Crete," said Stephen firmly, "one of the Seven Wise Men of Greece and the man who introduced the temple to the country. While tending his flocks one day, he fell asleep in a cave for 57 years and, after he woke up, lived to be 289."

"Will you shut the fuck up about ancient Greeks beginning with E, or I'm going to have to kill you," said the man disguised as Mount Elbrus, the highest mountain in Europe, known to the ancients as Strobilos, Greek for spinning-top, and the place where Prometheus was chained for stealing fire from the gods.

SLIPPERY FROG

Ever wondered why you don't see many frogs in winter? That's because frogs melt away into slime in the autumn. Then, by what Pliny astutely describes as 'a hidden operation of nature', they magically turn back into frogs in the spring.

PLINY the ELDER's
WONDERS
of the
NATURAL WORLD

1,800 years before Darwin there lived a great naturalist known as Pliny the Elder. Pliny was responsible for *Naturalis Historia*, the first great encyclopaedia. Made up of a whopping 37 volumes, the contents section alone ran to 70 pages. Pliny spent many years compiling his definitive guide to natural history, and he claimed that his book contained some 20,000 'important facts'. However, some of his facts were more important, if not indeed more *factual* than others. Here is a small selection of Pliny's pearls of ancient wisdom.

CRAFTY BEAVER

The male beaver has a drastic method of avoiding predators. Pliny explained that beavers gnaw off their own testicles in order to throw hunters off their scent.

MANTICHORA

In Pliny's day African wildlife was a lot more diverse than it appears to be today. This is the *mantichora*, essentially a lion, but with the head of a man and a scorpion's tail.

Sadly these, along with *pegasi* (flying horses) and *catoblepas* (the mere sight of which turn a man to stone) are now extinct.

GIANT INDIAN LOCUST

Next time you're in India look out for the giant locusts, which grow up to three feet in length. Rather than creating a nuisance, these monster insects were in fact rather useful. Pliny suggested that once their bodies had been dried out, their legs could be removed and used as saws.

THE EFFECTS OF EATING RABBIT

Pliny was not a fool. He was a scholar and man of reason. For example, he was sceptical about the popular Roman belief that eating rabbits made you sexually attractive, pointing out that this was possibly a play on words ('lepos' meaning grace, and 'lepus' meaning a hare.) But Pliny deemed it such a strongly held belief that it could not be without *some* justification. So he qualified his final judgement. He said that eating rabbit would make you sexually attractive, but the effects would only last nine days at the most.

EARWIGS IN EARS

Pliny was of the opinion that earwigs were no more likely to crawl into your ear than any other insect. But he was mindful of the fact that no matter how remote, the possibility did remain. He therefore included a simple remedy in his book. If an earwig does crawl into your ear, ask a friend to spit into it. The earwig will then come out again.

44

Pliny Pearlers

- The colour of cows is determined by the colour of the water that they drink.

- Ostriches stare at their eggs aggressively in order to make them hatch.

- Certain types of tree are able to walk and talk.

- If a shrew runs across a wheel-rut in a road, it dies.

- When wheat gets diseased it turns into oats.

- Pregnant women who want their babies to be born with black eyes should eat a rat.

PEST CONTROL

There were no insecticides in Roman times, so a good deal of ingenuity was called for when dealing with troublesome pests. In Egypt, making a sacrifice to the goddess Isis was the standard procedure for exterminating flies. Pliny's top tip for ridding an apple orchard of insects was typically unconventional, yet remarkably simple. All you had to do was find a woman who was menstruating, and ask her, no doubt very politely, to walk around the orchard stark naked.

Gaius Plinius Secundus, to give him his proper name, lived from 23 to 79 AD. As well as a prolific author Pliny was a military commander of some repute. In August 79 he was serving as *praefectus* of the Roman navy at Misenum when he witnessed the great eruption of Mount Vesuvius. Eager to get a better view, he set sail across the Bay of Naples towards the disaster and, alas, his consequent demise. Pliny is still remembered in vulcanology, where the term 'plinian' refers to a very violent eruption of a volcano in which columns of smoke and ash rise into the stratosphere.

THE HEROIC ANTHIAE

Air is soluble in water, or so says Pliny. That is why fish are able to breath, smell and hear. Among the fish he describes is the *anthiae*, a public-spirited creature which rescues its companions from anglers by severing fishing lines with its fin.

SNAKE BITES

Pliny recorded that the traditional cure for a bite from an adder was to press a pigeon's arse against the wound. If the pigeon died the treatment was obviously working, so you applied the arse of another pigeon, and so on, until the pigeons eventually stopped dying, at which point you were cured. If no pigeons were readily available, Pliny personally recommended tearing open a live swallow, and applying its innards to the bite.

TOP DARTS

Porcupines can fire their quills! Although Pliny made no mention of their range, or their accuracy.

HEAVY SLEEPERS

Pliny believed that humans were heavy sleepers - quite literally. He claimed that the human body became heavier when a person slept. Similarly, he calculated that when a person died they put on weight.

CD 7/07

THE FUN-Es

'Eye of newt, wing of bat, E102 tartrazine...'

'Let's face it, buddy – you're never going to forget.'

'This was due back next week!'

'It's from Mr Cummings!'

'I have this awful feeling I'm going to evolve into Liam Gallagher.'

Newman

The Poetry of QI

MALE ANGLER FISH *by Stephen Fry*

Male angler fish truly are pathetic.
It must be the feeblest male in
Nature, six times smaller than the female.

When they find a mate,
They latch onto them with their
Teeth and immediately start to disappear.

Scales, bones, blood vessels, all merge
Into those of the female, and
After a week, all that's left are two tiny little testes,
Which leak sperm into the female.

There are some of these female angler fish
Going around with about eight testicles
Hanging off them.

Brilliant.
It's like an Essex disco.

OBSCURITY *by Ronni Ancona*

Did you know about the word 'obscurity' before it got famous?
How it was beaten by its adjective father,
And left on the doorstep abandoned by its mother
And then it was the only noun growing up in a house of verbs.

But the verbs, they're always going out doing lovely things,
Because they're *doing* words,
And poor old obscurity was stuck inside suffering from asthma.

And then after school,
After school it was surrounded by quotation marks,
It got beaten up terribly,
And then one day it entered into a reality TV show,
And it became very famous
And it was much in demand
And used to describe all the people that leave *Big Brother* house.

DAVID BECKHAM LIVES IN CHINGFORD *by Ronni Ancona & Stephen Fry*

The Battle of Culloden is quite complicated,
Because it was basically an Italian fop with a Polish accent,
A bunch of Highlanders, some Irish,
A few French, fighting some Scottish lowlanders and
English, led by a fat German from Hanover.

There were the Campbells and the Rosses
And the Grants and the Gunns
And many of the lowland families.

There were more Scots there beating
Prince Charles, Edward Stuart,
Than there were English.

It's so weird that these national heroes
Are not from the place that they're supposed to be.

William Wallace was from Kenya. His mother was Masai.

Not really
But David Beckham is definitely from Chingford.

THE TROUSER PEOPLE *by Stephen Fry*

Appropriately enough, this book on Burma
Is called *The Trouser People*.

To give you a foretaste,
It quotes the diary of Sir George Scott –
The man who introduced football to Burma
In the 19th century:

Stepped on something soft and wobbly.
Struck a match.
Found it was a dead Chinaman.

Those were very much the days, weren't they?
You wonder why the British are hated around the globe.

HONEY *by Alan Davies*

Eddie Izzard once observed,
It was very odd that bees make honey.
Earwigs, he said, don't make chutney.

It takes twelve bees an
Entire lifetime to make enough honey
To fill a teaspoon.

So the lifetime of twelve bees,
And you go into a
Supermarket and you see all those jars.

Think how many
Bees have been working away?
If it's a 125 ml jar,
It'll take three hundred bees.

I HAD WIND WHEN I MET THE QUEEN *by Julian Clary*

It was just a little smidge, as I thought.
And I tried to get rid of it
By internal squeezing, as can be done.

But it wasn't going to go –
So I thought, Well:
I'll discreetly let it go.

But unfortunately
On that occasion
I shat myself.

OMNIPOD *by Mark Steel*

The South Africans once picked,
For their cricket team,
A one-legged Norwegian.

And it was in the time of apartheid,
So it was, you know, quite poignant,
Because you were more likely to get
In the South African cricket team
If you were a one-legged Norwegian,
Than if you were black
With two legs.

*Euterpe, Greek for 'delight', is the Greek Muse of lyric poetry, music and rejoicing.

Eleventh-Century Escape

Are you one of the 'been there, done that' crowd? Run out of new places to go on holiday? Why not try a break in the early to mid-11th century?

by Fred Monk

We didn't go anywhere remotely like this, unfortunately.

In these days when it seems almost impossible to find a genuinely 'new' travel destination, perhaps it's time we stopped thinking about 'where' and started thinking about 'when'?

I don't think the kids (or their mum Jocasta for that matter) were convinced when I said that we were going to try an 11th-century mini-break, which my wife described as sounding like 'Butlins with typhoid'. But without even so much as an **au pair** in tow we packed our bags and headed off **en famille.**

We arrived in 1002, just in time to witness King Ethelred's massacre of the Danish population of England — which certainly proved to us that he wasn't as 'unready' as the history books make out! Our hovel was built out of local materials (mud and sticks) and blended beautifully with its environment (a mire). In these days

before large-scale stone building, it's good to see regionally sourced, environmentally friendly style is back in fashion.

There was a simple open fire in the middle of the room (no stuffy old chimneys here!) set on a beaten earth floor. Decoration consisted of a handloom in the corner (used to make the lively local textiles, often depicting battles), some authentic flint-tempered pottery and a wooden bench and table. A single small window enhanced the atmospheric gloom, and someone had thoughtfully stretched a piece of oiled cloth across it. That, and the choking smoke from the fire, ensured that any light that might have seeped in was most unlikely to blind us.

The locals seem to go in for 'studio living', and we found the sleeping area in the same room. The beds consisted of a lavish pile of animal skins and sacks of hay. If I had a complaint it would be with the laundry department as these were generously supplied with lice, which we'll be picking from the children's hair for months. The slave offered to drape our bedding over the cesspit so that the rising ammonia would kill the bugs, but Jocasta didn't like the idea of her bed smelling of wee-wee so we declined. We were also initially surprised to find that a number of other guests, including a cow and two goats, were sharing with us. We were firmly told that this was not a booking error but, being winter, animals are brought in both to protect them from the cold and to help to keep the human inhabitants warm.

The food, to be honest, took a little getting used to. On the plus side, it's fresh – apart from the smoked meats – homemade, seasonal and organic. On the minus side, it's relentlessly disgusting. We'd opted for the 'peasant food' package after a wonderful holiday on a Tuscan olive farm last year but this was frankly a long way from **cucina di campagna**. The main meal, eaten off stout wooden platters, was a thin stew of local vegetables ('weeds' Jocasta called them, and not without reason) livened up with some grain, a lot of grit and the merest hint of a piece of pork (meat apparently being rather expensive). The children were, not surprisingly, furious that chips hadn't been invented yet. This was all washed down with small ale (for the kids!) and a stronger brew for the grown-ups, although neither was bitter – hops not reaching England for another 600 years. Drinking the local water unboiled is frowned upon – mainly because this can prove fatal.

As with any family holiday, the first thing on our minds, after an initial, crippling bout of dysentery, was finding things to do. Coming from an age of theme parks and Playstations, what could the 11th century offer a kite-surfing, off-roading, seen-it-all modern family? Well, provided you like singing, drinking and casual violence – quite a lot! The Danish invasion of 1009 (repeated 1013) showed that the English are by no means the worst behaved tourists. The Danes, who arrived by boat after what was clearly a rather rough crossing, not only hogged the best seats but proved to be savagely brutal, subjugating the whole nation to their will. But as Jocasta pointed out, at least the furniture and bathing habits might improve.

The highlight, for the kids at least, had to be the battle of Hastings in 1066. These were the days when people had to make their own entertainment, and they put on a show as though their lives depended on it – which, of course, they did. Watching 15,000 exhausted men cutting each other to pieces for hour upon hour on Senlac Hill was a treat, although we'd have liked a sniff of some toilet facilities. I won't spoil it for you, but do make sure you stay for the last stand of Harold II's housecarls as they gather around him to fight to the death with their long-handled axes – pure cinema!

In the evenings, things quietened down a bit and, whilst the wounded were patched up using folk remedies from what they colourfully call 'leechbooks', the rest of us clustered around the fire for an evening of singing and spectacularly heavy drinking. Once a week, a local 'scop' or bard visits the hovel, his shout of 'Hwæt!' signalling the beginning of one of his Germanic stories, poems or songs. Jocasta found the epic poetry rather moving, although the kids got a bit bored. They livened up (as did I) when the obscene riddles started. My favourite began, **'I stand erect in a bed.'** Can you guess what I am?

As the sun dips and its last rays struggle to get past the oilcloth and the acrid fumes from the fire and the cow, the heady atmosphere and pints of mead begin to take their toll. Most of the locals fall comatose where they are, but we stagger off to our lousy beds for some well-earned rest. Tomorrow will start at dawn (they're all early birds here!) when our new local Norman lord has offered to 'harry' us. We'll have to wait until tomorrow to find out exactly what that means.

GETTING THERE

It takes over 1,000 years to get from the beginning of the 11th century to the present day. Travelling back to the 11th century is frankly impossible for a number of temporal and philosophical reasons. We pretended.

WHERE TO STAY

The accommodation in the 11th century varies from rude 'huts' (like the hovel we stayed in) to impressive wooden 'halls' – usually the homes of the aristocracy. There are almost no stone buildings, with the exception of a handful of churches, until after the Norman Conquest. Even then the early Norman castles are impressive on the outside but hardly comfortable.

WHAT TO TAKE

A good medical kit – although there are a number of sophisticated herbal remedies available, they won't really help with the endemic typhus, cholera (in built-up areas – not that there are many of these) and tuberculosis. Do take water-purifying tablets to avoid throwing up at both ends or stick to the mead and ale which is boiled during manufacture and hence sterile(-ish). Polio, diphtheria and smallpox are also common, as is the occasional outbreak of bubonic plague, so it's best to check with your doctor about vaccinations before you leave.

WHAT TO BRING BACK

There are a number of good-value craft items available, although some are a little 'rustic'. Look out for Stamford ware pottery with its lurid yellow-green glaze, the colour of stale urine. Weapons are good value, especially the local single-bladed knife or 'scramseax'. Everyone here carries weapons, although you'll get into trouble if you draw a sword in the King's hall. Handmade textiles are plentiful although remember what is often called a 'tapestry' is actually an embroidered cloth – William the Conqueror got this wrong. Ultimately, the 11th century is an unspoilt, pre-industrial world. The real traveller brings home only memories (and perhaps tapeworm).

An artist's impression of our hovel

The epistles we get - a dip into the QI mailbag...

Dear Sir,

In your last show, Stephen Fry Esq. confidently told the British public that the male iguana possessed two 'penises'. Not so!

Many years ago, I found myself in the happy situation of being posted with the British Army in the Amazonian rainforest. (Trouble with the natives!) I remember those days fondly. Pink gins on the veranda, pygmy hunts on Thursdays and a charming batman called Tufty. But I digress. As it so happens, our battalion kept a pet iguana. Fine fellow called Spartacus. Bit of a gammy leg, but he entertained the chaps for hours. Anyway, I distinctly remember that Spartacus had three cocks, not two. Splendid things they were. He was always showing them off to the gals.

Anyway, just thought you should know!

Pip, pip and keep up the good work.

Yours faithfully, Major Giles H. Ferguson, The Wirral

Dear Mr Alan Davies Sir,

May I call you Alan? Greetings! It is your friend Amobi Abachai from Nigeria. You must be remembering me as I emailed you chain letter and you then placed £1,500 in my offshore bank account for your share in the moneys left behind by my father, the late General Sani Abachai.

You may remember that my father, bless his soul in heaven glory glory hallelujah, was most regrettably ousted in the recent coup by Chief Olusegun Obasanjo. Although I promised you that you would get 10% of my father's $565 Million US Dollars inheritance fund, I must regrettably inform you that matters have become difficult for me in Nigeria. Chief Olusegun Obasanjo has captured me and put me in a very deep snake pit with only a packet of Kellogg Pop Tarts to keep me alive, and my wireless laptop to keep my sanity mind. As such, I am needing to commandeer a military force to help me escape and need to recruit British SAS. Please help my escape by placing £150,000 into my usual account BANK OF NIGERIA: 345454366, SORT: 349234. Thanking you!

Your friendship forever,

Amobi Abachai (P.S. Your money come soon!)

Dear Sirs,

I think I could help you get a bigger audience for your show. By implying that QI is only Quite Interesting, I am sure you are missing out on a lot of people who would want to watch a Very Interesting programme. In my last job (in politics), I had similar success by changing the name of a party from 'Labour' to 'New Labour'. Hey, presto! Everyone was fooled into thinking they were going to get a different kind of political party. For a mere £1.5 million (and a book deal afterwards), the advice is yours to keep.

All the best,

Alastair Campbell, Hôtel Enorme, Cap d'Antibes
(P.S. Or what about Amazingly Interesting?)

Dear Mr Titchmarsh,

Surely begonias bloom in shady spots during the summer and not the other way round?

Love, your admirer,

Sally Frimbly, Surrey (P.S. Knickers enclosed)

Dear Sir,

I recently chanced upon the Christmas episode of your television programme, IQ. Quite frankly, it wasn't a patch on Ant and Dec's Saturday Night Takeaway and Animals Do the Craziest Things but worse still you are grievously misinformed about the festive arrangements at Sandringham. You were, I grant you, correct in saying that members of the Royal Family open their gifts on Christmas Eve (a German tradition) and that Her Majesty drinks her own blend of Indian Tea. However, it is simply not true to suggest that the Queen's favourite presents of all time were 'a casserole dish and a gift-wrapped washing-up apron'. That is a damned lie, and you know it. This is just what we have come to expect of the bearded homosexual Communists and fellow travellers who run the BBC! By far the Queen's favourite Christmas present was when Andrew dumped Fergie.

Get your bloody facts straight!

Yours faithfully,

Philip, HRH The Duke of Edinburgh

Dear Sir,

Ahoy there!

As the founder of Anagram Weekly Magazine, I wondered whether you realised what a treasure trove of fun you can have with the name of your resident panellist, Alan Davies?! It occurred to me that Alan would drive 'a ladies van' on his way to the shopping centre to do 'a vandalise'. As a well-known pigeon fancier, he could go to the pet shop to pick up some 'avian leads' by paying on 'a laden Visa', or go to the doctor for 'a nasal dive', some 'anal advise' and 'a saved nail'.

If he was peckish and had 'a saliva den', I'd imagine he'd go and buy 'a salad vine'. Only a thought!

Yours,

Dean Vialas

Dear Stephen Fry,

Hi! I'm from Ukraine and I would like to meet kind man to be my guide and maybe more. So if you haven't wife or girlfriend now, you may reply please. I'm going to work in UK for five months. My friends tell I look well enough. Please send your letter directly to my email mary.svetlana@ukraimail.com and I send my foto to you. I am waiting for your reply.

Buy,

your Mary, Ukraine

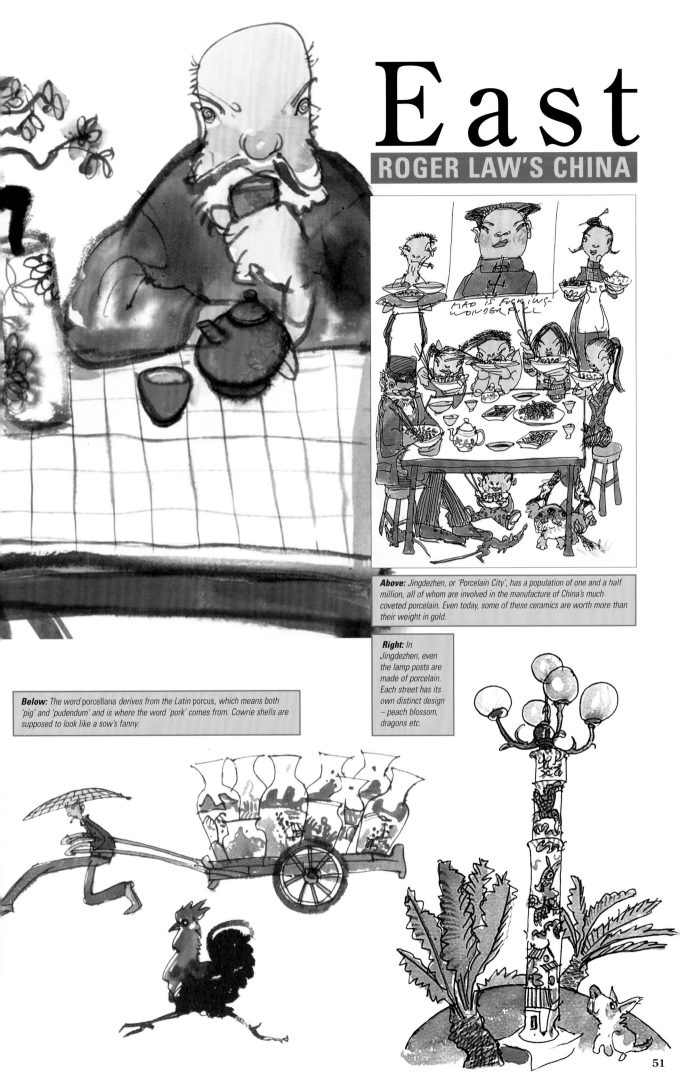

East
ROGER LAW'S CHINA

Above: Jingdezhen, or 'Porcelain City', has a population of one and a half million, all of whom are involved in the manufacture of China's much coveted porcelain. Even today, some of these ceramics are worth more than their weight in gold.

Right: In Jingdezhen, even the lamp posts are made of porcelain. Each street has its own distinct design – peach blossom, dragons etc.

Below: The word porcellana derives from the Latin porcus, which means both 'pig' and 'pudendum' and is where the word 'pork' comes from. Cowrie shells are supposed to look like a sow's fanny.

Right: McDonalds in China is known as 'The American Embassy'

Above: Each month, five million more Chinese acquire a mobile phone. The reception is often better in remote parts of China than it is in Norfolk. Many beauty spots (such as Guilin's famous limestone mountains) sport masts and barefoot peasants can be seen ploughing with oxen whilst yelling into their mobiles.

Below: In Mandarin, the word 'secretary' and 'honey' have the same pronunciation, and 'sweet honey' has the same sound as 'little secretary'. In President Jiang Zemin's new China, a 'little secretary' is an essential status symbol.

Above: The current slang for 'gay' in the new capitalist China is 'comrade'

Above: Nappies are not used in rural China. Instead, babies and toddlers have no seams in their trouser seats, allowing a quick-release action for number ones and twos.

Left: The Chinese barber or hairdresser is often a knocking shop. The Chinese character for 'leisure' also means 'brothel'. Under Mao, most towns and cities had a 'People's Square'. These have now been renamed 'Leisure Square'.

Right: The demonstrations and subsequent killings in Tiananmen Square are now referred to as 'The Accident'.

Above: Who killed cock sparrow? There are very few sparrows in China. Mao decreed that every family in China had to kill one a week to stop them eating all the rice. Sparrows do not eat rice.

Above: Mao awoke one morning and, in his wisdom, decreed that every Chinese family should present a set number of rats' tails to Communist officials each week. Unlike the sparrow campaign, the rats proved more elusive. Families found the solution by breeding rats to make up their quota of tails.

Above: Mao is the patron saint of Chinese taxi drivers. The Chinese have a popular urban myth that when Mao died, he descended into hell – whereupon Old Nick put him in charge of the traffic department.

Left: There is no such thing as a comfortable chair in the whole of China.

eyes

The vast majority of people entering a shop look left and turn right. Thereafter, women look down and men look up. Products placed 3–4 feet above the floor have the greatest overall sale potential, but exotic high-priced foods are placed on the higher shelves because very few women buy them.

The word 'pupil' is from the Latin *pupillus*, a little child or doll – after the tiny reflection of yourself you see when you look into someone else's eye. The same concept exists in all Indo-European languages as well as Swahili, Lapp, Chinese and Samoan. The ancient English word for pupil was 'eye-baby'.

Eyelash mites are tiny creatures with eight stumpy legs and wormlike bodies that live in the base of the eyelashes, as many as 25 to a follicle. They are so efficient at processing the dead skin they eat that they don't have an asshole.

Two men lay claim to the invention of false eyelashes. The first is Max Factor (1887–1938), who also invented the eyebrow pencil, lip-gloss and 'pancake' make-up, and was the first person to sell cosmetics for non-theatrical use. He started his career as an apprentice dentist in Poland. The other is the film director D. W. Griffith (1875–1948), who also invented the crane shot. His false eyelashes were made for Seena Owen who played Princess Beloved in the movie Intolerance *(1916). They were so cumbersome that she could only wear them a few hours at a time before her eyes swelled up and closed.*

About 15 babies in the UK each year are born without eyes, a horrific condition known as anopthalmia.

Only one creature on earth is normally born with one eye, a primitive fish called the Cyclops. Most insects have five eyes. The word senocular means 'having six eyes'. Most spiders have eight eyes. Grasshoppers have ten eyes. Caterpillars have 12 eyes, though the butterflies they turn into have only four.

According to former French president François Mitterrand, Mrs Thatcher has 'eyes like Caligula and the mouth of Marilyn Monroe'.

Luis Buñuel's Surrealist movie *Un Chien Andalou* (1929) featured a number of dead donkeys provided by Salvador Dali. He laid them out on grand pianos and cut out their eyes with a pair of scissors.

On July 16th 1945, the physicist Richard Feynmann was the only person to see the explosion of the first atomic bomb with the naked eye. Knowing that bright light alone can't harm the human eye, he refused to wear the regulation-issue dark glasses and watched it through the windscreen of a truck, which was sufficient to shield his eyes from harmful ultraviolet radiation.

'THE EYE OF GOD'

Left: The Helix Nebula is 650 light years away in the constellation of Aquarius.

In 1210, after a three-day siege of the town of Bram, Simon de Montfort seized the garrison. He cut off the noses and upper lips of more than 100 men and gouged their eyes out. Just one man was left with a single eye and ordered to lead his blind comrades to safety at the next town. De Montfort's strategy was to panic those defending the chateau at Cabaret into surrender as they saw coming down the road a party of living skulls, complete with grinning teeth and a triangular gap in the centre of the head topped by sightless eyes. This appears to us the act of a heartless monster, yet all those who knew de Montfort described him as handsome, charming, saintly, pious, noble, etc. Whatever his supposed charms and brilliant military strategy, de Montfort failed to capture Cabaret (HURRAH!), which eventually surrendered over a month later under diplomatic rather than military pressure.

I have eyes like those of a dead pig.
MARLON BRANDO

The human eye can take in a million simultaneous impressions and tell the difference between 8 million different colours. On a clear, moonless night the human eye can detect a match being struck 50 miles away.

An 'eye-servant' is someone who can only be trusted to do any work when his or her employer is watching.

The eyes are the spoons of speech. ARABIC PROVERB

Dante Gabriel Rossetti (1828–1882) had such bad eyesight that he wore two pairs of spectacles on top of each other.

The eyes of a buzzard are five times sharper than a human's. A person with exceptional eyesight may just be able to make out a rabbit flicking its ears from 100 yards away. A buzzard can do so from a distance of 2 miles.

11% of guide dogs in New Zealand are short-sighted. The eyesight of some of them is so poor that, if they were human, they would have to wear glasses.

Apart from the head chef, everyone who works at the Blindekuh ('Blind Cow') Restaurant in Zurich is either blind or partially sighted. Meals are served in pitch darkness, so that, in a reverse of the norm, sighted customers are entirely reliant on the help of the blind waiters and waitresses.

The philosopher René Descartes (1596–1650) had a fetish for cross-eyed women. He conquered this when he realised that the root of his fascination was a little girl with cross-eyes whom he had played with as a child. He used this insight to support his belief that human beings have free will.

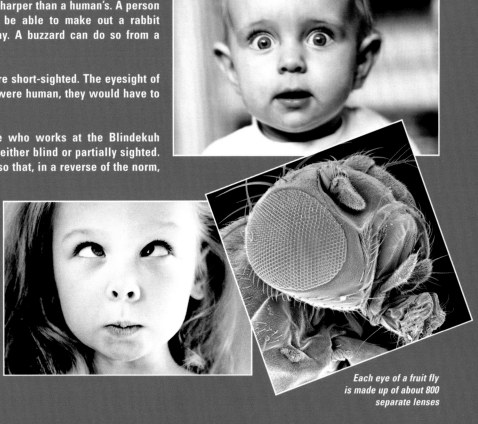

Each eye of a fruit fly is made up of about 800 separate lenses

WHOSE EYE IS THIS?

A: Meerkat   B :Swan   C: Human   D: Seal   E: Lion   F: Seagull   G: Dragonfly   H: Cow   I: Elephant   J: Pelican   K: Eagle Owl   L: Ostrich

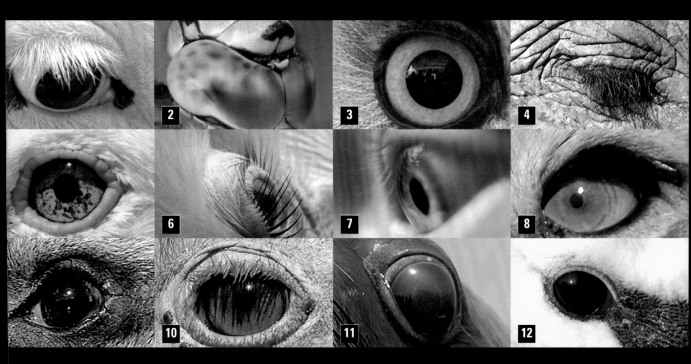

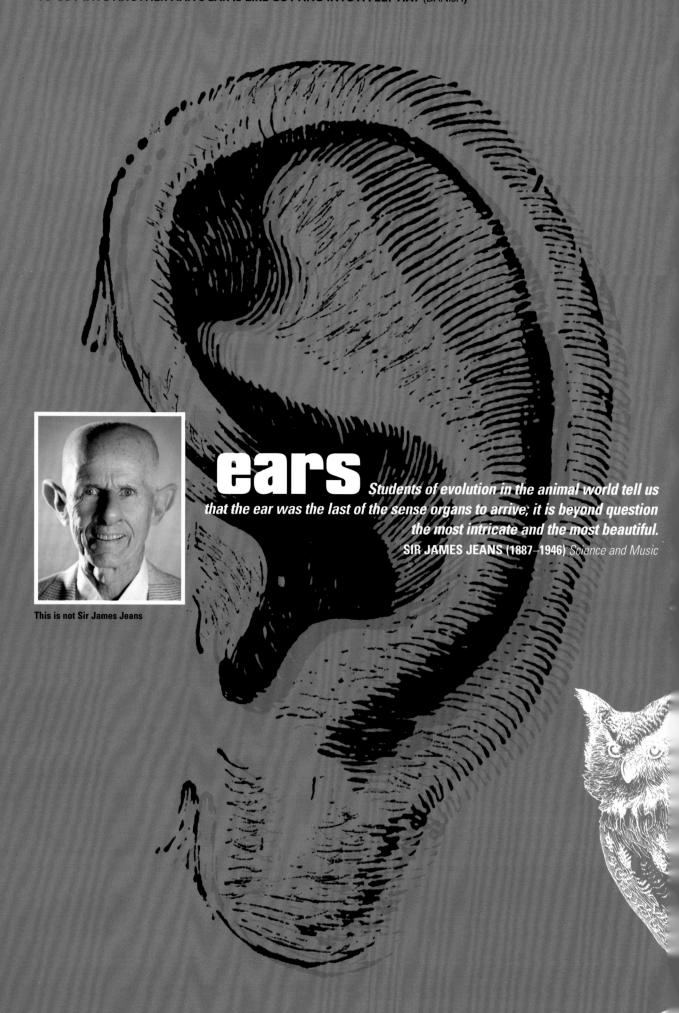

ears

Students of evolution in the animal world tell us that the ear was the last of the sense organs to arrive; it is beyond question the most intricate and the most beautiful.
SIR JAMES JEANS (1887–1946) *Science and Music*

This is not Sir James Jeans

The ancient Chinese believed that the ears indicated character and destiny. Long earlobes meant long life, thick ones wealth. They also believed that the longer a person's ears, the nobler he would be. Kings and emperors of Old China all supposedly had extremely long ears (as do all statues of Buddha). The ears of Liu Bei, founder of the Han dynasty in AD 221, are said to have reached his shoulders. He could see his own ears just by glancing round.

For women the best aphrodisiacs are words. The G-spot is in the ears. He who looks for it below there is wasting his time.
ISABEL ALLENDE

This woman is not an ancient Chinese. She's from Sarawak in Malaysia.

The smallest muscle and the smallest bone in the human body are in the ears. The smallest muscle is the *stapedius,* which is just over 1 mm long. Paralysis of this results in a condition called *hyperacusis,* which causes normal sounds to seem extremely loud. The second smallest muscle in the body is also in the ear. It's called the *tensor tympani* and is used to reduce the noise caused by chewing. The smallest bone is the stirrup bone. It's between 2 mm and 3 mm long and is shaped just like a tiny stirrup. It is also known as the *stapes,* from the mediaeval Latin for stirrup, *stapeda* or *stapedium* – literally 'foot-stand'. This is a made up word dating from the 14th century. There was no such word in classical Latin. Stirrups were unknown to the ancient Romans. They were a Chinese invention, dating from around the time of Christ. Later, they reached India, where the aristocracy both walked and rode barefoot. An Indian stirrup was originally just a ring for each big toe. Without stirrups, it is impossible to fight on horseback. Some historians believe that the adoption of stirrups by the cavalry of the Frankish King Charles Martel in AD 732 enabled the creation of the feudal system.

It is all very well to be able to write books, but can you waggle your ears?
J. M. BARRIE (1860–1937)

An okapi can wash its own ears inside and out with its tongue. Crickets have their ears on their forelegs. A cicada's ears are on its stomach. The praying mantis has only one ear, located in the centre of its chest.

Spiders do not have ears at all. They hear with minuscule hairs on their legs. This is not as strange as it sounds. Human hearing works the same way. Inside each human inner ear are approximately 15,000 extremely sensitive little hairs. These enable us to hear a whisper from many feet away, but loud noises (such as rock music or firing a shotgun without ear defenders) gradually destroy the hair cells. If you are standing next to someone and you have to shout to make yourself heard, you can be sure that the noise is damaging your ears. The hair cells in the ears are irreplaceable, and the loss of them is one of the principal causes of deafness. Human hearing starts to get gradually worse from the age of 20.

The inner ears of lobsters contain sand, which may explain why they can only hear things at very close range. Gravity keeps the sand at the bottom of their ears and tells the lobsters they're the right way up. Researchers replace the sand with iron filings. They use a magnet to move these around inside the lobster's head and fool it into flipping upside down. This greatly amuses the researchers.

The things that look like ears on an owl are tufts for display purposes only. Owls' ears are recessed into the sides of their faces, usually right at the outer edge of the ring of feathers around the eye. This feathery disc acts like a parabolic dish, focusing the sound waves into the ear canal entrance. The ears are positioned at different heights on each side of the head, enabling the owl to hear which vertical (as well as which horizontal) direction any sound may be coming from.

EAR-BASED PARTY TRICK
The oils and fats in earwax destroy the froth on beer by lowering the surface tension of the bubbles, which burst. People who wear glasses can get the same effect by using the sweat that collects on the bridge of the nose. Even the smallest traces of fat have this effect, but western earwax works better than oriental; most Asians have dry earwax, with a lower fat content.

John Bennet, aged 36, a Londoner, was today ordered to seek treatment at a psychiatric hospital after biting off the ear of a Danish Labour Exchange Official. Mr Bennet, from Hendon, who has lived for four years in Denmark, was found guilty of knocking down the official and chewing off his ear when he was refused public funds to go to Norway to look for a job. The local court was told that when the official recovered consciousness after the attack, he found his ear on a desk with a note that read 'Your Ear'. **THE TIMES**

Excommunication Exclusive!

Q1 is proud to present the first extracts from the recently discovered (unauthorised) Calendar of Saints featuring the Merry Month of May, by Frederick the Monk

3rd May St James The Lesser is perhaps not a title you'd aspire to but, as a cousin of Jesus, he certainly had a few stories to tell. The two most famous are that he prayed so frequently that the skin on his knees thickened until it looked like a camel's and that, after the crucifixion, he vowed to fast until Jesus returned. Jesus promptly then not only appeared unto James but also rustled up a spot of lunch for him. He was eventually martyred by being thrown from a tower of the temple in Jerusalem and then beaten to death with sticks.

4th May A day for firefighters to raise a glass to their patron, St Florian, an officer in the Roman army who is said to have put out a fire in the town of Noricum in modern-day Austria using a single bucket of water. This could be considered miraculous, or alternatively he might have overstated the scale of the fire.

6th May St Evodius was traditionally one of the 72 disciples commissioned by Jesus. He was ordained by St Peter and became Bishop of Antioch. What is quite interesting about him is that he's the first person on record to use the term 'Christian'.

8th May St Gibrian didn't do anything too miraculous but he came from a really wonderfully pious family – his siblings included St Tressan, St Helan, St Germanus, St Abran, St Petran, St France, St Promptia, and St Possenna. Just imagine what fun Sunday lunch must have been!

10th May St Simon the Apostle has to make any list of cruel and unusual martyrdoms, having been sawn in half. And it wasn't a trick.

11th May St Gengulphus, tiring of his wife's numerous affairs but not wishing to embarrass her publicly, retired to a hermitage in his castle at Avallon. One would have thought that his wife and her lovers would have been delighted that they could now get on with whatever they fancied without Gengulphus breathing down their necks, but no, one of the lovers tracked the poor old chap down and murdered him in his bed.

12th May Move right down the platform... it's St Pancras' day! St Pancras was an orphan brought by his uncle St Dionysius to Rome where he promptly converted to Christianity and was just as promptly martyred, aged only 14. Some 350 years later, Pope Vitalian had the wizard idea of digging him up and sending his remains to England, where the natives were proving unwilling to convert. St Pancras was duly shipped off to a delighted St Augustine of Canterbury, who'd only recently got his feet under the Archbishop and Primate of All England's desk. He split up the remains and immediately went about installing them in the altars of all the new churches he was busy building, each of which he dedicated to the saint.

13th May St Imelda Lambertini was a student at a Dominican convent who showed particular dedication to St Agnes, to whom she frequently prayed. As a reward for this she received her first communion 'miraculously' when aged only 11 and then promptly died in an ecstasy of love and joy.

15th May We should perhaps say 'Hats Off' – or, considering the form of his martyrdom 'Heads Off!' – to St Boniface of Tarsus, who had the pleasure of being converted by a Roman matron with the unusual name of Algae. And let's not forget St Matthias the Apostle, the patron saint of alcoholism.

16th May On May 10th 1657, St Andrew Bobola was living in Pinsk in Russia trying to persuade Russian Orthodox Christians to convert to Catholicism when Cossacks raided the city. Cossacks weren't all that fond of Jesuits, so when they caught him they first beat him, then tied him to a horse and dragged him through the streets. They then attacked him with knives, skinned him alive and finally beheaded him, just to be sure.

18th May St Felix of Cantalice was not necessarily someone you'd want to invite to a dinner party or any other social gathering. His great trick was that he could 'see' your sins – a ability so disconcerting that sinners used to hide from him i the street. A man of great piety, his funeral was so well attende that a hole had to be knocked in the church wall to get all th mourners out after the service without being crushed.

19th May St Calocerus was a eunuch made Governor Anatolia by the Roman emperor Decius. When Deci accused him of the twin crimes of embezzlement a Christianity, Calocerus chose to defend Christianity. One o only assume this meant he felt he didn't stand a chance on the embezzlement rap. Sadly he was convicted on both counts and Decius ordered him burnt alive. As is often the way with saints, however, the flames refused to burn him, so his guards had to beat him to death with the fiery brands.

20th May This is a good day for advertisers, public relations personnel and compulsive gamblers (all of which amounts to roughly the same thing), as it's their patron's day. St Bernadino of Siena made his name as one of the most charismatic of all medieval preachers, enlivening his act with bonfires of the vanities, collective weeping (always fun) and exorcisms – a sort of righteous Paul Daniels. The Blessed Columba of Rieti also knew some neat tricks. She was prone to mystical out-of-body ecstasies, in one of which she toured the Holy Land, thus saving her the time and inconvenience of having to visit in person.

21st May St Godric wrote the song 'Sainte Nicholaes', the earliest surviving piece of lyric poetry in English. He was a serious ascetic living in Finchale, Co. Durham, in a mud hut. To make this even more miserable he insisted on going barefoot, wearing a hair shirt (under a metal breastplate just to make sure it rubbed), living only off gathered fruits and berries and standing in a bucket of icy water to control his lust. To his further satisfaction, no doubt, Scottish raiders repeatedly arrived to beat him up, under the inexplicable impression that he had some buried treasure lying about. 'Look! – there's a bloke in a hut wearing a hair shirt and standing in a bucket of water. He must be rich – let's mug him.'

23rd May St William of Rochester was not actually from Rochester, he was from Perth in Scotland. However, he did go to Rochester, which is rarely a wise move. A bit of a wild child before he had a sudden conversion to Christianity and decided to become a baker, for a while he lived a good and simple life baking bread, giving one in 10 of his loaves to the poor and attending Mass each day. Then one day he was on his way home from Mass when he found an abandoned baby on his doorstep. Being a lovely man, he took the lad in, called him David and brought him up as his own – even teaching him the baking game. Everything was going swimmingly until William suggested to David that they should go on a pilgrimage to the Holy Land. After making a suitably large supply of professionally turned-out sandwiches for the trip, the two headed off. They had only got as far as Rochester when it all went a bit wrong. For some reason (hormones??) David turned on William and hit him with a club. He then cut his throat and stole his money and ran away. Fortunately, there was a happy ending. An insane old woman found William's body, put a garland of honeysuckle on it and was promptly cured of her madness. Some monks who had been watching this got very excited. It just so happened that they were looking for a saint to put in their cathedral in Rochester to cash in on the pilgrimage trade (or to 'venerate' as they liked to put it) – and there right in front of them was a bona fide miracle! So everyone went home happy. Except St William, of course.

24th May Things started going wrong for St Simon Stylites the Younger with his father's death, when he was just 5 years old. Thankfully, a kindly monk took Simon in, but it soon turned out he was a sociopath, and, when Simon was 7, he suggested they both move to the top of pillars to get a bit of peace and quiet. The plan didn't quite work out as expected as, once everyone heard there were two blokes living on pillars, they naturally wanted to throng to them. The two unlucky hermits had to keep building their pillars up to get away from the crowds. Starting at a perfectly sensible dwelling height of

3 feet, after 13 years they were 60 feet up in the air. At this point, Simon climbed down his pillar and hid in the mountains to get away from everyone and particularly from the kindly monk whose rotten idea it was. Eventually, a group of would-be students tracked him down and persuaded him to start a monastery for them. This he did, placing at its centre a brand new pillar for him to live on. He was then ordained a priest, which was rather tricky for the bishop doing the ordaining. Simon wouldn't come down, so the bishop had to go up. This made things even more difficult for the monks, as every time they wanted their new priest to celebrate communion they had to fetch a ladder. St Simon died up there at the ripe old age of 76. Of those 76 years he had spent 69 on pillars.

26th May At the age of 10 St Mary Ann de Paredes decided to become a hermit, not in the traditional mud hut/cave etc. but in her sister's house, which must have made for some awkward moments at dinner parties. She chose to live entirely on consecrated wafers and communion wine, supplemented by one ounce of dry bread every 8 to 10 days. ('The Eucharist Diet' – it could well catch on!) After the 1645 earthquake in Quito, Ecuador (where she lived), there was (as so often happens after earthquakes) an epidemic, and Mary Ann decided to offer herself as a sacrifice to God to spare the city. God seems to have liked the idea because she dropped dead – a white lily blossoming from her blood as she did so.

27th May St Augustine of Canterbury was the first Archbishop of Canterbury and the first English prelate, at least in the south where Roman Christianity seems to have died out. Whilst on his way to Britain to evangelise the pagans he got frightened by the stories of the nasty English (all true of course) and scampered back to Rome. Here he asked the Pope (Gregory the Great no less) if he could go somewhere nicer, but the Pope was very cross and told him he HAD to go to England. So he did.

30th May It's St Joan of Arc's day today. I'm sure I needn't bore you with the details of her life and her fight to overthrow English rule in France and restore the French royal line, but I did want to mention one thing. During the First World War the US Treasury department issued a series of patriotic posters urging the women of America to buy War Saving Stamps to help the war effort. The most famous of these showed Joan of Arc under the stirring headline 'Joan of Arc Saved France'. They were apparently blissfully unaware that Joan had saved France from their allies – the British.

31st May St Petronilla has her day today. Medieval hagiographies claimed that she was the daughter of St. Peter and was so beautiful that he locked her up in a tower to keep the men away, but the Catholic Church has dismissed this (well they would wouldn't they). Tradition also has it that a pagan king called Flaccus wooed her. He presumably had a key to her tower (as it were). But she wasn't impressed with the nasty pagan and refused all his advances. When he absolutely insisted on marrying her, she went on hunger strike and died three days later. She should have stuck to the Eucharist Diet! (see 26th May). She is the patron saint of treaties between Frankish emperors and Popes – which is, let's be honest, quite a niche patronage – and, given the lack of Frankish emperors these days, leaves her with plenty of time on her hands.

EUROPEAN LANGUAGES

No. 3: Spanish

Spanish is the third most widely spoken language in the world after Mandarin Chinese and English. The Spanish alphabet has 30 letters as compared to 26 in English and about 50,000 characters in Chinese.

In Spanish the word *esposas* means both 'wives' and 'handcuffs'. The word *matador* is Spanish for 'killer'. The Spanish for a restaurant bill is *dolorosa,* meaning 'painful', and 'hummingbird' is *chupamirtos* (literally 'a suck-myrtles').

The Spanish are a proud people, and their language reflects this, endowing the humble with magnificent nomenclature. An *escaparatista* is not an escapologist but a window-dresser. An escapologist is an *evasionista*, rather than a tax-dodger. The romantic-sounding *fontanero* means plumber (literally 'spring-man'). It's also used in political slang to mean someone who investigates leaks. A plumber's mate goes by the sonorous title of *desatascador de fregaderos,* which sounds like a Spanish Admiral of the Fleet but in fact just means 'unblocker of sinks'. A *balconero* is not someone who hires a box at the opera but a cat burglar and a *zapador* is someone who uses a spade for a living (like 'sapper' in English).

* * *

SPANISH DICTIONARY

baldada	bucketful
bolso	bag
bombo	gobsmacked
juicioso	wise
kodak	a small camera
pluto	sloshed
podredumbre	pus
propaganda	advertising
zambo	knock-kneed
zambombo	yokel
zambombazo	bang, explosion

SPANISH PHRASEBOOK

Así te tragues un pavo y todas las plumas se conviertan en cuchillas de afeitar
May all your turkey's feathers turn into razor blades

Estoy hasta los cojones de este jodido hijo de puta
I'm fed up to the male organs of generation with this very badly damaged son of a lady of ill repute

ELVIS FROM A WELSH VIEWPOINT
BY ROB BRYDON

There exist recordings of Elvis singing the following Beatles songs – 'Yesterday', 'Something', 'Get Back', 'Lady Madonna' and a particularly ill-advised stab at 'Hey Jude' in a key not fit for human consumption.

Songs about Elvis: 'Black Velvet' (Alannah Myles), 'King of the Mountain' (Kate Bush), 'Advertising Space' (Robbie Williams), 'Jordan the Comeback' (Prefab Sprout), 'Walking in Memphis' (Marc Cohn), 'Calling Elvis' (Dire Straits). Paul Simon says his song 'Graceland' is not about Elvis. Hmm... he's obviously not listened to it.

While playing in Memphis on his Born to Run tour in 1976, Bruce Springsteen scaled the wall at Graceland, hoping to visit Elvis and present him with the song 'Fire', written with the King in mind. Elvis wasn't in – he was performing in Lake Tahoe, and Bruce was escorted off the premises by a security guard. In the end the song was released by The Pointer Sisters.

Elvis was a big fan of Monty Python and Peter Sellers.

The American Secret Service's code name for President Clinton was 'Elvis'.

When Clinton played his saxophone on a US chat show, the tune was 'Heartbreak Hotel'.

Of George Bush, Clinton said: 'You know, Bush is always comparing me to Elvis in sort of unflattering ways. I don't think Bush would have liked Elvis very much, and that's just another thing that's wrong with him.'

The last song, 'It's Easy for You', on Elvis's last album, *Moody Blue*, was written by Tim Rice and Andrew Lloyd Webber.

In Las Vegas in the 1950s Elvis saw Billy Ward and the Dominoes performing a version of his then hit 'Don't Be Cruel'. He was so taken with it that he began to sing it just like the version he'd heard. If you listen to his live performances of the song he often sings the line 'at least please telephone' in the style he'd heard: 'at least please uh telephone'. It's very difficult to explain in print, but you can hear it on *The Million Dollar Quartet.* The singer in the Dominoes who performed the song was a then unknown Jackie Wilson. Elvis talked about Wilson's unique dance style. Years later, in one of his many films, when Elvis sang 'Return to Sender', he danced in the Jackie Wilson style. Incidentally, when Dexy's Midnight Runners played the Van Morrison song 'Jackie Wilson Said' on *Top of the Pops,* the BBC mistakenly put up a picture of Jocky Wilson, the popular darts player.

After visiting Graceland in 2004, I left my camera in a photo booth in a Memphis amusement arcade. When I went back it was gone. Do you have it?

ELVIS WAS OF WELSH DESCENT. BOTH HIS PARENTS HAD WELSH CHRISTIAN NAMES. HIS MOTHER WAS CALLED GLADYS LOVE SMITH, AND HIS FATHER WAS CALLED VERNON ELVIS PRESLEY.

The tiny parish of St Elvis is less than 20 miles from the Preseli Hills in Pembrokeshire, South Wales.

The igneous rhyolite and dolerite 'bluestone' of the Preseli Hills is said to have provided the altar and ring stones for Stonehenge, which were were supposedly transported there by land and water. But similar stones have been discovered across southern Wales and England and even on Salisbury Plain itself.

About 4 miles from St Davids, St Elvis is on the shore of St Bride's bay in St George's Channel. The small rather undistinguished church is dedicated to St Teilaw.

St David, the patron saint of Wales, had an older cousin named 'Ailfyw' (the Welsh rendering of Elvis), who was once Bishop of Munster in Ireland and was famous for baptising St David at Porthclais.

In Welsh, the village of St Elvis is known as Llaneilfyw (Church of Elvis). In 1833 it had a population of 44 people spread over two farms and 200 acres.

Near Solva, 3 or 4 miles east of St Davids, there is a 'St Elvis Farm' which lies close to the 5,000-year-old St Elvis cromlech. The site of the former St Elvis Church and St Elvis Holy Well are also nearby. Local islands off the coast near Solva bear the name St Elvis Rocks.

'Elvis foot' is climber's jargon for being so tired that your foot trembles on the rock.

One of St Elvis's few recorded utterances seems to indicate a tolerance of homosexuality.

In 1955, Elvis Presley was signed to the record company RCA. Though he had not yet had a hit record, he was paid $40,000, at that time the highest transfer fee ever paid to a recording artist.

During his whole life, Elvis never went to the home of his manager 'Colonel' Tom Parker.

Right: Jackie Wilson, easily confused with (far right) Jocky Wilson

BIG SCIENCE FOR SMALL KITCHENS

Experiments
...you can do at home

The elite **QI** research cadre doesn't spend all day with its noses in books. We are on a constant mission to understand and to measure the real world around us. Here, five senior 'action elves' demonstrate three experiments you can try at home. And one that you won't want to bother with as it is a completely futile waste of time, money and cats.

1: How to Measure the Speed of Light

You will need:
A microwave oven
A ruler
Some grated cheese*

Step 1: Disable the turntable on your microwave by removing the turntable or flipping the dish over. The experiment will not work if the cheese is rotating.

Step 2: Spread the grated cheese evenly on a plate and put the plate in the microwave.

Step 3: Turn microwave on for around 20 seconds. As soon as you see some of the cheese start to melt, STOP.

Step 4: Examine the grated cheese. You will see that some areas have melted and others haven't. Now measure the horizontal distance between the melted spots.

Step 5: Retire to perform your calculations.

The calculations
Microwaves are electromagnetic waves tuned to 2.5 GHz – the exact frequency to make water molecules rotate. The rotation causes friction and the friction heats the food. Now, the one thing everyone knows about microwave ovens is that they don't heat things evenly. This is usually a bad thing, but for us it's really useful.

The key element in our measurement is that the microwaves in the oven are 'standing waves' – that is, they are stationary in space with only the amplitude (the up and down bit) oscillating. Microwaves heat at the high and low points of the wave only (that's why they heat so unevenly and why the food inside is usually rotated).

A wavelength is the distance from one wavetop to the next. So we can measure the length of the wave, which will be twice the distance between the melty spots in the cheese (as they melted at both the top and the bottom of each wave). Now that we have the wavelength of the microwaves (and we already know their frequency) we can calculate the speed of light using the following equation:

Speed of light = frequency x wavelength

So:
Wavelength (in metres) x frequency (in Hz) = speed of light (in metres per second)

Or, more cheesily:
Twice the distance between melty spots (in metres) x 2,500,000,000 (frequency in Hz) = SPEED OF LIGHT

Final Step: *Eat cheese*
**chocolate chips are an acceptable substitute*

2: How to Measure the Circumference of the Earth

Eratosthenes first devised this experiment in the 3rd century BC. Are you as good with your hands as an ancient Greek? Let's find out.

You will need:
A piece of string
A protractor
A clock
A stick
A friend with a piece of string, a protractor, a clock and a stick
A sunny day

Step 1: Your friend needs to be on roughly the same longitude as you (i.e. due north or due south) but a few hundred miles away – and also in the northern hemisphere. Ghana is nice and sunny.

Step 2: Agree between you on a day to perform the experiment. Remember it must be sunny – so perhaps plump for summer?

Step 3: On that day, at exactly midday GMT, both go outside and place a stick vertically on the ground (your protractor may help with the verticality, or you could use a plumb bob or a spirit level). Take the string and hold it taut between the top of the stick and the end of the shadow it casts on the ground, forming a triangle.

Step 4: Measure the angle between the top of the stick and the string using your protractor. This is the angle at which the sun's rays are reaching the Earth.

Step 5: Retire indoors to phone your friend to get their measurement. Or you could use your mobile right where you're standing. Very much your choice.

The calculations

For this calculation, we are going to assume that the sun is SO far away that the light rays hitting the Earth are effectively parallel. At midday at two different longitudes we measured the sun's angle in the sky using sticks and strings. These measurements will be different because the world is spherical(-ish).

The difference in angle will tell us what proportion of the 360 degrees of a full circle the slice between our two observers is. By finding out that proportion and multiplying it by the distance between the observers we can then calculate the circumference of the Earth.

Let's do the sums…

Step 1: *The first thing we need to calculate is the difference between the two readings. Take the higher number (lets call it Angle 'a') and subtract the other reading (lets call that one 'b') from it. This tells us how many degrees of a circle there are between the two observers.*

Step 2: *Now we need to find out how many of those arcs would make up a full circle so let's divide it into 360. This tells us how many of the arcs between our observers it would take to make a full circle.*

Step 3: *Now we need to know the distance (we'll call it 'd') between the observers. You should be able to look this up online or in an atlas.*

Step 4: *Multiply this distance by the number you got in Step 2 and you've got the circumference ('C') of the Earth! Roughly. Hurrah! Treat yourself to more cheese.*

To put it in mathematical terms:

$$C = d \times [360/(a - b)]$$

Should you now wish to show off, you might care to calculate the surface area and volume of the Earth. You'll need first to calculate its radius 'r' using your measurement of the circumference C. This equation will do the trick:

$$r = C/2\pi$$

The surface area of the Earth will then be $4\pi r^2$ and the volume will be $v = 4/3 (\pi r^3)$

3: How to Extract Your Own DNA

You will need:
Yourself
1 tablespoon of salt
3 or 4 tablespoons of water
Diluted washing-up liquid
Some (very cold) gin (or vodka)
A receptacle like a glass beaker
A stirrer

Step 1: Mix the salt and water together to make salty water.

Step 2: Swish the salty water around your mouth, being careful not to swallow too much. Spit it back into the glass. It will now be swimming with DNA from your cheeks.

Step 3: Dip the stirrer first in the washing up liquid and then in the glass. Stir gently.

Step 4: Very carefully dribble a small amount of neat alcohol (the gin or vodka) down the inside of the glass. You might want your local cocktail waiter to help you with this. Hold the glass at a slight angle: you want the alcohol to sit atop the salty water. Keep going until you have a 2cm layer of alcohol.

Step 5: Stand by and wait. The DNA in the solution will find its way into the alcohol in the form of small white strands. This is the very essence of you, the unique code that makes you what you are.

Why it works:
By swishing the salty water you have displaced some cells from the inside of your cheeks. These cells contain your DNA, which is released by the washing-up liquid because the soap breaks down the fatty membranes that make up the cell walls. The DNA strands are then free to migrate gradually up to the alcohol and clump together while other cell parts dissolve in the alcohol.

Final step:
Either use the DNA to create a thousand clones of yourself and take over the world, or send it to the police in case they ever want to convict you of something, or drink the gin (or vodka) with ice, tonic and a twist of lime. Or all three.

And here's that experiment we DON'T think you should try at home.

Operation 'Acoustic Kitty' was a CIA experiment in the 1960s in which they bugged a cat in the hope that it would eavesdrop from window sills, park benches and the like. It cost about £10 million to wire up the first cat, and five years of experimenting before it was ready. It was then run over by a taxi.

AUNTY JO'S PROBLEM PAGE

Dear Aunty Jo,
I am a married woman in my forties with three children. Both my husband and I work full-time. Consequently, my house is very untidy and dirty. Do you have any tips?
Love, Betty.

Dear Betty,
If you can hang on for a while, I am in the process of writing a book for the stressed housewife called *Fuck It, That'll Do.* This will help you cut corners to the point of not doing any housework at all. But do bear in mind you can always clean the house when you retire. Let's be honest, nobody is going to look back over their life and say: 'Oh dear, the house was very messy on the third Tuesday after Whitsun 1991,' are they? I also find alcohol helps to dull the nagging voice of Mrs Domestic Goddess in your head.
Good luck!
Love, Aunty Jo

• • • • • • • • • • • • • • • • • • • •

Dear Aunty Jo,
Why are men so crap at multitasking?
Love from Ted.

Dear Ted,
I think you'll find this is because they do things so thoroughly. Last week, I popped to the shops and asked my husband to tidy the front room while I was out. When I came back, all the furniture was in the garden and he was using an attachment on the Hoover I've never even bloody seen before. Excuse my inappropriate language, but it was very irritating.
Yours, Aunty Jo

Dear Aunty Jo,
Is there a God?
Love, Bernard Manning.

Dear Bernard,
Yes, there is. She is a fat black woman in a wheelchair.
Love, Aunty Jo

• • • • • • • • • • • • • • • • • • • •

Dear Aunty Jo,
I have an irritating itch on my left side.
Love from Stephen.

Dear Stephen,
That is Alan.
Love, Aunty Jo

• • • • • • • • • • • • • • • • • • • •

Dear Aunty Jo,

I am on a television show called QI and I keep coming last. What shall I do?
Love, Alan.

Dear Alan,
As you are quite attractive, I think a sex change might help. Then all you need to do is smile becomingly and giggle a bit and people will ignore the fact your minus score has gone into free fall. Your other alternative is to overturn thousands of years of misogynist expectation single-handedly, which might take a bit longer.
Good luck!
Aunty Jo

• • • • • • • • • • • • • • • • • • • •

Dear Aunty Jo,
I have a very small penis. What can I do?
love from
(Name and
address supplied)

Dear Jeremy Clarkson of Chipping Norton,
It's what we all expected.
Love, Aunty Jo

E-GRATULATIONS! ANNOUNCING the arrival of our PRIDE, our JOY, our NEW WALLPAPER.

EMILY ROSARIO PERLMUTTER BORN: ?? 2007 in GUATEMALA
ARRIVED HOME: January 25th, 2008 to the loving carbon-neutral arms of WENDY and ROSS PERLMUTTER

Isn't she precious? Please note that the picture is a result of conversion for viewing on your screen and in no way represents Emily's true pigmentation. If you wish to print off Emily's pic, please, please use recyclable paper.

ABOUT HER NATURAL PARENTS: All I can say is Emily now has a real family, not a pretend one. Nothing against the Guatemalans (those pan-flute bands are amazing) but whereas her real mother gave her a nationality, we are here to give her the World… and to teach her how to protect it!

A FUTURE FOR OUR CHILD: Every child, no matter how precious, leaves a teensy tiny carbon footprint. During adoption proceedings, Ross and I made seven round-trip flights to Guatemala City. Calculated at 5 tons CO_2 emissions per person per trip* that comes out to – well, you do the math – 70 tons! To give you an idea of how much CO_2 that is, imagine drinking 64,000 Pepsis (Diet or Regular) a day for the rest of your life. Thus you can see that Emily arrives in this world with quite a substantial CO_2 debt on her little shoulders. Let's start planting those trees people!

A VISIT: Emily can't wait to see all her new friends and admirers! We strongly insist if you plan to pay a visit, please 'green' it. Carpooling is highly recommended. Ross is organizing a VanPool (hybrid 8-seater) for next Tuesday, February 1st at 4:00 p.m. Just let us know if you want a ride.

GIFTS: Riddle – what kind of showers don't carry acid rain? Answer: Baby showers! (LOL). They can, however, impact on nature in other insidious ways, so be very careful what you choose to bring as a gift. No gratuitous wrapping paper, ribbons or bows please. I don't need to tell you what that's doing to our forests. We recommend 100% cotton clothing, dye-free and of course any baby wear made from recyclable products. No Nike or Baby Gap stuff. The jury's still out on their 'fair-trade' claims. We really want to keep little Emily logo-free. And oh yes, Gina Ford books are strictly no-go in our household. That woman's murdered a lot of trees with her Nazi child-rearing manifestos.

In fact we would like to suggest a wonderful alternative: Ross has set up a carbon-offset account in Emily's name. Why not forgo those Teletubbies and fluffy booties and make a donation in Emily's name to the Vivo Project of Uganda which is currently attempting to build a wood-fired biomass boiler which operates on a 30 kilowatt photovoltaic turbine system!! Little Emily will love you for it!

THE BIG QUESTION – CLOTH VS. DISPOSABLE: Ross and I have agonized endlessly over what kind of impact Emily's diaper usage (a period we conservatively estimated to be 2 years) will have on the environment. Obviously we will eschew disposable diapers, given that a billion trees per year are cut down to make the wood pulp for disposables, not to mention the bleach used to whiten them producing organochlorine (Dioxin: the primary ingredient of Agent Orange! And you thought baby poop was toxic!).

Unfortunately, cloth diapers, though recyclable, utilize a large number of pesticides and chemicals to harvest the cotton they're made from. Even more detrimentally, washing them would use approximately 30,000 gallons of water annually – a cumulative total of 75,000 gallons of water. My, what a dilemma! After some serious back and forth on the issue, we realized maybe introspection was the answer: Physician heal thyself, if you will. By calculating that Ross and I personally flush about 60,000 gallons per year down the toilet the solution became obvious: all three of us are going to wear cloth diapers for the next two years. By our calculations, this will result in a net gain of 90,000 gallons of water per year.

A FEW FINAL WORDS: Having endured fourteen failed in-vitros, Ross and I were having a tough time understanding what was happening to us. We felt Nature had singled us out for punishment. We now appreciate that Ross's nugatory sperm yield was not a cruel twist of Nature, but in fact a Hidden Blessing (though I still maintain it's the result of a lifetime of ingested pollutants and industrial effluvia on Ross's part). The Adoption Process, for us, was clearly meant to be. Parenthood is a path, no matter how one arrives at it, though we both could have done with a little less paperwork and a more expeditious delivery. I know you're all sick of seeing us in those matching 'Expecting from Guatemala' T-shirts. Take our word for it – the wait was worth it!

* * * *

* The 5 tons of CO_2 per person is a conservative estimate based on a full plane. In fact, the flights we took to Guatemala City were only half-full, so a truer calculation would be 7.5 tons of CO_2 emissions per person. However, Ross and I are not going to accept undue blame. It's not our fault if Guatemala City is a shithole and no one wants to fly there!

Love from Wendy and Ross

EMILY

FROM RICH HALL'S JUNKMAIL FOLDER

Where's Johnny?

67

Egghead Corner

ESSAY ON THE EIGHTEENTH CENTURY*

by Garrick Alder, Esquire

Firstly, which eighteenth century do we mean? It's not enough to say '1701 to 1800'. Historians speak of a 'short' and a 'long' eighteenth century. The first fits somewhere inside the calendar dates of the real century, the second overhangs both ends of the calendrical one.

The 'short' and 'long' centuries are defined by the events that bookmark the key developments of the period, and these depend on the tastes and cultural prejudices of whichever historian is doing the defining. For example, the 'long' eighteenth century can mean the entire period between 1688 (Britain's Glorious Revolution) and 1832 (the passing of the Reform Act).

For QI purposes, we will consider a 'smudged' eighteenth century, which contains all the events of the 100 years but leaks a bit around the borders.

LISTS: The great linguistic achievement of the eighteenth century was Dr Samuel Johnson's *Dictionary of the English Language*, published in April 1755 after nine years of compilation. It was not the first dictionary of the English language, though. That was arguably Richard Mulcaster's 8,000-word *Elementarie* (1582). In a separate development, Mulcaster, a headmaster by profession, also gave the world the word 'football' and was the first person to describe its metamorphosis into a team sport (compared to the near-riot that it had been in early Tudor times).

Mulcaster's aim was to stabilise the 'hard words' in the English language, which he believed could supplant Latin in education. In his foreword he wrote: 'I do not think that anie language, be it whatsoever, is better able to utter all arguments, either with more pith, or greater planesse, than our English tung is, if the English utterer be as skillfull in the matter, which he is to utter.'

All of which shows the chaotic flux of everyday spelling before Johnson's *Dictionary* came on the scene. By Johnson's time, Mulcaster's optimism had been rewarded: mass literacy was on the rise, and the world needed an English-language 'rulebook'. Johnson's great achievement was to take a 'family portrait' of the language at the time, illustrated with quotations that would clarify every usage he described. Naturally, the book was huge in every sense. The first edition had 2,300 pages that were 46 inches tall and 56 inches wide, and came in two volumes (A–K and L–Z), together weighing 20 pounds.

However, Johnson's achievement is dwarfed by the publication (completed in 1725) of dynastic China's answer to the *Encyclopaedia Britannica*. This was the Gujin Tushu Jicheng, which translates into the modest claim: 'Complete Collection of Illustrations and Writings from the Earliest to Current Times'. Weighing in at 800,000 pages, spread over 10,000 individual scrolls, it was the first major publication in China to be set in movable copper type and contained 100 million individual Chinese characters. Only 60 copies were ever produced.

TOURETTE'S SYNDROME: Johann Sebastian Bach died aged 65 in 1750, seven years before Dominico Scarlatti (aged 72) and nine years before Georg Frideric Handel (aged 74), all three composers having been born in 1685. Of the three, only Scarlatti had not gone blind after being operated on by an English quack named John Taylor. Scarlatti's compositions are catalogued with K-numbers, his K30 being the so-called 'Cat Fugue', which was supposedly based on a theme produced when his cat walked across the keyboard of his harpsichord. The 'K' in question is American musicologist Ralph Kirkpatrick, who compiled the definitive list of Scarlatti's works during the 1930s and 1940s.

The other composer whose works are catalogued with K-numbers is Joannes Chrysostomus Wolfgangus Theophilus Mozart, who was born in 1756 and who died of an unknown complaint in 1791, leaving over 600 compositions to posterity. The 'K' associated with Mozart's work is Ludwig (Ritter) von Köchel, who published his catalogue of the composer's work in 1862. Mozart's first two baptismal names (Joannes Chrysostomus) are from the patron saint of 27th January (his birthday), John Chrysostom. 'Chrysostom' was added to the name of St John of Antioch (c.350–400) to distinguish him from several other St Johns, and the word itself means 'Goldenmouth', in reference to the eloquence and piety of his preaching.

In other words, St John had little in common with Mozart, whose potty-mouthed outbursts are legendary. St John Chrysostum once wrote: 'What good is it if the Eucharist table is overloaded with golden chalices when your brother is dying of hunger? Start by satisfying his hunger and then with what is left you may adorn the altar as well.' Mozart once wrote a song called 'Lick out My Arse'. Mozart was very odd. He was physically pained by the sound of a trumpet and clung to childhood rituals such as strict bedtimes. Eyewitness accounts describe him fidgeting endlessly, talking nonsense and miaowing like a cat while jumping on furniture, apparently not caring that his behaviour was strange to everyone else. Behaviour such as this has earned him (along with Dr Johnson) a speculative 'diagnosis' of Tourette's Syndrome. If such analysis is correct, Mozart had a very rare form of the syndrome. Fewer than 1% of Touretters are compulsively obscene in their 'tics'. We will never know, not least because Tourette's Syndrome was only first described in 1895.

The middle name 'Amadeus' is merely a Latinised version of Mozart's Greek-derived forename Theophilus, meaning 'loved by God'. It comes from a period in the 1770s in which he toured Italy, calling himself variously 'Wolfgang Amadè' or 'Wolgang Amadeo' in order to ingratiate himself with the locals. He never referred to himself as 'Amadeus', although he did sign his marriage certificate with 'Amadè' when he got married to Constanze Weber and once, in a light-hearted personal letter, as 'Wolfgangus Amadeus Mozartus' (also adding the cod-Latin '-us' suffix to each word of the date on which he was writing).

DIVING: Given the name 'Sir Edmond Halley' (pronounced 'Haw-ley'), most people will not recognise it. When you mispronounce it as 'HAL-ee', more people will recognise it and most of them will immediately mention comets. They might spell his first name 'Edmund' too, but that's their problem. While it is true that, in 1707, Sir Edmond Halley predicted the return of a comet that now bears his surname, he did other things as well: such as inventing (in 1690) and testing (in 1717) the world's first diving bell. The trial took place in the Thames. Sir Edmond and five fellow researchers remained submerged at a depth of 60 feet for nearly two hours. During this time, their atmosphere was replenished by sealed barrels of London air sent down on weighted cables.

Sir Edmond was also (and rather embarrassingly for science-worshippers) a founder and diehard proponent of the 'Hollow Earth' theory. The Auroras Borealis and Australis were, in his view, likely to be the escape of ionised gases from holes at the Earth's poles. Inside the Earth were four other spheres, nested like Russian *Matrioshka* dolls, roughly corresponding to the sizes of Venus, Mars and Mercury.

HEIGHT: In the eleventh century, the average height of a European male was just over 5 feet 8 inches (1.73 metres). Over the next two centuries, this fell slightly to just under 5 feet 7 inches (1.7 metres) but, by the eighteenth century, it had dropped to under 5 feet 5½ inches (1.662 metres). The cause was probably poor crops and diseases resulting from the Little Ice Age (LIA).

The eighteenth century marked the high point (or rather low point) of the LIA, a dip in the Earth's temperature that began at some point between 1200 and 1500 and ended between 1850 and 1900. The resultant crop failures (and the consequent skyrocketing of the price of flour) are the likely culprit for the bread riots that supposedly led Marie Antoinette to say 'Then let them eat cake'. But, if she ever said it at all – which is very unlikely – she certainly wasn't the first.

For a start, the legendary quote is *Qu'ils mangent de la brioche* ('Then let them eat brioche') and for a finish, Book Six of Jean-Jacques Rousseau's 12-volume autobiographical work *Confessions* was written around 1767 and contains the following passage: 'At length I recollected the thoughtless saying of a great princess, who, on being informed that the country people had no bread, replied, "Then let them eat pastry!"' Whoever this 'great princess' was, it wasn't Marie Antoinette, who first arrived in France from her native Austria in 1760 – the same year Rousseau's *Confessions* were published.

* For people who think pictures in books are a little bit babyish.

A HIPPO DOES NOT HAVE A STING IN ITS TAIL, BUT THE WISE MAN PREFERS TO BE SAT ON BY A BEE (POLISH)

REVOLUTIONS: There were three major revolutions in the eighteenth century: the French Revolution, the American Revolution and the Industrial Revolution. All historians agree that the American Revolution happened in 1776 and the French one in 1789, but when the Industrial one happened appears to be a matter of opinion. It either began in 1780 (Eric Hobsbawm), or in 1760 (T. S. Ashton), or it had already started by around 1400 with the invention of the printing press and was just a bit slow to get going (Lewis Mumford).

France, at that time still ruled by a monarchy, was the key ally of the fledgling American nation, mainly because it annoyed the British so much. The French supplied arms and ships to the revolutionaries until the final victory in 1783. France gained very little from the whole affair. In fact, seeing as the French monarchy was overthrown by a mob inspired by the American Revolution you could actually say that the French did as badly out of it as the British.

The Glorious Revolution, as discussed, can be said to mark the start of the long eighteenth century, but since it wasn't very glorious and it wasn't really a revolution (more of a coup d'état with the aim of installing a Dutch Protestant on the English throne), we'll let that pass.

PIRACY: The eighteenth century saw the Golden Age of Piracy, which started in 1716 and lasted until 1826 or 1830 or 1850, depending on whom you listen to. This was partly due to the high unemployment rate among European sailors following the signing of the Treaty of Utrecht, which ended the Spanish War of Succession and meant naval budgets could safely be cut back. It was also partly due to the expansion of the colonial supply lines in the Atlantic and Pacific, with cargo ships sailing back and forth to ferry the riches of the frontiers back to their European homes – a development which may in turn have been driven by the widespread crop failures in Northern Europe noted above. As twentieth-century economists have apparently so far failed to notice, high unemployment + expanding prosperity = rising crime.

Another lesson that hasn't been learned is that speculation without sound foundations – as happened during the South Sea Bubble – leads to a crash. The South Sea Bubble was inflated by the excitement at the opening up of the new trade routes. Suddenly, it seemed, there would be fantastic opportunities to get filthy rich if one invested one's money in the South Sea Company, which was backed with £10,000,000 by the Government of George I – a sum beyond the dreams of eighteenth-century avarice and still enviable today. Unhappily, the same thought occurred to crooks, who promptly set up their own 'south sea' companies promising investors such delights as perpetual motion machines, the restoration of English vicarages and the establishment of a 'company for carrying on an undertaking of great advantage, but nobody to know what it is'. Shares in these ludicrous ventures sold like bread to pigeons, and before long the whole thing went 'pop', depriving many people of their savings and making a few rascals very rich indeed. The same thing happens in the present day, most obviously with the dotcom bubble of the 1990s. Far be it from the present, however, to suggest any similarities between market traders and pirates.

COWS: A cow called Blossom changed the course of world history in 1796, when she passed the disease of cowpox to a London dairymaid called Sarah Nelmes. A doctor called Edward Jenner took pus from her 'poxes' (blisters) and injected it into the arm of a nine-year-old boy called James Phipps. The result was that (after a short fever) Phipps became the first recorded human being to be deliberately inoculated against smallpox, a far deadlier disease that had ravaged the human race since time immemorial. Edward Jenner entered the history books by publishing his results in 1798 and giving the world the word 'vaccination' – derived from the Italian word 'vacca', meaning 'cow'. But was Phipps really the first inoculated human? Jenner had embarked on his experiments after hearing a well-attested piece of country lore to the effect that cowpox prevented smallpox, so there must have been other instances before. Indeed, a Dorset farmer called Benjamin Jesty had already done the same thing to his family by 1774. Rather sadly, Jenner was unsuccessful when he inoculated his own son, who later died of smallpox. Jenner was also the first scientist to state that hatchling cuckoos push the rightful eggs out of their host nests using a special hollow in their backs. Previously it had been believed that the adult cuckoo did this while the 'victim' bird wasn't looking. Jenner wasn't proven right until the advent of photography.

KINGS:
George the First was always reckoned
Vile, but viler George the Second.
And what mortal ever heard
A good word of George the Third
But when from earth the Fourth descended
God be praised the Georges ended.
(Walter Savage Landor, b. 1765)

George I, Elector of Hanover, inherited the English throne at the age of 54 thanks to the Act of Settlement (1701). This named his mother as the only eligible successor to the faltering English monarchy. There were actually fifty European royals with better claims, but none of them were Protestant. In 1720, the South Sea Company collapsed and the ensuing economic chaos made George and his ministers extremely unpopular. Robert Walpole was appointed First Lord of the Treasury in April 1721 to take care of the mess, and from this date forth the monarchy became less and less involved in government. George retreated into the arms of his mistresses, the fat Charlotte Sophia Kielmannsegge (whom he created Countess of Darlington) and the thin Eherngard Melusina von Schulenberg (created Duchess of Kendall). The two were more popularly known as 'The Elephant' and 'The Maypole'. George had imported them to Britain along with his wife, and they ransacked the jewellery boxes of Britain so thoroughly that George's wife had to be enthroned in hired glass. Their scrounging became so notorious that a torch-wielding mob waylaid their coach and threatened to sack it. 'Goot pippil!' called the Maypole in her thick German accent, 'Vot vor you abuze uz? Ve came for all your goots!' This prompted one wit to reply: 'Yes, and all our chattels too, damn ye!'

George I's son George II deserves a place in history as the only monarch whose heart has been overheard exploding. His valet reported hearing a louder report as the King sat on the lavatory on the morning of October 25th, 1760. This was followed by a heavy thump and a moan. The valet rushed in to find the stricken king sprawled dying on the floor. At autopsy, it was shown that a ventricle had burst in his heart and that this was the noise the valet had heard. Alas, his first son, Frederick, Prince of Wales, was not around to rejoice, having died of a burst abscess in his lung after being hit by a cricket ball ten years earlier. George and Frederick hated each other with a passion truly beyond measure, and after a row over allowances in 1736, George barred Frederick from the deathbed of his own mother, saying: 'Bid him go about his business, for his poor mother is not in a condition to see him act his false, whining, cringing tricks now, nor am I in a humour to bear his impertinence; and bid him trouble me with no more messages, but get out of my house.' Mind you, it was probably for the best. One of the last recorded utterances by Frederick's mother was about him: 'At least I shall have one comfort in having my eyes eternally closed – I shall never see that monster again.' (In life, she had once seen him through a window and shouted, 'Look! There he goes! That wretch! That villain! I wish the ground would open at this moment and sink the monster to the lowest hole in Hell!') The family's generally unsympathetic attitude towards the son known widely as 'Poor Fred' inspired a folk rhyme (recorded by William Makepeace Thackeray):
Here lies Fred,
Who was alive and is dead.
Had it been his father,
I had much rather;
Had it been his sister,
No one would have missed her;
Had it been his brother,
Still better than another:
But since 'tis only Fred,
Who was alive and is dead,
Why, there's no more to be said.

The throne next fell to Frederick's son, who became George III. Under his reign, Britain's most visionary poet, William Blake, flourished quietly and wrote the poem now known as 'Jerusalem', which was set to music in the early twentieth century by Hubert Parry. Blake was once ordered to cut the grass in his front garden by soldiers of King George III and replied: 'Damn the King and damn his soldiers, they are all slaves!' By contrast, when George V first heard Sir Edward Elgar's orchestration of Parry's setting of 'Jerusalem' in 1922, he said he wished it could become the national anthem instead of 'God Save the King'.

WHAT GOES ON IN A BOFFIN'S BRAIN?

Qi The ENGINEER SIMULATOR

by Ted Dewan
(BSc Engineering)

Although you may appreciate the shiny things they design that go fast and make music, engineers (often simply referred to as 'They') subject you to ever more subtle forms of daily abuse as society becomes increasingly perverted by technology.

They work day and night to exploit every opportunity to humiliate the public, often concealing their aggression behind sensible-sounding unimpeachable practical explanations. 'Khegh-hegh-heghh!' They chuckle merrily as you stand in the rain for eternity, waiting at pelican crossings for permission to interrupt the flow of their motor vehicles. 'Hunh hunh hunnnh!' They snigger, savouring your delicious frustration as you attempt to set a digital alarm clock using only two buttons labelled with nonsense engineer words like 'mode' and 'enter'. '*Ha ba!*' They guffaw as you willingly part with another tenner on a guide that refers to you in its title as part of a widespread tribe of 'dummies' merely to comprehend one of their products. But what is it that causes such deviant behaviour in the sociopaths who create the systems that surround us?

You see, most sensible people wouldn't dream of serving their golden years of higher learning incarcerated in the fluorescent-lit gloom of a windowless engineering classroom. While the rest of the world youthfully frolics under the cherry blossom and snoozes in 'media studies', trainee engineers endure years of gruelling problem-solving and science-lab BO.

But once their brain-grinding apprenticeship is completed and the trainee engineers begin to flap their wet and sticky young wings, they gravitate towards the secretive international brotherhood of Them. Embedded within their dreary cubicles, They tirelessly shower the world with enslaving widgetry and extract their revenge on non-engineers for their frivolous merrymaking and ignorance. And so the non-technical public enters into a destructive cycle of dependency with the engineering fraternity, responding with untiring enthusiasm to the bogus promise of a better life through evermore developed technology while simultaneously increasing their psychological and physical dependency upon their products.

The engineer's vision of the world, however skewed, is consistent with the fruit of their disturbed and insular minds. Although it is clearly too late for most citizens of the technology-consuming societies to wean themselves off the goodies, it is never too late or hopeless to seek understanding and enlightenment, and perhaps attain some peace with the propellor-heads. Because in spite of the fact that They daily defecate upon the non-technical public through the medium of technology, They are largely to be pitied. Many engineers are victims of defects at birth, cursed with the likes of Geek Personality Disorder (GPD) and inadequate bodies that deviate substantially from optimum weight.

The QI Engineer Simulator gives you insight into the mental workings behind those who create the insults to dignity that are computer printers and retro toasters. It helps to understand the roots of the engineers' antisocial behaviour in order to forgive the boffins behind the bewildering devilry of burglar alarm control panels. They despise the non-technical public simply for the casual ease with which they succeed at being human. These poor creatures are only trying to make others feel stupid and inferior in an effort to persuade people that machines, and They who understand them, are in control of the world.

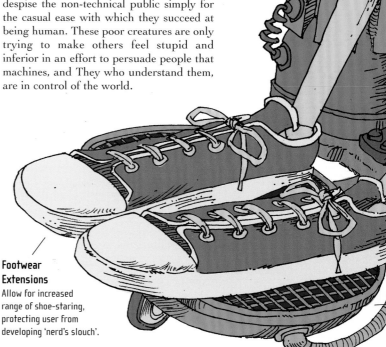

Inamorata Aversion Relay
External hormone detection unit directs user to masturbatory material so as not to waste time dealing with the social aspects of enchanting a sexual partner (coupled to *Libido Diverter*).

Indifferent Sartorial Pattern Projector
When projected upon plain, light-coloured material, creates the illusion of disastrous taste in clothing. User advised to wear plain white boiler suit for maximum fidelity of projected image. Choice pre-programmed by user's mum.

RSS Tension Bands
Simulates the symptoms of repetitive strain syndrome brought on by computer-based lifestyle, further enhancing obsession with one's own internal sensory environment.

Moral Neutralysis Ballast Tank
Facilitates cheerful obliviousness to the immoral consequences of user's actions while toiling with prolific abandon on over-engineered money-sucking delusional enterprises such as building weapons systems and transparent vacuum cleaners.

Footwear Extensions
Allow for increased range of shoe-staring, protecting user from developing 'nerd's slouch'.

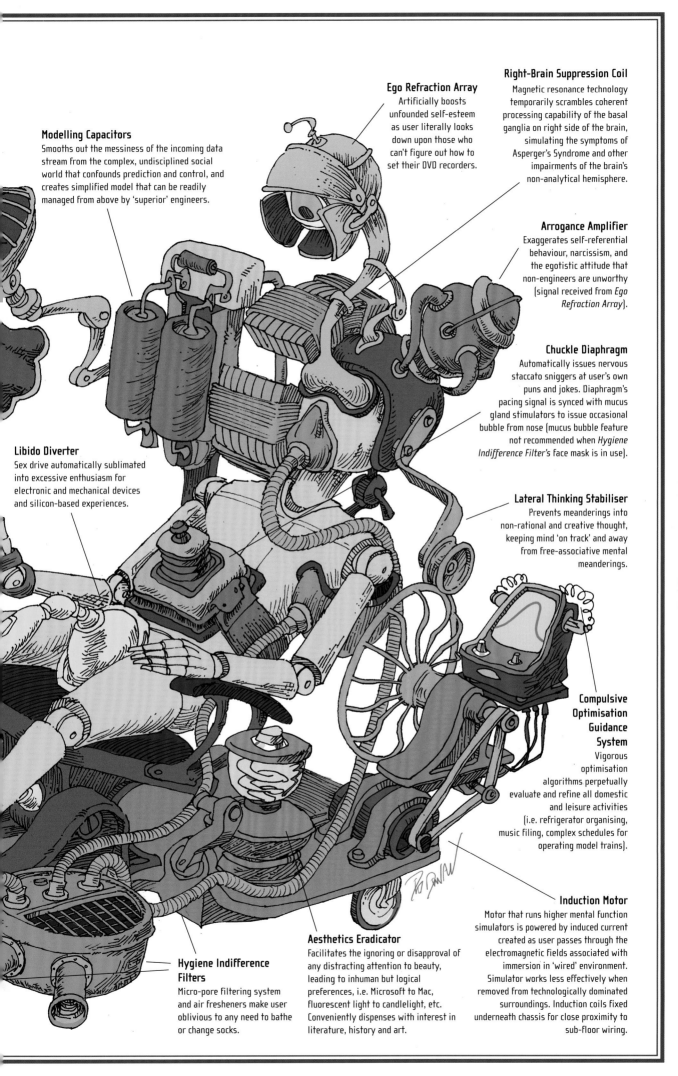

Modelling Capacitors
Smooths out the messiness of the incoming data stream from the complex, undisciplined social world that confounds prediction and control, and creates simplified model that can be readily managed from above by 'superior' engineers.

Ego Refraction Array
Artificially boosts unfounded self-esteem as user literally looks down upon those who can't figure out how to set their DVD recorders.

Right-Brain Suppression Coil
Magnetic resonance technology temporarily scrambles coherent processing capability of the basal ganglia on right side of the brain, simulating the symptoms of Asperger's Syndrome and other impairments of the brain's non-analytical hemisphere.

Arrogance Amplifier
Exaggerates self-referential behaviour, narcissism, and the egotistic attitude that non-engineers are unworthy (signal received from *Ego Refraction Array*).

Chuckle Diaphragm
Automatically issues nervous staccato sniggers at user's own puns and jokes. Diaphragm's pacing signal is synced with mucus gland stimulators to issue occasional bubble from nose (mucus bubble feature not recommended when *Hygiene Indifference Filter*'s face mask is in use).

Libido Diverter
Sex drive automatically sublimated into excessive enthusiasm for electronic and mechanical devices and silicon-based experiences.

Lateral Thinking Stabiliser
Prevents meanderings into non-rational and creative thought, keeping mind 'on track' and away from free-associative mental meanderings.

Compulsive Optimisation Guidance System
Vigorous optimisation algorithms perpetually evaluate and refine all domestic and leisure activities (i.e. refrigerator organising, music filing, complex schedules for operating model trains).

Induction Motor
Motor that runs higher mental function simulators is powered by induced current created as user passes through the electromagnetic fields associated with immersion in 'wired' environment. Simulator works less effectively when removed from technologically dominated surroundings. Induction coils fixed underneath chassis for close proximity to sub-floor wiring.

Aesthetics Eradicator
Facilitates the ignoring or disapproval of any distracting attention to beauty, leading to inhuman but logical preferences, i.e. Microsoft to Mac, fluorescent light to candlelight, etc. Conveniently dispenses with interest in literature, history and art.

Hygiene Indifference Filters
Micro-pore filtering system and air fresheners make user oblivious to any need to bathe or change socks.

EBBREVIATIONS By Craig Brown

ET was a creature who tried to phone home,
ER is a monarch who sits on her throne.
EMU is the system controlled by Rod Hull,
ECT involves wires, attached to the skull.
EPO is a hormone – you will cycle like merde –
EH's what one says when one hasn't quite heard.
EX wants your money (and also your house),
EEK! oh my goodness! I just spied a mouse!
ERM is a mechanism or... um... hesitation,
ENO has no need for operatic translation.
ENO's also the producer of Bowie:
EG 'Boys Keep Swinging' – (now I'm just being showy).
EEC's both a trade group and lower-case poet,
ELO had a hit (but I'm damned if I know it).
ESA sends up rockets (but they're always unmanned),
ETA is the time we're unlikely to land.
ETA are terrorists, primarily Basque,
ETC indicates you're bored stiff with your task.
ENSA put on dresses to cheer up our lads,
EST it turned out was just one of those fads.
ESP means 'Hang on! I know what you're thinking',
E-mails I now manage to send without blinking.
E-numbers are terribly bad for the heart,
ETD is the time that the aircraft won't start.
EC is what EEC was (or was it EU?),
E17 were a boy band (but I preferred Blue).
EPs are recordings, neither albums or singles,
ELF registers the merest of tingles.
EMF is a novelist who makes most look inferior,
E-Coli potentially deadly bacteria.
ECG shows a line that bobs back and forth,
EE bah gum is the language they speak up in't North.
EMINEM's the white rapper who started a trend,
and that's all you're getting 'cos
this is the END.

EMU European Monetary Union ECT Electro-Convulsive Therapy EPO Erythropoietin ERM Exchange Rate Mechanism ENO English National Opera
EEC European Economic Community EEC Edward Estlin Cummings ELO Electric Light Orchestra ESA European Space Agency ETA Estimated Time of Arrival
ETA Euskadi Ta Askatasuna (Basque Country And Freedom) ENSA Entertainments National Service Association EST European Summer Time ESP Extra-sensory
Perception ETD Estimated Time of Departure ELF Extremely Low Frequency EMF Edward Morgan Forster ECG Electrocardiogram

E-QUIZ

WIN £1,000!

WE'RE GIVING AWAY £1,000 IN CASH TO THE FIRST PERSON TO PROVIDE CORRECT ANSWERS TO THE EIGHTEEN QUESTIONS BELOW. EACH ANSWER IS A SINGLE WORD...

For obvious reasons, the answers are not to be found in this book. To enter the competition – or simply to play the quiz for fun – visit www.qi.com/equiz

Follow the on-screen instructions. By typing your answers in the spaces provided, you'll be able to see your score immediately. You can play as many times as you like. When or if you score 100%, submit your answers online as instructed.

In the event of a draw, the winner will be the contestant who, in the opinion of the judges, provides the most interesting responses to questions 19–21. (For a chance of winning, it is advisable to attempt these tiebreakers.)

The winner and the eleven runners-up will be invited to a live recording of the QI 'F' Series to meet the stars of the show, followed by dinner with the QI Elves.

The deadline is 8.08 p.m. on the 8th of Eighpril '08. The winners will be notified by email within 8 days, and the answers will be posted on www.qi.com

To discuss the quiz and other quite interesting topics, visit www.qi.com/talk

Full terms and conditions apply when entering this competition. These can be seen at www.qi.com

YOUR TIME STARTS NOW...

1. What is the word for the part of the play where the plot thickens?
2. Who or what are Dunk, Mya and Mary?
3. Which medicine comes from a Greek hedgehog?
4. What did zoologist Frank Buckland describe as 'horribly bitter'?
5. ADTFIAT, WUEMG. What does the 'E' stand for?
6. What connects two Kings of England, an estate in Kennington and a room in Kingsmeadow stadium?
7. Who is this? (See Below)
8. Which spherical object owes its name to the Ye river?
9. How many people could live off a day's oxygen from one acre of fir trees?
10. Where would you find a labyrinth, an oval window and a round window?
11. What is Mr A. G. Dorsey's preferred first name?
12. What is the next letter in the sequence:
    А, Б, В, Г, Д … ?
13. Who does this eye belong to? (See Below)
14. What was the 28th most popular name for baby girls in England and Wales in 2006?
15. Which country flies this flag? (See Below)
16. What did we eat 173 times in 2006?
17. Where would you see beaks going up Judy's passage?
18. What is a korvalappu?

TIEBREAKERS
19. Tell us something Quite Interesting about Easington, County Durham.
20. Tell us something Quite Interesting about eagles.
21. Tell us something Quite Interesting about emails.

Whose eye is this? (Q13)

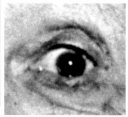

Who is this? (Q7)

Whose flag is this? (Q15)

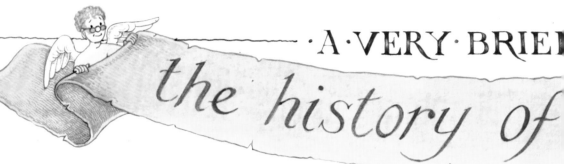

the history of

The first known erotic texts appeared in China in 1200 BC. Perplexing
instructions included 'Playing the Jade Flute' and 'Wailing Monkey Climbing a Tree'.

In ancient China, men developed a taste for tightly bound small feet. These were
considered to be another sexual organ – they would bend them into a loop and
have their way with them.

The Islamic world is rich in erotic literature, the most
famous of which is 'The Perfumed Garden' by Sheikh Nefzawi. The explorer Sir
Richard Burton (1821–1890) – who spoke 29 languages – translated it from the
Arabic. Shortly after completing his revised version, he died. His wife Isabel burned
it (and many of his other papers) before it could be published.

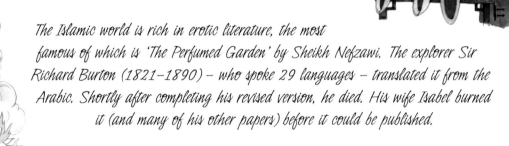

In ancient Japan, erotic prints known as 'shunga' were commissioned by bordellos
as advertisements. In 1002, Sei Shonagon, a lady at the Imperial Court, completed
'The Pillow Book' for the education of young women. Amongst many practical tips,
wives are advised to praise their husband's penis.

Ancient India gave us the 'Kama Sutra' (meaning The 'Love Thread' or
'Discourse on Pleasure') by Vatsayana. Contrary to common belief, it is not primarily a sex
manual, but doesn't shirk from the task if need be – including classics such as
'Lovely Lady in Charge' and 'Sucking the Mango'. It is advisable not to
turn over two pages at once.

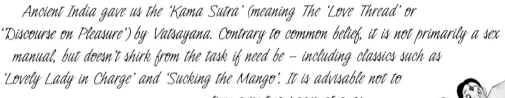

Ancient Greek erotica was rather more basic. Recommended positions included
'The Posterior Venus' and 'Hector's Horse'. Bottoms – male and female –
loom large in Greek texts. According to legend, two sisters, blessed with
beautiful big backsides, held a competition to decide which was the finer by
flashing them at total strangers in the street. Hence the useful English word
'callipygian', meaning 'superbly bottomed'.

A little more recently, Giovanni Boccaccio (1313–1375) wrote the
Decameron – 100 bawdy tales featuring disgraceful hanky-panky amongst the
clergy.

The erotic poems of Robert Herrick (1591–1674) include 'Upon the Nipples on Julia's Breast' and 'Upon
Julia's Sweat'.

The lewd verses of John Wilmot, Earl of Rochester (1647–1680), included 'Signior Dildo', a scandalous satire
on the engagement of the future James II.

Giacomo Casanova (1725–1798) was actually rather a tragic figure with a weakness for women
dressed in men's clothes.

Before settling down, late in life, to write his 'Life of Samuel Johnson', James Boswell (1740–1795) was a
tremendous libertine, struggling with addictions to alcohol, gambling and prostitutes.

'This day show that you are Boswell, a true soldier. Take your post. Shake off sloth and spleen, and just
proceed. Nobody knows your conflicts. Be fixed as a Christian, and shun vice. Go not to Amsterdam.'
JAMES BOSWELL, 'Journals', 1764

In modern China, 'blue' movies are yellow; in Japan they're green.
But surely they should be pink...

The difference between pornography and erotica is lighting.
GLORIA LEONARD

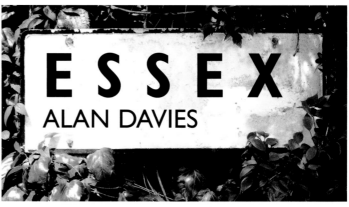

E S S E X
ALAN DAVIES

The road was typical of many in the area in that it was made up of good-sized detached houses for the aspirational middle classes. My Dad was a chartered accountant. When the railway reached Loughton in 1856, the Eastern Counties Railway did not allow 3rd-class ticket holders to board there or at any of the stations beyond it on the way to Epping. They didn't want the trains full of workers paying low fares, heaven forbid. That's why the North East London suburbs grew the way they did, with smaller houses closer to the centre in areas like Leyton and Walthamstow, from where workers were allowed to board the trains, and larger ones further out in places like Woodford and Loughton.

We pointed towards London because we were on the Central Line and we had an 01 telephone number, and because as teenagers we did not aspire to travel to Bishop's Stortford or Saffron Walden, nice as they are. We wanted to go to Camden Market and Carnaby St.

This was partly because London was perceived as trendy and exciting, and partly because if you go too far north you can end up being anally raped in a Norfolk boys' school and that is much less fun than buying bootleg tapes of The Jam in Camden Town.

Here is your introduction to my home county of Essex.
I will disavow you, is that right? Disinter? No. Er... challenge your preconceptions. Yes, that's it. Apologies in advance for having a preconception of your preconceptions, but I'm sticking to it. My bit of Essex points towards London. I grew up in Epping Forest. Actually, in a house near Epping Forest, in a road called Spring Grove in Loughton.

I did venture out to Chelmsford and Southend to watch Essex play cricket. I was raised to enjoy cricket and I'd go with my older brother who would rather have gone alone. Chelmsford was capital of England for 5 days in 1381 when Richard II regained control of the country after the Peasants' Revolt. This is never mentioned at the cricket because I suspect no one knows about it. I have a cousin called Richard. He was called Dick until he rejected the name when he reached adolescence. Understandable. Cousin Richard is unrelated to Richard II, to my knowledge. Cricket excursions were always peaceful affairs. Leather on willow and all that. However, things have changed. During the modern floodlit Twenty20 games, boozy lads are liable to shout 'Jonathan' at me and then point their mobile phone cameras in my face. It's pointless telling them I'm not Jonathan Creek as they will only say 'Yes you are' and take more pictures.

The atmosphere can become a little testy, and in those circumstances I shudder to recall the infamous match between Essex and Kent in 1776 when a spectator was bayoneted, a soldier was shot dead and one of the Kent players killed a member of the Essex team. The match took place at Tilbury Fort (built in 1672) and featured the worst violence the Fort ever saw.

I don't think I like that phrase 'Richard II regained control of the country'. How was that done in 1381, when the peasants were revolting? I suspect it wasn't a matter of asking them nicely and was possibly more in the spirit of Tiananmen Square or Hungary in 1956. The peasants were revolting in Brentwood, which is now home to a posh private school. It also has good access to the M25. I was caught speeding on the M25 in 1987 and went to court in Brentwood. They said I was doing between 106 and 108 mph. In a subsequent stand-up routine I claimed that I then said, 'That'll be 107 then.' I didn't really. I was cowed into silence. The magistrates banned me for two weeks. At the next-door police station I asked how to get back to Loughton. They wouldn't tell me, so I got in my car and drove anyway,

thinking that if I was stopped I'd tell them I was going to a phone box to get help. Brilliant, I'm sure you'll agree. They watched me leave and arrested me after a 50-yard, *Life on Mars* pursuit with full flashing blue lights. While I was locked up in custody I was pitifully scared and realised I would be a rubbish criminal. A few weeks later I received a second ban (four weeks). Nowadays the police no longer have to watch through the window for miscreants flouting driving bans – in 1994 Brentwood became the first town in the UK to install colour CCTV.

Essex has a history of zero tolerance for criminality. William Calcraft from Little Baddow exemplified this spirit. As Britain's longest-serving hangman, he is thought to have hanged between 400 and 450 people in a 45-year career. It sounds a lot until you realise it's less than one a month. Lazy Bill.

Loughton is home to the Royal Mint, where all of Britain's bank notes are printed. When the M11 was being built, everyone I knew had 'Stop the M11' stickers in their cars. From Loughton it's only possible to gain access to the southbound carriageway. This is because there was a fear that if a gang robbed the Mint (in order to become minted) they could flee north up the M11 to an airfield. From there it's just a short hop to.... nowhere you can spend any pounds. As far as I know, the Mint has never been robbed but the potential is there. After all, more cars are broken into in Loughton than anywhere else in the UK. If Loughtonians are shocked and would like to move to a safer place, Southend is recommended as the safest large town in the UK, with just 30.91 crimes per 1,000 people.

> While I was locked up in custody I was pitifully scared and realised I would be a rubbish criminal.

Although Essex is generally safe, Britain's Best Earthquake shook the village of Wivenhoe in 1884. The chimney of the gasworks collapsed and masonry fell from the church tower. Records show that someone 'later died of shock'. That's not what shock means to me. Something that hits you later? No, no, no. You die of shock there and then: 'Aargh!' (thud). To die of shock 'later' suggests someone who had had a dream about an earthquake in which the chimney of the gasworks fell on him or his name was Mason and he fell off the church tower. Or something. Wivenhoe is tranquil enough now, but if you want real security you could book a spot in Kelvedon's nuclear bunker for £30,000. (This will secure you a place for 10 years.) Be warned, though. In the event of a nuclear attack, you may be joined by 600 government types.

Colchester lords it over Chelmsford as Britain's oldest town. It was probably for a time the capital of Roman Britain and has the distinction of being written about by Pliny the Elder in AD 77. He is generally as reliable as the interweb for information. He described it as Camulodunum, though I suspect he was dictating after too much bacchanalian revelry and was just trying to say Colchester. There has always been plenty of wine in Essex. Ten vineyards are currently operational, two more than in the 11th century. The star grape is the bacchus. The vineyards survived the late 20th century despite the countywide practice of only drinking wine at Christmas and traditionally drawing it from a cardboard box stored next to a radiator. It's the temperate climate that leads to all the wine-growing. St Osyth (never heard of it) is the driest place in the UK, with only 513 mm of precipitation per year. I've no idea how that compares to anywhere else, but I'm sure that if everyone in St Osyth went out and a had a pee in the garden they'd probably double it.

Ignoring Colchester's rich history, Chelmsford leapt ahead in 1893 when The Eclipse, the world's first electric toaster, was invented there. Five years later Marconi opened the world's first 'wireless' factory.

It seemed nothing could stop Chelmsford from taking its place at the hub of the world's burgeoning electronics industry. Sadly, progress halted on the opening of the world's first naturist site in a back garden in Wickford. A member of the English Gymnosophist Society made her garden available for naked air-bathing, and Essex, with its collective eye off the ball and on the balls, was soon electronically eclipsed by the Japanese.

Mistakes are still sometimes made – in 2003, a museum in Leigh-on-Sea was forced to abandon plans to exhibit a 150,000-year-old woolly mammoth tusk when a second opinion from a geologist identified it as a length of Victorian drainage pipe – but Essex has recovered from missing out on hundreds of billions of yen with a characteristic and innate cheeriness epitomised

by the dazzling smile of its three famous beauties: Vicki Michelle, out of 'Allo, 'Allo!; Daniella Westbrook, out of Eastenders; and Jodie Marsh, out of her clothes. Where does that sense of humour come from? The answer is Braintree, home of Nicholas Udall who created England's first comedy, Ralph Roister Doister, in the early 1550s. He was also headmaster of Eton College but left in disgrace when he was accused of stealing a silver plate from the College Chapel.

YOU CAN TAKE THE BOY OUT OF ESSEX BUT YOU CAN'T TAKE ESSEX OUT OF THE BOY...

NOW SOME POETRY:
*There was a young boy from Chelmsford
Who soon discovered the futility of trying to write a limerick about his home town as there is no word in English that rhymes with Chelmsford, apart from an obscure town in New York called Elmsford.*

SO HE WROTE:
*There was a young boy from Chelmsford
Who spent all his life in Chelmsford
He had a Capri
And a wife called Tracey
And they shared a house in Chelmsford.*

Jodie Marsh, almost out of her clothes

EUROPEAN LANGUAGES

No. 4: Italian

That soft bastard Latin which melts like kisses from a female mouth. LORD BYRON

The Italian alphabet uses only 20 letters. There are hardly any words beginning with H, J, K, W, X or Y in an Italian dictionary and all of them are borrowed directly from other languages.

The Italian for 'pencil-sharpener' is *temperamatite*, a 'drug-addict' is *tossicodipendente* and 'goo' is *sostanza appiccicosa* ('sticky substance').

Tasso in Italian means both 'yew' and 'badger' and the Italian for a 'crack' is *botto*.

ITALIAN DICTIONARY
The key divisions of the Italian language are as follows:

1. Italian words that look convincingly Italian.

babbo	dad
baffo	moustache
bollo	stamp
bosso	box
buffo	funny
bullo	tough
buzzo	paunch
dotto	duct
fatto	fact
fitto	thick
flusso	flow
fosso	moat
frizzo	witticism
goffo	clumsy
golfo	gulf
gozzo	throat
grillo	cricket (grasshopper)
groppo	tangle
grullo	silly
gruppo	group
mozzo	buoy
tappo	cork

tatto	touch
tetto	roof
tocco	touch
tozzo	stocky
trucco	make-up
tutto	all
zoppo	wobbly

2. Italian words that look like English

bimbo	child
bonzo	Buddhist monk
brillo	pissed
bronco	bronchial tube
bruno	brown
frodo	contraband
garbo	grace
gobbo	hunchback
gonzo	dolt, simpleton
monaco	monk
montgomery	duffel-coat
tonto	stupid, dumb, silly
zappa	hoe
zeppo	jam-packed

3. Italian words that look like Finnish

battipanni	carpetbeater
bendisposto	well-disposed
bighellone	moocher
bussolotto	dice-shaker
frangiflutti	breakwater
fuggifugg	stampede

3. Italian words that look like German

krapfen	doughnut
transfert	transference

4. Italian words that are English but where some Italian's got the wrong end of the stick somewhere along the line.

big	an industrial mogul or movie star
boy	a male ballet dancer
flipper	a pinball machine
footing	jogging
miss	a beauty queen
mister	a professional body-builder
mole	a massive shape

tip tap	tap-dancing
torpedo	a touring car

5. Italian words that only Italians apparently feel the need for

balillo	a member of a Fascist youth group
bambolotto	a male doll
mammismo	an excessive attachment to one's mother
zampata	a blow from the paw of an animal
zimarra	a long shabby coat
zirlare	to sing like a thrush
zuzzurullone	an over-grown school kid

6. Wonderfully evocative Italian words

blatta	cockroach
buggerare	to swindle
friggere	to fry
tamponare	to plug
turlupinare	to cheat
zanzana	mosquito
zazzera	a shock of hair
zoccolo	hoof, clog

7. Peculiar Italian noises

bau bau	bow wow!
bum	boom!
tictac	tick-tock

8. God knows how these came about

boato	a roar
boato sonico	sonic boom
bradipo	sloth
zampognaro	bagpiper

9. Other stuff

bozzettista	sketch-writer
zenzero	ginger
zizzania	discord
zolphanello	match
zolletta	lump, cube
zoppicante	limping

ITALIAN PHRASEBOOK

vai a farti friggere!
get lost! (literally, 'go screw yourself')

ENGAGED

Lavatories
THROUGH THE AGES

The world's oldest discovered lavatories date back to 2500 BC. The Harappan or Indus Valley civilisation, in what is now Pakistan, invented the first known basic flush system. They would tip a pot of water into a bowl with a hole that would wash the waste away through a pipe into an underground drain.

There were also quite advanced lavatories in ancient Rome, Persia and Egypt. Most Roman cities had large public lavatories that became social meeting places. By 315 AD there were 144 in Rome, and people would gather to chat and gossip, much like in the public baths. For cleanliness they would use a communal 'sponge on a stick' which would be cleaned after each use in a moving stream of water in a gutter by their feet. Hence the unfortunate terminology 'getting the wrong end of the stick'.

After the Roman Empire fell, the sophisticated drainage systems were less widely used. The rough and ready Saxons and their counterparts generally used basic pots or shat in holes in the ground.

In the Middle Ages, the aristocracy demanded more sophisticated ablutions. The most advanced recorded was that of John the Fearless (1409–1413), the de facto King of France. His lavatory was attached to a 25-metre shaft that descended to the bottom of his palace where a stone septic tank collected his waste. It also had a padded seat and a heating and cooling system. John also had the pleasure of using cotton and linen as an early forerunner to lavatory paper.

In Norman and Tudor times, the populace did not enjoy much luxury. Some homes simply had holes in the wall to crap onto the street. The slightly richer may have had a small room extension sticking out of the side of the house with a hole in the wooden floor (still crapping in the street though). Most commonly, the contents of chamber pots would be thrown out of the window in the hope of eventually finding an open drain. Needless to say, the streets were not pleasant.

King Louis XIII (1601–1643) allegedly had a commode built under his throne that he would happily use while receiving visitors. Perversely, he preferred to eat undisturbed.

> ### ❧ CRAP FACT ☙
> • Only 40% of the world's population have access to lavatories, and only 30% of the world's population use lavatory paper.

Henry VIII had a luxury padded lavatory covered with silk ribbons and gold fittings which emptied into a water tank rather than a pit. It was called a 'stool of easement', hence the wordage 'stool'. A high-ranking, but probably not very coveted, job in Henry's Court was the 'groom of the stool'. This official cleaner of the royal rear was employed to wipe his arse, sometimes, in lieu of any decent parchment, leaf or sponge, with his bare hand!

The courtiers and guests at Hampton Court would share the 'Great House of Easement' that contained 28 seats. These led to drains lined with brick which would wash into the Thames. These drains would be cleaned by 'gong scourers', young boys small enough to fit down them!

> ### ❧ CRAP FACT ☙
> • The average Briton (78 years) deposits 2.86 tons of faeces in their lifetime. We eat, however, an average of 50 tons.

> ### ❧ CRAP FACT ☙
> • We each use an average of 80 miles of lavatory paper and visit the lavatory an average of 230,000 times in our lifetime.

LAVATORY ETIQUETTE QUIZ

This quiz is taken from the excellent website for the renowned World Toilet Organization, and compiled by Expert Rating

1. A man enters the Gents and finds one other man at the long bank of urinals. The other man is using the first urinal near the door. Which urinal should the new customer choose?
a. ○ The one furthest from the door
b. ○ One at least 3-4 away from the first man
c. ○ One within 3-4 urinals of the first man
d. ○ The one smack in the middle of the bank of urinals

2. What if a man enters the Gents and finds that every other urinal is in use (ie: the first, the third, the fifth)… which urinal should he choose then?
a. ○ The one nearest the smallest man in the room
b. ○ Any urinal, since they are all equal distance apart at this point
c. ○ None of them; the man should fix himself in the mirror until someone leaves, or leave and return later when there are fewer people in the restroom
d. ○ The free urinal furthest from the door

3. Women like to socialise in the Ladies. In what part of the restroom is it inappropriate to casually chat?
a. ○ Over the lavatory doors
b. ○ At the sinks
c. ○ While waiting in line
d. ○ While primping in front of the mirrors

4. Even if there are partitions between a group of urinals, standard urinal rules still apply, meaning don't use one next to someone else.
a. ○ True   b. ○ False

5. When is it appropriate to begin a conversation with a fellow urinal user?
a. ○ When you need to say something important to the other person, especially if in a business setting
b. ○ When you have some comment to make about the lavatory
c. ○ When the other person speaks to you first
d. ○ Never

6. What is the proper protocol for flushing a toilet?
a. ○ Flush once, make sure no second flush is necessary
b. ○ Flush twice, always
c. ○ Flush before using the toilet, then flush after
d. ○ Flush before using the toilet, then flush twice after

7. Let's say there are three stalls in the Ladies and all are empty. Which one should you use?
a. ○ The first   b. ○ The middle
c. ○ The last   d. ○ Any of them

8. Many people use a paper towel to open the door of a public lavatory after washing their hands to prevent picking up new germs from the door. But experts say that, in fact, there is something else in the bathroom with more germs. What is it?
a. ○ The toilet handle
b. ○ The handle on the bathroom stall door
c. ○ The sink tap
d. ○ The toilet-paper dispenser

Quiz Answers: 1.a, 2.c, 3.a, 4.a, 5.d, 6.b, 7.b, 8.c. These answers are not necessarily endorsed by the authors.

The World Toilet Organization also encourages the enthusiast with some inspired computer games. Go to www.worldtoilet.org and click on the Toilet Entertainment banner. We particularly enjoyed Catch A Shit (pictured to the left), Toilet Splash is another favourite for the whole family

> ### ❧ CRAP FACT ☙
> • The bidet, an 18th-century French invention, translates as the word for 'pony', and comes from the way you sit on it as though straddling or riding one.

> ### ❧ CRAP FACT ☙
> • World Toilet Day takes place on 19th November each year.

and the joys of THE LAVATORY

BY
OSCAR AND
ANTHONY PYE-JEARY

The World's Greatest Lavatory
THE MAGNIFICENT TOTO NEOREST 600

The inspired precision-engineered functions available in this hi-tech masterpiece make it the most advanced lavatory in the world today.

1. The lid automatically opens as you approach, then closes and automatically flushes as you walk away.

2. The remote-controlled adjustable seat warms using variable temperature settings.

3. The revolutionary multi-sequential cyclone-siphon jet flushing system delivers higher levels of performance than you have ever experienced.

4. An automatic washing and cleansing system that provides a gentle front and back aerated warm water spray, which can be regulated for preferred water pressure and temperature.

5. It also has an automatic warm air dryer, and automatic power catalytic air purifier and deodorizer and an optional oscillating spray massage.

6. All remote-controlled with a wireless LCD panel, plus a discreet yet accessible manual overdrive.

Sir John Harrington invented the first semi-automatic flush lavatory for his godmother, Queen Elizabeth I, in 1596. She refused to use it, though, because she complained it made too much noise.

Alexander Cummings, a watchmaker, invented a much more sophisticated flush lavatory in 1775. His revelatory idea was to retain some water in the bowl after the flush so that it blocked sewer gases wafting up the pipes.

In the 19th century the population in Britain increased dramatically, and with no adequate sewerage system more and more waste was going into the cesspits. A survey in the 1840s estimated 200,000 cesspits in London alone. The drains overflowed before they could reach the Thames, and before anyone realised the dangers of water-carried disease, tens of thousands of Londoners died of cholera. In 1858, as a result of an unusually hot summer, the smell became so bad that work stopped in the House of Commons and plans were made to evacuate as far afield as Oxford. It became known as 'The Year of the Big Stink.'

When Joseph Bazelgette, the Chief Engineer with the Metropolitan Board of Works, devised a scheme to carry water away from people's houses and from the Thames into the estuary, he laid the foundations for the London Sewerage System.

Subsequently, Thomas Crapper helped to popularise the lavatory due to a number of pioneering plumbing techniques and renowned good craftsmanship. He was given a Royal Warrant to King Edward VII to install 30 lavatories in Sandringham, and the modern lavatory as we know it today was born.

EVOLUTION
AND THE FRENCH STILL HAVEN'T CRACKED IT! ↓

HOLE

FEET

THE BRISTOL STOOL CHART
Developed by K.W. Heaton at the University of Bristol and first published in the *British Medical Journal* in 1990

Type 1	Separate hard lumps, like nuts (hard to pass)
Type 2	Sausage-shaped but lumpy
Type 3	Like a sausage but with cracks on its surface
Type 4	Like a sausage or snake, smooth and soft
Type 5	Soft blobs with clear-cut edges (passed easily)
Type 6	Fluffy pieces with ragged edges, a mushy stool
Type 7	Use your imagination! You really don't want to see this illustration.

eighty per cent

80% of the human race lives in Asia. 80% of first pregnancies end in abortion. 80% of Botswana is covered by the Kalahari Desert. 80% of the soldiers in the Zimbabwean Army have AIDS. 80% of aircrashes happen within one kilometre of the airfield. 80% of Americans die in hospital. 80% of all the almonds in the world are grown in California. 80% of the world's oxygen is produced by plankton. 80% of tigers do not live long enough to reproduce. 80% of a bee's day is spent doing absolutely nothing. 80% of all the motor vehicles in Thailand are in Bangkok. 80% of top-flight Japanese students have regular sex with their mothers. 80% of the world's opals are produced in the town of Coober Pedy, Australia. 80% of the lead produced by Italy is mined in Sardinia. 80% of the world's population ingests caffeine every day. 80% of Scotch whisky is made for export. 80% of American women own a diamond ring. 80% of Bolivian children do not go to secondary school. 80% of Britons cannot name the English King executed by Parliament in 1649. An ear of corn is 80% water. The human brain is 80% water, more watery than blood.

eighty thousand

West Bank terrorists are believed to possess more than 80,000 illegal weapons. There are more than 80,000 streets in London. About 80,000 Americans are injured by lawnmowers every year. About 80,000 Japanese were killed by the atom bomb attacks on Hiroshima and Nagasaki. More than 80,000 Nepalese refugees fled to India in 2006. The US has arrested over 80,000 terrorist suspects worldwide since 2001. The US government provides airlines with a list of 80,000 terrorist suspects. About 80,000 Assyrian Christians have fled Iraq since the fall of Baghdad in 2003. 80,000 US women every year undergo unnecessary hysterectomies. About 80,000 new weblogs are created every day. British parents drive their children 80,000 miles before they reach 17. About 80,000 people have died in the conflict in Darfur, Sudan, through violence, starvation and disease. 80,000 people in the US have contracted cancer as a result of nuclear testing.

QI ELEGANCE

A pot-pourri of style and how to acquire it

by Kathy Phillips
International Beauty Director, *Vogue Asia*

I ALWAYS WEAR MY SWEATER BACK-TO-FRONT; IT IS SO MUCH MORE FLATTERING.
Diana Vreeland

Diana Vreeland (1903–1989) was the doyenne of US fashion editors – the *Devil Wears Prada* of her day. In her youth, she danced with the Tiller Girls, sold lingerie to Wallis Simpson and played tennis with Gertrude Lawrence. She shared a masseur with Queen Mary and was taught to ride by Buffalo Bill. She was a friend of Coco Chanel, Evelyn Waugh, Cecil Beaton and Cole Porter. She discovered Andy Warhol. She and her banker husband insisted on having all their footwear made in Budapest 'where they make the best shoes'. They were made of Russian calf and polished by the butler with cream and rhinoceros horn. The butler also broke in all his master's new shoes for him until they were as 'soft as butter'. Mrs Vreeland was once in her office at *Vogue* when she heard a clacking noise and asked what it was. Told it was a woman's heels, she replied: 'Fire her. I will not tolerate such distraction.' It was said her own shoes never touched the pavement. She was Editor-in-Chief of *Vogue* until 1971, when she was herself fired.

Few women, perhaps, have gone to quite so much trouble to achieve style, but many have gone to more trouble than you might imagine.

NEVER FEAR BEING VULGAR, JUST BORING, MIDDLE CLASS AND DULL.
Diana Vreeland

CLEOPATRA'S DEEP RED LIPSTICKS WERE MADE FROM FINELY CRUSHED CARMINE BEETLES MIXED WITH ANTS' EGGS

Body

Tattoos – from a Tahitian word meaning 'to strike' – originated in ancient Nubia in the 4th century BC. To puncture the skin and inject dyes, tattooists originally used boars' tusks or the shards of sea turtle shells.

According to the *Oxford English Dictionary*, the word 'corset' was first used in 1299, in an account of the wardrobe of the household of King Edward I.

Elizabeth Arden launched her Eight Hour Cream in 1930. The apricot coloured balm was not just for her clients: she also used it to soothe the legs of her thoroughbred horses.

The Miss Americas of the 1960s were five feet six inches tall and weighed a hundred and twenty pounds. Twenty years later they had gained two inches in height but remained at the same weight. The torch-bearing woman in the Columbia Pictures logo was slimmed down to look right in 1992.

Butt Glue: American beauty contestants use this to keep their swimsuits from riding up during competition. Flying High Enterprises offer it as 'a gentle roll-on body adhesive available in a 2 oz bottle. Washes off with soap and water'. Price: $8.50 per bottle. 'Put an end to those mid-floor routine wedgies,' says the ad.

Proportionally speaking, more people in the US die every year from liposuction operations than in car crashes.

Breast implants are so yesterday. *Perfect 10*, the United States' newest porn magazine, guarantees the first silicone-free pornography, with models guaranteed to boast only the real thing.

Lips

In the US today, 1,484 tubes of lipstick are sold every minute. Many women feel as designer Betsey Johnson does: 'If I were dying, I would be in the hospital wearing lipstick.'

Pink is the navy blue of India.

Diana Vreeland

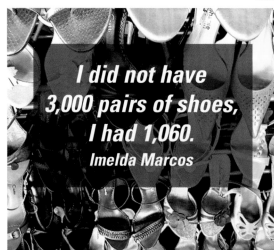

I did not have 3,000 pairs of shoes, I had 1,060.

Imelda Marcos

The word 'boudoir' was first used in English in 1781. Its literal meaning is 'a place to sulk in', from the French *bouder*, to pout or sulk.

Pots of red oxide of iron have been found inside ancient Sumerian and Egyptian tombs. Apparently lipstick is a timeless last request.

Before collagen injections, women repeatedly puckered their lips with words beginning with 'p' to plump up their mouths. The early women's rights campaigner Elizabeth Cady Stanton (1815–1902) once said that she would not give any feminist literature to women with 'prunes and prisms expressions'.

Despite this, in her 1963 *Beach Book*, the young Gloria Steinem admitted to sucking against the heel of her hand: 'This makes thin lips full, full lips firm, and fat cheeks lean.'

Lipstick Pistol: Referred to as 'The Kiss of Death', the lipstick pistol was employed by female KGB operatives during the Cold War. The 4.5 mm single shot weapon was disguised as a tube of lipstick, easily hidden in a purse. For male Russian spies, an alternative was the KGB's single shot Rectal Pistol, which was encased in rubber and secreted where you might imagine.

Hands

Night Sky, a sparkling dark-blue nail varnish, was a best-seller for Chanel. One woman bought hundreds of bottles to paint her bathroom ceiling.

Silkworm Cocoons: These are the latest thing in Japan. Known as *mayutama*, each one measures 3 x 2 cm and fits neatly onto the end of the fingertips. The sericin (silk) protein from the cocoon stimulates the epidermis and will naturally exfoliate and smooth your pores as you rub it over your face and hands. Order online.

Face

Makeup was an advanced art by the time of the ancient Egyptians. Both sexes shaved and pumiced their bodies and wore wigs, sometimes in combination with their own hair (a look later adopted by Andy Warhol). When archaeologists opened the tomb of King Tutankhamun they found a pot of 3,000-year-old makeup made from perfumed animal fat.

The ancient Roman physician Galen (AD 129–216) is credited with the original recipe for cold cream. It was based on beeswax, olive oil and rose water. He also recommended finely ground garden snails as an effective moisturiser.

Ancient Greeks wore false eyebrows made from dyed goats' hair, attached to the skin with natural gums and resins.

High foreheads and the absence of eyebrows were made fashionable by Elizabeth I. During the reign of Charles I, children's brows were covered in walnut oil to decrease hair growth. Adults' eyebrows were shaved and replaced with fake ones made with mouse skin.

Botulinum toxin (sometimes called 'sausage poison') is one of the most toxic naturally occurring substances in the world. Under the trade name Botox, it has been used since 1980 to smooth out lines and wrinkles on the face and neck.

There are no ugly women, only lazy ones. Helena Rubinstein

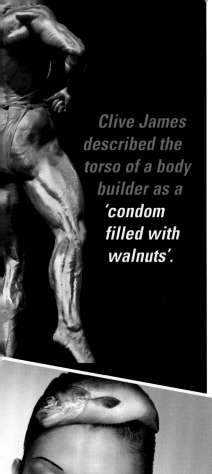

Clive James described the torso of a body builder as a *'condom filled with walnuts'.*

DONNA TROPE

FURE A L'ÉCHELLE, CARICATURE DU XVIIIᵉ SIÈCLE

Contrary to scaremongering, its history shows it to be profoundly safe. The minute doses used would need to be 60 times the size to cause any ill effects.

The Korean Society of Plastic and Reconstructive Surgeons lists 1,300 members, almost twice as many as there are in California. Most of the world's rhinoplasty operations aim to reduce noses, but Koreans routinely have bridges put into their noses to give them more character. (Botox, on the other hand, is used to reduce big calf muscles, which cause Korean women psychological distress.)

Women will do anything to conceal, bleach and blush. For two thousand years, European face makeup was made from white lead, which was combined with chalk or applied in a paste with vinegar and egg whites to mask completely the skin's surface and colour. The Spanish physician to Pope Julius III, Andreas de Laguna, complained that women's makeup was so thick he could 'cut off a curd of cheesecake from either of their cheeks'.

In the Middle Ages in Britain, to fight the destructive effects of the lead paste on the face, noblewomen prepared their skin with ground asparagus roots and goats' milk. This was rubbed into the skin with pieces of warm bread. They used hair gel made from a mixture of swallow droppings and lizard tallow.

As well as poisonous lead and mercury, women attached leeches to their bodies and swallowed arsenic wafers. To mimic skin translucency, the Greeks and Romans and, later, Queen Elizabeth I, painted the veins on their breasts and foreheads blue.

Today, haemorrhoid cream is a well-known make-up artist's secret for de-puffing a model's eyes before a show. Preparation H is available from all good chemists for around £5.00.

'Age Dropping' (starting plastic surgery in one's thirties rather than fifties) is the latest trend in America. The idea is never to age visibly at all.

All the American women had purple noses and gray lips and their faces were chalk white from terrible powder. I recognized that the United States could be my life's work. Helena Rubinstein

Legs and Feet

Doctor fish are named for their ability to produce healthy results from even the most crusty or diseased skin. They are currently all the rage in spa treatments across Japan, China, Turkey and Europe. The idea is that you immerse your feet, hands or, if you're brave enough, your entire body in a warm pool that swarms with hundreds of hungry minnow-sized feeders. The fish zoom in on your flakiest, most scabby parts and chomp away at it to reveal the fresh layer beneath. According to enthusiasts, you emerge refreshed, buffed and glowing. Gara Rufa are toothless little fish originally from Turkey – they nibble but can't bite. They eat dead skin because they evolved in hot springs where very few plankton and other animals live, so they take what they can get.

The Roman poet Ovid advised women, 'Let no rude goat find his way beneath your arms and let not your legs be rough with bristling hair.' Supermodels don't walk the runway with hairy legs.

Hair

The tallest recorded hair belonged to European aristocrats of the late 18th century, who stuffed their coiffure with wool or horsehair pads and kept it in place with wire, pomade and flour. Women had to crouch in carriages because their heads were too big to sit, and they had to sleep on their backs in order not to ruin the 'do'. In 1780, the doorway of St Paul's Cathedral had to be raised four feet to accommodate big-haired women.

Dolls don't sell well unless the little girl can indulge in what toy manufacturers called 'hairplay', coiffing and combing the doll's hair. The makers of Barbie, the most popular doll of all time, produced a special 'totally hair' version in 1992: her hair reached to her toes. It became the best-selling Barbie ever.

In ancient Rome, women bleached their hair using pigeon droppings. Blonde hair was considered to be the mark of a prostitute.

Of all 88 screen Tarzans, only one, Mike Henry, had a hairy chest.

166 years after John Keats died, Dr Werner Baumgartner analysed a lock of his hair and found traces of the opiate laudanum. Each strand of hair has its own blood supply and reflects whatever is coursing through us. Drugs from aspirins to anticoagulants to thyroid medications can all affect the health of hair. Hair is such a sensitive indicator that drug companies are now experimenting with hair analysis rather than urine analysis.

Perfume

Assyrian men and women wore their hair elaborately braided, oiled and perfumed. Inside their hairdos, close to the scalp, they tucked tiny balls of scented wax. Melted by body heat, this trickled down the neck, allowing the wearer to remain fragrant throughout the evening.

The Glove-makers' and Perfume-makers' Guilds were both founded in Grasse, Provence, in 1582. Perfume was closely linked to the development of glove-making. It was used to mask the unpleasant odour caused by tanning the leather.

On the day before her desperate flight from Paris with King Louis XVI to escape the mob, Marie Antoinette hurried to Houbigant's store in Rue Faubourg St Honore to have her perfume bottle refilled.

William Penhaligon, Queen Victoria's barber, created his first fragrance ('a subtle accord of jasmine and sandalwood') in 1872. He named it Hammam Bouquet, after the Turkish Baths near his shop in St James's, London.

It takes one metric tonne of petals (8 million individual blooms) to obtain just over 2 lb of Jasmine de Grasse (the distillation of the flowers to make scent). To make 2 lb of the essential oil of roses you need five metric tons of flowers.

One bottle of Chanel No. 5 is sold in airports every 9 minutes. There are nine ritual operations involved in sealing each bottle. One of these is *baudruchage*, in which a fine natural membrane is secured by cotton thread and knotted four times. This seals the top of the bottle to ensure that it's perfectly airtight. The term comes from French *baudruche*, slang for 'false optimism' or 'a windbag'.

A little too stylish for my taste

Charlemagne owned eight hundred pairs of fine gloves. His excuse would have been that, at that time, gloves were difficult to produce and to clean.

The Duke and Duchess of Windsor had their lavatory paper hand cut, and footmen served their dogs from silver bowls.

The 2nd Duke of Westminster (1879–1953) had his shoe-laces ironed.

The singer, dancer and 1930s movie star Josephine Baker (1906–1975) used to take her pet cheetah to the cinema.

The New York socialite Rita de Acosta Lydig (1880–1929) owned eighty-seven identical black velvet coats that differed only in their lace trims.

The Italian shoemaker Salvatore Ferragamo once sold seventy pairs of his shoes to Greta Garbo in a single sitting, and a hundred pairs to the Maharani of Cooch Behar, who then sent him pearls and diamonds to adorn them.

The London residence of the designer Valentino has linen curtains that are taken down, washed, ironed and re-hung every day.

EUROPEAN LANGUAGES
No. 5: French

The French are sawed-off sissies who eat snails and slugs and cheese that smells like people's feet. Utter cowards who force their own children to drink wine, they gibber like baboons even when you try to speak to them in their own wimpy language.

P. J. O'ROURKE

The average country French person has as much difficulty with irregular French verbs and with words agreeing with each other and with grave and acute accents as an English person does. Not only are most French people over the age of 50 unable to write grammatically – they cannot speak French properly either.

The circumflex accent (the little hat over a letter) represents an ancient missing 's'. It makes no difference to the way a word is spoken, so an attempt was made to abolish it by the Académie Française. This created such a storm of protest, particularly by those people who had one in their name, that the Académie was forced to reinstate it.

In 1880, a third of the population of London's Soho was French. British diplomats were trained by being sent there to learn the language.

The word 'etiquette' is French for 'label'. In French, a *brassière* is a baby's long-sleeved vest. A *chauffeur* in French means a stoker or fireman. Chauffeurs were originally French medieval bandits who drove their victims over hot coals.

There is no exact French translation of the English expression 'front door'.

FRENCH DICTIONARY

gland acorn
grappe bunch
prune plum
raisin grape

Grace
COCK
FLAVOURED
soup mix
spicy
AUTHENTIC
JAMAICAN

Euroshag

Mini Risk®
SOAP
NAAF
Asma och Allergi Förbundet
YHTEISTYÖSSÄ ALLERGIA- JA ASTMALIITON KANSSA

Mahe ja tõhus. Koostöös Põhjamaade Allergialiitudega.
Нежное и эффективное.
Одобрено Союзами Аллергологов Северных Стран.
Maigs un efektīgs.
Izstrādāts sadarbībā ar Ziemeļvalstu alerģijas savienībām.
Švelnus ir efektyvus.
Gaminami su Šiaurės šalių
alergijos asociaciju leidimu.
75 g

BON
TUES
NATUR
C

WONKA®
HOPPIN' Candy
NERDS®
Pink Rainbow
rainbow

SPUNK

ASS-ratiopharm®
Wirkstoff: Acetylsalicylsäure 500 mg
30 Bei Schmerzen und Fieber
Tabletten N2
ratio

Teller
SCHOVIT
Kakaohaltiges Getränkepulver
Sofort löslich
NEU!
mit 6 Vitaminen
+Traubenzucker
+Calcium

Knorr
Bitte zu Tisch!
Knoblauch
Suppe

FRECKLED EGGS CANDY
WONKA
runts
Net Wt
5 oz (49.6 g)
ARTIFICIALLY
FLAVORED

uff
MAX
CROCCANTINI
DI MAIS
4 FORMAGGI

Knorr®
ock
ube
COCK SOUP
FLAVOUR
BOUILLON
NET WT.

Super
Dickmann's®
Super gross – mit Schokolade
Mach dick
das dumme
Gesicht!
...die Echten
in der
Frischebox

CRIPPLE
COCK
PREMIUM WESTCOUNTRY CIDER

HB

Hardon Tea
25 Class A
Teabags
redients: 100% Tea

Snack
TANKE
SCHON!
Pfanni
Kartoffel
Snack
mit Fleischbällchen
& Röstzwiebeln

Casino
PLOPSIES,
RIZ SOUFFLÉ ENROBÉ
AU CHOCOLAT
BON

EIGHTY-EIGHT USES FOR SAUSAGES

According to the British Pig Executive, there are more than 400 named varieties of sausage in Britain, and an estimated 1,720 uses for them.
We could only think of 88:

1. Pincushion.
2. Doorstop.
3. Paperweight.
4. Bottle stopper.
5. Low-maintenance pet.
6. Comical false moustache.
7. Novelty dog turd.
8. Faintly sinister buttonhole for Mafia wedding.
9. Biodegradable key fob.
10. Emergency cricket bails.
11. Aromatic candles for people who hate the smell of vanilla.
12. Stoat coshes.
13. German currency.
14. Speed bumps for model village.
15. Draught excluder for doll's house.
16. Show-jumping fences for mice.
17. Pick-up Stix for the short-sighted.
18. Butcher's bunting.
19. Relay batons for pre-school children.
20. Shoe trees for people with small, tubular feet.
21. Flush tester for lavatory factory.
22. Hair rollers for ladies whose husbands like them to smell of meat.
23. Handicap baseball bat for top player in game against toddlers.
24. Ten chipolatas will keep a pair of gloves shapely.
25. Nuclear submarine for fish tank.
26. Paint roller for creosoting shed.
27. Hand warmer.
28. Hamster bolster (place in baby's cotton sock).
29. Instant pork stuffing for roast snake.
30. Fingers for snowman.
31. Massive compensatory cock for Action Man.
32. Substitute torch batteries for torch that wasn't working anyway.
33. Flagpole for small, stout flag.
34. Pretend cigar for non-smoking movie mogul.
35. Voodoo doll for militant feminist.
36. Jiggle-it-yourself energy-saving vibrator.
37. Splint for broken finger.
38. Conversation piece for short, not very interesting conversation.
39. Device for distracting guard dog when breaking into stately home.
40. Horrible warning example to naughty pig.
41. Ornament which changes colour and texture over time.
42. Bookmark for one of those cardboard children's books with only four pages in.
43. Subbuteo flicker.
44. Ostentatious earplugs to impress upon others that you're not listening.
45. Sex doll for a slug.
46. Wind chimes for people who don't like the sound of wind chimes.
47. Window dressing for condom shop (if there is such a thing).
48. Scaled-down logs for foyer display of large timber merchant.
49. Incentive to dangle in front of carnivorous donkey.
50. Non-chicken drumsticks.
51. Replacement for lost lead-piping piece in game of Cluedo.
52. Easy-to-conceal truncheon for non-violent secret policeman.
53. Travel bathplug.
54. Rehearsal harmonica.
55. Edible perch for baby eagle.
56. Bait for dogfish.
57. Barrel cleaner for sawn-off shotgun.
58. Altogether more interesting *Big Brother* contestant.
59. Teether (exposes baby to salmonella, improves immune system).
60. Stylus for records you don't want to listen to any more.
61. Paint white and use as smart fenders for 1/72 scale yacht.
62. Pin two to an Alice band for instant rabbit costume.
63. Pin four to underpants for instant cow costume.
64. Glue parsley onto top to make realistic baobab tree for train set.
65. Use instead of air for puncture-proof inner tube for bike tyre.
66. Placebo in scientific tests of sausage-shaped drugs.
67. Retirement home for maggots.
68. Hands of unusual clock.
69. Tusks of unusual walrus sculpture.
70. Manlier alternative to liquorice in sherbet fountain.
71. Charisma implant for the discerning Speedo-wearer.
72. Necktie to distract attention from someone with weird neck.
73. Temporary stopcock for strange hole in wall of public toilet.
74. Hollow out and use as straw for milk.
75. Daub with ketchup, pretend to have amputated finger.
76. Now you too can practise circumcision without fear!
77. Ian Hislop action figure.
78. Something to produce when asked if you have a Nectar card.
79. Darts you can use in complete confidence that no one will die.
80. Stick several up bottom and tell doctor you think you might have haemorrhoids.
81. Eye-catching alternative to tinsel.
82. Edible solution to runny noses.
83. Crime-proof jemmy for burglars.
84. Non-vegan Rawlplugs.
85. Banana boat for frogs.
86. A common enemy for Israelis and Palestinians.
87. Leatherette-look gear stick.

88. Can be eaten with mashed potato, baked beans and gravy.

EGYPT

THE EGYPTIAN NAME FOR EGYPT IS MISR, WHICH MEANS 'THE COUNTRY'. IT IS THE WORLD'S OLDEST NATION, HAVING EXISTED CONTINUOUSLY FOR 5,000 YEARS. ✱ IT IS THE 30TH LARGEST COUNTRY IN THE WORLD, FOUR TIMES THE SIZE OF THE UK, HALF THE SIZE OF SAUDI ARABIA AND THE SAME SIZE AS NIGERIA. ✱ ITS 79 MILLION PEOPLE MAKE IT THE MOST POPULOUS COUNTRY IN THE ARAB WORLD AND THE SECOND MOST POPULOUS COUNTRY IN AFRICA AFTER NIGERIA. ✱ IT IS ALSO THE WORLD'S DRIEST NATION, WITH LESS THAN A QUARTER OF AN INCH OF RAIN EACH YEAR. ✱ BECAUSE 90% OF THE COUNTRY IS DESERT, THE POPULATION DENSITY IS NOT HIGH OVERALL (IT'S THREE TIMES LOWER THAN THE UK'S) BUT ALMOST EVERYONE LIVES ALONG THE BANKS OF THE NILE AND A QUARTER OF THEM IN CAIRO, WHICH IS AFRICA'S SECOND MOST CROWDED CITY AFTER LAGOS. ✱ 98% OF THE POPULATION IS EGYPTIAN, 80% ARE MUSLIM AND THE NATIONAL LANGUAGE IS ARABIC. ✱ THIS IS QUITE SURPRISING GIVEN ITS SUCCESSIVE WAVES OF INVASIONS, NOT JUST BY MUSLIM ARABS BUT ALSO BY LIBYANS, NUBIANS, ASSYRIANS, PERSIANS (TWICE), GREEKS, ROMANS, BYZANTINE ROMANS, OTTOMAN TURKS AND NAPOLEONIC FRENCH. ✱ THE WORD 'EGYPT' COMES FROM AIGYPTOS, THE GREEK MISPRONUNCIATION OF THE ANCIENT EGYPTIAN NAME, HWT-KA-PTAH, 'THE HOUSE OF THE SOUL OF PTAH' (PTAH WAS AN EARLY EGYPTIAN GOD). ✱ 'COPTIC', THE NAME NOW USED FOR EGYPTIAN CHRISTIANS, WAS AN ARABIC MISPRONUNCIATION OF AIGYPTOS. ✱ BUT EGYPTIAN CIVILISATION HAD STARTED LONG BEFORE THESE CONFUSIONS: THE GREAT PYRAMID AT GIZA WAS COMPLETED 1,000 YEARS BEFORE STONEHENGE. ✱ IT TOOK 20 YEARS TO BUILD, USING A LABOUR FORCE OF 100,000 (ABOUT A TENTH OF THE WHOLE POPULATION) WORKING AN AVERAGE TEN-HOUR DAY. ✱ ALTHOUGH IT DEPENDED ON SLAVERY, THE WORKMEN WERE PAID — THE FIRST RECORDED PAYROLL IN HISTORY. ✱ THE GREAT PYRAMID WAS THE WORLD'S TALLEST BUILDING FOR 4,000 YEARS, ONLY OVERTAKEN BY LINCOLN CATHEDRAL IN AD 1300 . ✱ OVER THE FOLLOWING 300 CENTURIES, AS WELL AS BUILDING OVER 100 MORE PYRAMIDS, THE EGYPTIANS — WITH A POPULATION NO LARGER THAN THAT OF MODERN BIRMINGHAM — INVENTED PAPER, INK, WRITING, METALWORKING, CONCRETE, WOODEN FURNITURE, BOATS WITH SAILS, WEIGHING SCALES, SHOES, CANDLES, TAPS, METAL SWORDS, CHARIOTS, MUSEUMS, SUNDIALS, THE 365-DAY YEAR, ALCHEMY, COSMETICS, PERFUME, FIBREGLASS AND A CONTRACEPTIVE MADE FROM CROCODILE DUNG AND HONEY. ✱ THEY ALSO INVENTED THE BUSINESS HANDSHAKE, THE WILL, MONOTHEISM, THE NOW UNIVERSAL MORAL PRECEPT 'DO AS YOU WOULD BE DONE BY', AND — WHILE MOST OF THE REST OF THE WORLD WAS STILL HUNTING AND GATHERING — THE WORLD'S FIRST GUIDE TO ETIQUETTE. ✱ THEY ALSO HAD THE WORLD'S FIRST FEMALE RULER — MERITNIT IN 2950 BC. ✱ MODERN EGYPT'S INNOVATION RATE IS, INEVITABLY, SLOWER, BUT IT REMAINS THE ONLY ARAB COUNTRY WITH AN OPERA HOUSE.

89

EXECUTIONS

BEHEADING

1535 – Severed heads were usually boiled in salt then stuck on poles where they would stay for months. The head of John Fisher – executed by Henry VIII – 'grew daily fresher & fresher', leading to cries that it was a miracle.

1541 – Margaret, Countess of Salisbury, a game old lady well over 80, was condemned to death by Henry VIII in place of her absentee cardinal son. She refused to kneel with her head on the block and was chased, screaming, round the scaffold. Eventually the executioner had to push her over and hack off her head as she wriggled on the ground.

1685 – Lord Monmouth, sentenced by the notorious Judge Jeffreys, was still alive after three hefty swings of the axe. The headsman had to finish off the job with a knife.

1747 – The last person to be beheaded in Britain was Lord Lovat, an 80-year-old Jacobite. There were so many spectators that the grandstand collapsed, killing 22. 'The more mischief, the better sport!' chortled the ancient rebel.

1792 – About 10,000 people were guillotined in France between 1792 and 1799. Contrary to popular belief, more than 80% of them were commoners. The guillotine was also popular with the Nazis who used it to execute over 20,000 people.

1905 – A Doctor Beaurieux attended the execution of a criminal called Languille and called on the newly severed head by name. Opening its eyes, it fixed him with a penetrating gaze and was conscious for 30 seconds after the blade fell.

1977 – The last execution by guillotine took place in Marseilles, more than eight years after men first landed on the moon.

BOILING & BAKING

570 BC – The sculptor Perillus of Athens designed a life-size hollow bronze bull for the Sicilian despot Phalaris. The condemned man was to be placed inside and a fire lit beneath, so that his screams came out of the bull's mouth. To test the device, Perillus was selected as the first victim.

1531 – Richard Roose, the Bishop of Rochester's cook, was convicted of poisoning 17 people and killing two. A special Act of Parliament was passed to allow him to be boiled to death in his own pot.

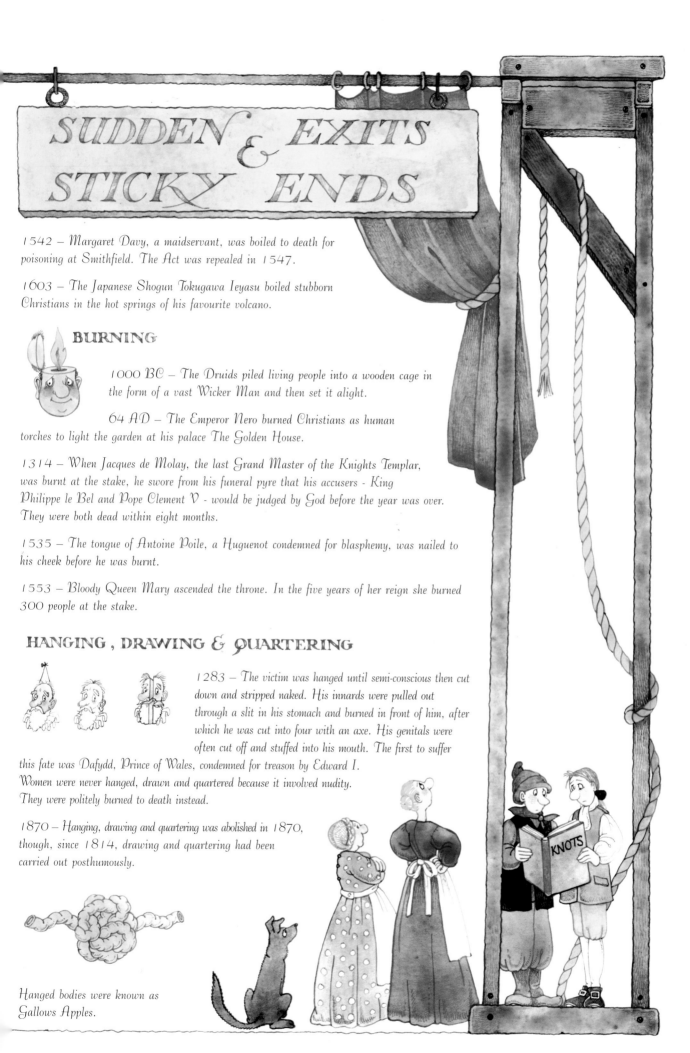

SUDDEN EXITS & STICKY ENDS

1542 – Margaret Davy, a maidservant, was boiled to death for poisoning at Smithfield. The Act was repealed in 1547.

1603 – The Japanese Shogun Tokugawa Ieyasu boiled stubborn Christians in the hot springs of his favourite volcano.

BURNING

1000 BC – The Druids piled living people into a wooden cage in the form of a vast Wicker Man and then set it alight.

64 AD – The Emperor Nero burned Christians as human torches to light the garden at his palace The Golden House.

1314 – When Jacques de Molay, the last Grand Master of the Knights Templar, was burnt at the stake, he swore from his funeral pyre that his accusers - King Philippe le Bel and Pope Clement V - would be judged by God before the year was over. They were both dead within eight months.

1535 – The tongue of Antoine Poile, a Huguenot condemned for blasphemy, was nailed to his cheek before he was burnt.

1553 – Bloody Queen Mary ascended the throne. In the five years of her reign she burned 300 people at the stake.

HANGING, DRAWING & QUARTERING

1283 – The victim was hanged until semi-conscious then cut down and stripped naked. His innards were pulled out through a slit in his stomach and burned in front of him, after which he was cut into four with an axe. His genitals were often cut off and stuffed into his mouth. The first to suffer this fate was Dafydd, Prince of Wales, condemned for treason by Edward I. Women were never hanged, drawn and quartered because it involved nudity. They were politely burned to death instead.

1870 – Hanging, drawing and quartering was abolished in 1870, though, since 1814, drawing and quartering had been carried out posthumously.

Hanged bodies were known as Gallows Apples.

Escoffier v. Mitchell

Georges Auguste Escoffier (1846–1935) was not only a legendary chef, he also existed and, to this day, is probably the most famous chef who's dead, and is likely to remain so until Delia dies.

Above all, keep it simple.
AUGUSTE ESCOFFIER

'Food, glorious food, nothing quite like it for cooling the blood' is a mixture of two well-known songs and reflects the views of neither.
DAVID MITCHELL

ESCOFFIER DOSSIER

Escoffier was the world's longest-serving chef: he worked professionally for 62 years.

He was the first great chef to work for the public. Before him, master chefs worked exclusively for the aristocracy.

He was the first chef to be awarded the Légion d'Honneur. He was very short and had to wear built up shoes to reach the stove.

His wife was called Delphine Daffis. They were married for 55 years. He died aged 89, a few days after she did.

But what did Escoffier actually do that was so great? Well, among others, these things:

He pioneered the 'brigade system' for running kitchens (which replaced the previous 'help yourself to whatever's in the fridge' system, which was a bit of a mean system until the fridge was invented).

He created the two most famous Melba foods (Peach and Toast).

He introduced 'service à la russe' to France, where, perhaps understandably, 'service à la française' had previously prevailed. (The difference between these services being that, in the old French one, all the dishes came all at once and sat there getting cold like bloody tapas, whereas in the 'à la russe' system things arrived course by course, as is now normal). And he basically made it okay and even a bit cool to be a chef.

A really terrific cook, then, he was also an astute businessman who co-founded (with César Ritz) some of the most famous hotels in the world.

Many would say he dedicated his whole life to food lovers.

I would not say that.

I would say that we should not mistake gourmets for food lovers. Gourmets are just fussy eaters – they have no love for food in its purest form: as it is found in a newsagent's. I, on the other hand, count myself a genuine foodie because, when I'm hungry, I find almost anything delicious.

No one who has lost touch with the deliciousness of a Scotch egg and a packet of Quavers, or a mouthful of shrink-wrapped ham followed by a KitKat can call themselves a genuine food lover.

Escoffier famously said of cookery, 'Above all, keep it simple.' Clearly he did not mean this. It's just the same twinkly dishonesty as when Gary Rhodes claims to be demonstrating a good old-fashioned fry-up breakfast and then advocates making your own baked beans. 'Keep it simple'?!? Escoffier invented 10,000 recipes! I don't think I've eaten 10,000 different things in my life. I say, 'Have a cheese sandwich for lunch every day for a month' – that's keeping it simple. Only a real food lover could get through that.

So I propose to take him on: gourmet versus food lover, master chef versus trencherman, Le Creuset versus Uncle Ben's.

• •

There are two things I like stiff, and one of them's jelly.
DAME NELLIE MELBA

Round One: Starter

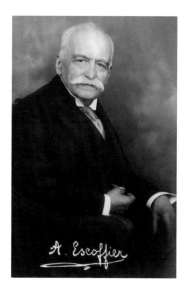

Escoffier (left) *vous propose 'Nymphes à L'Aurore' or 'Nymphs in the Dawn'. This was a dish created for the Prince of Wales and is actually 'lukewarm frogs' legs in a white wine and fish sauce with paprika, garnished with chervil and tarragon and served in champagne jelly'. He said it was 'nymphs' to make it sound more palatable to the prince, who presumably thought eating a river-dwelling mythical maiden was absolutely the kind of thing he should be doing more of.*

My starter (right) *is also served lukewarm: 'Crisps That Have Been in the Car'. I was going to go for something more complex but there's been a massive run on chervil at my local Londis. Nevertheless, I'm not stinting on service as I'm putting them in a bowl. Sophisticates may like to accompany their crisps with a tub of red goo – which you can usually find by the tills of any good video rental shop.*

Round Two: Main Course

Escoffier (left) *vous propose 'Tournedos Rossini'. This is actually made of beef, not the famous composer, but there is no record of whether this made it sound more or less delicious to royalty. Some anecdotes claim that it was actually invented by Antoine Carême, an earlier French chef.*

My creation (right) *for the main course has also been attributed by the envious to other chefs: 'Chicken Korma with Pilau Rice'. Ingredients: 1 Packet of Chicken Korma with Pilau Rice (feeds one). Certainly there have been dishes of this name in the past, but my breakthrough was to see the advantages of limiting my cuisine to foods that already have cooking instructions printed on the outside. Not only is this convenient but it also guarantees that gratifyingly delicious amounts of salt and sugar will already have been added at the factory stage. Eat that, Escoffier! (He'd probably rather not, he's fussy.)*

Round Three: Pudding

Escoffier (left) *vous propose 'Peach Melba'. Again dedicated to a muso, this time the opera singer Dame Nellie Melba, it's a sort of ice-cream sundae with peaches and, for some reason, raspberry sauce. I would have thought that kind of chocolate sauce that goes hard on the ice cream forming a sort of negative Alp effect would have been a lot better.*

My offering (right) *is 'There Isn't Any Pudding – Shall We Go to the Pub?' I must say my guests always find this very popular, particularly in the summer months when the smell of my kitchen bin can be a little bit ripe for some Korma-stuffed stomachs. And I find that two or three pints of strong lager really can perform digestive miracles.*

And who is the winner, Mitchell or Escoffier? You must be the judge. Just ask yourself which of the above menus you've eaten most from in your life, and give that chef a hundred points.

The EGGHEAD ADVENTURES of THOMAS EDISON

Eggheaded inventor Thomas Alva Edison (1847-1931) was an extraordinary character. The true story of this oddball American's crazy capers makes comic book reading.

Young Thomas Edison was a prodigious reader, encouraged by his father, who paid him for every book he read. When he wasn't reading, Thomas would carry out scientific experiments. One of his earliest experiments was sitting on a bird's egg to see whether it would hatch.

It didn't.

COME ON! ONE MORE MOUTHFUL AND WE'LL HAVE LIFT OFF!

PARP!

SQUELCH!

OH CRUMBS! I THINK I'VE FOLLOWED THROUGH!

In another childhood experiment Edison induced a friend to swallow a large quantity of Seidlitz powders - a laxative containing tartaric acid, sodium bicarbonate and potassium sodium tartrate - in the hope that the gas generated would enable his unfortunate pal to fly.

Thomas Edison's schooldays lasted all of three months. That was as much as his teacher could bear. Edison is thought to have suffered from Attention Deficit Disorder, but his schoolmaster had another name for it...

AND DON'T COME BACK, YOU ADDLED RETARD!

OOPS! BETTER MAKE MYSELF SCARCE!

TAKE THAT!!

Thomas was almost totally deaf, and he blamed this on an assault he suffered at the hands of an irate railway guard whose train he had accidentally ignited during an impromptu chemistry experiment.

As well as an egghead, Thomas was an entrepreneur. He earned money selling newspapers, confectionary and home-grown vegetables to train passengers.

WAR DECLARED! CONFEDERATES ATTACK FORT SUMTER...

APPLES, BANANAS, 2 CENTS A PAAHND!

CANDY, CHOC-ICES!

He saved up his profits and invested them in a second-hand printing press...

...and at the age of 14 he was producing his own newspaper, which he edited, printed and distributed, on board a train.

ROLL UP, ROLL UP! WEEKLY HERALD, ON SALE HERE!

I DON'T BELIEVE IT!

GADZOOKS! HE'S PRODUCING THAT NEWSPAPER... FROM A TRAIN!

Edison built his own telegraph system using bottles, nails and stove-pipe wire. He tried to generate power for it by *rubbing a neighbour's cat* to create static electricity.

HISSSS!!

That didn't work, but the system did... until the day it was wrecked by a stray cow.

1,000 patents weren't enough - He just kept on inventing stuff!

Edison worked as a telegraph operator and was constantly coming up with new inventions. But he had no joy selling them. In 1869 he arrived in New York, penniless, and was offered a job repairing telegraph equipment.

His big breakthrough was the Universal Stock Ticker, a telegraphic printer used for communicating stock prices to New York brokers' offices.

Edison was hoping to sell the rights to this little invention for $3,000, but he didn't have the nerve to ask for such a large sum. Which was just as well...

He spent the proceeds setting up the world's first industrial research laboratory, at Menlo Park, New Jersey. It was the ultimate garden shed! Inside it, Edison beavered away day and night, aiming to come up with a new invention every week.

Edison employed a large team of scientists and engineers who worked alongside him, but his hard-working assistants didn't always get the credit, or rewards, that their work deserved.

He was such a frequent visitor to the US Patent Office, Edison received an annual invitation to their Christmas party.* He held 1,093 US patents in total, as well as many patents in England, France and Germany.

* Joke

Edison is credited with inventing, among other things, the phonograph (record player), the quadruplex telegraph (an early form of broadband, sort of), the movie camera, the fluoroscope (X-ray) and, of course, the incandescent light bulb...

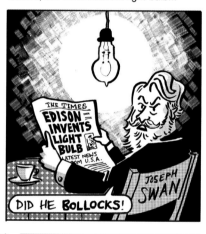

Edison was definitely the first man to execute an elephant in public using electricity. He accomplished this dubious feat in 1903. The victim was Topsy, a homicidal pachyderm from Coney Island circus. Edison hoped that by pumping 6,600 volts of alternating current through the hapless beast he could convince the public that his DC electricity supply system was safer than AC. Topsy died in vain, and the AC system, promoted by Edison's arch-rivals George Westinghouse and Nikola Tesla, won the day.

A big concrete tower topped by a giant glass bulb now stands on the site of Edison's Menlo Park laboratory, a fitting tribute to his inventive genius.

And Edison's name lives on, at least in the pubs of Devon and Cornwall, where a band *claiming* to be the original line-up of the sixties chart-toppers Edison Lighthouse (whose name was inspired by the concrete memorial) perform their one and only hit, 'Love grows where my Rosemary goes', to ever decreasing audiences.

Coffee isn't
My cup of
Tea.

sam Goldwyn

Tea is not
like VODKA -
which you can
drink a LOT of
BORIS
YELTSIN

If this is coffee please
bring me some coffee
If this is tea please
bring me some tea

Abraham Lincoln

The best quality tea must have
creases like the leathern boot
of Tartar horsemen, curl like
the dewlap of a mighty bullock,
unfold like a mist rising out of a
ravine, gleam like a lake touched
by a zephyr, and be wet and soft
like a fine earth swept by rain.

Lu Yu (733-804 AD)

Where there's tea
there's hope.

Sir Arthur Pinero

The Institute
For Tropical Diseases

Do Not Remove

Anyone
remotely
interesting
is mad in
one way or
another.

John Green

I never drink
coffee for lunch:
I find it keeps
me awake for
the afternoon

Ronald Reagan

Nobody can teach you
How to make a perfect
cup of tea.   It just
happens over time.
Wearing cashmere
helps, of course.
Jill Dupleix

Is there no Latin word
for tea? Upon my soul
if I had known that I would
have left the vulgar stuff
alone.

Hilaire Belloc

PLAN
AHEA
D

Go not to the
Elves for advice
for they will say
both no and yes.

JRR Tolkien

The QI Annual was written, researched, illustrated and otherwise enhanced by Garrick Alder, Ronnie Ancona, Clive Anderson, Rowan Atkinson, Pablo Bach, Bill Bailey, Jo Brand, Craig Brown, Rob Brydon, Jimmy Carr, Jeremy Clarkson, Julian Clary, Mat Coward, Alan Davies, Cherry Denman, Ted Dewan, Chris Donald, Jenny Doughty, Geoff Dunbar, Piers Fletcher, Stephen Fry, Justin Gayner, Howard Goodall, Christopher Gray, Rich Hall, Martin Handford, James Harkin, Tony Husband, Phill Jupitus, Kate Kessling, Sean Lock, Roger Law, David Mitchell, John Mitchinson, Nick Newman, Dara O'Briain, Molly Oldfield, Kathy Phillips, Sandra Pond, Justin Pollard, Matt Pritchett, Anthony Pye-Jeary, Oscar Pye-Jeary, Vic Reeves, Arthur Smith, Mark Steel, Vitali Vitaliev and Tim Watts.

Edited by John Lloyd.

Designed by David Costa and Nadine Levy at Wherefore Art?
Cover illustration: David Stoten.

Project Manager: Victoria de Wolfe.

Picture research: Jon Petrie.
Etymological and Punctuational Adviser: Neil Titman.

Thanks to New Holland Publishing for the picture of the blowfly from *Nick Baker's Bug Book*, to NASA for the photography of the Earth and the Helix Nebula, and Donna Trope and *Vogue* (China) for the fashion photos in QI Elegance.

Respect and admiration to the anonymous geniuses of the qi.com forums, especially barbados, djgordy, dr.bob, Fudgie, grizzly, Mr Grue, Hans Mof, Neotenic, Not a Number, Peetay, samivel, Sebastian flyte, smiley_face, snophlake, strukkanurv, suze, Tas, Twopints, violetriga and 96aelw for thinking up 88 uses for sausages and for being generally good eggs.

Dedicated to Peter Ainsworth, Sophia Bergqvist, Christopher Broadbent, Jason Brooks, Richard Burridge, Simon Linnell, Ranjit Majumdar, Brendan May, Jill Parker, Lucy Parker, and Andrew Sunnucks – 'The Friends of QI' – who got the point before anyone else.

Photography: Chris Craymer, Harry Lloyd, Sarah McCarthy, Brian Ritchie, Dan Schreiber and Rebecca Waite.
Embroidery: Elizabethe Townsend.

QI Logo design: Jules Bailey.

With special thanks to Tony Cloke, Brett Croft, Olly Fetiveau, Mike Gornall, Brian Greenwood, Sarah Lloyd, Lise Mayer, Simon Papps and Jan Peter Werning.

No animals were harmed during the making of this annual apart from the ones eaten by Jeremy Clarkson.

Additional photo credits:
pp. 25, 30, 31, 48, 55, 56, 57, 65, 85, 88 *(Corbis)*
pp. 61, 85 *(Getty Images)*
pp. 12, 13 *(iStockphoto)*
pp. 17, 20, 33, 34, 35, 85, 92, 93 *(Mary Evans Picture Library)*
p. 54, final endpaper *(NASA)*
pp. 61,79 *(Rex Features)*
pp. 22 *(Topfoto)*

How inappropriate to call this planet Earth when clearly it is Ocean.
ARTHUR C. CLARKE

The Earth was small, light blue, and so touchingly alone, our home that must be defended like a holy relic. It was absolutely round. I believe I never knew what the word 'round' meant until I saw Earth from space.
ALEKSEI LEONOV, *USSR cosmonaut*

My experience helped me to see how isolated and fragile the Earth really is. It was also beautiful. It was the only object in the entire universe that was neither black nor white.
FRANK BORMAN, *US astronaut*

The world is but a school of inquiry.
MICHEL DE MONTAIGNE

'If the King's English was good enough for Jesus, it's good enough for me!' *Miriam 'MA' Ferguson (1875–1961), first woman Governor of Texas.*

THE QUITE INTERESTING DICTIONARY: **eaglify** v To make into an eagle. **ean** v To bring forth lambs. **earn-bleater** n (SCOTS) A snipe. **earthling** n A ploughman. **eassin** v To lust after bulls. At the time of writing, this word is so rare that it cannot be successfully Googled. It appears only once on the net – as the chathandle of a contributor to Wikipedia: someone who clearly enjoys interesting evenings. **eavesdrip** v The dripping of water from the edge of a roof, or the patch of ground the rainwater drips onto. The word became **eavesdrop**, which originally meant 'to stand under the eaves to listen to secrets inside the house'. **eavesdrop** n In Scottish law, the right to shed rainwater onto an adjoining property. **ebberman** n One who fishes beneath bridges. **ebrangle** v To shake violently. **eccle-grass** n The Orkney Islands name for common butterwort *(Pinguicula vulgaris)*. *Pinguicula* is Latin for 'slightly fat'. Butterworts are carnivorous flowers whose shiny leaves look as if they've been buttered. This was first pointed out in 1561 by the Swiss botanist Conrad Gesner (1516–1565). Four years later, he also became the first man to describe a pencil, after which he died of the plague. **ecdysis** n More than 1 million species of animal – 80% of the total known – regularly undergo ecdysis, the moulting of the skin of a snake or the outer covering of a lobster. After ecdysis, the naked animal is said to be 'teneral', a word also used to describe a soft new-born butterfly after it emerges from the chrysalis. An ecdysiast is a fancy word for a stripper. **echinal** adj Of or belonging to a sea-urchin. **echinology** n The study of sea-urchins. **echinulate** adj Covered with small prickles. **eclipse** n From a Greek word meaning 'a failure to appear'. **economics** n Economics originally meant 'household management', from the Greek word *oikos* (house) + *nomos* (law) from the verb *nemo* (to manage). So the expression 'home economics' is not, in fact, pretentious, but it is tautologous. **ecru** adj The colour of unbleached linen. **ecstasy** The word ecstasy is from the Greek *ecstasis* ('put out of place'), originally meaning 'insanity' or 'bewilderment'. Later it came to mean a mystic trance where the soul supposedly left the body. Its original English meaning was not the modern one of intense delight, but the state of being 'beside oneself' in either a frenzy or a stupor of fear, anxiety, astonishment or passion. **ectoproctous** adj Having an external anus. **ecumenopolis** n The world viewed as one single enormous city. **eczema** n Eczema in cattle *(E. epizooticum)* is called foot and mouth disease. **edacious** adj Extremely keen on eating. **edentata** n The toothless ones: the former name for sloths, armadillos and anteaters, lumped together because they lack front teeth. The word comes from the Latin verb *edentare* ('to knock someone's teeth out'). **eduction** n Sticking one's tongue out; also, the exit of waste steam from a steam engine. **eel-drowner** n (SCOTS) Someone who can do the impossible: an exceedingly clever person. **eedle-doddle** n (SCOTS) A nonchalant person. **eeksie-peeksie** adj (SCOTS) Absolutely even or equal. **eerock** n A hen in its first year. **eetle-ottle** v (SCOTS) To choose by counting out: the Scots version of 'Eeny-meanie-miney-mo'. **effendi** n Turkish title of respect, applied to government officials and other big-wigs. The word comes from the Greek *authentis* (a murderer). Fortunately, Turkish big-wigs are unaware of this. **efflagitate** v To demand eagerly. **effodient** adj Used to digging. **effrenable** adj Violently rebellious. **egagropile** n A hairball found in the insides of horned cattle and goats. **eggler** n An egg-dealer; hence eggling, what an eggler does. **egomism** n The belief that one is the only being in existence. **eidoloclast** n One who demolishes idols. **eik** n (SCOTS) Sheep-sweat. **elambication** n The analysis of mineral waters. **elaphine** n Resembling or belonging to a stag. **elapidate** v To clear a place of stones. **elaqueate** v To set free from a noose. **elastician** n An expert in elasticity. **elenctic** adj Cross-examining. **elfhood** n The state of being an elf. **elfship** n The personality of an elf. **elger** n An eel-spear. **elinguate** v To cut the tongue out, hence elinguation. **ell** n A shed placed against a building. **elocular** adj Without partitions. **elozable** n Open to flattery. **elucubrate** v To write by candlelight. **eluscate** v To blind in one eye. **elutriate** v To purify by straining. **elvish** adj Irritating, weird. **ely** v To disappear gradually from sight or drop off one by one. **elychnious** adj Of or like a wick. **elyzianize** v To praise with rapturous or extravagant admiration. **emacity** n A fondness for shopping. **emaculate** n To remove spots. **emblustricate** n To bewilder. **embock** v To plug the mouth of a cannon. **embog** n To plunge into a swamp. **embogueing** n The place where a river or lake flows out. **embolus** n Something moving in, or inserted into, something else, such as a door bolt, a wedge, or the top part of a syringe. **empasm** n A perfumed powder used as a deodorant. **emphanist** n An informer or professional spy. **emulatrix** n A female emulator. **emunction** n Wiping, blowing or picking the nose. **emunctory** adj & n Something that removes waste from the body: a nose, kidney or armpit. **emuscation** n Cleaning the moss from a tree-trunk. **enarthrosis** n A ball-and-socket joint. **encarpa** n Festoons of ornamental carved fruit. **enchorial** adj Used in a particular country. **encycliglotte** n The string that connects the tongue to the base of the mouth. **endoss** v To write on the back of a document. **energumen** n A person possessed by a devil. **engastration** n Stuffing one bird with another. **engastrimyth** n A ventriloquist. Ventriloquist is Latin for 'belly-speaker'. Engastrimyth means exactly the same in Greek. **enlimn** v To paint in bright colours. **enneacontahedral** adj Having ninety faces. **enneagonal** adj Having nine angles. **enneahedral** adj Having nine faces. **enneatic** adj Occurring one time in nine. **enodate** v To unknot or remove difficulties. **enode** v To solve a riddle. **enoisel** v To fly at a bird like a hawk. It's not quite clear what flies at a bird like a hawk, except for a hawk. **enoptromancy** n Divination by mirrors. **enorn** v To lay a table. **ensate** adj Sword-shaped. **enseam** v To remove the superfluous fat from a horse. **enseel** v To sew a hawk's eyelids together. **ensiform** adj Sword-shaped. **ensky** v To put in the sky. **ensynopticity** n The ability to take a broad view. **entapisse** v To carpet. **entasis** n The widening of architectural columns towards the top to make them seem parallel from the ground. **enterodelous** adj Having an intestine plainly visible. **enteroid** adj Resembling a bowel. **enthusiasm** n Enthusiasm was originally not something you would want to be accused of. It meant 'frenzied possession by a god'. **entophyte** n A plant growing inside an animal (or another plant). **enturret** v To surround with towers. **entwit** v To rebuke or reproach. **enubilous** adj Cloudless. **enumber** v To overshadow. **enurny** adj A heraldic term meaning 'decorated with beasts'. **eoan** adj Dawnish; dawn-like; dawny. **eohippus** n The oldest known genus of the horse family; Greek for 'dawn horse'. Eohippus was a small animal no bigger than a fox, with four toes on each forefoot and three on each hind foot. Modern horses have only one whole toe on each foot. **eont** n Ancient word for a giant. **epalpate** adj Without feelers. **ephemeral** adj An ephemeral insect, flower, fever or disease is one that only lasts for a single day. **ephemeromorph** n A member of the lowest form of life, not an animal, not even definitely a vegetable. **epidendral** adj Growing on trees. There ought to be a useful word anepidendral meaning 'not growing on trees'), which could be used to describe money. But there isn't. **epinyctis** n A pustule that only comes out at night. **epistaxis** n A nose-bleed. **epistolarian** n One who is addicted to writing letters. **epitasis** n The part of a play where the plot thickens. **epitrite** adj In a relationship of four to three. **epitrochasm** n Several points made in a hurry. **epotation** n Drinking up. **epulation** n Indulging in dainty morsels. **equirotal** adj Having back and front wheels of equal sizes. **equivorous** adj Horse-eating. **erostrate** adj Without a beak. **erse** adj or n (SCOTS) Gaelic. Or an arse. **eruciform** adj Caterpillar-shaped. **erugate** v To remove wrinkles. **erumpent** adj Bursting out.

escalade v To scale a rampart using ladders. **eschansonnery** n A butler's pantry. **eschellett** n A small ladder. **esclavage** n A necklace composed of several rows of jewellery, resembling the chains of a slave. **escopette** n An ancient Mexican rifle. From the Latin *stloppus*, the sound made by slapping an inflated cheek. **esculent** adj Eatable. **escume** n Froth. **escutcheon** n The crotch of a four-legged animal. **espagnolette** n The fastening of a French window. From the Spanish word meaning 'Spanish'. Go figure. **espiegle** adj Sprightly; frolicsome; roguish. **esplanade** n Originally an outward-sloping parapet on a castle, then an open, flat piece of ground separating the castle from the town. **espontoon** n A half-size pike carried by an infantry officer. Use the space to write a witty remark about Captain Mainwaring from *Dad's Army*...

esquillous adj Splintery (as of a fractured bone). **esquisse** n The first sketch of a picture or a rough design drawn with a crayon. **esplumoir** n The cage that a moulting hawk is kept in. **essaykin** n A small essay. Also essaylet. **estaminet** n A café where smoking is allowed. **estrap** n A day's ration for troops. **estivate** v To 'hibernate' in the summer. **ethmoid** adj Full of little holes like a sieve. **etymon** n The 'true', literal or original meaning of a word; the primary root word from which another word is derived or corrupted. **eyewall** n A layer of turbulent, funnel-shaped clouds surrounding the calm centre, or 'eye', of a storm.

THE END

The sequel to the long-awaited 'A', 'B', 'C' and 'D' annuals . . .

Featuring Clive Anderson, Rowan Atkinson, Bill Bailey, Jo Brand, Rob Brydon, Jimmy Carr, Alan Davies, Stephen Fry, Rich Hall, Phill Jupitus, Sean Lock, Dara O'Briain, David Mitchell, Vic Reeves and Arthur Smith.

With cartoons by Roger Law and the Spitting Image team; Newman and Husband from Private Eye; Chris Donald of Viz; Cherry Denman, Geoff Dunbar and Ted Dewan; and Matt from the Daily Telegraph.

ff

According to both Greek and Scandinavian mythology, the **first man** was made from ash wood. The **first known tools** date to 2,600,000 BC, but the fir
evidence of agriculture is only 10,000 years old. The **first human beings to survive the Ice Age** were Neanderthals. They lived in tents and huts, r
in caves, and were expert makers of stone knives, axes and lance heads. The **first King of Egypt** was killed by a hippopotamus. The **first know**
individual human being in history is the Egyptian pharaoh Akhenaten, father of Tutankhamen and the inventor of monotheism. The **first person to i**
circumcised was the prophet Abraham, who was also the **first Christian**, the **first Jew** and the **first Moslem**. On God's instructions, he snipped off
own foreskin aged 99. The **first letter of the Yiddish alphabet** – *alef* – is silent. The Babylonians devised the **first telescope** in about 750 BC. They a
invented insurance. The **first coinage** and the **first shops** appeared in ancient Lydia in the 7th century BC. The **first man to make a map of the wor**
was the ancient Greek philosopher Anaximander (c 610- 546 BC), who also invented the sundial. The **first recorded instance of scalping** was by t
ancient Scythians in the 5th century BC. They were also the **first people to smoke marijuana**. The **first person to realise that diseases were n**
punishments from the gods was Hippocrates (460-379 BC), the inventor of diagnosis. The **first Emperor of China** was Shih Huang Ti (c 259-209 B
also known as Chao Cheng. He claimed his Empire would last 10,000 generations, but it collapsed four years after his death. The world's **first regul**
news service (*Acta Diurna* or 'Daily Doings') was founded by Julius Caesar in 59 BC and distributed free to the people of Rome. Julius Caesar was al
the **first person to fold scrolls** and thus became the inventor of pages. The leader of the **first stable Japanese government** emerged in the 4th centu
The Chinese called him 'The Great Wa' and the Japanese called him 'Hatsu-kuni-shirasu-sumera-mikoto'. The **first Christian martyr in Britain** was
Alban, executed in 303 AD under the persecutions of the Emperor Diocletian. In 305, Diocletian retired to his farm to raise cabbages. The **first abbey**
Britain was founded in the 7th century at Glastonbury, which means 'woad town' in Celtic. The **first person to write down the recipe for nettle so**
was St Columba (521-597). The **first crossbow** appeared in Italy in the 10th or 11th century: no one knows who invented it. The **first variety of apple**
be named was the Pearmain, recorded in Norfolk in 1204. Mountaineering was invented in 1336 when the Italian poet Francesco Petrarch became t
first person to climb a mountain simply 'because it was there'. The peak he scaled was Mount Ventoux, which today is the hardest stage of the *To
de France* cycle race. The **first use of the word hedgehog** was in 1450. It was spelt 'heyghoge'. The **first person to use the word 'adder' in print** w
Sir Thomas Malory (1405-71) in *Le Morte D'Arthur*, which was published by Caxton in 1485. It was a mistake. An adder was originally 'a nadder'. The fi
known use of the @ symbol dates from Italy in 1536. The **first European sighting of a potato** was in 1537 in what is now Colombia. A group
Spaniards under Jiménez de Quesada entered a deserted village where some potatoes had been left behind, and ate them mistaking them for truffles.
1572, the Danish astronomer Tycho Brahe (1546-1601) became the **first man to observe a new star with the naked eye** since Hipparchus (170-120 B
Richard Morton published the **first medical case history of anorexia** in 1689. The **first human being to see bacteria, algae, blood cells a**
spermatozoa was Antonie van Leeuwenhoek (1632-1723), the uneducated son of a Dutch basket maker, whose hobby was grinding lenses. The fir
European to see Alaska (in 1741) was the Danish explorer Vitus Jonassen Bering, after whom the Straits are named. Denis Diderot (1713-84), compi
of the world's **first encyclopaedia**, *L'Encyclopédie Française*, excluded any reference to insects because he thought them 'unworthy'. Wolfgang Amade
Mozart (1756-91) composed his **first symphony** at the age of eight and his **first two operas** at twelve. All five of his violin concertos were written ag
19. The **first country to recognise the USA** was Morocco, in 1789. The same year, to get to the **first inauguration of a US President**, Geor
Washington had to borrow money to travel from his home in Virginia, to the USA's **first capital**, New York City. The **first seven US presidents** were
born British subjects. The **first man to be run over by a train**, William Huskisson MP (1770-1830), had narrowly survived death some years earlier wh
a horse fell on him during his honeymoon. Dr John Gorrie of Apalachicola, Florida built the world's **first practical fridge** in 1844. The **first person to p**
a rabbit out of a hat was the Scottish conjuror John Henry Anderson (1814-74), known as the Great Wizard of the North. The **first person to discov**
what turnips are made of was the Scottish chemist Thomas Anderson (1819-74). In 1871, Thomas Adams became the **first man to make chewing gu**
commercially. He had tried without success to make toys, masks, gumboots and car tyres out of chicle gum before eventually putting some in his mou
The world's **first professional baseball game** was played in Fort Wayne, Indiana on 4th May 1871. The **first telephone directory**, issued by The Ne
Haven District Telephone Company in Connecticut in February 1878, contained only fifty names. In 1884, James Murray planned the **first Oxford Engli**
Dictionary as a four-volume, 6,400-page work that he estimated would take about ten years to write. Five years later, he and his tiny staff had only g
as far as 'ant'. The world's **first electric trolley bus system** opened in Montgomery, Alabama in 1886. The world's **first aquarium** opened in Chicago
1893. The same year, New Zealand became the **first country in the world to give women the vote**. The **first female mayor in the United Stat**
was Susan Madora Salter, elected to office in Argonia, Kansas in 1887. She had originally been nominated by a group of men as a joke. She died in 19
aged 101. The world's **first Woolworth's** opened in Lancaster, Pennsylvania in 1897. The **first man to sail single-handed around the world w**
Captain Joshua Slocum in 1895-8. He disappeared on his boat in 1909 while traversing the straits of Magellan. The **first known asteroid**, Ceres, w
discovered on the first night of the nineteenth century. The **first vacuum cleaner**, invented in 1901, was horsedrawn. The **first cinema in the wor**
opened in Los Angeles on 2nd April 1902. The **first jail sentence for speeding** in the USA was imposed on 28th August 1904 in Newport, Rhode Isla
Rhode Island was the site of the **first pub in America** (1673) and the **first circus** (1774), the **first polo match** (1876), the **first National Lawn Ten**
Championship (1899), and the **first open golf tournament** (1985). The **first painting that Matisse gave Picasso** was a portrait of his daugh
Marguerite in 1907. Picasso hung it up in his studio for friends to use as a dartboard. The **first man to die in an air-crash** was Lt Thomas Etholen Selfrid
in 1908. The pilot was Orville Wright, who broke his leg. Earlier that year, Selfridge had successfully piloted a plane designed by Alexander Graham B
Harry Houdini made the **first solo flight in Australia** in 1910. In 1913, Igor Sikorski (1889-1972) invented the **first enclosed aircraft cabin** for both pi
and passengers, something that didn't catch on elsewhere for another ten years. The **first King of Albania** arrived to take up his position on 7th Mar
1913 and left again (never to return) on 3rd September the same year. The world's **first aircraft carrier** was HMS *Furious*, commissioned for the Ro
Navy in 1917. Vincent Burnelli (1895-1964) designed the world's **first airliner** (the 26-seater Lawson C-2) in 1919. He was disappointed with the res
which he said looked like 'a street-car with wings'. The **first shopping mall** opened at Country Club Plaza, Kansas City in 1922. The novelist Barb
Cartland (1901-2000) invented the **first aeroplane-towed glider** in 1931. The **first two wives of Rudolph Valentino** shared the same lesbian lover. I
second wife was Winifred Kimball Shaughnessy de Wolfe Hudnut from Salt Lake City. On 2nd December 1942, Enrico Fermi and a small team of scienti
and engineers built the world's **first nuclear fission reactor** in a squash court under the football stadium at the University of Chicago. When R
Hayworth was told that the **first atomic bomb to explode on Bikini Atoll** in 1946 had her picture on it, she burst into tears. In 1947, the **first Articho**
Queen to be crowned in Castroville, California, the 'Artichoke Capital of the World', was Norma Jean Baker, who went on to become Marilyn Monroe.
his **first twenty-seven films**, David Niven only ever played Mexicans. Gary Cooper was the **first person to be called Gary**. An illiterate ex-cartoon
and baby-photographer, he took the name from his agent's hometown of Gary, Indiana. The **first Japanese tape-recorder**, devised by Sony in 1950, h
a tape made of paper and was sold to a noodle-shop for use as a karaoke machine. Roger Bannister, the **first man in the world to run a mile in le**
than 4 minutes (on 6th May 1954) held the record for only 46 days. The **first McDonald's** opened in Des Plaines, Illinois on 15th April 1955. The first u
of the word 'album' to mean a 'long-playing record' or a collection of songs was in 1957, the year that Ghana declared independence. The **first Pri**
Minister of Ghana was Kwame Nkrumah (1909-72). In Akan, the language of Ghana's largest tribe, his name means 'Born-On-Saturday Ninth-Born-Chil
Yuri Gagarin (1934-68), the **first man into space** in 1961, was 5' 2". When John Glenn became the **first American to orbit the Earth**, about halfw
round he informed Mission Control that he needed to go for a pee. That this might happen had not occurred to anyone at NASA, so he had to go in
pants. John Glenn, along with Orville Wright, the **first man to achieve manned flight**, and Neil Armstrong, the **first man to walk on the moon**, we
born in Ohio. The **first Prime Minister of Nigeria** – Sir Abubakar Tafawa Balewa (1912-66) – is the only one the country has ever had. He w
assassinated in 1966. One of the **first reported incidents of air-rage** involved a passenger in first class who shat on top of a food trolley after be
refused another drink. In 1995, Heather Whitestone of Alabama was elected as the **first disabled Miss America**. In September 1995, scientists at CE
in Geneva made the **first nine atoms of anti-matter**. Each lasted about 40 billionths of a second before being cancelled out by matter-matter. Today, m
than ten million particles of anti-matter are produced by CERN every second. In 2001, astronomers at Berkeley, University of California, studying a faint s
51 light years from Earth in the constellation of The Plough, claimed to have found the **first solar system that remotely resembles our own**. The wor
first underwater post office opened in May 2003, in Vanuatu in the South Pacific. Special waterproof postcards are provided. The **first serious attem**
to contact alien civilisation was made by beaming radio waves to a star cluster in the constellation of Hercules in 1974. If there are any aliens the
and if they intercept the message, and if they are able to reply, we will, if we are still here, receive their answer in approximately 48,000 years time.

Edited by John Lloyd and John Mitchinson

Art Direction by David Costa

A Birthday FFib

*There was only ever one Faber – Geoffrey – who founded the publishing house Faber & Gwyer in 1925.
When he bought out Lady Gwyer's stake in 1929, the poet Walter de la Mare suggested he add a second fictional
Faber because it sounded good and 'you can't have enough of a good thing'.
And so it has proved. Happy 80th Faber!*

faber and faber

Other books from QI

The Book of General Ignorance
The Book of General Ignorance: Pocket Edition
The Book of Animal Ignorance
The QI 'E' Annual
Advanced Banter: The QI Book of Quotations
The Sound of General Ignorance

First published in 2008
by Faber and Faber Limited
3 Queen Square London WC1N 3AU

Printed in Great Britain by Butler Tanner and Dennis Ltd, Frome and London

The right of QI Ltd to be identified as author of this work has been asserted in accordance
with Section 77 of the Copyright, Designs and Patents Act 1988

A CIP record for this book
is available from the British Library

ISBN 978–0–571–24414–0

2 4 6 8 10 9 7 5 3

CONTENTS

A Foreword by Stephen Fry

Once more I find myself in the business of introducing you to this year's *QI Annual*. It's an interesting business to be in and one I would certainly recommend that young people get involved with.

You don't need much experience, knowledge or expertise – just enthusiasm, diligence and a reasonable grasp of punctuation. You might be interested to know about hours? (There's an example of a punctuation option. I added a question mark to that last sentence, even though it wasn't strictly necessary. In this business you have to have the strength of mind and confidence to make this kind of individual choice. For me the question mark just works. Same goes for these brackets.) Well, to answer your question, the 'introducing you to this year's *QI Annual* business' hours are far from punishing. I started some oh, four minutes ago and fully intend knocking off in about fifteen, so not really too demanding. Does this business have a pension scheme, I can hear you scream, and what about holidays? Whoa, my young friend, steady on and calm right down this minute, you're getting hot and excited and that's not good in this business. Pension schemes, no. Holidays, again, no. In a small business like this, you are master/mistress of your own hours. It's all about the work. I'm not in the business of laying down hard and fast rules. I used to be in that business but I sold out. The business of laying down hard and fast rules is a career option for some, but I found it both exhausting and unrewarding: I would lay down what I thought were hard and fast rules all morning and then find that some of them had been hard but not fast while others were plenty fast enough but a very long way from being hard, all of which meant I had to pick them up and only lay them down again when I was sure that they were truly hard and verifiably fast. So I moved out of the business of laying down hard and fast rules and went instead into the business of introducing you to this year's *QI Annual*, which is not only rewarding but also pleasingly varied. It's a one-time business of course. The moment the project is completed I'll have to think of other businesses to get into. For instance, I'm considering, once I've closed down the business of introducing you to this year's *QI Annual*, the business of going for a walk. Not the most glamorous or well-regarded business, but one which has its own pitfalls. There's one just by the hedge about a quarter of a mile from my house as a matter of fact, dug by my neighbour. Or there's always the business of attending to emails, which is a business I don't much enjoy being a part of but which does provide an essential service. I could attend to your emails, I suppose, but *your* emails, I feel, are not really my business and I hope I'm not in the business of attending to things that aren't my business. Folly, madness and despair lie waiting for those in that kind of business.

Well, we've reached the end of this business of introducing you to this year's *QI Annual*, you've been well and truly introduced and there's nothing more for me to do but wind the business up and cease trading. Where does that leave you? Well, my recommendation is that you think about the whole business of turning the page and flicking through *The Annual*. Thanks to the elves, guest writers and editors, it's quite a business to be in.

Good afternoon to you.

Illustration by Derren Brown

An (F) word from the Editors

Hello there again chums, and welcome to the second *QI Annual* – which this year is all about the letter 'F'. Only another 24 years to go and you'll know something quite interesting about every single letter of the alphabet! Bet you can't wait for 2027 and the amazing 'X' Annual with its super 34-page article on Xylophones and an interesting fact (probably) about Xylobalsamum, the fragrant wood that yields the resin called Balm of Gilead!

For now, though, the *F Annual* is co-edited by the two plumpish gents on the right, both of whom are called John but only one of whom has an enormous beard. He looks quite like a badger (see below). The other, less badgerly chap would like it to be known that he is perfectly capable of resembling a badger if and when he so chooses.

Many species of animal have a convenient Latin-derived adjective to describe them. If this was the 'A' Annual, for example, we might describe a skylark as *alaudine*, a goose as *anserine* and a ram as *arietine*. As this is the *F Annual*, however, we will confine ourselves to mentioning that the word *fuliguline* means 'like a sea-duck'. Ask Mummy and Daddy to take you to the seaside this Christmas so that you can impress them. Or you could just be *limacine**.

Oddly enough, there is no Latin-derived word for 'badger-like'. This is surprising because quite a lot of people (and almost all badgers) look like badgers so it would be a good word to have around. On the other hand, absolutely no one in the universe looks like a sandpiper or a leopard, which is one good reason why you don't hear the words *tringoid* and *pardine* bandied about in the pub. Apart from *badgerly*, the nearest we could come up with for 'badger-like' is *musteline*, but that also means 'like a weasel' or 'like a stoat', which would be confusing since neither of us looks like one of those. They are slim, beady-eyed little fellows, who have kittens instead of children and who do not drink beer or eat pies.

But we digress – this is supposed to be all about 'F', after all! Don't worry, there's all sorts of fascinating efformation (a useful word meaning 'F-related information' that we just made up) to come. Plus (in case you just can't wait) two whole pages illustrated with Xylographs!*

Meanwhile, why not try buttering up your teacher by describing her as *turdine* (thrush-like) and the headmaster as *ratite* (resembling or pertaining to a flightless bird)? You are sure to get top marks**.

*Look it up! **Hem, hem. Fat chance!

Fig. 1 (above): left, John L. and right, John M.

Fig. 2 (left): A badger

Four is the number of wholeness, balance and solidity: **four** legs on a table, **four** sides to a square, **four** wheels on a car, **four** human blood groups (A, B, AB, O), **four** humours (blood, black bile, yellow bile, phlegm) and corresponding temperaments (sanguine, choleric, melancholic, phlegmatic), **four** points on a compass and **four** apostles.

The DNA of all livings things is composed of **four** sub-units A, G, C and T (adenine, guanine, cytosine and thymine). Theoretically, therefore, no living thing can be less than ¼ similar to any other, even if they have no apparent similarities whatsoever.

Four is the only number in the English language that has the same number of letters in its name as the number itself; this is also the case in Dutch, German, Afrikaans (*vier* in all three) and Hebrew (*arba*).

One in **four** in animals is a beetle.

Four times as many plants live on the land as in the sea.

We can live **four** times as long without food as we can without water.

Human beings have **four** nostrils: the two you can see and two internal passages, called *choannae* (Greek for 'funnels') that connect to the throat allowing us to breathe through our noses.

In Japanese, Cantonese and Mandarin Chinese, **four** has the same unlucky associations that we ascribe to thirteen. 'Fear of **four**' (or tetraphobia) probably derives from the fact that the word for **four** (si) is very similar to the word for death. Japanese and Chinese hospitals have no **fourth** floor and no rooms numbered **four**, and significantly more Chinese and Japanese people die on the **fourth** day of the month than in the West.

Never sweep. After four years the dust gets no worse.
QUENTIN CRISP

Hundreds of sites on the internet will tell you that fingernails grow **four** times faster than toenails because fingernails get more light, warmth and air. This is not true. Toenails grow at about half the rate of fingernails and this seems to be genetically rather than environmentally determined. However, the growth of our fingernails does seem to be in phase with the rate of movement of the Earth's tectonic plates – both move at about **four** centimetres per year.

You can't move your little finger without moving your **fourth** finger because the *flexor digitorum* muscle moves the middle, **fourth** and little finger as a unit. This finger has often been connected with healing powers. In Latin, German, Japanese and Korean it is known as the 'medicine' or 'doctor's' finger. The tradition in Western culture of wearing a wedding ring on the **fourth** finger of the left hand may have begun because it was thought that the *vena amoris* vein in that finger directly connected to the heart.

The Czech idiom, 'rozhovor mezi čtyřma očima' – a dialogue between **four** eyes – means a conversation conducted in private.

If you play first at Connect **Four** you can win, no matter what your opponent does, as long as you start in the middle column and play the right moves thereafter. Start in any of the **four** outer columns and you hand this advantage to your opponent. James D. Allen and Victor Allis discovered this within **four** weeks of each other in October 1988.

The **four**-colour theorem states that for any map separated into regions, you only need **four** colours to ensure no sections of the same colour touch one another. Despite being first proposed in 1852, it wasn't proved until 1976 by a team at the University of Illinois. It was the first major theorem to be proved using a computer. Checking the permutations took the computer hundreds of hours and, perhaps for this reason, pure mathematicians consider the solution 'inelegant'.

In the 19th century, '**four**-ale' was the cheapest beer, so named because it was sold at **four** pence a quart (2 pints or 1.2 litres). Hence a '**four**-ale pub' was a way of describing a particularly low-class boozer.

'**Four**-membered rings' may sound suggestive, but they turn out to be fairly uninteresting chemical compounds. Similarly the '**four** Wangs' were Chinese landscape painters of the 17th century (Wangs Jian, Hui, Shimin and Yuanqi).

Five-part symmetry recurs throughout nature: humans, primates and most reptiles and amphibians have **five** fingers and toes; most starfish have **five** arms and many flowers, like wild roses, have **five** petals.

To Pythagoras and his followers, the number **five** was the sum of the first even number (2) and the first odd number (3) and therefore symbolised marriage. (The Greeks did not consider 1 to be a number at all.) The Pythagoreans also characterised **five** as rebellious, perhaps because they knew of only 4 Platonic solids, or convex regular polyhedrons – the tetrahedron, cube, dodecahedron and octahedron. About 100 years after the death of Pythagoras, Theaetatus (417-369 BC) discovered a **fifth** Platonic solid (the 20-sided icosahedron). He also proved that there are **five** and only **five** such objects.

The number **five** is associated with Venus, the goddess of love; her symbol is the pentagram or **five**-pointed star. In old England, a knot tied in the shape of a pentagram was known as a lover's knot.

Only **five** planets can be seen with the naked eye: Mercury, Venus, Mars, Jupiter and Saturn.

There are **five** galaxies visible with the naked eye from Earth. These are the Andromeda Galaxy (M31); the Large Magellenic Cloud; the Small Magellenic Cloud; the Triangulum Galaxy (M33); and, of course, our own Milky Way – though not all of them are visible from any single point on Earth at once.

The **five** stars of the Southern Cross may represent the smallest of the 88 constellations, but they are extremely important in many cultures of the Southern Hemisphere, being used to point south in the same way that the Pole Star shows north. The **five** stars appear on the national flags of Australia, New Zealand, Brazil and Papua New Guinea, as well as those of the island nations of Niue and Samoa. In traditional tales, the **five** stars are variously described as a stingray, two birds in a gum-tree, an anchor or a giant sky-canoe.

A child of five would understand this. Send somebody to fetch a child of five. GROUCHO MARX

The Nepalese flag is the only national flag that has **five** sides (it takes the form of two overlapping triangles on top of each other).

In Islam, there are **five** pillars, **five** prayers a day and **five** law-giving prophets (Noah, Abraham, Moses, Jesus and Mohammed).

In Hinduism, there are **five** concentric sheaths that envelop the soul: material, mental, vital, intellectual and bliss.

Christians refer to the **five** books in the Jewish Torah as the *Pentateuch* (literally 'five vessels'). These are Genesis, Exodus, Leviticus, Numbers and Deuteronomy and are also known as the **Five** Books of Moses. In Judaism, the Torah is formally known as *Chamisei Chumshei Torah* – the '**Five-Fifths** of the Teaching'.

The **five** Ks are symbols worn by Sikhs: uncut hair, a steel bracelet, a wooden comb, a steel sword and cotton underwear.

In many non-European cultures there are **five** cardinal directions, the extra being 'towards the centre'. In Dynastic China these **five** directions each had their own colour: East was green/blue; Centre, yellow; South, red; West, white; and North, black.

The Mandarin Chinese word for **five** is *wu*, which also means 'enlightenment'. (And much else besides: there are more than 80 different meanings of *wu* in Chinese.) In Chinese internet slang **555** means 'crying' because it sounds like *wu wu wu*; in Thai internet slang the same number sounds like *ha ha ha* and so is used to denote laughter.

The 'Big **Five**' is a term used to describe Earth's mass extinctions, which took place 4**5**0, 37**5**, 2**5**1, 20**5** and 6**5** million years ago.

In US slang, '**five** by **five**' means everything is OK - this comes from radio communication where the phrase is used to mean 'Loud and Clear' - the first **five** relates to reception strength while the other is a rating of the signal clarity. A '**five** by **five**' can also be used to mean a very fat person.

The television series Hawaii **Five**-0 is named after a fictional Hawaiian police force (Hawaii has never had its own state police) but was so named because Hawaii was the 50th state of the union.

The poet Ted Hughes had **five** desks in his study. Francis Ford Coppola was fired **five** times during the making of *The Godfather* in 1972. Gummo, the **fifth** Marx brother, quit the act in 1919 to take up a career selling women's clothing.

FRANKS in FLIGHT

Throughout history men called Frank have been at the forefront of Man's eternal quest to conquer the skies...

In 1910, pioneering American pilot **FRANK COFFYN** was granted his wings by non-other than Wilbur Wright. Frank became a regular member of the Wright brothers' exhibition flying team, and in 1912 he flew a Wright Model B plane above New York City. He thrilled the thousands of onlookers by swooping down and flying beneath the Brooklyn and Williamsburg bridges. Coffyn is credited with having taken the first aerial photographs of New York city. He became an army flying instructor during World War I, and later in life he qualified as a helicopter pilot.

On June 2nd 1933, record-breaking US aviator **FRANK HAWKS** set a new trans-continental airspeed record when he flew his Northrop Gamma non-stop from Los Angeles to New York in 13 hours, 26 minutes and 15 seconds. Hawks was the man who introduced Amelia Earhart (right) to flying when, on 28th December 1920, he took her for a ten minute flight at Long Beach, California. In 1932 Earhart became the first woman to fly solo across the Atlantic. She died in 1937, when her plane vanished during an attempt to circumnavigate the globe. Frank Hawks died the following year, when his Gwinn Aircar hit telephone wires shortly after take-off at East Aurora, New York.

Balloon busting **FRANK LUKE** was America's second highest scoring air ace during World War I, destroying 18 enemy aircraft in one frantic spell between September 12th and 29th, 1918. A hot-headed former bare-knuckle boxer, he was disliked by some of his colleagues for his aggressive nature and tendency to fly alone. His luck ran out when he was shot down over enemy lines near Murveaux in France. Despite having been wounded in the shoulder by anti-aircraft fire, Luke drew his pistol and shot dead a further 7 German soldiers before he himself was shot and killed. In 1921 Frank Luke was awarded a posthumous US Medal of Honor for his act of heroism.

Squadron Leader 'Fearless' **FRANK DAY** lost a thumb and was shot in the knee when his Spitfire was downed off the coast of Crete in 1942. After 24 hours in the water, Day was rescued by an enemy ship, and sent to the notorious Stalag Luft III POW camp, scene of the real-life 'Great Escape'.

Frank acted as a 'penguin', dispersing spoil from the escape tunnel in his trouser legs. Another claim to fame was that in 1938, whilst serving as an RAF flying instructor, Frank taught Kiang Chai-shek to fly. His pupil later became the first president of the Communist Chinese republic.

On February 6th 1958, a plane carrying Manchester United back from a European Cup tie against Red Star Belgrade crashed during take-off at Munich airport. The only Frank to perish in the disaster was **FRANK SWIFT**. Ironically, Swift made all of his 338 football league appearances for United's arch-rivals Manchester City. Having retired in 1949, he was working as a reporter for the *News of the World* when disaster struck.

FEB 6th 1958

MUNICH

WILLS CIGARETTES

FRANKS IN FLIGHT

Teenage fraudster **FRANK ABAGNALE** flew over 1,000,000 miles on over 250 Pan-Am flights, visiting 26 different countries, without paying for a single ticket. He simply posed as an airline pilot travelling between jobs. As well as free flights, all Frank's hotel expenses were charged to Pan-Am. In the movie *Catch Me If You Can* Frank's character was played by Leonardo DiCaprio.

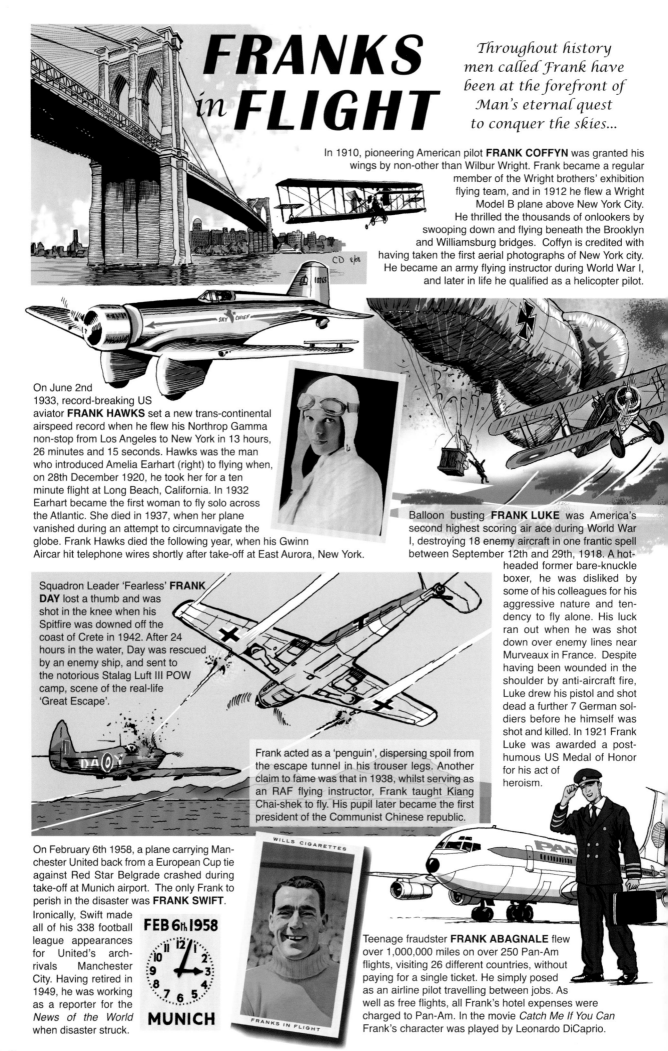

FRANKS in SPACE

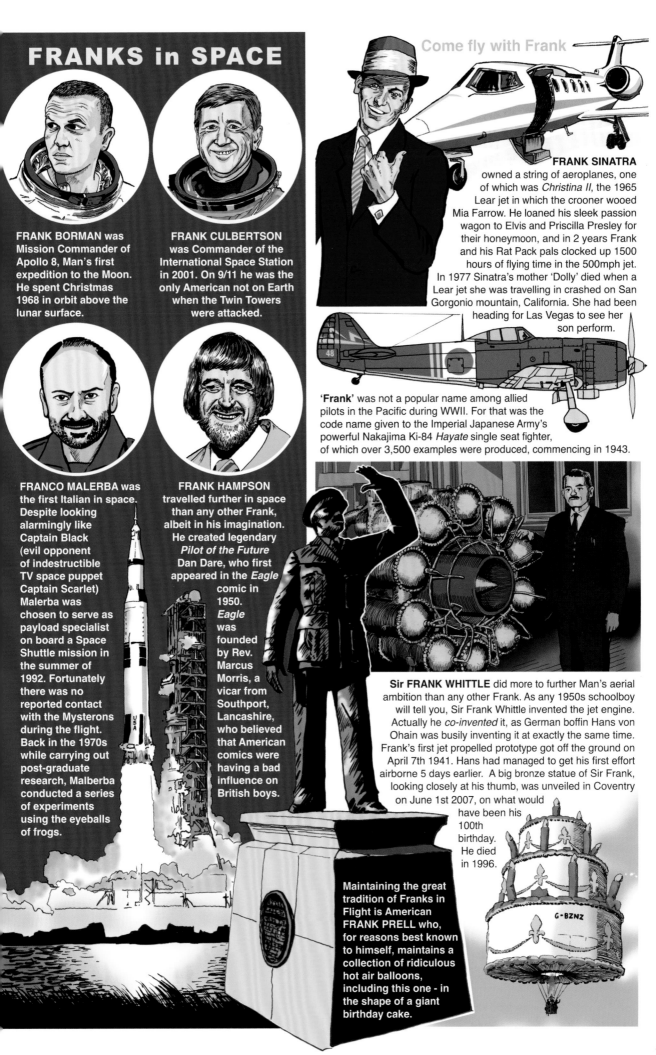

FRANK BORMAN was Mission Commander of Apollo 8, Man's first expedition to the Moon. He spent Christmas 1968 in orbit above the lunar surface.

FRANK CULBERTSON was Commander of the International Space Station in 2001. On 9/11 he was the only American not on Earth when the Twin Towers were attacked.

FRANCO MALERBA was the first Italian in space. Despite looking alarmingly like Captain Black (evil opponent of indestructible TV space puppet Captain Scarlet) Malerba was chosen to serve as payload specialist on board a Space Shuttle mission in the summer of 1992. Fortunately there was no reported contact with the Mysterons during the flight. Back in the 1970s while carrying out post-graduate research, Malberba conducted a series of experiments using the eyeballs of frogs.

FRANK HAMPSON travelled further in space than any other Frank, albeit in his imagination. He created legendary *Pilot of the Future* Dan Dare, who first appeared in the *Eagle* comic in 1950. *Eagle* was founded by Rev. Marcus Morris, a vicar from Southport, Lancashire, who believed that American comics were having a bad influence on British boys.

Come fly with Frank

FRANK SINATRA owned a string of aeroplanes, one of which was *Christina II*, the 1965 Lear jet in which the crooner wooed Mia Farrow. He loaned his sleek passion wagon to Elvis and Priscilla Presley for their honeymoon, and in 2 years Frank and his Rat Pack pals clocked up 1500 hours of flying time in the 500mph jet. In 1977 Sinatra's mother 'Dolly' died when a Lear jet she was travelling in crashed on San Gorgonio mountain, California. She had been heading for Las Vegas to see her son perform.

'Frank' was not a popular name among allied pilots in the Pacific during WWII. For that was the code name given to the Imperial Japanese Army's powerful Nakajima Ki-84 *Hayate* single seat fighter, of which over 3,500 examples were produced, commencing in 1943.

Sir FRANK WHITTLE did more to further Man's aerial ambition than any other Frank. As any 1950s schoolboy will tell you, Sir Frank Whittle invented the jet engine. Actually he *co-invented* it, as German boffin Hans von Ohain was busily inventing it at exactly the same time. Frank's first jet propelled prototype got off the ground on April 7th 1941. Hans had managed to get his first effort airborne 5 days earlier. A big bronze statue of Sir Frank, looking closely at his thumb, was unveiled in Coventry on June 1st 2007, on what would have been his 100th birthday. He died in 1996.

Maintaining the great tradition of Franks in Flight is American **FRANK PRELL** who, for reasons best known to himself, maintains a collection of ridiculous hot air balloons, including this one - in the shape of a giant birthday cake.

9

THE QI CUP FINAL
The most interesting game of football sadly never played, in which Stephen's effortless aristos and brainboxes take on Alan's naturally gifted squad of backstreet heroes.

FRY'S GENTLEMEN'S XI

Goal Keeper: Niels Bohr (1885-1962)
Some say that Nobel Prize winner Bohr played internationally for Denmark and that Albert Camus played for Algeria, but in fact they're wrong: neither ever represented their country. Niels Bohr once let in an outrageously long shot due to being distracted by a mathematical problem, while Camus once claimed 'All I know most surely about morality and obligations, I owe to football.'

Left Back: C.B. Fry (1872-1956)
As well as being one of the greatest English cricketers of all time and a holder of the world long jump record, Fry was a full back for England, Southampton, Portsmouth and Corinthians (a team of such sportsmen that they deliberately missed penalties, refusing to believe the other team had meant to foul them). One of Fry's party pieces was to jump backwards from the floor onto a mantelpiece.

Centre Back: Max Woosnam (1892-1965)
Cambridge University's Max Woosnam fought alongside Siegfried Sassoon in WWI and once beat Charlie Chaplin at table tennis using a butter knife instead of a bat. He played football for Chelsea, Man City and England as well as winning a gold medal in tennis at the 1920 Olympics. Woosnam was also on the board of ICI and drove a bus during the General Strike of 1926.

Centre Back: Henry VIII (1491-1547)
The first known pair of football boots were catalogued in Henry VIII's possessions when he died. Although he once banned the game, this certainly implies that he played it, and while we don't know of his preferred position, his ample frame would surely complement Woosnam's natural ability in the centre of defence.

Right Back: Arthur Conan Doyle (1859-1930)
Arthur Conan Doyle was a keen sportsman, a founder member of Portsmouth FC and the team's first ever goalkeeper. 'Pompey' (Sherlock Holmes himself would struggle to pick the right origin for this nickname - there are *at least* 8 different theories) were very successful in their first season, only losing 3 of their first 22 games, and beating the Royal Marines 10-0.

Left Midfield: Cuthbert Ottaway (1850-1878)
Cuthbert Ottaway was the first-ever captain of the England football team. Educated at Eton, he also played cricket for England. In those days, footballing skills didn't stretch to passing: players would just dribble with the ball until they got tackled. Ottaway was the epitome of elegance on and off the field. A barrister, he died at the age of 27 from a chill caught in the course of a night's dancing.

Right Midfield: al-Saadi Gaddafi (1973-)
The son of Libya's leader often benefited from somewhat dubious refereeing decisions. His position of captain of the Libyan football team was helped by his position as president of the Libyan football federation. A move to play in Italy was ill-fated. Gaddafi played only one game for Perugia before failing a drugs test; he was once trained by the disgraced Canadian athlete Ben Johnson.

Central Midfield: Sócrates (1954-)
Brazilian legend Sócrates Brasileiro Sampaio de Souza Vieira de Oliveira, better known simply as Sócrates, earned his degree in medicine while simultaneously playing professional football. Sócrates was also a political activist, co-founding the Corinthian Democracy, an ideological movement that helped overthrow Brazil's military dictatorship in 1982.

Attacker: Simen Agdestein (1967-)
Simen Agdestein played professional football for Norway, and is perhaps the only person in the world to be an international footballer and a chess grandmaster. Though he has not yet broken into the world elite, he was Norwegian champion at 15, a grandmaster at 18, and came second at the 1986 World Junior Chess Championships.

Attacker: Alfred Lyttelton (1857-1913)
Yet another Etonian, Alfred Lyttelton was the *first* man to represent England at both football and cricket. He went on to become a liberal MP and was president of the MCC. In 1900 he was sent to South Africa to oversee the country's reconstruction after the Boer War, and was an advocate of women's suffrage. Alfred Lyttelton was the great-uncle of *I'm Sorry I Haven't A Clue's* late great Humphrey.

Attacker: Luther Blissett (1958-)
According to football folklore, England international Luther Blissett only got to sign for AC Milan because they mistook him for John Barnes. He has had the last laugh, though, as the inspiration for the 'Luther Blissett Project', a collection of anonymous Italian *avant garde* artists whose manifesto states: 'Anyone can be Luther Blissett simply by adopting the name.' Blissett himself is a member.

Goalkeeper: William Foulkes (1874-1916)
William 'Fatty' Foulkes was a 25 stone 'keeper for England, Sheffield United, Bradford City and Chelsea; he also played cricket for Derbyshire. It took six men to carry him off the field when he was injured. Once when playing Liverpool, he picked up their centre forward, turned him upside down and planted him in the mud.

Left Back: Jesper Olsen (1961-)
Perhaps more of a left winger, but Olsen takes his place in our back four thanks to a terrible defensive pass in the 1986 World Cup in Denmark's game against Spain which allowed Emilio Butragueño to score and has since made Olsen's name synonymous with error. 'Rigtig Jesper Olsen' (a right Jesper Olsen) is now Danish slang for a gaffe of any kind.

Right Back: Billy Meredith (1874-195[...]
Meredith played for Manchester Utd and Wal[...] at the turn of the 20th century, but began h[...] working life driving pit ponies. He w[...] instrumental in setting up the first footballe[...] union. Banned for 10 years for allegedly bribi[...] an opposition player, Meredith liked to che[...] tobacco 'for concentration'. He changed [...] chewing toothpicks after the cleaners refused [...] wash his tobacco-stained shirts.

Centre Back: Jah Bless Youth (c 1981-)
The Players' XI answer to Mr Fry's polymaths, Jah Bless Youth is not only a professional footballer – playing in the heady heights of the Swiss and Irish 3rd divisions – he is also a reggae-ragga-ska-dub rapper and drummer. His music aims to bring the 'message of the Almighty' to the younger generation. He has released four albums including 2004's *Babylon Stop Abusing Human Kind.*

Centre Back: Charlie Oatway (1973-)
The former Brentford and Brighton defender is actually called Anthony Philip David Terry Frank Donald Stanley Gerry Gordon Stephen James Oatway – he is named after the QPR's entire 1973 first-team squad. He is called 'Charlie' because when his parents told his aunt the proposed name, she said 'he'd look a right Charlie', and the name stuck.

Left Midfield: José Moreno (1916-197[...]
No, not Jose Mourinho. Known as *El Char[...]* (the cowboy), this Argentinian legend playe[...] for River Plate in the 1940s and was famo[...] for his unusual training regime. He believe[...] the best possible training for a football mat[...] was to dance the tango until late and then be[...] a couple of women. For lunch before kick-o[...] he would eat chicken stew and drink a bott[...] or three of red wine.

Right Midfield: Garrincha (1933-1983[...]
According to his biography by Ruy Castro, th[...] well-hung Brazilian legend lost his virginity t[...] a goat. One of his legs was two inches shorte[...] than the other, which gave him a distinctiv[...] gait; hence 'Garrincha,' meaning 'little bir[...] He never trained, and once stored the cas[...] bonus from a World Cup win in a mattres[...] only to find some years later it had rotted du[...] to his child wetting the bed.

DAVIES's Players' XI

Central Midfield: Milene Domingues (1979-)

The only woman (and Buddhist) in the team, Domingues is a former model and the ex-wife of Brazilian striker Ronaldo who first saw her on TV practising her ball-juggling skills (aged 17, she set a new world record of 55,187 keepy-uppies). She currently plays for Italian team Fiamma Monza — her £200K transfer in 2002 made her the most expensive woman player ever.

Central Midfield: Diego Maradona (1960-1997)

Maradona is the only member of the Players' XI to have a religion named after him; the Church of Maradona has over 80,000 worshippers. Maradona has been suspended twice for drug abuse and once opened fire with an air rifle on journalists. Now a successful television presenter, he is one the few talk-show hosts to have interviewed his hero, Fidel Castro (he has his portrait tattooed on his leg).

Attacker: Héctor Castro (1904-1960)

Uruguayan international Héctor Castro scored the winning goal in the first ever World Cup final in 1930 in Montevideo. He remains the only one-armed person to have achieved this. Known as 'el Manco', the 13-year-old Castro accidentally amputated his right forearm with an electric saw. It didn't hold him back: he used his stump as a club when leaping for headers and had a reputation as a serious womaniser.

Attacker: Eduard Streltsov (1937-1990)

Eduard Streltsov was known as the Russian Pelé. His loyalty to Torpedo Moscow meant he refused to join either the Army's CSKA Moscow or the KGB's Dynamo Moscow. As a result, he was accused of rape and sent to work in the Siberian Gulag for seven years. When he returned, commentators noted that he had lost a few yards of pace, but still led Torpedo to the Russian championship.

Fugloy easternmost of the Faroe Islands, means 'bird Island' in Faroese. It has one road, no trees, 200,000 puffins and a mountain called Klubbin. No one is quite sure about how many people live there: the official records say 44, but that doesn't include the huldufolk or 'other people' who lead a parallel existence but cannot be seen unless they choose to be. It is also supposed to be full of trolls (or trølls, as they are called in Faroese). It would be a good place to lie low if you practised the dark arts: the Faroes are the only country in Northern Europe never to have burned a witch.

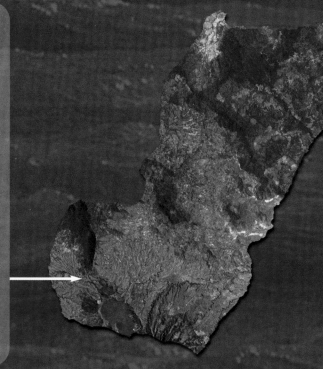

Fernando Póo part of the former Spanish colony of Equatorial Guinea (now the richest country in Africa), is named after the Portuguese explorer who first charted it in 1472. He himself called it Formosa ('beautiful'), a name also later given to Taiwan by another Portuguese in 1544. In 1973, the dictator of Equatorial Guinea renamed the island Masie Nguema Biyogo after himself: since his overthrow in 1979 it has been called Bioko. One of Nguema's many crimes took place in the island's football stadium in 1973, where 150 alleged conspirators were put to death as speakers blasted out the President's favourite song, *Those Were the Days* by winsome Welsh songstress, Mary Hopkin. The main residents of Fernando Póo are the Bubi people, also called the Bube, the Boombe, the Ibubi and the eVoové. Their name for the island is Otcho.

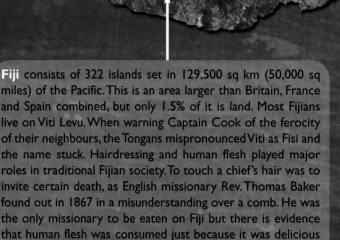

Fiji consists of 322 islands set in 129,500 sq km (50,000 sq miles) of the Pacific. This is an area larger than Britain, France and Spain combined, but only 1.5% of it is land. Most Fijians live on Viti Levu. When warning Captain Cook of the ferocity of their neighbours, the Tongans mispronounced Viti as Fisi and the name stuck. Hairdressing and human flesh played major roles in traditional Fijian society. To touch a chief's hair was to invite certain death, as English missionary Rev. Thomas Baker found out in 1867 in a misunderstanding over a comb. He was the only missionary to be eaten on Fiji but there is evidence that human flesh was consumed just because it was delicious – the best bits being thigh, heart and bicep.

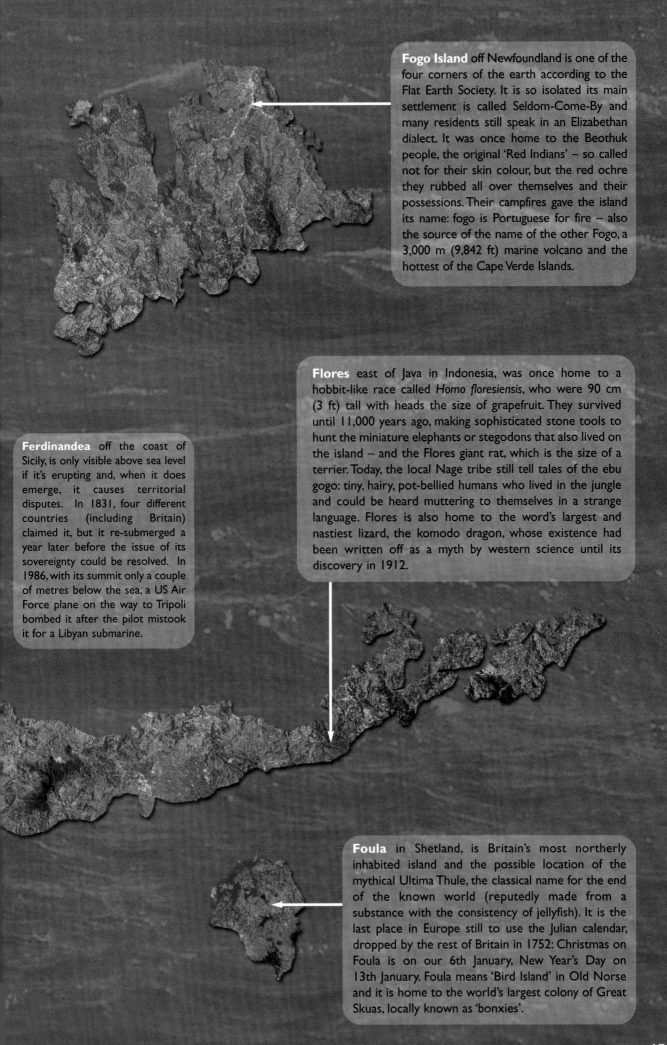

Fogo Island off Newfoundland is one of the four corners of the earth according to the Flat Earth Society. It is so isolated its main settlement is called Seldom-Come-By and many residents still speak in an Elizabethan dialect. It was once home to the Beothuk people, the original 'Red Indians' – so called not for their skin colour, but the red ochre they rubbed all over themselves and their possessions. Their campfires gave the island its name: fogo is Portuguese for fire – also the source of the name of the other Fogo, a 3,000 m (9,842 ft) marine volcano and the hottest of the Cape Verde Islands.

Flores east of Java in Indonesia, was once home to a hobbit-like race called *Homo floresiensis*, who were 90 cm (3 ft) tall with heads the size of grapefruit. They survived until 11,000 years ago, making sophisticated stone tools to hunt the miniature elephants or stegodons that also lived on the island – and the Flores giant rat, which is the size of a terrier. Today, the local Nage tribe still tell tales of the ebu gogo: tiny, hairy, pot-bellied humans who lived in the jungle and could be heard muttering to themselves in a strange language. Flores is also home to the word's largest and nastiest lizard, the komodo dragon, whose existence had been written off as a myth by western science until its discovery in 1912.

Ferdinandea off the coast of Sicily, is only visible above sea level if it's erupting and, when it does emerge, it causes territorial disputes. In 1831, four different countries (including Britain) claimed it, but it re-submerged a year later before the issue of its sovereignty could be resolved. In 1986, with its summit only a couple of metres below the sea, a US Air Force plane on the way to Tripoli bombed it after the pilot mistook it for a Libyan submarine.

Foula in Shetland, is Britain's most northerly inhabited island and the possible location of the mythical Ultima Thule, the classical name for the end of the known world (reputedly made from a substance with the consistency of jellyfish). It is the last place in Europe still to use the Julian calendar, dropped by the rest of Britain in 1752: Christmas on Foula is on our 6th January, New Year's Day on 13th January. Foula means 'Bird Island' in Old Norse and it is home to the world's largest colony of Great Skuas, locally known as 'bonxies'.

FINANCE
101 Uses For a Dead Hedge Fund Manager...

no. 4

no. 17

no. 31

no. 35

no. 42

no. 59

no. 63

no. 75

no. 82

no. 87

no. 94

no. 101

YE FRAUDULENTE HISTORIE OF FAKENHAM

Fakenham is an ancient Saxon town in Norfolk, mentioned in the 'Domesday Book'. It became famous in the 1990s when it was widely described in the national newspapers as 'the most boring place on earth'. That was not true*, and nothing else on this page is true either. Apart from this bit, of course.

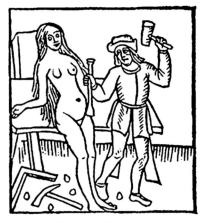

One of the earliest known sex-change operations nears its grisly conclusion.

Turbulent seas during the Roman occupation caused a pasta supplies ship to sink off the north Norfolk coast some nine miles from Fakenham. For almost a year afterwards, ships had great difficulty navigating the Vermicelli Straits.

Novice Agnes Queate pummelling Slime Tuber, a kind of acidic parsnip, to a mulch. Widely used as a shaving balm by penitent monks at the Abbey.

Inigo Thucke, a pioneer of selective breeding programmes, demonstrates his flock of micro-sheep. These tiny animals proved very popular with the gentry of Fakenham for the sweetness of their meat and the fact that they would fit inside a bun. Just visible in the background is Thucke's extraordinary floating goat that was propelled skywards by bodily gas emissions. Sadly, the animal exploded over Little Snoring and Inigo was so depressed he never bred another.

Dark Days – The fear of witches was taken to bloody extremes during the Fakenham Assizes of 1646-50, when almost any physical deformity was treated as a sure sign of Demonic affiliation. In one notable incident, the artist Enoch Butters was hanged as a witch merely for having an excessively pointy chin.

Gathering in the Fakenham hemp harvest often had a soporific and, occasionally, aphrodisiac effect upon the reapers. The harvest was often delayed for several days because of amorous mishaps - leading, nine months later, to the arrival of so-called 'Hash-a-bye Babies'.

Dr Napkin's free school. Napkin advocated that students should be free to express themselves in any way they felt appropriate. Here we see a small group of pupils expressing themselves by planning to sear the doctor's backside with a cattle brand while his dog is forced to eat a skunk's tail.

Warwick Soyle takes the stand to defend himself against the charge that he has made the crappiest desk in history.

*The error arose from the fact that a single contributor to the internet site The Knowhere Guide (www.knowhere.co.uk) had described Wednesday afternoons in Fakenham (early closing) as 'the most boring place on earth'. This was taken out of context and Fakenham hit the national headlines as 'having been voted the most boring place on earth', causing the town council considerable expenditure of time and money trying to prove otherwise. Current attractions in Fakenham include The Museum of Gas and Local History, which is open every Thursday.

FIFTEEN FINLAND FACTS

The statements below are all absolutely true. Finland is the most truthful place on earth*.

1. It is polite to remove shoes when entering a
Finnish home.
2. St Henry, patron saint of Finland, was
neither Finnish nor a saint.

3. A third of Finland is covered in peat.
4. In the 17th and 18th centuries,
Finland's major export was tar.

5. Only three of the lakes in Finland
are more than 91m (300 ft) deep.
6. Local handicrafts include making
wooden reindeer-milking bowls.

7. Finland is the world's largest producer of farm-raised foxes.
8. The log cabin was invented in Finland.

9. Helsinki is the smallest city in the world ever to host the
Olympic Games.
10. The last Peasant's Revolt in Europe took place in Finland in 1596-7.

11. The World Air Guitar Championships are
held annually in Oulu, Finland.

12. There are some two million saunas in Finland. Almost
every building in the country has at least one.
13. The second-largest religion in the country is the Finnish
Greek Orthodox Church, which reports to the
Bishop of Constantinople.

14. The maximum number of reindeer
permitted by law in Finland is 224,900.
15. Swedish is compulsory in Finnish
schools but most Finns never really learn
to speak it properly.

*Finland is officially the world's least corrupt country. Transparency International, a Berlin-based research group, produces an annual Corruption
Perception Index, grading every nation state. In the 2007 report, Finland was narrowly beaten to the top spot by Denmark - with New Zealand
coming third, the UK 12th and the USA 20th. But this is an aberration. Finland has consistently won the poll since the millennium, coming top in
2001, 2002, 2003, 2004 and 2006 with another second place in 2005 (won by Iceland). The bottom four in 2007 were: Haiti, Iraq, Burma
(Myanmar) and Somalia (judged the world's most corrupt state).

FROG SALAD

DECLARE A GREEN ALERT!

The world is losing its frogs. A third of the 5,250 recorded species are threatened with extinction through disease and climate change; since the 1950s at least 120 species have already joined the great froggy chorus in the sky. This must stop.

HERE ARE FOURTEEN REASONS WHY.

1. Glass Frogs, or Ghost Frogs, are lime green on top, but translucent below. Get underneath one and you can see its heart beating, its skeleton and its intestines. Why? Is this an evolved defence against dissection by biology students?

2. Bion, a popular philosopher of Athens, born around 325 BC, wrote: 'Boys throw stones at frogs for fun, but the frogs don't die for fun, but in sober earnest.' But it's hard to imagine a sober earnest frog, alive or dead. Look ...

3. *Pipa pipa* is the Surinam Toad from South America. It looks like a pancake. For three centuries after it was discovered, no one knew how it reproduced. *Pipa pipa* knew. The male and female perform a simultaneous underwater somersault, at the peak of which the female lays eggs which fall onto the male's belly. During the descent, the male fertilises the eggs and presses them upon the female's honeycombed back. Over and over, they somersault. Once she has about 100 fertilised eggs on her back, her skin swells up and envelops them. Months later, she moults her skin and fully formed tiny toads emerge.

4. All toads are frogs. Not all are Surinams. In some species, it is almost physically impossible to separate a mating pair, so solid is their embrace. They will part when they are ready. Leave them be, can't you?

5. But frogs have never been let be. The Florida Department of Agriculture, in 1952, published 50 recipes for bullfrog meat, including:
Bullfrog Pot Pie
Bullfrog à la King
Bullfrog Shortcakes
Bullfrog Omelette
Bullfrog Clubhouse Sandwich
French Toasted Bullfrog, and ...

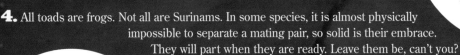

Bullfrog Salad.

6. In the Middle Ages, great houses employed servants whose sole job was to interrupt the brouhaha of croaking frogs by throwing stones into ponds all night, so that their masters might sleep.

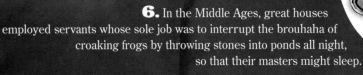

CROOAK OOH-ARR!

7.

The Northern Pool Frog croaks in a Norfolk accent. It went extinct in England in the 1990s, but was re-introduced into the Fens in 2005. From Sweden.

8. In Windham, Connecticut, in 1754, the people waited trembling for war to reach their village bournes. One steamy midnight in June, a deafening tumult of hatred and terror woke them all, and sent them screaming from their beds. The Day of Judgement, or Indians attacking? Either way, the villagers ran. In the morning light, they returned and found their foe: thousands of bullfrogs, drawn to a local pond by a freak drought.

8.

9. Not all frogs sing chorally. Spring Peeper Frogs form trios: one frog plays an A; a second soon responds in G sharp; after a while of this duetting, a third frog joins in with a B. And so it goes on: A, G sharp, B ... A, G sharp, B ... Even if part of a gathering of hundreds, each Peeper ignores the songs of all the others, only responding to the members of its own combo.

9.

10. Frogs, like birds, communicate with songs instead of smells. The song of the American Toad reminds many of the opening movement of Beethoven's 'Moonlight Sonata'. The Colorado River Toad's call resembles a ferryboat whistle. Others sound like pigs, like hounds or squirrels, like two carpenters banging in nails out of synch. The distress call of the bullfrog is endlessly mistaken for a human scream. And not only in Connecticut.

OINK! **WOOF!** **TOOT!**

10.

11.

11. Green Tree Frogs have been known to respond to sounds other than Green Tree Frog calls, including the mating calls of washing machines, popcorn makers, car alarms, and the cannons roaring in a film about the US Civil War.

12.

12. Sometimes, in mass mating sessions triggered by sudden downpours, male toads will attempt to mount other males. The male underneath gives a harsh, high-pitched croak of protest, repeatedly, until the one on top gets off. This is the most commonly heard of all toad calls, which must tell you something.

13. In many lands, frogs are good luck symbols. In Japan especially, the bullfrog is propitious, being descended from a fabled ancestor capable of sucking all the mosquitoes out of a room with one mighty inhalation.

14. 2008 is the official International Year of the Frog.

And also International Year of the Potato.

And of Sanitation.

And of The Planet Earth.

And of Astronomy, and of the Coral Reef, and of Languages.

13.

But mostly, surely, of the Frog.

There are over 100,000 species of **fungi** and 250,000 known species of **flowering plant**. The **flower auction** at Aalsmeer in the Netherlands is largest in the world: 19 million **flowers** pass through its halls every day. The '**Flower of Kent**' is a large green-skinned variety of apple, thought to h been the one that inspired Sir Isaac Newton to **formulate** his theory of gravity. There are about 12,000 known species of **fern**. **Ferns** range in size f the tiny **fragile** *Ophioglossaceae* that produce just one **frond** a year and the **filmy ferns** *Hymenophyliaceae* whose **fronds** are only one or two c thick, to the monstrous triffids in the genus *Cyathea* that have stems like tree trunks and can grow up to 80 **feet** (24m) tall. **Ferns** have more chromosor than any other living thing. The '**futhork**' or '**futhark**' is the Runic alphabet, named after its first six letters f, u, th, o or a, r and k. In the year 2000, ab 185,000 **foetuses** were aborted in Britain – more than 3,500 a week. You are 20 times more likely to be involved in a **fatal car accident** in the T World than in Europe. The last **fatality** caused by an adder sting in Britain was a **five-year old girl** in 1977. A **fatal dose** of chocolate for a human be is about 10kg (22lb) and for a dog about 2kg. A small songbird can succumb to a single Smartie. Birds are **feathered reptiles**. The **fear of feather** called pteronophobia. Xenophon of Kos, personal physician of the Emperor Claudius, murdered his patient by sticking a poisoned **feather** down his thr The **faster** a bird runs, the **fewer** toes it has. No bird has more than **four toes** on each **foot**. The abalone is a huge marine snail that has only one f – though this accounts for two-thirds of its body weight. Andorra is the only country in the world with a **free postal service**. PETA, the **fundamenta animal rights** group, claims that cows can suffer from humiliation if people laugh at them. There are **fourteen** species of crocodile. **Florer Nightingale** owned 60 cats. Before the banning of **fox hunting** in Britain, an average 16,000 **foxes** were killed by hunts each year, compared with aro 300,000 **foxes** that died of natural causes or in road accidents. Hitler banned **fox hunting** in Germany because he thought it was cruel and immora Siberia in 1623, a single black **fox-fur** pelt could be exchanged for a cabin with **fifty** acres of land, **five** horses, ten cows and twenty sheep. Horses w originally hunted for **food**. The largest **food company** in the world is Nestlé SA of Switzerland. Modern Americans spend more money on **fast food** t on higher education, personal computers, computer software or new cars. A single potato crisp production line uses in one hour as many potatoes could be planted, grown and harvested from a **full-size football pitch**. Robert Mitchum could memorise his lines from an entire **film script** after a sir read-through. He chose most of his **films** on the basis of how much time off he could get to go **fishing**. The greatest depth at which a **fish** has b caught is 27,200 feet (8,370m). **Fishermen** kill about 100,000 albatrosses a year. They die on the baited hooks of **fishing lines** that can be up to 80 m long. **Forty-three** per cent of British 7 year olds do not understand the word 'amber'. Amber is the **fossilised resin** of pine trees. Wombats have cu shaped **faeces**. St **Fidelis** of Sigmarigen's skull is buried in **Feldkirch**, Austria but the rest of him is buried in Chur, Switzerland. **Four million peo** visit the tomb of St **Francis of Assisi** every year. Gabriele **Falloppio** (1523-62), also known as **Fallopius**, was the **first man** to describe the clitoris to name the vagina. Though he described the **Fallopian tubes** that are named after him, he was not the **first to do so** and didn't understand what t were for. He called them 'the trumpets of the uterus'. **Fromology** is the study of cheese. Aerodontia is the branch of dentistry dealing with proble caused by **flying**. In Croatia, so many may**flies** hatch on the rivers that **farmers** scrape them off the surface and use them as **fertiliser**. There are m than **forty** different ethnic groups in Gabon, but one third of the population belong to the **Fang** tribe. The **Fang** are the only ethnic group in Gabon have always opposed slavery. The lovely stained glass windows in the Süleymaniye Mosque in Istanbul were crafted by the **famous glazier** Ibrahim Drunkard. According to Canadian scientists, winning an Oscar extends an actor's life by **four years**: winning two Oscars by six. Crickets have their e on their **forelegs**. Bhutan and Nepal are the only two countries in the world where **female life expectancy** is less than the male. Admiral of the **Fl** Lord 'Jackie' **Fisher** (1841-1920), the **First Sea Lord**, sent his **favourite niece** £10 in cash for her wedding, accompanied by a note saying he wc never speak to her again because she was marrying an Army officer. The **flag of Liechtenstein** had a crown put on it in 1937, to distinguish it from **flag of Haiti**. Modern Haiti is one of the **four most corrupt countries** in the world. One of principal exports of Liechtenstein is **false teeth**. The **name** of the novelist **F. Scott Fitzgerald** (1896-1940) was **Francis Scott Key Fitzgerald**: he was named after his second cousin three times remo **Francis Scott Key**, author of *The Star Spangled Banner*. The real name of the novelist **Ford Madox Ford** (1873-1939) was **Ford Hermann Huef** Robert **FitzRoy**, captain of the *Beagle* (on which Darwin **first formulated** the Theory of Evolution) was the inventor of weather **forecasting**. Otto Ro **Frisch** (1904-79), an Austrian physicist sacked by Hitler from Hamburg University for being Jewish in 1933, went on to conceive the atomic bomb. **F Haber** (1868-1934) invented chemical warfare in Germany during the **First World War**. He called it 'a higher **form of killing**'. After the war, he esca to Switzerland in a **false beard**. In 1918, he was awarded the Nobel Prize for Chemistry. **Friedrich** Wilhelm Heinrich Alexander von Humboldt (17 1859) is said to have been the last man in history who knew everything that could be known. Thomas Jefferson (1743-1826), 3rd President of the Un States, invented the **foldaway bed**. In her **final movie**, made in her mid-80s, Mae West remained convinced she was a sex symbol, even though was nearly blind, stone deaf and so elderly that, when she had to turn round on camera, a stage hand crouching out of shot would swivel her by ankles. W.C. **Fields** called her 'a plumber's idea of Cleopatra'. The names Honda and Toyota both come from Japanese words meaning '**field of ri** Honda means 'main rice **field**' and Toyota means 'abundant rice **field**'. In 'Cow Bingo', a **field** is divided into squares that players can 'buy'. A cow is into the **field**, and the player on whose square the **first cowpat** lands wins. **Fair Isle**, lying between the Orkneys and the Shetlands, is Britain's remo inhabited island. The **Faroe Islands** are **famous** for **fog**. On Mykines, it is **foggy** for 100 days a year. **Faroe islanders** claim that it is possibl experience all **four seasons** in a single day. The name **Funchal**, the capital of the island of Madeira, comes from the Portuguese for **fennel**. The Gr for **fennel** is 'marathon'. Only 100 people in the world are **fluent** in Cornish. The last person to speak Cornish as their **first language** was Dolly Pentre of Mousehole, who died in 1777. There are **four hundred and twenty-seven thousand villages** in India. The world's most **fertile bull**, Itofuku died in Japan in January 2002. In a 20-year career, he **fathered** 39,157 calves, averaging over **forty-nine** a week. The Kalashnikov is the most wi used **firearm** in the world, more than **fifty** national armies have them in their arsenal. A bullet **fired** from a Kalashnikov weighs only a quarter of ounce, but leaves the barrel at over 1,500 mph. This gives it a **force of impact** equivalent to that of a brick dropped from the top of St Paul's Cathe **Falling coconuts** kill 150 people a year, ten times as many people as are killed by sharks. Henry **Ford**, William Durant (founder of General Motc Ettore Bugatti and Louis Delage all died in 1947, the year that **Ferrari** was founded. Carrara in Italy is the source of the world's most **famous marbl** is so plentiful that it is ground into sand for use in concrete. The town is almost as **famous** for salted, aged and spiced pig **fat** or lard, a Tuscan delic The **finest lard** - sometimes called leaf lard - comes from inside the loin and around the kidneys of a pig. This kind of pig **fat** is called the **flare**. Accorc to leading redneck authority Jeff **Foxworthy**, you may be a redneck if you have ever used lard in bed. All **fats** are composed of crystals. Most crys have an irregular shape, but the angle between their **facets** always remains constant. The German for **fat** is Schmalz. **Faggots** are a kind of ch sausage made with pork offal mixed with **fat**, breadcrumbs and onions. An accident with a batch of **faggots** started the Great **Fire of London** in Pudc Lane in 1666. Each year, up to 200 million tons of Chinese coal bursts into **flames** whilst still underground. There are at least 60 such **fires** ragin China at this moment. One of them, at Baijigou in northwest China, has been on **fire** continuously for 150 years. Such **fires** produce more greenho gases than all the cars in Germany put together. Golf was played in ancient China, more than **five hundred years** before it was first mentione Scotland. The **first recorded** mention of golf in Scotland, in 1457, made it a **felony**, punishable by death. During his lifetime, Benny Hill was the m **famous comedian** in the world. His biggest **fan** was Charlie Chaplin. He died at home alone watching television, his body undiscovered for two da The composer Rimsky-Korsakov (1844-1908) was a **full-time naval officer**. Thirty-six per cent of the EU is **forested**, compared to only 8.4% of Brit The world's largest protected **forest** is the Amana Reserve in Brazil. It covers 2,350,000 hectares (9,180 square miles), an area about the size of Belgi Technically speaking, an *idiot* is someone with the lowest possible grade of **feeble-mindedness**, having an IQ of less than 25, or a mental age of t When Liverpool **footballer** Ian Rush was signed to Juventus and was asked how he **found** living in Italy, he said it was 'like being in a **foreign coun** Since the year 2000, the **Federal Aviation Administration** can propose **fines** of up to $25,000 for unruly passengers. A single incident can resu multiple violations. There are **forty-four** muscles in the human **face**, enabling us to make more than 250,000 different **facial expressions**. The Ma word *bongking* means 'sprawling **face down** with one's bottom in the air'; *jeremak* means 'suddenly **face to face**'; and *jeremus* means 'to spraw one's **face**'. It is impossible to **faint** while lying down. It's **fascinating** that there are words for the **fear of dust**, clocks or hearing good news, but n for the common ones such as the **fear of school**, bats or bears. Arthur Conan Doyle and W.B. Yeats both believed in **fairies**. **Fairies** are suppose eat copious quantities of weeds. The scientific study of **fingerprints** is called *dermatoglyphics*, a word that has the distinction of being one of the longest in English with no repeated letters. The other one is *uncopyrightable*. The Yiddish for **finger** is 'toe'. **Fireworks** are illegal in Australia. **Faus** is Latin for 'lucky'.

A FARRAGO* OF FRUIT

Fruit are ovaries, simple as that. Suddenly doesn't sound quite so appetising, does it? Ovary smoothie, mmm…

Tomatoes, as everyone knows, are fruits not vegetables. Fewer people know that avocadoes, pumpkins, coconuts, cucumbers, peas, beans (green as well as all other beans), peppers, corn, aubergines and squash are also fruits.

All nuts are fruit. Acorns are fruit. Grains of wheat and rice are fruits.

Fruits can be fleshy like peaches, or dry like peanuts. They can have many seeds in them like watermelons, or a single seed like cherries. They can be as large as pumpkins, or as small as blueberries.

The fruits of the tiny floating plants known as water-meal are so small they are almost invisible. The tropical jackfruit, on the other hand, can weigh as much as 90 lb (40 kg).

With an apple I will astonish Paris.
PAUL CEZANNE

More than 40 million tons of apples are produced in the world each year. There are about 8,000 named varieties. The world's largest producer is China. Almost half the apple juice drunk in the USA is Chinese. The Chinese for 'apple' is *ping*. Apples are popular gifts because *ping* also means 'peace' but the Chinese never give apples to invalids because *ping* sounds a bit like *bing*, which is Chinese for illness. According to legend, Merlin sat under an apple tree to teach. The word *Avalon* means 'apple orchard' in Celtic. For some unknown reason, people always cut apples in half vertically. If you cut one in half horizontally, the core makes the shape of a perfect five-pointed star or *pentagram*. Try this for yourself, right now. It is quite strikingly beautiful and astonishing if you have never seen it before. The pentagram is an ancient occult symbol, first discovered by the mystic cult of Pythagoras and said to reveal the secret of good and evil. It would be typical of Pythagoras' originality to be the first man to think of slicing an apple crosswise.

A world without tomatoes is like a string quartet without violins.
LAURIE COLWIN

Tomatoes were originally yellow: hence their Italian name pomodoro ('golden apple'). Dame Anita Roddick, the founder of *Body Shop*, used to say that the secret of happiness is to eat tomatoes, on the grounds that Italians eat a lot of them and there is no such thing as an unhappy Italian. Whether this is true or not, eating any kind of cooked tomatoes regularly - tomato sauce, tomato soup, ketchup, or even pizza - gives you a much better chance of a long life. Tomatoes contain a substance called *lycopene* that gives them their red colour. This is a powerful anti-oxidant that counteracts dangerous 'free radicals' in the body, which cause heart disease, cancer and ageing. The human body cannot make lycopene and has to acquire it from food. It is much more active and easily absorbed into the blood after the tomatoes have been cooked. Oddly enough, raw tomatoes are not nearly so good for you.

*It means 'medley'. As opposed to medlar (which is a kind of apple) or medulla (which means 'pith', as found in oranges etc).

Intellectual property has the shelf life of a banana. BILL GATES

Bananas are the most popular fruit in Britain. The UK imports more than 7 billion bananas a year. More than 140 million bananas are eaten in Britain every week. More than 500 million people in the world depend on bananas for half their daily intake of calories. The largest exporter of bananas in Europe is Ireland. Fyffe's, the Irish multinational, buys up the entire banana crop of Belize each year. The European country that grows the most bananas, however, is (bizarrely) Iceland. They are produced in greenhouses heated by geothermal energy. Edible bananas are one of the world's oldest crops. The first one appeared about 10,000 years ago. There is a theory that the Forbidden Fruit with which the serpent tempted Eve might well have been a banana. It certainly wasn't an apple – apples are much more recent – and the Bible doesn't say what kind of fruit it was.

God sends almonds to those without teeth. SYRIAN PROVERB

Almonds are a kind of peach and peaches are a kind of rose. Almond trees have more beautiful flowers than peach trees and are arguably as lovely as roses. Pink flowers produce sweet almonds: white flowers produce bitter almonds, which contain cyanide, which smells of almonds. On 29th December 1916, Prince Yussupov and his cronies poisoned Rasputin by means of a plate of almond cakes and a bottle of wine. These contained enough cyanide to kill 500 people. Rasputin scoffed the lot with no apparent ill-effects. He was then shot in the back, beaten senseless with an iron bar, dragged to the River Neva and pushed through a hole in the ice. When the body was recovered, the cause of death was found to be drowning. The word 'almond' is from the Greek amygdala. The amygdala is the name for the small almond-shaped part of the human brain responsible for fear, depression and anger.

If you want to know what cherries taste like, you must ask birds and boys. JOHANN WOLFGANG VON GOETHE

Cherries, like almonds, are members of the rose family. The word comes from old Norman French, *cherise*. When the word first entered Middle English it was assumed to be a plural and that there must logically be a singular 'cheri' - hence the English word 'cherry'. Cherries have been eaten since at least 5,000 BC. First cultivated by the Greeks, they were thought to be an essential part of a Roman legionary's diet. It is supposedly possible to trace the routes of forgotten Roman roads in Britain by looking out for wild cherry trees - the soldiers spat out the stones of imported fruit as they marched around the country. According to Pliny the Elder, it was Lucullus (118-56 BC), the Roman general and gourmet who fought Mithridates the Great, that first brought sweet cherries to Rome. Later, he is said to have committed suicide because he feared he was running out of them. Cherries are almost 84% water.

The coconut trees, lithe and graceful, crowd the beach like a minuet of slender elderly virgins.
WILLIAM MANCHESTER

Coconuts are the stones of the fruit of the coconut palm, the most useful tree in the world. It provides food, timber, fuel, chemicals, medicines, alcoholic drinks, yeast for bread making, and materials to make thatch, baskets, ropes, brushes, brooms, mats and cloth. In Indonesia it is said that the coconut tree has as many uses as there are days in the year. There is no such thing as a wild coconut. All the coconut trees in the world come from palms that have been cultivated - even the ones on desert islands. Coconuts float: they can survive for 100 days in seawater and travel as much as 3,000 miles. In the Solomon Islands, there are nine different words for various stages of a growing coconut but no equivalent of the word coconut itself. Coconuts can produce pearls. These are just like the pearls found in oysters, but as big as cherries. No one understands the process by which they form.

Me said, 'Come rub it 'pon me belly With you guava jelly, Damsel.' Said, 'Here I stand. Come rub it 'pon me belly with you guava jelly.'
BOB MARLEY 'Guava Jelly'

Guavas are members of the myrtle family (which also includes cloves, pimentos and eucalyptus) and are the only commercially significant variety of myrtle to be cultivated in the USA. They taste like a mixture of pears and strawberries and they are the most nutritious fruit of all, with five times as much Vitamin C as oranges. A single guava has four times as much fibre and nineteen times as much vitamin C as an apple, and 25 times as much Vitamin C as a whole bunch of grapes. A single guava can weigh as little as an ounce or as much as a pound. In many parts of the world, guavas run wild, forming huge thickets called *guayabales* in Spanish. They overrun pastures, fields and roadsides so vigorously in Hawaii, Malaysia, New Caledonia, Fiji, the US Virgin Islands, Puerto Rico, Cuba and southern Florida that they are classed as a noxious weed. The Vietnamese for guava is *oi*, the same word Brazilians use when they answer the telephone.

When I was young, I said to God, 'God, tell me the mystery of the universe.' But God answered, 'That knowledge is for me alone.' So I said, 'God, tell me the mystery of the peanut.' Then God said, 'Well George, that's more nearly your size.' And he told me. GEORGE WASHINGTON CARVER

Peanuts are not nuts. They are members of the pea family, so they are fruit. They both grow and (strangely) ripen underground. Peanuts have more protein, minerals and vitamins than beef liver, more fat than double cream and more energy than sugar. They can also be made into cheese, milk, coffee, flour, ink, dyes, plastics, wood stain, soap, lino, medicines and cosmetics. Most of these uses are due to the brilliant research of George Washington Carver (1860-1943), the former slave who rose to become Director of Agricultural Research at the Tuskegee Institute, Alabama, where he devised 325 different uses for them. Today, half the peanuts harvested in the US are turned into peanut butter. Using extreme high pressure, it is possible to turn peanut butter into diamonds. Peanuts are also used in the manufacture of dynamite. Don't eat the peanuts on the bar. They contain traces of urine because most men don't wash their hands after visiting the lavatory.

All the nine songs known to bears are about wild pears. TURKISH PROVERB

Pears, like apples, are a kind of rose. Columbus believed the world was pear-shaped. The correct word for 'pear-shaped' is *pyriform*, though several varieties of pears are apple-shaped. There were no apples or pears in America before Columbus got there. Like apples, pears grown from seed do not stay true to the original stock but produce completely different varieties. In the 16th century, Duke Cosimo III of Florence, who was a vegetarian, had 232 different varieties of pear served at his court in a single year. It is extremely unusual to be allergic to pears. They are often used as part of a 'restriction diet' where, when testing for allergies, most foods are eliminated and then re-introduced one by one until the culprit is found. Other such foods include lamb, rice and sweet potatoes. *Jargonelles* are French pears that smell like 'pear drops'. The distinctive smell is amyl acetate, the main ingredient of nail polish remover.

FUNAMBULISM

THAUMATRON Ever since human beings first twisted cords of hemp and flax, the temptation to walk on rope seems to have been irresistible.

In Ancient Greece they were considered performers, like magicians, rather than athletes and never competed in the Olympics: what they did was too strange and dangerous. Instead they had their own prize – the Thaumatron, the award for 'wonders', given to anyone 'who shows people something amazing, out of the ordinary'.

In Rome, rope dancers became funambuli (from 'funis' rope and 'ambulare' to walk). Such was their hold on the popular imagination that play-wrights complained of them stealing their audience.

SPIRIT AND GRISTLE Through the Middle Ages, no fair would be without rope dancers. Acts became more and more daring. For the arrival of Isabel of Bavaria in Paris in 1385 a high-wire walker processed with two huge candles along a rope attached to the highest tower of Notre Dame.

In England, rope sliding became a craze. The most famous exponent was Robert Cadman, described by a contemporary historian as 'a small figure of a man, seemingly composed of spirit and gristle', who would attach a wooden plate with a groove in it to his chest and propel himself down an almost vertical rope from a high church tower, firing pistols, blowing a trumpet and trailing smoke as friction caused the rope to catch fire behind him.

He died in spectacular fashion on a frosty day in Shrewsbury in 1740, when a faulty rope snapped and he plunged into the crowd. 'The body, after reaching the earth, rebounded upwards several feet' according to one eyewitness.

As one epitaph had it: 'Good-night, good-night, poor ROBERT CADMAN, You lived and died just like a madman.'

BLONDIN The greatest of all high-wire performers was born Jean François Gravelet in 1824 in France. He took the name Blondin from the owner of the circus in which he first worked. As the Great Blondin, he took the high-wire walk to hitherto undreamed-of levels of daring.

BEING ON THE TIGHTROPE IS LIVING; EVERYTHING ELSE IS WAITING.
KARL WALLENDA (1905-78)

In 1859, when he was 31, and on a rope that was 160 ft (49 m) high, quarter of a mile (350 m) long and only 3 inches (7.5 cm) in diameter he crossed the gorge of the Niagara Falls no less than 17 times, ratcheting up the excitement with every 20-minute crossing. He did it on stilts, in a blindfold, with a wheelbarrow. He carried a 50-lb (23-kg) stove on his back and prepared, cooked and ate an omelette halfway across. He carried a large camera out on to the middle of the rope and took pictures of the tens of thousands of spectators on the opposite bank.

He only came close to losing his balance once, when carrying his cigar-smoking manager, Harry Colcord, on his back. Two guy ropes broke and the wire swayed wildly. Colcord had to dismount 6 times before they finally made it to the other side, with Blondin charging the thronging crowd in order to dismount safely. Often imitated, he was never equalled.

BIRDMAN Blondin's modern heir is Philippe Petit who, aged 24, was responsible for the most audacious sky walk of all. In 1974, after 6 years of meticulous planning, he broke into the still-unfinished World

LIFE IS ALWAYS A TIGHTROPE OR A FEATHER BED. GIVE ME THE TIGHTROPE.
EDITH WHARTON (1862-1937)

Trade Center and used a bow and arrow to fire a 3/4 in (1.9 cm) steel cable across the 140 ft (43 m) gap between the two towers. He made 8 crossings in all, sitting and lying on the wire and talking to a passing gull, before being arrested.

THE BLONDIN DONKEY Although this wasn't a real animal but a famous 'skin' act of the late 19th century in which the Griffiths brothers performed on a rope while dressed as a donkey, animal funambulism has almost as long a history as the human variety.

In 1734 an ill-conceived attempt to send a donkey rope-sliding from a church tower in Derby ended in disaster: 'A whole multitude was overwhelmed; nothing was heard but dreadful cries; nor seen, but confusion. Legs and arms went to destruction. In this dire calamity, the ass, which maimed others, was unhurt himself, having a pavement of soft bodies to roll over.'

This is the last record we have of a rope-dancing donkey, although Philip Astley, founder of the modern circus in the 1780s, claimed to have trained horses to rope walk.

More recently, Negus the Tightrope-Walking Lion (above) was a huge attraction for Bertram Mills' circus in the 1950s. After 6 months' intensive training, which involved a great deal of meat, the lion learned to walk along the ropes laid on the ground. These were then gradually raised until they reached 6 ft (3 m) in height, with Negus shuffling along them quite unconcerned.

'WHEN I FIRST **FELL IN LOVE** WITH THE TOWERS, THEY WERE NOT BORN. SO I SAW THEM GROW. AND THEN, WHEN THEY WERE OF AGE, I MARRIED THEM!' PHILIPPE PETIT

'Forgive me Father, for I am an identity thief.'

'Waiter, there's a flea in my dog soup.'

'This summer we're renting a flip flop in Spain.'

FRY'S ELVES: HOW QI RESEARCH GETS DONE

Each day starts with a brief lecture and rub-down from Stephen and Alan.

Today we're studying 'capnolagnia', in which one becomes aroused by watching people smoke.

Experimenting is a big part of the job.

We like to work with the local community: 'Look! English bond, the strongest bond for a one-brick-thick wall and popular from the late 1450s right up to the nineteenth century.'

'The dragonfly's penis is shaped like a spade, which it uses to scoop out any sperm previously deposited by a rival,' I tell passers-by.

Sometimes, when Stephen asks to see things, I get the wrong end of the stick.

Not everyone agrees with us. This Captain vigorously disputed my meaning of 'bottomry'.

If we don't find enough questions we have to stand on the naughty step.

Rich Hall likes to drop by and collect his appearance fee in person.

Elves are only paid in love so we supplement our income by selling prayer rugs whenever the opportunity arises.

After a hard day fact-finding we all like to settle down for a quiet evening in.

If we're very lucky, Stephen might invite us into his boudoir for a 'night cap'.

Buteo's Big Box

Probably the most influential attempt to sort out the Ark's logistics was French mathematician Johannes Buteo's *The Shape & Capacity of Noah's Ark,* written in 1554. He proposed that the bottom deck held animals, the middle deck provisions, and the top deck humans and birds ~ as well as dogs (who would be happy eating their own vomit). He imagined the Ark as completely dark on all levels except for the top ~ because 'wild animals and all kind of reptile will actively seek out darkness'. He left the smaller animals such as snakes and lizards out of his plans on the basis that they would 'live in small holes around the stabling and living areas'. And insects were com~ pletely excluded, as they were then thought to be the product of spontaneous generation.

Floating Factory

Buteo thought that the bottom two levels must have holes for animal excrement to fall into the bilge; he also thought that food could be dropped down to the animals from the middle deck, and that water could be passed around the ship through a system of siphons. He envisaged space for the storage of 'agricultural and urban equipment' and 'every kind of workman's tool', factoring in a pantry, kitchen, hand~mills, men's and women's quarters and smokeless logs for fuel. His food store contained a barn filled with every known kind of farmers' crop. He also worked out that the animals' enclosure had to be arranged to ensure their inhabitants stayed in perfect balance to prevent the ship capsizing.

The idea of building a ship that could carry representatives of every known species has haunted the imagination of scholars and engineers for millennia.

Part of the reason for this is that there are some apparently precise details in the biblical account of the dimensions and methods of construction of Noah's vessel. For example, we know it had a volume of 450,000 cubic cubits, or 1.5 million cubic feet, which is about a third of the volume of the auditorium of the Albert Hall. But arguments have raged about its shape, with most scholars going for the parallelepiped (that's a regular 'box' to you and me). But not the early Christian philosopher Origen (c 185 ~ c 254), who was convinced it was built in the shape of a pyramid, with a base that covered half a square mile. (But then again, he also castrated himself after mis~ reading a passage in the Gospels.)

WE'RE STUCK ON THE BOTTOM, BUT I HEAR WE GET OUR OWN DVD PLAYER!

No, YOU'RE NOT TAKING YOUR PONY PORNO!

FORM 2 LANES

Self~righting

Buteo's work inspired many other 'Ark designers'. The German Jesuit polymath Athanasius Kircher (1601~80) solved the instability problem by keeping the heaviest animals at the bottom of the boat as ballast ~ he used Galileo's research into floating bodies to calculate accurately. His triple~decker contained 50 rooms per deck, housing about 1,000 animals.

Oi! YOU'RE SUPPOSED TO STAY ASLEEP TILL WE HIT DRY LAND!

Green Herbs, No Ham

And what about the plants themselves? Most are much too delicate to survive a flood ~ maybe Noah could have kept an equivalent of the Doomsday Seed Vault that opened in Svalbard, Norway in February 2008 to preserve 1.5 million agricultural crop seeds.

As well as crops and seeds, the Ark would also have needed a supply of bamboo: not necessarily for the pandas, who can supplement their diet with insects and fruit, but for bamboo mites and bamboo mealy bugs who live on nothing else. In fact many insects can only feed on certain plants ~ including most of the 6,000 known species of plant~feeding mites.

Every Moving Thing that Liveth

So could it be done? For 1,000 animals maybe, but we're now looking at 2 million species, with as many as 30 million more waiting to be named. Taking the lowest reasonable estimate of 5 million species, that's 10 million individual animals to accommodate, or 0.15 cubic feet of space each.

In the world's zoos, there is a ratio of 25.4 animals per zoo keeper. Noah's family would have had 1.25 million animals each to look after. To feed them all once a day, Noah, his wife, three sons and their wives would have needed to get through 115 animals per second.

But that doesn't begin to solve the feeding problems. A polar bear can eat 50 lb (22.5 kg) of meat at a single sitting, while a walrus is able to eat around 5,000 clams in one meal. The short~nosed fruit bat can eat twice its weight in bananas in three hours (it has the biggest appetite of any mammal for its size). Perhaps Noah fed the carnivores with unicorn, griffin, and the like. That would have helped to keep the food fresh, as well as explaining why those animals haven't survived.

YUM--NOTHING QUITE LIKE A NICE JUICY JOINT....

Wood Worriers

Then there are the 3,000 species of termites. It's just possible that the mysterious 'gopher wood', which the Bible claimed the Ark was made from, was cypress pine, which is termite proof ~ but what about teredos, the strange saltwater clams also known as 'shipworms' or 'termites of the sea' that are notorious for devouring wooden hulls? Isambard Kingdom Brunel's engineer father Marc was inspired to build the world's first submarine tunnel (the Thames Tunnel) after watching teredos chomp through cellulose. Solitary confinement would be essential.

Two by Two?

The Ark would also need a 'sexing room', to make sure the right two individuals were selected. It's not as straightforward as it sounds. Male and female hyenas, sea cucumbers, starfish and gila monsters are almost indis~ tinguishable without specialist scanning equipment. And what about hermaphrodites, like the 650 known species of leech? Or the Amazonian Molly~fish whose species are all female?

Ordure

Then there's the question of shit. An elephant creates about a tonne of dung per week. Even the 4,500 species of dung beetle are going to have their work cut out chomping through that. A single cow belches about 300 litres of methane a day; along with all the other ruminants, the boat could easily have exploded if subjected to a naked flame. The risk might have been reduced by a giant lightning rod and perhaps a ventilation system powered by the 1,700 species of rodents running around in little wheels.

Odour

And it's not just the dung and the belching: some animals smell bad anyway. Ants were once called 'pismires' due to the urinous odour they give off; skunks smell like rotten eggs mixed with old garlic and burnt rubber and the anal secretion of the ferret~like zorilla can stun a chicken at twenty paces. Perhaps they could bunk up with some of the sweeter smelling denizens: binturongs, for instance, smell of freshly cooked popcorn; tapirs like a crate of lettuce; while koalas eat so much eucalyptus it's easy to mistake them for large furry cough~sweets.

I'm a Patriarch, Get Me Out of Here!

Finally, a year at sea is a long time. Birth control pills would be needed, especially for the 100,000 species of fly, whose descendants can number over 190 trillion within 6 months if left unchecked.

All things considered, it's enough to drive a man to drink. Which is precisely what happened to Noah when the voyage finally ended: 'And Noah began to be an husbandman, and he planted a vineyard: And he drank of the wine, and was drunken; and he was uncovered within his tent.' (Genesis 9:20~21)

After all that stench and sea water, who can blame him?

Illustration: Ted Dewan

FALLACYBUSTER

Facts are ventriloquist's dummies. Sitting on a wise man's knee they may be made to utter words of wisdom; elsewhere, they say nothing, or talk nonsense. ALDOUS HUXLEY

In 1973, Norman Mailer coined the word 'factoid'. He defined this to mean facts 'which have no existence before appearing in a magazine or newspaper.' Since then, the number of factoids in existence has increased a million-fold: the web is awash with them. Online, they are known as 'trivia' (a word which is much older – its modern meaning dates from 1922).

TRIVIA CAN BE FUN – BUT HOW MUCH OF IT IS TRUE?

Here we take on twenty of the most frequently cited internet factoids and subject them to the QI Fallacybuster Test:

1. A duck's quack does not echo (and no one knows why).
FALSE Somebody made this up (and no one knows who, when or why). Thankfully, in 2003 the good people at the University of Salford took the trouble to test it by placing a duck in a reverberation chamber; sure enough, the quack echoed just like every other sound.

2. Birmingham has more miles of canal than Venice.
TRUE Birmingham has 35 miles of canals, Venice only 26 (or 42 km). However, Venice covers 3 square miles (8 sq kms) compared with Birmingham's 103 square miles. Which means Brum is 35 times bigger than Venice, yet contains only a third more canals.

3. A 'jiffy' is an actual unit of time equal to 1/100th of a second.
FALSE The only recognised definition in physics for a jiffy is the time taken for light to travel half an inch in a vacuum: around 33 picoseconds (or 33 trillionths of a second).

4. The most common name for a pub in the UK is 'The Red Lion'.
FALSE A survey carried out by CAMRA in 2007 found that 'The Red Lion' was only the second most popular pub name: there were 668 of them. The winner was 'The Crown' with 704 examples. However, this may already be outdated. Since the smoking ban in 2007, so many pubs have gone bust that, in 2008, CAMRA claimed that more than half the villages in England are 'dry' for the first time since the Norman Conquest.

5. The average person consumes four spiders per year in their sleep.
FALSE This 'fact' was dreamt up by journalist Lisa Holst of *PC Professional* magazine in 1993, in an experiment to test the degree of absurdity people will accept simply because they come across it on the net.

6. When you lick a stamp you take in one calorie.
TRUE Or, at least, possible. According to the Royal Mail, the gum on the back of a stamp is made from a petroleum derivative and potato starch. A single standard postage stamp contains 5.9 calories, so it is conceivable that your tongue might absorb a calorie when licking the back.

7. The blue whale has a heart the size of a small car and its blood vessels are so broad that a child could swim through them.
TRUE (and FALSE) A blue whale's heart is around 6 feet wide (1.8m) and over 6 feet in length and weighs 1,000lb or 453.6 kg – not an unreasonable estimate of the size of a small car. However, its largest blood vessel, the aorta, is only 9 inches (22.5 cm) across: quite a squeeze for even the tiniest newborn baby, and certainly too narrow for any child old enough to swim.

8. Disneyworld is bigger than the world's five smallest countries.
TRUE Not just each of them, but all of them put together. The Walt Disney World Resort in Orlando, Florida, USA, is 28,000 acres (or 44 square miles) in extent, which is bigger than the total area of the five smallest independent nations combined. Vatican City, Monaco, Nauru, Tuvalu and San Marino cover just 42.7 square miles between them.

9. In space it is impossible to cry - the tears cannot run because of the lack of gravity.
FALSE (and TRUE) The second 'space tourist', South African entrepreneur Mark Shuttleworth, who joined the Russian Soyuz TM-34 mission in 2002, said: 'I am very happy to say that the only tears that I have experienced in space are tears of joy… It is a strange feeling because tears don't fall down they just build up.' So you can 'cry' in space – but, though the tears come to your eyes, they don't run down your cheeks.

10. Tarantulas do not leave any tracks on sand.
FALSE Fortuitously enough, a 2005 paper published by the Geological Society of America looked at this very subject.

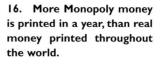

Effects of Slope and Temperature on the Morphology of Experimental Scorpion and Spider Tracks (J. Azain & J. Wright) concluded that tarantulas do not leave tracks on damp or slightly moist sand because the animals are too light, but on dry sand they certainly do.

11. It takes a week to make a jelly bean.

TRUE 'Jelly Belly', a premium brand of US jelly beans, states that, although they produce 347 jelly beans per second, each individual bean takes 7 to 21 days to make. It's a painstaking business, involving such mysterious procedures as 'engrossing', 'polishing' and 'printing' – in between which the beans are dried for periods of up to 48 hours.

12. In your lifetime your body will produce more than 25,000 quarts of saliva.

FALSE Although no one is quite sure how much saliva the average person produces in a day, most studies suggest it's about a pint. If so, this would mean that you'd have to live to approximately 137 to generate 25,000 quarts (or 50,000 pints, or 28,400 litres).

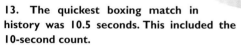

13. The quickest boxing match in history was 10.5 seconds. This included the 10-second count.

FALSE We managed to find an even quicker bout. When Al Carr fought Lew Massey in 1936 in New Haven, Connecticut, the contest was stopped (without a count) after 7 seconds.

14. *The Goodies* is the only British comedy to have killed someone.

FALSE On 24th March 1975, Alex Mitchell, a 50-year-old bricklayer from King's Lynn, England, died laughing while watching 'Kung Fu Kapers', an episode of *The Goodies*. But the syndrome struck again in 1989, when Danish ear doctor Ole Bentzen died of a heart attack after an extreme laughing fit brought on by John Cleese's *A Fish Called Wanda*.

15. It is illegal to impersonate Chelsea Pensioners in Britain.

TRUE Chelsea Pensioners are retired British soldiers who live free in a magnificent Grade I building called the Royal Hospital in Chelsea. It is illegal to impersonate them, insofar as you cannot claim a Chelsea pension to which you are not entitled. However the Chelsea and Kilmainham Hospitals Act of 1826 makes no mention of it being illegal to dress up in their trademark scarlet coat and tricorne hat, so a citizen's arrest of anyone so attired would be ill-advised.

16. More Monopoly money is printed in a year, than real money printed throughout the world.

FALSE There are 200 notes per game and, according to the manufacturers Parker Brothers, 200 million games have been sold worldwide to date. This means there have been about 40 billion Monopoly notes produced since 1934. As the US alone produces 10 billion banknotes per year, this factoid fails to pass go.

17. If you take the head of a raccoon to the town hall of Henniker, New Hampshire, USA, they will give you $10.

FALSE QI emailed Henniker city council. Their response was: 'Perhaps [the law] did exist in our history, of that I am not sure. If it did exist, it is nothing that has been followed for over 50 years.' In 1994, a raccoon captured in Henniker tested positive for rabies. But even if anyone had thought to decapitate it and deliver the result to the mayor, no reward, it seems, would have been forthcoming.

18. Residents of Hawaii eat an average of 4 cans of Spam per person, per year - more than any other place on earth.

FALSE According to the manufacturers, Hormel Foods Inc., the island of Guam in Micronesia currently has the highest per capita consumption of SPAM in the world, consuming 16 cans per head per year. With just 5.5 cans per person per year, Hawaii trails along a poor second.

19. 5 British people were injured last year in accidents involving out of control Scalextric cars.

ARGUABLY FEASIBLE This factoid is indiscriminately applied to several different countries, including Scotland and Australia, which makes it highly suspect. On the other hand, the Royal Society for The Prevention of Accidents records 3,000 - 4,000 accidents in the UK every year involving a 'Small Toy Car, Vehicle, Plane or Boat', so maybe there's something in it.

20. The average duration of sexual intercourse for humans is 2 minutes.

HIGHLY UNLIKELY Would enough people agree to be observed on the job to make a statistically viable sample? On the other hand, if researchers just took people's word for it, how many interviewees would confess to a mere two minutes? More worryingly, a recent survey by Durex found that the average Briton enjoyed 22.5 minutes of foreplay, while another by *Mens' Health* magazine found that the total sexual experience lasted 18.64 minutes. From this it can be calculated that the Great British Shag (without the foreplay) lasts minus 3.86 minutes – substantially less than the figure given.

The truth is more important than the facts. FRANK LLOYD WRIGHT

FLUENT FINNISH

'Finding a Finnish grammar book was like entering a complete wine cellar, filled with bottles of an amazing wine of a kind and flavour never tasted before.'

JRR TOLKEIN, Letters

TOP TIPS

The Finnish for 'we' is **me**

The Finnish for 'they' is **he**.

There is no verb 'to have' in Finnish.

Practice your Finnish vowels using the word

haeaeyoeaie — wedding-night intention

a	like 'u' in "shut"
e	like 'e' in "net"
i	like 'i' in "tip"
o	like 'o' in "pot"
u	like 'u' in "put"
y	like 'ue' in French word "rue"
ae	(a with two dots) - like 'a' in "I am"
oe	(o with two dots) - like 'ea' in "early"

FINNISH DICTIONARY - Useful rules of thumb:

You'll have some chance of being understood if you just speak English and add an 'i' on the end of all the nouns*. If the English word you want to get across already ends in a 'i' sound, add an extra 'tti' forgood measure.

bussi - bus	immuniteetti - immunity	posti - post
faksi - fax	kapteeni - captain	postikortti - postcard
filmi - film	kassetti - cassette	potti - pot
fossilli - fossil	kassettidekki - cassette deck	puberteetti - puberty
hamsteri - hamster	klubi - club	testi - test
hitti - hit	kuriositeetti - curiosity	voltti - volt
hotelli - hotel	ornamenti - ornament	watti - watt

This does not always apply. 'Flipperi' is the Finnish for 'pinball machine'.

MANY FINNISH WORDS THAT SOUND QUITE LIKE ENGLISH ONES HAVE TOTALLY DIFFERENT MEANINGS:

happi	oxygen		nappi	button
hapy	vulva		pussi	bag
(note: be careful with this when asking for oxygen)			pyssy	gun
hissi	elevator		siili	hedgehog
hyppy	jump		silli	herring
kokenut	veteran		sissi	guerrilla

IF A FINNISH WORD ALREADY LOOKS EXACTLY LIKE ENGLISH, YOU CAN BE PRETTY CERTAIN THAT IT MEANS SOMETHING COMPLETELY DIFFERENT.

into	eagerness		manner	continent
kate	roofing, funds, reliability		otto	withdrawal
korea	gorgeous		tie	road
lama	depression			
lima	phlegm		vain	just, only
lumme	waterlily		veto	pull

SOME FINNISH WORDS SOUND LIKE THEY OUGHT TO MEAN 'YES' BUT DON'T:

ei	no
ja	and
jaa	hmm
jo	already
yö	night

The Finnish for 'yes' is myönteinen vastaus.

SOME FINNISH WORDS SOUND LIKE THEY MIGHT MEAN 'NO' BUT DON'T.

ne	they (for some reason he also means 'they')
niin	so, then, and
niin no	hmm, let's see
no	well
no niin	oh well, OK, sure
no no	there there; now, now; come, come.

The Finnish for 'no' is kielteinen vastaus.

MANY SHORT FINNISH WORDS LOOK AND SOUND LIKE THEY COULD ONLY BE FINNISH.

lumi	snow		nuttu	jacket
nuppi	knob		pusu	kiss
nuppu	bud		puu	tree
nurka	corner		sinko	rocket-launcher
nurmi	grass			

SOME LONG FINNISH WORDS LOOK LIKE THEY OUGHT TO MEANING SOMETHING ELSE:

jaakobinpaini	inner struggle
jobinposti	bad news
kapalot	swaddling clothes
lennonjohto	air traffic control
lukenut	well-read
oveton	doorless
ptruu!	whoa!
pullopantti	bottle bank

WORDS THAT ARE UNIQUE TO FINNISH

eno	a maternal uncle
kaksikymmenvuotias	a twenty-year-old
kirkonkylä	a small village with a church

GOOD LUCK!

Or onnea yrityksellesi, as we say in Suomi!

EXERCISES
Using the first example as a guide, make a reasonable stab at translating the proverbs below back into their original Finnish (TIME ALLOWED: 8 years)

THE CAKE IS FINE ON TOP, BUT THERE ARE CRICKETS INSIDE.

1. A woodpecker in the forest is mottled, but a man's life is more so.

2. In heaven you won't hear the mosquitoes.(HINT: mosquito - moskiitto)

3. Life is uncertain so eat your dessert first.

4. War does not determine who is right, only who is remaining.

5. As bottomless as a priest's sack. (HINT: sack - säkki)

6. It shrinks like a partridge before the end of the world.

7. There's a man like any other, said the flea in the sauna.

8. Time enough for the mouse to yawn when it's half inside the cat.

9. Don't mistake a sheep's head for a roasted turnip.(HINT: turnip - turnipsi)

10. A bit of dirt adds to the soup, a spider to the dough. (HINT: throat disease - kurkkutauti)

VOCABULARY

cake	kakku
top	kärki
but	kuitenkin
crickets	krikettipeli
is	on
killiksi	enough
kirppu	flea
kissa	cat
kuula	to hear

39

She said she was approaching forty, and I couldn't help wondering from what direction.

BOB HOPE

40x40

1. Forty is the only number written in English that has its letters in alphabetical order. **2.** 40% of people are killed by water, air and soil pollution. **3.** 40 % of 3-month-old babies regularly watch TV. **4.** A baby takes 40 weeks to develop from conception to birth. **5.** According to the *Journal of Clinical Nursing*, people are at their most lonely at the age of 40. **6.** According to a study by the Orange Prize for Fiction, 40 % of people in the UK never read a book. **7.** Derived from a Venetian word meaning 40, 'quarantine' gets its name from the incubation period of the Black Death. Before that, it was used to describe the desert where Jesus fasted for 40 days. **8.** Despite the apparent biblical fondness for the number (40 days and 40 nights, 40 years in the wilderness, etc.), there are actually more incidences of the word 'thirty' in the King James Version of the Bible (166 as against 145). **9.** The religious significance of the number 40 dates back to the disappearance of the Pleiades for the 40 days before the winter solstice. These 40 days were a time of hardship for the Babylonians, and their reappearance was greeted with great celebration. **10.** In Buddhism, the *Kammatthana* is a list of 40 subjects of meditation that includes elements like earth, water, fire and air; colours like yellow and red; bright light; virtues like morality and liberality; and objects of repulsion such as corpses (swollen); corpses (festering) and corpses (worm-eaten). **11.** The *Tessarakonteres*, a galley built for Ptolemy IV of Egypt, was the largest ever man-powered vessel. Its name means 'forty', after the number of banks of oars it had. It was manned by 400 sailors and propelled by 4,000 oarsmen. **12.** Herod was crowned King of Judea by the Roman senate in 40 BC. **13.** According to tradition, the first apparition of the Virgin Mary happened in the Spanish city of Zaragoza. She appeared to St James the Greater in 40 AD – while she was still alive. **14.** To be a judge in the Spanish Inquisition, you had to be at least 40 years old. **15.** The Italian version of the Royal Society, The National Academy of Sciences, is known as the 'Academy of Forty'. The Académie Française is limited to 40 members known as 'The Forty Immortals'. **16.** The 'Forty' was an Athenian court called upon when a dispute could not be solved by arbitration. It would randomly pick a citizen over 60 years of age who would make a decision to which both parties had to adhere. **17.** According to the *Oxford English Dictionary*, a 'forty' was Australian slang for a criminal. Newly arrived convicts were given 40 acres of land – in contrast to native Aussies born of convict parents, who were allowed 60 acres. **18.** A tetracontagon is a shape with 40 sides. **19.** Forty is the atomic number of zirconium, of which 900,000 metric tons are mined every year, almost all of it for use in nuclear reactors. **20.** Most vodka is 40% alcohol by vol. This is due to Dmitriy Mendeleev, the Russian chemist who created the periodic table. He established that 40% was the optimal ratio of water to alcohol to create the smoothest tasting spirit. **21.** The name WD40 comes from the fact that it took so many goes to develop the product - it stands for Water Displacement, 40th attempt. **22.** Kyrgyzstan is a landlocked country in central Asia. Its name means 'Land of 40 Tribes', represented on the country's flag by 40 rays of the sun. **23.** The Neem Tree is known in Swahili as *mwarobaini* because it can be used to cure 40 illnesses (*arobaini* means 40 in Swahili). **24.** According to Turkish superstition, a wish will come true if you say it out loud 40 times. **25.** In 2008, there were only 40 New Zealand fairy terns left in the world. **26.** A professional kangaroo hunter has to shoot a minimum of 40 animals a night to make ends meet. **27.** The largest number of people ever eaten by a single lion is 40. This compares poorly with man-eating leopards and tigers, whose records are 400 and 5,000 respectively. **28.** 'Forty-legs' is an old name for the centipede, which is more accurate: centipedes can have 40 legs but never 100. The words for centipede in Russian, Greek and Persian also refer to just such a 40-legged animal. **29.** The sperm of the fruit fly is almost 40 times its body length. **30.** Porcupines, mice and peanuts all have 40 chromosomes. **31.** The shipping forecast area 'Forties' gets its name from a sandbank called 'Long Forties' which is a consistent 40 fathoms in depth. On a nautical chart, this looks like a long line with the number '40' printed by it repeatedly. **32.** The 'roaring forties' is a name given by sailors to the latitudes between 40°S and 50°S. The name comes from the blustery, gale-force winds that blow along the Southern Ocean; there is no land there to slow the gusts. **33.** At Port Martin, Antarctica, winds of over 40 mph can be felt on more than 100 days of the year; yet the least windy spot on earth is on the same continent – at the centre of the central Antarctic plateau, where there is a permanent high-pressure system. **34.** In 2003, NASA announced that the southern hemisphere of Neptune was about to enter Spring, a season expected to last about 40 years. **35.** Forty Hill, a suburb of Enfield, North London, was the site of the Royal Palace of Elsynge, where, in 1547, the 9-year-old Edward VI was told of the death of his father (Henry VIII) and of his own accession to the throne. **36.** In the 17th century, Torrington Sq, Bloomsbury was called the Field of Forty Footsteps, after a duel which 2 brothers fought over a girl. She watched from a nearby bank as they killed each other. So lively was their swordplay that the grass their feet wore out never grew back. **37.** In 1910, Blanche Stuart Scott became the first woman to fly solo in an aeroplane. Aviator Glenn Curtiss allowed Scott to borrow his 'plane, having first inserted a block of wood behind the throttle pedal to stop her from reaching the necessary speed to take off. However, 'something happened' and Scott managed to get the 'plane 40 ft up in the air. **38.** In 1778, Forty Fort, Pennsylvania, hosted the Wyoming Massacre, where 360 American men, women, and children were killed by British and Iroquois forces. **39.** In 1981, Ronald Reagan became the 40th President of the US and the oldest to be elected to office, at just three months shy of 70. **40.** Forty is the life expectancy for men in Swaziland and for women in Mozambique. 53.6% of Zambians don't even reach 40.

To live beyond 40 is bad taste. DOSTOEVSKY (who died aged 60)

FETISH

~FROM THE PORTUGUESE~

feitico ≈ sorcery & LATIN ~ *facticius* ≈ made by art.

'Fetish' is the name given to an AMULET thought to contain a specific spirit possessing magical powers. Most fetishes take the form of a doll or statue and the spirit they contain must usually be fed like a living thing.

:::::

THE WORD WAS ORIGINALLY USED TO DESCRIBE WEST AFRICAN AMULETS FROM THE GUINEA COAST ALTHOUGH THEY ARE ALSO FOUND IN POLYNESIA, AUSTRALASIA, NORTH & SOUTH AMERICA AND THE ARCTIC.

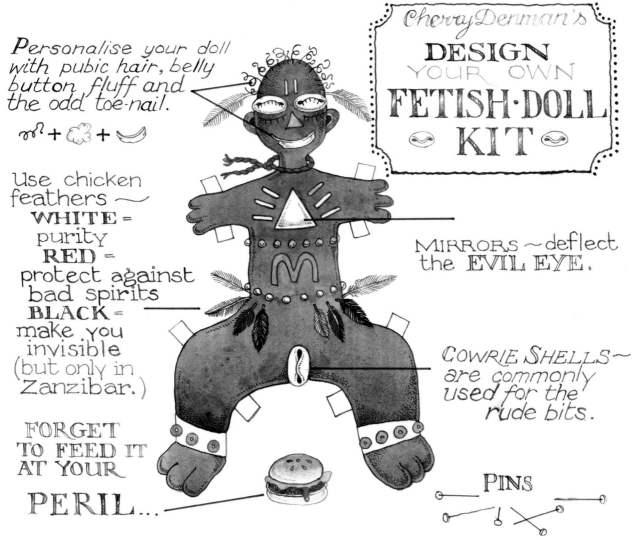

Personalise your doll with pubic hair, belly button fluff and the odd toe-nail.

Use chicken feathers ~
WHITE = purity
RED = protect against bad spirits
BLACK = make you invisible (but only in Zanzibar.)

FORGET TO FEED IT AT YOUR

PERIL...

Cherry Denman's

DESIGN YOUR OWN FETISH·DOLL KIT

MIRRORS ~ deflect the EVIL EYE.

COWRIE SHELLS ~ are commonly used for the rude bits.

PINS

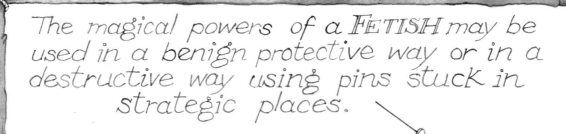

The magical powers of a FETISH may be used in a benign protective way or in a destructive way using pins stuck in strategic places.

∼: IN PSYCHOLOGY :∼

THE WORD IS USED TO DENOTE A CONDITION IN WHICH SEXUAL GRATIFICATION IS OBTAINED FROM HANDLING SOME OBJECT OR PART OF THE BODY OTHER THAN THE SEXUAL ORGANS.

OCHLOPHILIA

sexual love of crowds

ALTOCALCIPHILIA

a high heel fetish

UROLAGNIA

deriving sexual pleasure from urinating or watching others urinate.

A MYSOPHILIAC

is aroused by dirt, mud or filth.

FORMICOPHILIA

NOT A CHANCE

is sexual arousal caused by having insects crawl on one's genitals.

ENDYTOPHILIA

sexual love of people who are clothed.

ACROTOMOPHILIA

...hello sailor!

sexual attraction to amputees.

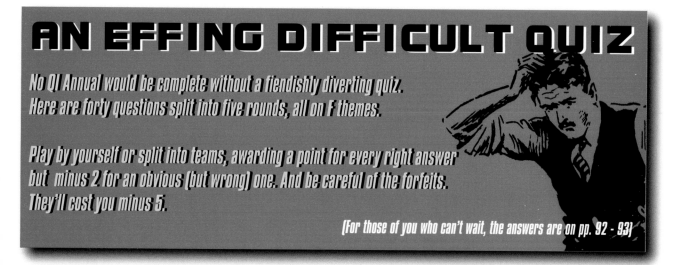

AN EFFING DIFFICULT QUIZ

No QI Annual would be complete without a fiendishly diverting quiz.
Here are forty questions split into five rounds, all on F themes.

Play by yourself or split into teams, awarding a point for every right answer
but minus 2 for an obvious (but wrong) one. And be careful of the forfeits.
They'll cost you minus 5.

(For those of you who can't wait, the answers are on pp. 92 - 93)

F WORDS

1. It's recently been shown that you can fold a piece of paper in half 12 times. If you had a piece of paper of normal thickness but infinite length and you could fold it in half as often as you liked, how many times would you have to fold it to make a stack of paper tall enough to reach from here to the sun?
2. Are fungi animals or plants?
3. What's quite interesting about the Southern Adder's Tongue fern?
4. Name the oldest, synthetic chemical process known to man.
5. What is a fylfot?
6. What creatures also known as *flying milk bottles* are Britain's longest-lived and most malodorous birds?
7. During the First World War, British soldiers in the trenches were issued with 'fish jam', which was so unpopular that most troops spent their own meagre wages to buy tinned sardines instead. What was it?

FRUIT

8. Which fruit, pulverised by NASA and used as thermal insulation in the nose cones of its rockets, has a Latin name that means 'the head of God's penis'?
9. Identify this fruit: its English name comes from the Latin for 'vagina', but it belongs to a family of plants whose name comes from the Greek for 'testicle'. (It doesn't smell like either.)
10. Which fruit was thrown at the bride and groom at ancient Roman weddings?
11. Where do most pineapples come from?
12. There are seven types of chicken comb. The first six are called single, rose, pea, buttercup, cushion and v-shaped. What is the name, commonly but wrongly described as a fruit, of the seventh kind?
13. What unusual labour force, organised into ten gangs of 50, was used to harvest plums in the Santa Clara Valley in California in 1905?
14. What fruit provides the flavour of the Italian soft drink 'Dribly' and the Greek soft drink 'Zit'?

FAITH

15. What is the fastest growing faith in the world?
16. In which faith is God a woman?
17. In which faith is it an article of belief that God took early retirement in 1914?
18. Which is the only major faith in the world not to use the swastika as part of its symbolism?
19. In Sufism, an ancient mystical offshoot of Islam, that some say is the root religion predating all others (and from whose Whirling Dervishes others believe Morris dancing is derived), adepts are able to practise telepathy. What do they mainly use their telepathic powers for?

20. In Zen, the paradoxical statements intended to jolt practitioners into enlightenment are called *koan*. The word for enlightenment itself is *satori*. What is *zazen*?
21. An illiterate blacksmith's daughter founded which faith in Toad Lane, Manchester, in 1736?
22. How many times have Popes issued infallible statements?

F FOLK

23. John Meade Falkner (1858-1932) rose to a senior position with a firm of Newcastle armaments manufacturers before becoming honorary librarian to the Dean and Chapter of Durham Cathedral. What famous book did he write?
24. What was the middle name of William Faulkner, Nobel prize-winning author of the tough novels *Soldier's Pay* (1926), *The Sound and the Fury* (1929) and *As I Lay Dying* (1930).
25. What was the film star Tula Ellice Finklea better known as?
26. What was the pen name of the writer Cecil Lewis Troughton Smith (1899-1966)?
27. Which French writer is known as the father of Entomology?
28. What world-famous song concerns something entirely made of *Foraminiferans*?

THE F WORLD

29. What's quite interesting about St Henry, the patron saint of Finland?
30. How much of France is in Europe?
31. Citroën is a world-famous French car company, but the word 'citroen' is not French. What language is it from?
32. Where in the world is the Florin still legal currency?
33. In Solomon Islands pidgin, an *envelope* is 'trouser belong letter' and a *saw* is 'this fella pull-him-he-come push-him-he-go brother belong axe'. What is a 'hat belong finger'?
34. What is the name of the bay (beginning with F) where the world's highest tides occur?
35. Between 2000 and 2005, what extraordinary percentage of the forests of Guyana was cut down?

FLORILEGIUM

36. What did the fathers of Christopher Marlowe (1564-93), Joseph Stalin (1879-1953), Hans Christian Andersen (1805-75), Louis Braille (1809-52), Thomas Traherne (1637-74) and Patrick Kavanagh (1904-67) have in common?
37. What was the responsibility of the Roman god Fabulinus?
38. In which country was the use of the word 'fall' to mean autumn first used?
39. What was shot on the island of Gozo in 1982?
40. Who or what is Fafnir?

French Abuse: Find the Fake French Fraise

As everyone knows, a 'French letter' is slang for a condom and the 'French pox' for venereal disease. For hundreds of years, it has been traditional for the English to ascribe French origins to anything they see as dirty or disgusting.

But can you tell which of the following are real pieces of actual English slang, and which ones have been made up specially for the F Annual?

French abacus
A clitoris

French afternoon
Long lunch followed by sex with a member of staff

French bath
Fellatio

French bathe
To cover oneself in perfume to avoid washing

French bench
A woman's face

French butter
Vaseline

French cannibal
Syphilis

French clock
Cockerel

French cream
Brandy

French culture
Fellatio

French deck
Pornographic playing cards

French dip
Vaginal pre-coital fluid

French dressing
Semen

French Embassy
Any location, such as a gym or YMCA, allowing unbridled homosexual action

French entry
Manhole

French flies
Wasps

French-fried ice-cream
Semen

French girl
Prostitute who specializes in fellatio

French inhale
To blow smoke out through the nose

French job
Fellatio

French lady
Woman who specializes in fellatio but isn't a prostitute.

French lamb
Horse

French language training
Teaching fellatio**

French Malteser
Something that won't flush down the lavatory

French marbles
Syphilis

French marriage
Unscheduled sexual encounter
with a total stranger in the toilet on a train

French marzipan
Chicken skin

French measles
Syphilis

French mistress
A female tapir

French muesli
Scabs

French onions
Testicles

French overcoat
Thong

French pig
Syphilis

French plumbing
Violent rattling, thumping and gurgling
coming from next-door's bedroom

French poke
Intimacy with a bar of soap and a radiator

French policeman
Gynaecologist

French polishing
Rubbing oneself between two
ecclesiastical candles

French prints
Unusual heterosexual pornography

French screwdriver
Hammer

French spaghetti house
A brothel that also serves pasta

French towel
Wiping your cock on the curtains

French tricks
Oral sex

French uncle
Milkman

French vanilla
Black term for a sexy white woman

French vowels
The noises made during vigorous homosexual sex

French walk
The posture adopted by someone being thrown out of a
saloon

French wasps
Lisping Italian homosexuals

French window
1. Pants with a rear-entry flap
2. A mirror on the bedroom ceiling

French woman
Fortune-teller

French wrench
Something a plumber has to go and fetch,
allowing him to take an extended lunch
(with sex afterwards)

French yashmak
Panties with a hole in the front

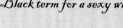

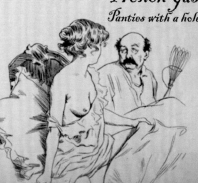

Answers on Page 67

FORAGING with SEAN LOCK.

As a moderately successful comedian I often find myself travelling up and down the country performing my humorous routines for the good townsfolk of Britain. Sounds like a good life, and it is. Apart from one thing: <u>food.</u> The only sustenance you can find in the average British city after 10 pm is a kebab or a curry. Eat that for 46 consecutive nights and you'll have a liver the size of a church Bible, no hair, and rickets due to the hours spent in cubicles. You'll be clumsy and slow and have the reflexes of a walrus.

My solution is not a Wild Bean Café or a packed lunch. No, I get out there in the countryside and <u>forage</u>. There are 10,000 species of edible plant in Europe, millions of insects and... mmm.... <u>squirrels.</u>

Coupled with rising food prices, there's never been a better time to put your boots on, march past the supermarket and into the woods.

Here are my DOs and DON'Ts of Foraging

DOS...

Pine needles make good tea.

Birch has a delicious sap you can drink – even more delicious if you've just been drinking pine needle tea.

Acorns and dandelion roots can be roasted for coffee. And if you grind up clover and ivy you get a Decaf Macchiato. (Only joking. What am I like! See how much fun you can have foraging!)

46

Hen-of-the-Woods fungus smells like mushrooms. And if you know where to find the right kind of mushrooms, it even looks like a hen too.

My favourite is cauliflower fungus. It smells like aniseed and tastes like walnuts. (What more could you want? **Jam on it**.)

The seed cases of wild roses contain more Vitamin C than any other fruit. (And supermarket oranges contain less Vitamin C than slippers.)

Poplar, willow and spruce bark are edible. (NB Look up **edible** in the dictionary before you try them. It doesn't mean 'tasty'…)

Grind insects between two stones and add them to stews. Insects are more nutritious than vegetables and, if you're eating them, they're not crawling up your trouser leg.

Woodlice, starfish, bees and whirligig beetles are all edible. But then so is a pasty from Sandbach Services.

FOREST FEAST

Baby squirrels are delicious! Pluck them from their nests inside hollow trees.

All lizards are edible but do not attempt to eat a Komodo Dragon! (You'll upset the greenies!)

Dazzle frogs at night with a bright light then club them to death. (Not as much fun as it sounds.)

Remember what they say in foraging circles: **'A snake is a steak'**. (It's not, of course: I'd much rather have a steak but it's preferable to a spruce bark wrap and it rhymes.)

Do trap! It requires less skill and leaves more time to forage.

Traps follow these 4 principles. **Mangle, Strangle, Dangle, Tangle.**

A balanced weight MANGLES, a snare STRANGLES, springy saplings whip the prey into the air so they DANGLE, and a net TANGLES.

But don't let it get stuck in your head like a mantra. And ignore anything that BANGLES or WANGLES – they won't help at all.

BAIT HINT

If you want to trap a particular animal, break open its droppings to find out what it's been eating and bait the trap accordingly. Or, if you're not keen on rummaging in poo, use chocolate buttons.

47

Don's...

It's been 3 days now, it must be dead

...Bastard Cashew nuts... Bastard Cashew nuts...

Never pick up a snake until you are certain it is dead. Snakes feign death convincingly.
(Well, there's only one way to feign death.)

Wild potato fruits (which look like tomatoes) are poisonous. Wild tomato plants are edible but look like wild potatoes. So my advice is to get a couple of rocks and some earwigs and start grinding.

Cashew nuts are poisonous unless peeled and boiled and if you do boil them the fumes can blind you. So let's have a minute's silence for whoever found that out.

DON'T EAT WASPS!

They are the master-race and they don't like it.

There you are Grandad, your Lupin tea

Sigh... Not tonight dear, I've a headache

TIME FOR A TREAT

Gather blackberries from brambles and then use the bramble canes to extract rabbits out of their sleeper holes. Sounds nasty but if you've been grinding earwigs all week...

Lupins cause inflammation of the stomach and intestines that can prove fatal.

Buttercups cause severe inflammation of the intestines. I don't feel sorry for whoever found this out 'cos they are flowers and you're not meant to eat flowers.

Cowbane causes death within minutes. Ow!

Shark liver is poisonous. (It's all the neoprene from the wetsuits: they can't digest it.)

Don't Hunt! It's illegal.

I hope this modest guide will encourage you to plunder meadow, hedgerow and fen till there is nothing left. Happy Foraging!

And remember – mangle, strangle, dangle, tangle, mangle, strangle, dangle, tangle, mangle, strangle, dangle!

ROWAN ATKINSON'S
FURNITURE MASTERCLASS

One of the maddening things about ready-assembled furniture is that it never comes with instructions. If you buy a new video camera or an iron or something and you can't get it to work, at least you can always blame the manual. But with furniture, it's always your responsibility.

Here's my essential guide to Getting It Right.

Incorrect use of Planter

49

BASIC CHAIR TECHNIQUE

A chair is a very difficult object. LUDWIG MIES VAN DER ROHE

The domestic chair didn't become a common object until the 16th century. For thousands of years, only the powerful and important sat on them. Now, you too can learn to do it.

Good but feet should be a bit nearer the floor.

Bottom not near enough to chair.

Ideal if frightened of mice.

'The Sprinting Mantis' (advanced).

Commuter-style 'Reserved Seat' option.

Ideal if frightened of chairs.

Ideal if wet indoors.

No. (Newspaper is missing.)

CHAIR PLUS

You've now mastered single-chair operation. Let's move on. It's quite common to find several identical pieces of multiple-legged furniture clustered together. Powerful and important people use these for 'dinner parties' (long meals in the dark).

WRONG
Wine glass completely absent.

WRONG
Wine glass upside down.

WRONG
Wine glass too big.

BATHROOM FURNITURE

As a trained engineer, I tend to divide furniture into 'hardware', 'software' and 'wetware'. Hardware is stuff like tables, software is armchairs, beds and so forth. Wetware is my term for stools (also known as plop-plops) plus wee-wee and soaping the unmentionables.

English-style.

Scottish-style.

Couldn't get to the lavatory in time.

Not a shower (notice absence of soap-dish).

**IMPORTANT!
IT IS BAD
MANNERS TO PUT
YOUR FEET ON
THE FURNITURE.**

WRONG

Nearly right.

Nowhere near right.

Just plain silly.

51

FALCON VS FERRET

Which would you take home? Both are fearless, both are able to make a contribution to the family budget by bringing home a steady stream of furred and feathered game, both have been domesticated for millennia, but which one edges it for fun, form and function?

HERE'S HOW THEY SCORED ON OUR 10-POINT RATING SYSTEM.

TRAINABILITY: 9
You can get a falcon to perform to a very high standard by understanding its instincts. Training them is painstaking work and very rewarding but don't ever expect them to talk, or to hang upside down, or to adopt a baby rabbit.

ECONOMIC VALUE: 5
A well-trained falcon can be used to catch rabbits or quail but the hundreds of hours of training and supply of food probably mean you'll always be down on the deal in purely monetary terms.

EDIBILITY: 0
Even if you were desperate they're hardly worth the bother – their feathers weigh twice as much as their bones. Imagine the body of a thrush with huge talons and an abnormally large hooked beak – that's what a plucked falcon looks like.

DRESSING UP: 7
They look good in a hood, which can be quite flash and decked out with gaudy feathers and embroidery. And, at a pinch, their jesses (restraining straps) could be picked out in gold lamé. They look great on your arm at a party.

FERTILITY: 2
You don't have to breed them, so unlikely to be an issue. If you do want 'baby falcons', get help, much as you would if you decided to keep pandas. It's about that easy.

THERAPEUTIC VALUE: 6
Watching a falcon fly, dive, swoop an strike is exhilarating, particularly if you've trained it yourself. But don't expect empathy or affection – their small reptilian brains don't have room

CONTRIBUTIO TO THE LANGUAGE:
Few animals have contribut more: if you'r 'fed up', 'at th end of your tether', 'in a bate', 'alluring live in a 'mews act like a 'cad' go for an evening's 'boozing', you owe it all to falconry.*

CUDDLEABILITY: 0
Falcons are magnificent and aloof. They're wonderful to look at, but remember you are only interesting to them as a source of food. So don't be surprised if they try to bite you.

BOTHER: 3
Lots of equipment, need for exercise, incompatability with other birds, risk of losing them altogether when they're flying. Difficulty in explaining 'accidents' to next-door neighbours' now hamsterless children.

SUPERPOWERS: 9
The peregrine falcon in a dive is the fastest animal on the planet reaching speeds of 215 mph (346 kph). A falcon's visual acuity is 8 times better than ours: they can spot a hamster from 2 miles/3.2 km away. As they dive, their eye muscles adjust the curvature of the eyeball to maintain sharp focus. When they hit, tendons in their claws snap shut to break their prey's neck (imagine being able to shatter a full wine bottle by squeezing your hand shut).

OVERALL SCORE: 52

CONTRIBUTION TO THE LANGUAGE: 2
Not much other than 'ferreting' in the sense of searching for something. Allegedly, 'ferret' comes from the Sanskrit root, 'bher-' meaning 'to carry or bear' from which we also get 'furtive', 'pheromone', 'fertile' and 'suffer'.

SUPERPOWERS: 7
One of the hardest bites in the animal kingdom, a ferret can snap a pencil without blinking and will crunch up every scrap of a bunny's bone, nail and fur for roughage. They can smell prey from hundreds of metres away, can drag a load 3 times their weight and leap 4 times their body length from a standing start. And they never get tired: they will kill rabbits non-stop, for as long as you let them.

THERAPEUTIC VALUE: 9
Ferrets are such cheerful, perky little animals they even get used as therapy animals for the severely depressed or trauma victims. They make very cute chirpy noises and do silly slightly unco-ordinated dances when you pay them attention. They aren't needy (like dogs), but are always pleased to see you (unlike cats).

TRAINABILITY: 6
You can teach a ferret to come to its name and roll over, but that's about it. They have absolutely no homing instinct and have a talent for getting themselves wedged in dark and difficult places. You don't really train them to catch rabbits – it's just what they do.

DRESSING UP: 7
There's quite a sub-culture of dressing up pet ferrets. 'Ferret World', the one-stop ferret shop, stock football strips, Hallowe'en and Father Christmas costumes, waxed jackets and a 'Phantom of the Opera' cape bought by ferret-owning barristers because it looks like a legal gown.

ECONOMIC VALUE: 9
A morning's ferreting can bring in a dozen or more rabbits: nutritious, delicious, free protein. To overcome any resistance from rabbit-lovers, mince the meat and make bunny burgers: much less squeam-inducing.

CUDDLEABILITY: 5
They look cute and will happily curl up in your lap and wriggle inside your jumper. But beware: their latin name, 'Mustela putorius furo', translates as 'musk-bearing, stinking thief' and it's not without cause. Ferrets stink. Be prepared to change clothes after handling (if it's a male, or hob, burning the clothes may be cheaper).

EDIBILITY: 0
Mustelids are edible, but it's hard to imagine a ferret fricassee (it's the smell). Besides, eating them is expressly forbidden in Leviticus 11:30: they are nailed as 'unclean' along with chameleons, lizards, snails and moles.

FERTILITY: 2
Slightly tricky – the jill (female) can die if they aren't mated when they're on heat, which is twice a year and a single jill could easily produce 27 kits a year. That's more than anyone needs. Try to borrow a vasectomised male (hoblet) but be warned: even safe ferret sex is rough, noisy and can go on for hours.

*'Bate' means pointless wing flapping. 'Booze' or 'bouse' is the term for the bird's drinking; a 'cadger' or 'cad' was the lowly person who carried the falcon for the falconer.

BOTHER: 8
No more work than a hamster – they sleep 18 hours a day. If you do take 'em out ferreting, all you'll need are 20 nets, a shovel (in case they fall asleep on the job) and the 'cojones' to knock a rabbit on the head.

OVERALL SCORE: 55

53

WHAT'S A FOOT?

FOOT: *the lower extremity of the leg below the ankle*

Feet excrete up to half a pint of moisture every day. They have over 250,000 sweat glands.

~HYPERHYDROSIS~ otherwise known as **SWEATY FEET**

FOOT~SOLDIER

THE *LARGEST* FEET IN THE WORLD BELONG TO ~*MATTHEW McGRORY* HIS FEET ARE A SIZE **28½ US**

BROMOHYDPOSIS
IS
THE MEDICAL TERM FOR
FOOT ODOUR

£ FOOTSIE $

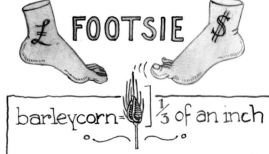

barleycorn = ⅓ of an inch

Feet size in England are measured in **BARLEYCORNS**

MADELINE ALBRECHT HOLDS THE WORLD RECORD FOR "MOST FEET SNIFFED" SHE WORKS FOR A RESEARCH COMPANY TESTING FOOT-CARE PRODUCTS FOR SCHOLL AND HAS SNIFFED APPROX-IMATELY 5,600 FEET.

FOOTWORK

athlete's foot

in-growing toenail

PODOMANCY IS DIVINATION BY MEANS OF EXAMINING THE FEET

love
death
health
wealth
misery

Your big toe is the most likely part of your body to be bitten by a vampire bat.

bunion

verruca

FOOTNOTE~

ELEPHANTS CAN LISTEN TO AND COMMUNICATE WITH EACH OTHER THROUGH THEIR FEET.

CAPTIVE ELEPHANTS CAN SUFFER BADLY FROM ATHLETE'S FOOT.

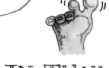

IN THAILAND IT IS EXTREMELY OFFENSIVE TO SHOW SOMEONE THE SOLE OF YOUR FOOT.

There is a significant correlation between foot-size and hand-size (but not between foot-size and penis size.)

— AS A CHILD, CHARLES DARWIN HAD PARTICULARLY SMELLY FEET —

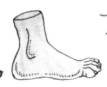

FOOTSTOOL

Charlie Chaplin's feet were insured for $150,000

Michael Flatley's were insured for $40,000,000

8% OF AMERICANS ARE SO FRIGHTENED OF GERMS FROM LAVATORIES THAT THEY FLUSH THE LOO WITH THEIR FEET.

FOOTLIGHTS

INVITE A PIG TO YOUR TABLE AND HE'LL PUT HIS FEET ON IT.

Russian Proverb

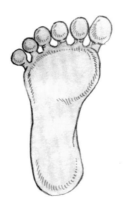

A QUARTER OF THE BONES IN THE HUMAN BODY ARE IN THE FEET.

FOOT-FAULT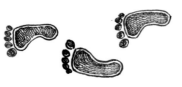

FI, FIE, FOE, FEMME! - a foto luv

Rob 'n' Ronni

A wise man once said the reason men and women fight is that each assumes the other has their own characteristics. A wise woman immediately disagreed with him. 'Women are tough, unsentimental creatures,' she said, 'subduing horses with a glance and lifting molten metal with our bare hands, whereas men are simple and kind and enjoy cooking.' 'That's what I just said,' said the wise man under his breath. 'Don't you take that tone with me!!' screamed the wise woman, furiously packing her suitcase and folding some tea towels the while.

My point is this. Women think men know how to carve meat and that all they want is sex. But what men really yearn for is *love*, expressed in the form of pre-sliced hot food. Men think that if women ask a question they want to know the answer, when what they're really after is a long argument followed by chocolate. Try to see things *her way*. Walk a mile in her shoes (vacuuming and remembering birthdays as you go). Then complain that your feet hurt. That should do the trick…

So I set out to woo Ronni by turning up 45 minutes late…

…and then asking if she needed any light bulbs changed.

He's insane

Soon, we were getting on like a house on fire. I made her laugh by regaling her with intimate descriptions of my girlfriend's accessories…

Omg! Prada trainers!!

…then I asked her if she fancied something to eat.

This was a mistake, probably because she thought I was implying she was anorexic.

…so I hurriedly went off to take out the rubbish.

56

While I was away, I asked myself some pretty tough questions. Like, what's the difference between an elephant's bottom and a postbox.

When I returned, I tried to get back into Ronni's good books with a typically feminine non-sequitur. 'Fylfot!!' I exclaimed.

'What exactly do you mean by that?!?' she demanded icily.
'I'll show you, cow!' was my rejoinder.

'Fylfot' is the Old English word for a swastika, as I was able to demonstrate visually.

After beating my brains out, she seemed to relax a little.

'Come with me', she said, 'I've got something I think you'll find interesting.'

It was a portal into the underworld!!!

No, not really.
She wanted to show me her new belt.

We're happily married now, I'm pleased to say.

Though not to each other, thank God….

TO BE DISCONTINUED

57

FARSI PROVERBS

There are about 144 million speakers of Farsi (also known as Persian or Tajik) in the world. About half of them live in Iran, Afghanistan and Tajikstan where it is an official language. Persian is written in Arabic script, and Tajik in Cyrillic (Russian) script. In Afghanistan, Farsi is known as Dari. In some parts of Iran, Azerbaijan and Russia, it is known as Tat. This includes Christian-Tat and Judeo-Tat.

I   Not everything that is round is a walnut.

II   Not everything with a beard is your dad.

III   It is a mistake to point out the errors of elders.

IV   The wise man sits on the hole in his carpet.

V   He who wants a peacock must put up with India.

VI   If my aunt had a beard, she would have been my uncle.

VII   Two watermelons cannot be carried in one hand.

VIII   For every grape there are a hundred wasps.

IX   The bird in the air cannot be grilled.

X   I used to feel sorry for myself because I had no shoes, until I met a man who was dead.

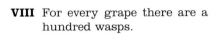

XI   He who wears dark glasses, sees the world as dark.

XII   Harvesting is not the work of a goat.

XIII   A drowning man is not troubled by rain.

XIV   He who has been bitten by a snake fears a piece of string.

XV   Death is a camel that sleeps in everyone's house.

XVI   Write kindness in marble and injuries in the dust.

XVII   Wherever you go, the sky is the same colour.

XVIII   Slanting baggage never reaches home.

XIX   Somersault in front of a buffoon!

XX   A kind word can bring a snake out of a hole.

XXI   If the sky falls, we shall all catch larks.

XXII   The chicken has one leg.

FACRONYMS

by Craig Brown

FBI are detectives, searching for clues;
FTSE's your cue to switch off the news.
FIAT is the car giant once owned by Agnelli;
FFJ dress in tights and appear on the telly.
FCUK is for preppies who want to be Chav;
FAQ answers everything but the problem you have.
FOH is the theatre crush prior to the show;
FYI is a note sent by those in the know.
FDR (i) was the Pres behind the New Deal;
FDR (ii) is for spouses to holler and squeal.
FDR (iii) is a vestige that precedes a seizure;
FDR (iv) is the People's Democratic Front of Indonesia.
FDR (v) is the technical term for Black Box;
FLAK is the ultimate school of hard knocks.
FRL's famous tome is *The Common Pursuit*;
FO is for toffs who are awfully astute.
FYR means more work (and more waste of ink);
FT is a paper, pretty in pink.
FOE ride on boats, saving dolphins and whales
FBRs are no danger (except when one fails).
FSB's what the KGB calls itself now;
FIFA's perpetually caught up in a row.
FANY arrive at each battle wreck quick;
FIRST is Forschungs Institut fur Rechnerarchitektur und Software Technik.
FRSL is the authors you remember but dimly;
FAX is no acronym (it's short for facsimile).
FM or AM? It's always a wrench;
FFS is For Fuck's Sake (pardon my French).
FSA monitors those who beg, steal or borrow;
FSH is Full Service History (I'll read it tomorrow).
FOAF is geek-speak for Friend Of A Friend;
FIN is an airport in Papua New Guinea,
But also means Finnish, or Finis –

The End.

FTSE - *Financial Times* Stock Exchange; FBI - Federal Bureau of Investigation; FIAT - Fabbrica Italiana Automobili Torino; FFJ - Fathers For Justice; FCUK - French Connection UK; FAQ - Frequently Asked Questions; FOH - Front of House; FYI - For Your Information; FDR (i) - Franklin Delano Roosevelt; FDR (ii) Family Dispute Resolution; FDR (iii) Firearm Discharge Residue; FDR (iv) Front Democrasi Rakjat; FDR (v) Flight Data Recorder; FLAK - FlugAbwehrKanone (German for Anti-Aircraft Guns); FRL - Professor F. R. (Frank Raymond) Leavis; FO - Foreign Office; FYR - For Your Reference; FT - *Financial Times*; FOE - Friends of the Earth; FBR - Fast Breeder Reactor; FSB - Federainaya Sluzhba Bezopasnosti; FIFA - Fédération Internationale de Football Association; FANY - First Aid Nursing Yeomanry; FRSL - Fellow of the Royal Society of Literature; FM - Frequency Modulation; FSA - Financial Services Authority; FIN - Three-letter shortcode for Finschhafen Airport, Papua New Guinea.

Grim Fairy Tales

Little Red Riding Hood

In 1697, a French poet named Charles Perrault (1628-1703) published eight traditional oral tales for the first time. In his version of Little Red Riding Hood, 'Le Petit Chaperon Rouge', the wolf (dressed as the Grandma he has just eaten) is a werewolf. To distract him and play for time, Red Riding Hood performs a full striptease, taking off one article of clothing at a time until she is stark naked and the werewolf is mad with lust. When he begs her to come to bed with him, she makes the excuse that she needs a pee. 'Do it in the bed,' gabbles the desperate werewolf, but the girl goes outside and escapes.

My what a big willy you have, Grandma!

Sleeping Beauty

In Giambattista Basile's bracingly titled 1634 collection, 'Lo cunto de li cunti' (that's 'The Tale of Tales' in Neapolitan, of course), a piece of flax gets under Sleeping Beauty's fingernail, which sends her to sleep. A foreign king stumbles upon her and finds her so irresistible he ravishes her, despite her death-like slumber. (Oh, perlease, what has monarchy sunk to!) Nine months later she gives birth to twins – while still asleep – and only wakes up when one of these, while searching for a nipple, sucks on her finger and removes the bewitching flax.

You came back...

Cinderella

In the 7th edition of the Grimm Brothers' collection (1857), Cinderella's step-sisters are as evil as we have come to expect them to be, but they are also beautiful – a chilling touch. Their mother, equally beautiful and a psychopathic sadist to boot, presents them with a knife and tells them to cut their feet down to size until the golden slipper fits. 'When you are queen you will no longer have to go on foot,' is her icy rationale. The mutilated feet are only discovered when a pigeon sees blood pouring out of the slippers. The sisters hobble along to Cinderella's wedding anyway, but the pigeons are on hand to peck their eyes out.

Off with her feet!

Many fairy stories started as traditional tales told by adults, to adults. They were passed on, spoken aloud, for hundreds of years before they were ever written down. Here are some early versions of familiar scenes from what have since become best-loved children's classics

Pinocchio

In Carlo Collodi's original story, first published in 1883, Pinocchio falls asleep in front of the fire and his feet burn off. (By this point he's already murdered the talking insect that will one day become known as Jiminy Cricket with a wooden mallet.) Later, a cat and a fox hang Pinocchio by the neck from an oak tree and wait for him to die. He then gets turned into a donkey, tied to a rock and thrown over a cliff. This is because the man who bought him wants to kill and skin him in order to make a drum.

'ev you gotta light boy?

Hmmm, pleasant little vintage!

Snow White

In the Grimm Brothers' version of 1812, the huntsman is sent by Snow White's jealous real mother (not her step-mother) to bring back her daughter's lungs and liver, which she plans to salt, cook and eat. (In earlier variants of the tale, she also asks for a phial of the girl's blood to drink, helpfully suggesting that the murderer uses her severed toe as a stopper.) The queen gets her come-uppance when she is forced to attend Snow White's wedding wearing red-hot iron shoes and dance in them until she drops down dead.

The Frog Prince

One of the oldest-known versions of the story is a folktale from Hungary. The frog is guarding a well and won't allow the girl to draw water for her family. His suggestions become ever more bold until finally he demands that the girl's father let him go to bed with her. The thirsty father agrees and next morning the family find a handsome young man lying in her arms. Just to remove any doubts over what has happened, the tale ends: 'they hastened to celebrate the wedding, so that the christening might not follow it too soon.'

... but this is a Grimm Fairy Tale, my dear - you'll have to go a lot further than that...

Finger Games

How to win at
Rock-Paper-Scissors*

The oldest game

Recent research into the human brain has revealed that the same area that controls our tongues and larynx also controls the movement of our hands and fingers. Some even think we used our hands to talk before our voices. So humans may have been playing RPS even longer than we've been talking (replace scissors with knives and paper with leaves and a Neanderthal version is perfectly possible). After all, it is a universal way of solving problems, is played everywhere and requires no board or fancy equipment.

Pure luck

Most beginners make the fatal error of believing RPS is a game governed by the laws of chance. In fact it is as psychologically charged and complex as chess. It even has its own international regulatory body, The World RPS Society based in Toronto, who mount annual world championships.

RPS Tactics

Here's our cut-out-and-keep guide to winning the oldest game of all.

Stage 1: Beginners

There are two fundamental RPS maxims:

MAXIM 1: Rock is for rookies

Never play rock as your first move.
As the old adage goes, 'rock is for rookies.'

The best move is to play paper, but most people can work this out, so play scissors.

However, due to this fact appearing in pieces like this; the top strategy is now to play rock.

MAXIM 2: Know your opponent

If your opponent appears aggressive they are most likely to play rock.
Action: Play paper.

If your opponent appears thoughtful, they are most likely to play paper.
Action: Play scissors.

If your opponent seems cocky or devious, they will probably play scissors.
Action: Play rock.

Stage 2: Intermediate

In best-of-three play, there are a number of combinations that will keep your opponent guessing.

The Avalanche

Rock-Rock-Rock – ultra-offensive strategy that works because after a single aggressive throw most opponents assume you would be reckless to throw a second, and a complete nutter to throw a third.

The Bureaucrat

Paper-Paper-Paper – the ultimate softly-softly strategy. This works particularly well against rock-throwing show-offs with a serious avalanche habit. Also, the risk of coming up against scissors is lower: it's easily the least popular throw, only played 29.6% of the time.

The Toolbox

Scissors-Scissors-Scissors – not to be used against beginners (owing to their fondness for rock) but can be particularly effective if you 'spring-load', i.e. push your scissor fingers against the inside of your hand so that they get fired out quickly when throwing.

The Crescendo

Paper-Scissors-Rock – this gambit gives the illusion of weakness with its opening throw but ends in a devastating rock climax which will shatter your opponent's confidence.

Fistful of Dollars

Rock-Paper-Paper – the swift switch from offence to defence will unnerve even the best opponent. Most effective against a player who is trying to control his/her temper.

Stage 3: Advanced

Tells

All but the most professional RPS players reveal tiny changes to their behaviour or expressions that help give away their next move. Inexperienced players tend to change their stance as they change their throw and stay in the same position if they plan to repeat the previous throw.

Here are some useful pointers.

Jaw-clench – adrenalin causes people to clench their jaws to better absorb a punch in the face. A jaw-clencher will always throw rock.

Little finger knuckle – if the knuckle of your opponent's little finger moves slightly inwards, this means he or she is about to extend his/her ring and index fingers into a scissors. You can also tell a lot about a player by the angle of their scissors.

Curve-ball – in professional play, a paper-throw must have the palm parallel to the ground, to avoid confusion with scissors. As a result, players often slightly curl their forearm towards their face when playing this move.

Professionalism and borderline cheating

Cloaking – making it look like you are throwing one move before switching at the last moment to another. Be careful: push this too far and the referee will award the game to your opponent.

Throw counting – paying careful attention to your opponent's throws to find a pattern. Humans are driven by patterns. This can be difficult, especially if your opponent clocks that you are a counter, and responds with lively, off-putting banter.

Crystal ball – this technique requires the gift of the gab – pretend to predict your opponent's next move – 'You're going to choose scissors again' – to narrow his/her options.

Overwhelming your opponent – if you have a physical advantage, try flexing your muscles, grunting and generally acting like a testosterone-fuelled Neanderthal before playing an unexpected scissors.

RPS: THE FACTS

The modern version of RPS is a Far Eastern game originally played during Chinese New Year.

When it first arrived in Japan in the late 19th century it was an adult drinking game played in the bars of Tokyo's red-light district.

In 2005 Christie's won a $20 million contract to sell a corporate client's collection of Picassos and Van Goghs after a game of rock, paper, scissors.

The elements alter from country to country: in France it's 'Rock-Scissors-Well'; in Malaysia, 'Rock-Beak-Well' and in Vietnam, 'Elephant-Human-Ant.'

The apology – making your throw extremely late and responding to the inevitable complaint with: 'Sorry, my fault. Let's do it again.' Reverse psychology dictates he or she will almost always attempt the same throw again. Use this gambit sparingly – some referees consider it cheating.

Further reading

The RPS bible is *The Official Rock Paper Scissors Strategy Guide* by Douglas & Graham Walker (Simon & Schuster, 2004) or you could visit their website: www.worldrps.com

* still called 'Scissors-Paper-Stone' by older British players.

RPS INTERNATIONAL

Jenken or Jan Ken Pon (Japan)
Kai bai bo (Korea)
Janjii (Thailand)
Roshambo (Southwestern USA)
Shnik Shnak Shnuk (Germany)
Farggling (USA)
Ching Chong Chow
(South Africa)

'My mum told me, "don't throw stones, don't play with scissors," I bet you're choking on those words now, eh mum?'

- Dave Bradbury, 1943 UK RPS champion.

FORM

Toroid

Infundibuliform

Please take a few moments to answer the following short questionnaire.

1. How many times have you been lost for words when trying to describe the shape of something?

a) Literally millions of times, it drives me mad!!
b) Fairly often, it bothers me quite a lot.

c) Relatively rarely, I am rather articulate.
d) Who are you? How did you get this number?

That's it. Well done. If you answered a, b or c, score two points - your worries are over. By memorising the list of *form*-type words on these pages, you will soon be '*top* of the form' and get to Cambridge University with the chance to become the next Stephen Hawking, Stephen Fry or Stephen Poliakoff. Pretty well everyone at Cambridge called Stephen becomes world-famous and nearly all of them managed it simply because they understood correct *form*. Don't worry if you're not called Stephen *at the moment*, your tutor or spymaster can help you fill in The Form in due course.

If you answered d, you may be interested to know that you are suffering from Rajasthani Call-Centre Syndrome, where you imagine that you are hearing voices in your telephone with impenetrable sub-continental accents asking for the second digit of your security code. Regrettably, this condition is incurable, but can be relieved by being incomprehensible back. Pepper your responses generously with some of the words here and just hear those voices ring off in despair!

Acorn-shaped: Balanoid
Apple-shaped: Pomiform
Arrow-shaped: Beloid; sagittal
Awl-shaped: Subulate
Axe-shaped: Securiform
Barrel-shaped: Dolioform
Basin-shaped: Pelviform
Bell-shaped: Campanulate
Berry-shaped: Aciniform
Boat-shaped: Cymbiform; navicular; scaphoid
Boil-shaped: Bulliform
Bonnet-shaped: Mitrate
Book-shaped: Libriform
Bristle-shaped: Setiform
Brush-shaped: Aspergilliform; muscariform
Bunch-of-grapes-shaped: Uvelloid
Buttock-shaped: Natiform
Cake-shaped: Placentiform
Cap-shaped: Pileated
Caterpillar-shaped: Eruciform
Chisel-shaped: Scalpriform
Claw-shaped: Unguiform
Cloud-shaped: Nubiform
Coin-shaped: Nummiform
Comb-shaped: Pectiniform; cteniform
Cone-shaped: Infundibuliform
Cow-shaped: Boviform
Crescent-shaped: Lunate; menisciform
Cucumber-shaped: Cucumiform
Cup-shaped: Poculiform; scyphiform
Cushion-shaped: Pulvilliform
Dagger-shaped: Pugioniform
Dart-shaped: Belemnoid

Doughnut-shaped: Toroid
Drop-shaped: Guttiform
Drum-shaped: Tympaniform
Ear-shaped: Auriform
Egg-shaped: Ooidal
Fan-shaped: Rhipidate; flabelliform
Feather-shaped: Pinnate
Flowerpot-shaped: Vasculiform
Fork-shaped: Furcular
Fringe-shaped: Laciniform
Frog-shaped: Raniform
Funnel-shaped: Chaonoid
Girdle-shaped: Zosteriform
Goat-shaped: Capriform
Groove-shaped: Sulciform
Half-moon-shaped: Semilunate
Hammer-shaped: Malleiform
Handle-shaped: Manubrial
Hatchet-shaped: Pelecoidal
Helmet-shaped: Cassideous; galeated
Herring-shaped: Harengiform
Hood-shaped: Cuculate
Hook-shaped: Unciform
Horn-shaped: Corniculate; corniform; ceratoid
Horseshoe-shaped: Hippocrepian
Ivy-shaped: Hederiform
Jellyfish-shaped: Medusiform
Jug-shaped: Urceolate
Keyhole-shaped: Clithridiate
Kidney-shaped: Nephroid; reniform
Knife-shaped: Cultriform
Ladder-shaped: Scalariform
Leaf-shaped: Phylliform; foliform
Mosquito-shaped: Culciform

Mouse-shaped: Muriform
Mulberry-shaped: Moriform
Needle-shaped: Acicular
Net-shaped: Clathrate
Nipple-shaped: Mamilliform
Nose-shaped: Nasutiform
Nostril-shaped: Nariform
Nut-shaped: Nuciform
Oar-shaped: Remiform
Oat-shaped: Aveniform
Oval-shaped: Vulviform
Owl-shaped: Strigiform
Oyster-shaped: Ostreiform
Paintbrush-shaped: Pencilliform
Palm-leaf-shaped: Spadicious
Partition-shaped: Septiform
Pea-shaped: Pisiform
Pebble-shaped: Calciform
Pincer-shaped: Cheliform
Pine-cone-shaped: Pineal
Pipe-shaped: Fistuliform
Plate-shaped: Lamelliform
Pouch-shaped: Scrotiform
Purse-shaped: Bursiform
Ribbon-shaped: Taenioid
Rice-shaped: Riziform
Ring-shaped: Cingular; circinate; cricoid
Rod-shaped: Vergiform
Rodent-shaped: Gliriform
Roof-shaped: Tectiform
S-shaped: Annodated
Saddle-shaped: Selliform
Saucer-shaped: Acetabuliform
Sausage-shaped: Allantoid
Saw-shaped: Serriform
Scimitar-shaped: Acinaciform

Screw-shaped: Helicoid
Seaweed-shaped: Fucoid
Shark-shaped: Squaliform
Shield-shaped: Aspidate; peltastiform; scutiform
Sheep-shaped: Oviform
Sickle-shaped: Drepaniform
Sieve-shaped: Coliform
Slipper-shaped: Soleiform
Slug-shaped: Limaciform
Socket-shaped: Glenoid
Spade-shaped: Palaceous
Spinning-top-shaped: Trochiform
Spur-shaped: Calcariform
Stirrup-shaped: Stapediform
Sword-shaped: Xiphoid
Tail-shaped: Caudiform
Tear-shaped: Lachrymiform
Thorn-shaped: Spiniform; aculeiform
Toad-shaped: Bufoniform
Tongue-shaped: Linguiform
Tower-shaped: Pygoidal; turriform
Tree-shaped: Arborescent; dendriform
Trumpet-shaped: Buccinal
Turnip-shaped: Napiform
U-shaped: Hyoid
Umbrella-shaped: Umbraculiform; pileiform
Violin-shaped: Panduriform
Wedge-shaped: Sphenoid; cuneiform
Whip-shaped: Flagelliform
Wolf-shaped: Lupiform
Woodpecker-shaped: Piciform
Worm-shaped: Vermiform

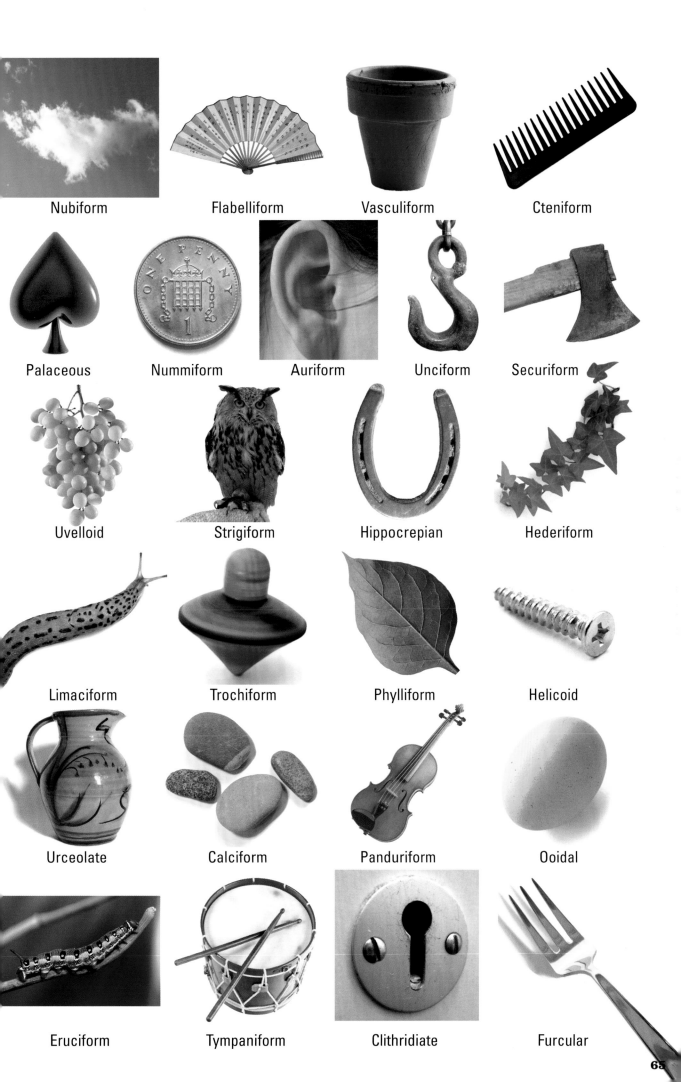

Nubiform

Flabelliform

Vasculiform

Cteniform

Palaceous

Nummiform

Auriform

Unciform

Securiform

Uvelloid

Strigiform

Hippocrepian

Hederiform

Limaciform

Trochiform

Phylliform

Helicoid

Urceolate

Calciform

Panduriform

Ooidal

Eruciform

Tympaniform

Clithridiate

Furcular

FOOTBALL
IN MOUTH

Think of a number between 10 and 11.
RON ATKINSON

Argentina are the second best team in the world and there is no higher praise than that. KEVIN KEEGAN

Chile have three options - they could win or they could lose. KEVIN KEEGAN

When England go to Turkey there could be fatalities - or even worse, injuries.
PHIL NEAL

I'd like to play for an Italian club, like Barcelona.
MARK DRAPER

I can see the carrot at the end of the tunnel. STUART PEARCE

It all went a bit grape-shaped. JASON McATEER

I always used to put my right boot on first, and then obviously my right sock. BARRY VENISON

I'd love to be a mole on the wall in the Liverpool dressing room at half time. KEVIN KEEGAN

Don't ask me what a typical Brazilian is because I don't know what a typical Brazilian is. But Romario was a typical Brazilian.
BOBBY ROBSON

If you can't stand the heat in the dressing room, get out of the kitchen. TERRY VENABLES

Goalkeepers aren't born today until they're in their late twenties or thirties. KEVIN KEEGAN

The Germans only have one player under 22, and he's 23.
KEVIN KEEGAN

People will look at Bowyer and Woodgate and say, 'Well, there's no mud without flames'. GORDON TAYLOR

Unfortunately, we keep kicking ourselves in the foot.
RAY WILKINS

You can't say my team aren't winners. They've proved that by finishing fourth, third and second in the past three seasons. GERARD HOULLIER

Well, Clive, it's all about the two Ms - movement and positioning. RON ATKINSON

And Seaman, just like a falling oak, manages to change direction. JOHN MOTSON

The tide is very much in our court now. KEVIN KEEGAN

We must have had 99% of the match. It was the other 3% that cost us. RUUD GULLIT

That could have been his second yellow card - if he'd already got his first one of course. TREVOR BROOKING

I was feeling as sick as the proverbial donkey. MICK McCARTHY

We don't want our players to be monks. We want them to be better football players because a monk doesn't play football at this level. BOBBY ROBSON

Viv Anderson has pissed a fatness test. JOHN HELM

At this level, if five or six players don't turn up, you'll get beat. KEVIN KEEGAN

You're on your own out there with ten mates.
MICHAEL OWEN

He may well yet pull his team from the edge of the cliff by the scruff of its neck into the land of milk and honey.
JONATHAN HAYWARD

He dribbles a lot and the opposition don't like it - you can see it all over their faces. RON ATKINSON

I felt a lump in my throat as the ball went in.
TERRY VENABLES

If someone in the crowd spits at you, you have just got to swallow it. **GARY LINEKER**

That kind of ball is meat and two drink for the Palace defence. **DENIS IRWIN**

I wouldn't be surprised if this game went all the way to the finish. **IAN ST JOHN**

We didn't underestimate them - they were just a lot better than we thought. **BOBBY ROBSON**

He's started anticipating what's going to happen before it's even happened. **GRAEME LE SAUX**

If I had a blank piece of paper there'd be five names on it. **KEVIN KEEGAN**

I don't think there's anyone bigger or smaller than Maradona. **KEVIN KEEGAN**

I never make predictions and I never will. **PAUL GASCOIGNE**

I'm not a believer in luck, but I do believe you need it. **ALAN BALL**

Mark Hughes crossed every i and dotted every T. **ROBBIE SAVAGE**

It's understandable that people are keeping one eye on the pot and another up the chimney. **KEVIN KEEGAN**

The world is my lobster. **KEITH O'NEILL**

Celtic manager Davie Hay still has a fresh pair of legs up his sleeve. **JOHN GREIG**

I definitely want Brooklyn to be christened though I don't know into what religion yet. **DAVID BECKHAM**

BECKHAM

Aston Villa are seventh in the league. That's almost as high as you can get without being one of the top six. **IAN PAYNE**

That was the perfect penalty - apart from he missed it. **ROB McCAFFREY**

He had defenders swarming around him like a wet blanket. **GERRY ARMSTRONG**

I just wonder what would have happened if the shirt had been on the other foot. **MIKE WALKER**

FILL IN THE BLANK

Fun mini-quiz

1. Wong
2. Lee
3. Chan
4. Chen
5. Li
6. Leung
7. Lam
8. ......
9. Ng
10. Chow
11. Wang
12. Liu
13. Wu
14. Ho
15. Nguyen
16. Huang
17. Cheung
18. Lin
19. Lau
20. Kim

(Answer on credits page)

French Abuse Answers

The real ones (copied from Cassell's Dictionary of Slang by Jonathon Green) are: French bath, French bathe, French cannibal, French cream, French culture, French deck, French dip, French dressing, French Embassy, French-fried ice-cream, French girl, French inhale, French job, French lady, French language training, French marbles, French measles, French pig, French prints, French screwdriver, French tricks, French vanilla, French walk and French woman.

And there is one trick one: French polishing is a real piece of English slang, but it doesn't mean 'rubbing oneself between two ecclesiastical candles'. It means fellatio.

67

For thousands of years China had a tradition of witty and influential court jesters with fantastic names. Their skill in using humour to escape punishment or gently ridicule their employers seems peculiarly modern. Which one are you?

BALDY CHUNYU

King Weiwang, ruler of the state of Qi from 378 to 343 BC was rescued from a life of drink and womanising by his fool Baldy Chunyu who told him a riddle in which the King was portrayed as a rather ineffective large bird squatting on the palace roof.

TWISTY POLE

The feckless emperor Qin Er Shi (229-207 BC) decided he wanted to lacquer the Great Wall. The famous fool and dwarf Twisty Pole subverted this lunacy by declaring it a brilliant plan but wondered how practical it would be to build a drying room large enough for the lacquer to harden.

NEWLY POLISHED MIRROR

The Emperor Zhuangzong (ruled 923-926) had a particularly feisty fool called Newly Polished Mirror who was once bold enough to strike the emperor's face, plunging the court into shock. Luckily, the emperor saw the funny side and rewarded him generously.

IN FULL STREAMER

A fool who was kidnapped by rebels during the reign of Emperor Xuanzong (685-762) and kept himself alive by entertaining his captors. He later managed to persuade the emperor of his loyalty by recounting dreams he'd had which showed the rebellion would fail and he would be released.

FITTING NEW BRIDLE

When threatened by a thuggish governor (who had recently burnt a rival city to the ground), he saved

WHAT KIND O

Have you ever told a funny joke in your entire life?

YES

NO

Are you a particularly brave person?

YES

YES

Do you have a witty response for every occasion?

NO

Do you like wine, women and DIY?

NO

YES

Do you like to fight dirty?

YES

NO

YES

· YOU ARE · **· TWISTY POLE ·**

· YOU ARE · **· BALDY CHUNYU ·**

· YOU ARE · **· NEWLY-POLISHED MIRROR ·**

· YOU ARE · **· GRADUALLY STRETCHING TALLER ·**

· YOU AR **· WILD PIG ·**

CHINESE FOOL AM I?

You are definitely NOT an ancient Chinese fool.

NO

Do you hate your boss?

NO

YES

Do you resent paying your taxes?

Are you popular at parties?

NO

NO

Are you a fan of the outdoors?

NO

NO

YES

Do you prefer *A Question of Sport* to *The Apprentice*?

YES

NO

Do you think you have psychic powers?

YES

YES

• YOU ARE •

• NOT A CHINESE FOOL •

• YOU ARE •

• TRULY ASSISTING UPRIGHTNESS •

• YOU ARE •

• FITTING NEW BRIDLE •

YOU ARE

SCORCHING VIRTUE

• YOU ARE •

• IN FULL STREAMER •

himself through the speed of his wit. When asked if he would beg for mercy, he said he had no need to beg as he could live by selling the charcoal produced by the governor's pyromania.

TRULY ASSISTING UPRIGHTNESS

Chinese fools often pushed it too far. This one was executed by Emperor Dezong (742-805) for satirising tax policies by dressing as a pauper. This was an unpopular decision: most people felt strongly it was the place of jesters to 'provide indirect advice' through humour.

SCORCHING VIRTUE

Scorching Virtue was severely punished for criticising the prime minister of the Emperor Huizong (1082-1135) who had flattened a village to build a new park. Wittily comparing it to another park which looked like a bank of clouds, the new park, he said, was like a downpour, because it had caused so many tears to fall.

GRADUALLY STRETCHING TALLER

Gradually Stretching Taller persuaded Emperor Liezu (d 949) to stop overtaxing his subjects by suggesting that even the rain was refusing to enter the city for fear of being taxed. The emperor laughed, repealed the offending law and the heavens immediately opened.

WILD PIG

Emperor Xizong (1119-1149) fancied himself as a great footballer. 'If I sat an exam in dribbling, I'd come top of the class' he told his fool, Wild Pig. 'Yes, but you'd end up at the bottom of the league of good rulers,' came the quick retort. The Emperor laughed and gave up his dreams of football glory.

Oo-er! Sounds a bit rude...

TINKLING FANNY

Fanny Mendelssohn was the older sister of the composer Felix. The more famous male Mendelssohn readily admitted that she was a better pianist than he was, but due to 19th-century attitudes towards women, she never reached the fame that her talent deserved. Fanny composed 466 pieces of music, several of which were published under Felix's name. Queen Victoria's favourite Mendelssohn song was 'Italien' from his Op. 8 collection: it was actually written by Fanny. Fanny's father is reported as telling her: 'For you music can and must only be an ornament. You must prepare more earnestly and eagerly for your real calling, I mean the state of a housewife.' Fanny and Felix both died of a stroke in the same year, 1847. She was 41; he was 37.

FLYING FANNY

Francina 'Fanny' Blankers-Koen was a 30-year-old Dutch athlete and mother of two known as 'Amazing Fanny' or 'The Flying Housewife'. At the 1948 London Olympics, she won 4 gold medals, trouncing the entire British Olympic team single-handed – Britain only won 3 golds that year – and remains one of just four people (and the only woman) to win 4 track and field golds at a single Games. During her career, she set world records in 7 different events. In 1999, the IAAF voted her 'Female Athlete of the Century'.

ROCKY FANNY

Fanny is a minor planet orbiting the sun, otherwise known as Asteroid 821. Discovered in 1916 by German astronomer Max Wolf (1863-1932), nobody knows why he chose that name. Wolf, a pioneer of astrophotography, also discovered 247 other asteroids, including the equally mysteriously named 456 Abnoba, 810 Atossa, 866 Fatme, 868 Lova, 1661 Granule, 449 Hamburga and 1703 Barry.

BRAWNY FANNY

Fanny Brawn was the love of the poet John Keats's life. Only 1.5 m (5 ft) tall and generally uncomfortable in the company of women, Keats's letters to Fanny are classics in the art of love letters, and the two secretly became engaged before the affair was brought to an end by Keats's untimely death from tuberculosis at the age of 25. Fanny later married and had 3 children but never took off the ring given to her by Keats, and never told her husband about her former love.

FUSSY FANNY

Fanny Owen was a close friend of Charles Darwin's sisters and became his girlfriend while he was at Cambridge. He used to go riding with her, they played billiards together and he taught her how to shoot pheasants. She ended the relationship early in 1930, because Darwin preferred to spend the Christmas holidays organising his beetle collection rather than staying with his potential in-laws.

PRAWNY FANNY

Pioneering 60s TV chef Fanny Cradock was abandoned by her mother Bijou on her grandmother's billiard table at the age of one and was bought up by her grandparents for the next 9 years. She was married 4 times (twice bigamously), and believed that she was psychic, getting expelled from boarding school for holding a séance in the library. This Fanny is credited with inventing the prawn cocktail.

PRETTY FANNY

Former Prime Minister Arthur Balfour (1848-1930) was nicknamed 'Pretty Fanny' at Eton and Cambridge due to his lovely manners and the great importance he paid to appearance. Nephew to former Prime Minister Robert Gascoyne-Cecil, 3rd Marquis of Salisbury, he got his big break in politics when his uncle made him Minister for Ireland.
It was this act of nepotism that led to the phrase 'bob's your uncle'. Balfour was also nicknamed 'Clara', 'Niminy-Pimminy' and Lisping Hawthorn Bird'. He never married.

TINNED FANNY

Fanny Adams was originally the name given by British sailors to tinned meat (especially mutton) and the stew or hash made from it, first recorded in print in a dictionary of slang in 1889. The origin of the term is grisly and relates to the famous murder of an 8-year old girl in Alton, Hampshire in 1867. The murderer, a solicitor's clerk named Frederick Baker, was hanged in front of 5,000 people at Winchester later that year. In 1869, the Royal Navy introduced a new 'convenience food' mutton ration. This looked so unpleasant that sailors compared it, with macabre humour, to the horribly dismembered remains of 'Sweet Fanny Adams'. Sailors adapted the large packing cans in which the tinned meat arrived for use as impromptu mess tins, and, in today's Navy, mess tins in general are still referred to as 'fannies'. The expression 'sweet FA' (meaning 'nothing') and used as a euphemism for 'F*** All', derives from the coincidental similarity of the letters FA.

KISSY FANNY

One tradition in the French game of pétanque, or *boules*, is that when a player fails to score a single point, he must kiss the bottom of a girl called Fanny. At many pétanque courts, you can see a bare-bottomed statue or picture of 'Fanny', in case there is no obliging young lady of that name available. Legend has it that the original Fanny was a waitress from the Savoie region of France who, just after the First World War, offered the local mayor a kiss on her nether regions as a consolation prize for coming last. You can purchase your very own fanny here: www.labouleblue.fr/en/Catalogue/Boutique.htm

NAUGHTY FANNY

Fanny Hill is considered to be the first modern erotic novel. It was written in 1748 by John Cleland and was originally called *Memoirs of a Woman of Pleasure*. Many believe that this is where the rude sense of the word 'fanny' comes from. It caused a scandal at the time, and despite his careful use of euphemisms (the male member is referred to by 50 different names) Cleland was imprisoned briefly and the Bishop of London blamed the book for causing 2 small earthquakes.

Fantastic Flushers

Underwatercloset

with
Sir John Flushing
and Dr Lulu Ubenda

by Ted Dewan

This WWII submarine toilet (or "head") was shared by 20 men. The queues for the heads were long because they were so complicated to flush.

Bombs Away!

Submarine toilets had to flush waste into the sea at high pressure (30 - 100 psi). To achieve this, a reservoir tank was connected up to the main compressed-air line. The reservoir pressure had to be high enough to overcome sea pressure. Before flushing, it was essential to ensure the discharge-to-sea valve was fully open. Levers which controlled the flushing system and positioned a non-return flap had to be manipulated in a strict operational sequence.

SPLOOFSH!

Turn red valve above the toilet to fill the bowl with water halfway

Flushing the toilet was nearly as lethal as launching the other sort of "torpedoes". If a sailor got it wrong, it could result in painfully high-pressure sewage blasting out the toilet back in the sub. This was known as *"getting your own back"*.

Nazi Poop Deck

The toilet on the German WWII U-boat submarine *U-1206* proved to be too much for one Captain Schlitt who made an error when flushing the toilet during a drill. Captain Schlitt's fumbled flush forced gushes of seawater into the sub which leaked down into the battery compartment. The sub then had to rise to the surface to ventilate the toxic chlorine gas given off by the water-logged batteries. Once on the surface, the *U-1206* was spotted by an RAF aircraft and depth-charged, sinking the entire ship.

When finished, lift and lower this lever to flush, but only after reservoir pressure is high enough to discharge waste, and a non-return flap is engaged

The Toilets of the WWII Submarine USS Pampanito

72

TARGET PRACTICE

Men and boys seem to have difficulties aiming their pee due to a combination of inattention, carelessness, and unexpected diversions of the urine stream caused by the occasional partial obstruction in the nozzle of the penis. Since it seems that the guys never learn to take preventative action, here are several solutions to the undesired effects of this age-old problem and the related disharmony between the sexes.

The Ups and Downs of Toilet Sharing

Women complain about men failing to lift the seat and peeing all over it. A Japanese design solves the problem by featuring a seat that lifts itself into an upright position.

But women also complain to men for leaving the seat up when they've finished urinating. The gracious thing for men to do is lift the seat, urinate, and then return the seat to its down position for the next female user.

If this sounds like too much work for the lads, the celebrated mathematician John Banderob once put it in precise mathematical language, "a woman's need to have the seat down is greater than a man's need to leave it up."

etched fly

Aiming to Keep the WC Clean

Inspired by a Victorian innovation that first appeared in London, these modern urinals in Amsterdam have a picture of a fly etched into the porcelain. If a guy sees a fly in a urinal, he aims at it. And because the guy is thinking and aiming at the fly, the mens' room stays five times cleaner than it would without the fly because there's less urine spraying in an unruly fashion. By the end of the session, it becomes apparent that the fly is a fake. But such is the joy of the ingeniousness of this idea, it is likely that 'aim for the fly' might become incorporated into a repeat user's private peeing ritual.

Uro-Cap

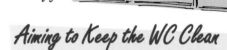

This urinal employs a device for improving aim by once again appealing to male instincts. The toy plastic football goal has a ball hanging from the top which changes colour when soaked in urine. However, this solution is not a serious attempt to keep public mens' rooms cleaner, because the goalposts deviate the streams of urine somewhat haphazardly.

NOW WASH YOUR HANDS

Fried Fish

Butter Hamlets are small, brightly coloured tropical fish which live in the western Atlantic. They come in 10 different colours – this one was a lovely purplish hue. Butter hamlets make distinctive low-frequency mating calls that are too deep to be heard with the human ear, which scientists believe may prove they are actually 10 different species. They are hermaphrodites that carry both ripe eggs and fertile sperm and mate by intertwining, so that the hamletty part goes in the buttery bit and vice versa. Try not to think about it.

The *Death Valley Pupfish* (*Cyrinodon salinus salinus*) is the last known species of fish still living in Death Valley, California, in a creek called Salt Creek that used to be a lake called 'Lake Manly'. The entire world's population lives within a half-mile radius of each other. Also called the Salt Creek Pupfish, the salty nature of its habitat means seasoning is unnecessary. Not to be confused with the Devil's Hole Pupfish, found only in a single desert spring in Nevada. Or with what's in the picture, which, of course, is haddock.

Humuhumunukunukuapua'a (*Rhinecanthus rectangulus*) as shown here is the state fish of Hawaii. Its name means 'triggerfish with a snout like a pig' and it is also known as the Picasso Triggerfish, although its wildly glowing patterns make it look more like a Mondrian or an African national flag. It has blue teeth. It's not the longest name for a fish in Hawaiian: that belongs to the *lauwiliwilinukunuku'oi'oi* ('long-snouted fish shaped like a wiliwili'). A *humuhumunukunukuapua'a* can change colour startlingly if threatened, but is drab if asleep or in fishcake mode.

The male *Sunset Gourami* (*Colisa lalia*) is one of the most beautiful and distinctive of aquarium fish. It is a metallic pale blue, with bright red vertical stripes. The females are not nearly as attractive as the males, being a plain grey with the faintest trace of stripes. We chose to fry a male one, for obvious reasons. An alternative might have been a 'balloon pink' kissing gourami – or possibly a green one. But, though these have luscious-looking lips, the effect is rather spoiled by them being lined with horny teeth.

Siamese Fighting Fish (*Betta splendens*) are used to being battered. They are bred in Thailand especially to fight, and, before being popped into hot oil, are kept in jam-jars out of sight of other fish, as they can try to swim through the glass to get at a potential opponent and injure themselves. Though ordinary looking and dull green or brown in their natural habitat, selective breeding has produced varieties with spectacular colours and wafting, feathery fins, leading them to be nicknamed The Jewels of the Orient. This one is an iridescent, electric-blue veiltail.

Upside-down Catfish (*Synodontis nigriventis*) are found in the Central Congo basin of Africa and are notable because they swim upside down. Tremendous fun to watch! They have been admired for countless centuries: pictures of them have been found in ancient Egyptian art. They adapted to swimming upside down in order to feed on insects on the surface of the water. To get an idea of what one looks like in the wild (or in ancient Egyptian art), turn the page upside down.

Orange Clownfish live symbiotically with anemones. These protect the clownfish from people who want to fry them (or other predators) and, in return, the fish groom the anemones and bring oxygen to them by swimming about. Their bold colouring is strikingly attractive: vibrant orange with three blue-white bands edged with a thin black border. This one is actually a false-clownfish. It has an extra 11th spine on its back; regular clownfish have only 10. That's how you tell them apart. (You can't do that here obviously, because this is a fillet).

FIVE GO
FACT FINDING ON
FORMOSA

Dick - likes cake and fighting and funambulism

Anne - likes the sort of things girls like, but not girls like George

Georgina - likes to be called 'George' and is a bit of a tomboy

Julian - would like to be an actuary or an exotic dancer

... and not forgetting Timmy the dog!

Formosa is a Fabulous Island in the Thames just brimming with "F"s and we're out to spot every one. Here we are at the "Tarry Stone" in Cookham which doesn't begin with an "F".

But how will we find Formosa? Julian has spotted a clue. "Why don't we follow this clearly marked Footpath? Come on, Timmy!"

But what's this? George is flummoxed by a mysterious sign. "Surely Heidegger conjectured there is no such thing as nothing? This really is jolly confusing."

But despite this logical inconsistency we decided to go on. The first "F" we find is... our Feet! "We'll need them to get to Formosa," says Dick, with no apparent irony.

Formosa, it turns out, is Full of Fruity Food. George decides to try what looks like a crab apple. "Hedgehogs like rolling in crab apples," George reminds us.

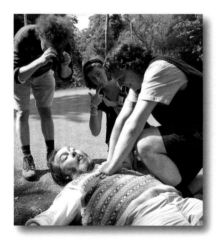

Oh Fiddlesticks! George has gone into anaphylactic shock which sounds like it should have an "F" in it but doesn't. Fortunately Dick knows First Aid.

George has made a Famous recovery and we're back on the hunt for "F"s. Flint! - the state gemstone of Ohio - Fascinating.[1]

Anne has found a Feather. "Look at me, Julian, I'm demonstrating the language of the Fan! This means 'lend me a Fiver!'"

Dick wants to go Fishing, but fears he might be committing a Felony if he does. Frightening.

"Come on, boys," cries Anne. "I fancy a spot of Feaguing!" But there are no eels to be found anywhere.[2]

"I say, Julian, is that a Filthy Fag in your Face?" "F*** off, Dick. 73% of the population of Manila smoke. If it's good enough for them it's jolly well good enough for me."

1. A man told us that flint was harder and sharper than steel, not bad considering it's actually made of dead sponges.
2. Apparently feaguing is an old term for sticking a root of ginger or a live eel up an animal's backside to make it perky.

FIGHT! "Stop!" cries Anne. "Aren't you boys aware that Pope Urban II expanded the 'Truce of God' (an edict which outlawed fighting) to last from Wednesday night to Monday morning, and it's only Thursday!"

The Fury is soon Forgotten however and we all settle down to a Feast. With lashings of ginger beer, of course. "Aristotle believed candied ginger gave men erections," quips George.

Dick eats a bit like a Foreigner. "Here's something else a bit Foreign," quips Dick. "In French, *un biscuit* is not a biscuit at all but a cake. A sponge cake, to be precise. A biscuit in the English sense is *un biscuit sec*."

Anne has found a forked stick. "If only dowsing wasn't such a bucketful of unproven arse-gravy," she sighs, delicately.

George is one of a rare group of "grass-spotters." "Look! Fescue, a genus of around 300 species of perennial tufted grass belonging to the family Poaceae," she squeals with delight.[3]

"My, it's hot. I Fancy I might Float, like most species of Ctenophores," hazards George.[4] "No, George!" cries Anne. "There are boys around. Cover your modesty!"

"Why should it always be the boys who have the Fun?" cries George.

But on Formosa no-one can be Fed up for long and soon we're all Frolicking across a Field.

It's time to say Farewell to Formosa. Thanks for showing us all your "F"s. They were great! What stories we'll have to tell when we get back home.

---

3. George should be careful. Some fescues carry a fungus which can cause weight gain, rough coat, panting and high rectal temperatures.
4. Ctenophores are a special type of fast-breeding hairy jellyfish. One species called 'The Monster' has destroyed all the fish in the Black Sea.

As I was going to QI

by Phill Jupitus

As I was going to QI

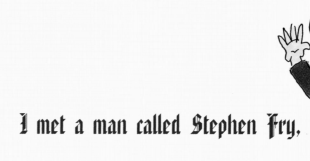

I met a man called Stephen Fry,

Alan Davies followed on,

Pursued by artist Jasper Johns,

After whom a circus bear

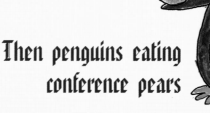

Then penguins eating conference pears

Chewbacca with a ping-pong bat,

Some meerkats
wearing party hats,

A mighty horseman, name of Lars

A Dalek juggling Marmite jars,

A cow in an MCC tie,

How many were going to QI?

79

FAGS OF THE WORLD

The fags elderly beagles long for.

Made in the Ukraine, but sensibly not smoked there.

Old fags for old lags.

Emphysema here we come!

What sort of wood do you want your coffin made of sir?

For thin scary teachers.

For thin scary pupils.

Easily concealed in the operating theatre.

Smoked by Joan Collins lookey-likeys.

Smoked by Joan herself.

South Korean fags North Koreans can only dream of.

Gold-coloured to piss off the North Koreans.

Will bring up a lung with your first toke.

Can use one to poke your lung back in.

Swanky yet wanky.

Popular with girls who like pictures of flowers.

Popular with asthmatic girls who like pictures of flowers.

The perfect fag to smoke in church.

Not a lucky strike for your lungs.

Makes your breath smell like faeces.

For weirdos who like beige.

For the cowboy with cancer.

Japanese, not mild and there aren't seven in a pack.

You are not allowed to mention them in Monte Carlo.

The Malaysian Coffin Nail.

Over a hundred years old, unlike its smokers.

Bafflingly called Los Angeles Blast.

Perfect for making Yorkshire pudding with.

Originally made with caustic soda, so shove one down your drain or your husband to freshen them up.

Popular with chain smoking MPs.

Popular with chain smoking lady MPs.

Slim and weak like an oiled seabird.

Probably smoked by God.

Actually God probably smokes these.

Certainly not these.

Packet design by an acid casualty.

Usually only smoked as a bet.

Make you very intelligent.

They should pay you to smoke these.

Dullest fag in the world.

Its very tedious little brother.

Its enormously emotionally disturbed maiden aunt.

Designed for young professional women like me.

Named after the famous anorexic tennis player.

The medieval sex offender of the fag world.

80

Does my corpse look big in this?

German über fags.

You won't be able to run to the shop for a packet of these.

Worth a whack from the headmaster.

These will help you get fitter, but only if you throw them away.

Made out of old settees.

Made out of young settees.

Not to be confused with Dabitoff.

Dead posh fags which will make you dead.

Shroud matching not a problem.

Strong fags smoked in Hungary.

Strong fags smoked when you're hungry.

The Samurai's choice.

The Geisha's choice.

Popular with asthmatic girls who like pictures of flowers and God forbid, pink as well the silly cows.

Very thin ones for very thin ones.

Symbolises luxury… my arse.

The original gasper.

Silly little fags with attitude.

The perfect fag to smoke after you've shagged your best friend's husband.

The perfect fag to stub out on a hoodie.

You are allowed to mention them in Monte Carlo but only at the weekends.

You are allowed to mention them in Monte Carlo but only if your child is called Givenchy.

The perfect accompaniment to Complan.

Thin and green like snot.

The probation officer's fag of choice.

The supply teacher's fag of choice.

The probation officer who wants to be a supply teacher's fag of choice.

A big packet for someone with a big packet.

A small packet for someone with a small packet.

A pointy packet for someone with a pointy packet.

'Call this Mister'.

George Bush can't read this.

Germans love 'em and I love Germans!

Smoked by Poles and some Planks.

Make you very pretty.

Tasty and satisfying… unlike John McCririck.

An anagram of 'meals.'

Smoked by teenagers who can't spell.

The Caretaker's fag

Soft enough to smoke anally.

Rarely found in the pockets of builders.

The ballet dancer's fag of choice… although people often smoke a ballet dancer by mistake.

Popular in smaller branches of Debenhams.

Rhymes with chest and will get you wheezing.

Smoke West in your best vest, sex pest.

Perfect after a fight on the beach.

Often left in the machine.

A cunt of a fag. (Just checking you made it to the end.)

81

FRANCE
by Clive Anderson

France is a beautiful country, conveniently located just a few miles across the English Channel from Kent.

It boasts a wide range of stunning land and seascapes: a long stretch of Atlantic coastline, miles of Mediterranean beaches, a portion of Alps, half of the Pyrenees and a variety of other spectacular mountains, gorges and rivers. It is the most visited country on Earth.

The French people produce fine wines and even finer foods and have a high reputation in art, music, literature, philosophy and science.

Given all that, naturally we have spent most of the last thousand years waging war with them.

So engrained is the attitude of Anglo-French hostility that during the Crimean War when Britain and France were on the same side fighting Russia, the British commander Lord Raglan persisted in referring to the enemy (the Russians) as the 'French'.

And in 1944, wanting to bolster British morale in the final stages of the war against Germany, the government funded Laurence Olivier's film version of Shakespeare's *Henry V*, featuring England's glorious victory over the French (our allies in 1944) at Agincourt in 1415.

In recent years, France has enjoyed a poor reputation for military prowess in the English-speaking world. If you searched for 'French military victories' Google used to ask you, 'Do you mean French military defeats?' Homer Simpson - or was it George W. Bush? - called the French 'cheese-eating surrender monkeys'. This might be based on the French disinclination to support the invasion of Iraq in 2003 but is more likely harping back to the Second World War when French forces resisted the German advance for only 6 weeks before their government collaborated with the German occupation. As was said at the time:

Q: *Why do French roads have trees planted alongside them?*
A: *Because German soldiers like to march in the shade.*

And of course, at the beginning of the 19th century, the great French war leader Napoleon Buonaparte was defeated by Britain (and her allies) at Waterloo and Trafalgar, and by the Russians (and their winter) in Moscow.

Despite all this, the French military track record is actually rather better than the selective memory of Britain (and America) might suggest.

1066 BATTLE OF HASTINGS

This, the most famous English defeat in history, is remembered as a victory for the Normans rather than the French. King Harold and the English nearly won, but were beaten in the end by fixture build-up, having had to fight against the Norwegians at Stamford Bridge only a couple of weeks before. Plus William the Bastard used typically sneaky, continental tactics. His troops fought on horseback instead of riding to battle, getting off their horses and fighting on foot like proper Englishmen.

But, let's face it, Normandy was (and is) part of France. Contemporary documents from the *Anglo-Saxon Chronicle* to the Bayeux Tapestry refer to the invaders as French rather than Norman, and their arrival imposed a French-speaking aristocracy on England for hundreds of years.

One-nil to the French in anyone's language.

THE HUNDRED YEARS WAR, 1337-1453

In England, this conflict is largely remembered for its extraordinary length and for the glorious English victories at Crécy (1346), Poitiers (1356) and Agincourt (1415). However, the French also won important victories at Patay (1429) and at Castillon (1453), which are never mentioned in English history lessons but which brought the war finally to an end.

At the beginning of the war, English kings had pretensions to rule all of France, but by the end of it they possessed only the town of Calais. Though it had taken a while, it must count as another victory for France.

Not that the English were prepared to give up their claim on French territory just because they'd lost one small war. The symbol of France, the *fleur-de-lis* was only removed from the British Royal Coat of Arms nearly 350 years later, in 1801.

If you add in victories over the Moors in 701 (Tours); against Spain in 1603 (Rocroi); the British in America in 1781 (Yorktown); and Austria and Russia in 1805 (Austerlitz), the French batting average isn't so shabby. According to historian Niall Ferguson, out of a total of 168 important battles fought since 387 BC (which takes it back to some time before anything recognisable as 'France' quite existed), they have won 109, lost 49 and drawn 10.

THE AULD ALLIANCE

Until Great Britain came into existence, Anglo-French rivalry was very much an English-French thing (though the Welsh provided the 'English' bowmen at many important battles). Scotland had its own reasons for opposing England and so, in treaties from 1295 until the 16th century, it was as often as not allied to France, against England. The Auld Alliance, as it was known, was always old. It doesn't appear to have been called the New Alliance even in its early days. And it doesn't appear to have done Scotland very much good. Rather like the so-called Special Relationship between Britain and America, the smaller country puts the greater store on the deal, but gains less.

An Army of Scotland fought for France to great effect in the Hundred Years War. But France provided precious little help in the Scottish Wars of Independence at the beginning of the 14th century. The King of France even tried to get Robert the Bruce to go on a Crusade with him in 1309, which might have meant him missing the Battle of Bannockburn in 1314. And it was to honour the Auld Alliance that the Scots attempted their foolhardy invasion of England, leading to their bloody defeat at Flodden in 1513.

Later that century, again as part of the Auld Alliance, Mary, Queen of Scots also became Queen of France, but her abnormally short, stammering husband Francis II promptly died from an ear infection, less than 18 months after ascending the throne, aged 16. Mary went home to Scotland, where in due course she was arrested, imprisoned and executed in England.

Merci beaucoup.

FRENCH IN COURT

As mentioned above, the Normans introduced French to England and it was over 300 years before English once again emerged as the language of polite society and literature. Geoffrey Chaucer's *Canterbury Tales* (1387) was the first work of note in the mother tongue since 1066. The lawyers were even slower to catch on. Courtrooms clung to French long after even kings and queens had got round to communicating *en Anglais*. This meant that ordinary people couldn't follow what was going on in court – which is the way lawyers like it – and, if there was any opposition from the judges, it was probably because they would rather use Latin.

In 1362, a Statute of Edward III had required all court pleadings be in English. But the lawyers just wouldn't be told. As late as 1631, an ordinary criminal case is recorded as being in what amounts to courtroom Franglais, including the phrase: 'the prisoner ject un brickbat que narrowly missed'.

It wasn't until 1731, not far short of eight centuries since the Norman Conquest, that Parliament again enacted that English and not French should be used in all public legal proceedings. And this time the legislators got their way. (Though they did have to pass another Act in 1733 because they had forgotten to include Wales.) *Au revoir, enfin.*

FRENCH MILITARY TERMINOLOGY

Their business is war, and they do their business. RUDYARD KIPLING (1865-1936) in 1915

The British rightly pride themselves on their naval superiority, but this was largely born out of the certain knowledge that we would never win a war on the continent. Over its long history, the French army was usually the largest, best-equipped and most strategically innovative army in Europe. The language of modern warfare is French; all the following English words are of French origin; many even keep the original spelling.

arms, army, arsenal, attaché, artillery, attack, bandoleer, barracks, battery, bayonet, bombardier, brigade, cadet, camouflage, captain, carbine, colonel, combat, company, corporal, détente, division, dragoon, ensign, exercise, fort, fusilier, cavalry, charge, corps, epaulette, espionage, esprit de corps, garrison, general, grenade, grenadier, lieutenant, lance, marines, manoeuvre, melée, militia, military, mine, munitions, naval, offensive, ordnance, parachute, pilot, platoon, quarters, reconnaissance, recruit, regiment, ricochet, sabre, sergeant, soldier, sortie, standard, surrender, tent, terrain, trench, uniform, volley and volunteer.

It is well known with what gallantry the [French] officers lead and with what vehemence the troops follow. GENERAL SIR WILLIAM NAPIER (1785-1860)

FAIRLY FAMOUS F FRENCHMEN

1. Franz Fanon (1925-61)

A psychiatrist, philosopher, author and revolutionary from the French colony of Martinique, his father was descended from African slaves. After France fell to the Nazis in 1940, he left the island and joined the Free French. Although decorated with the *Croix de Guerre*, he was forbidden to enter Germany with the victorious army because he was black. He dictated his greatest book *The Wretched of the Earth* (about Algeria's bitter struggle for independence) whilst dying of leukaemia.

2. Henri Farman (1874-1958)

Pioneering French aviator who was born in Paris, but was in fact English: his father was a foreign correspondent and he was christened Henry. Farman broke a number of early aviation records (including two world records for duration and distance) but there are two distinctions he will hold forever. In 1908, he became the first person in Europe to carry a passenger in an aircraft and the following year he was the pilot of the first aeroplane in the world to carry two passengers.

3. Felix Francois Fauré (1841-99)

Son of a small-time furniture maker, he rose to become President of France and died of apoplexy while having oral sex in his office with his mistress, 28 years his junior. Georges Clemenceau, who was born in the same year but outlived him by 30 years, commented: 'Il voulait être César, il ne fut que Pompée.' This had the deliberate double-meaning: 'he wanted to be Caesar, but ended up being Pompey' or 'he wanted to be Caesar but ended up being pumped'.

4. Gabriel Fauré (1845-1924)

The foremost French composer of his generation, his father sent him to music school in Paris aged nine, where he was considered so gifted that they charged no fee. Taught by Saint-Saens, he later taught Ravel. He is best known for his *Requiem* (which, he said, was not written for anyone in particular but just 'for the pleasure of it') and for *Berceuse* from his *Dolly Suite* (which was used by the BBC for 32 years from 1950 as the closing music for the children's radio show *Listen With Mother*).

5. Pierre Fermat (1601-65)

One of the greatest mathematicians of his day, Pierre Fermat was a lawyer and government official during the reign of Louis XIV. He was not a very good lawyer because he spent all his time on his hobby, but he rose to a senior position largely because many of his colleagues were struck down with the plague. Fermat himself was (wrongly) reported dead of the disease. His famous *Last Theorem*, whose proof he himself mysteriously failed to provide, was finally proven 328 years later.

6. Georges Feydeau (1862-1921)

Son of a beautiful Polish woman and rumoured to be the illegitimate son of Napoleon III, the master of French farce wrote the first of his 60 plays at the age of 7. Successful during his lifetime, but dismissed as lightweight, his works are continually revived and still widely performed today. A lover of high

living, Feydeau had a table permanently reserved at Maxim's in Paris. In 1918, he contracted syphilis and for the rest of his life gradually descended into madness.

7. Gustave Flaubert (1821-80)

Flaubert was born into a family of doctors but he himself was always ill, suffering from epilepsy and outbreaks of boils. 'I'm liquefying like an old Camembert', he said. World famous for his novel *Madame Bovary*, he achieved his first literary success at the age of 15 with a school essay on mushrooms. He had copied it off someone else and was later expelled. Although he had various mistresses, he lived with his mother until he was 51 and in later life was a compulsive frequenter of brothels.

8. Ferdinand Foch (1851-1929)

Marshal of France and commander of the allied forces at the close of the First World War, he was noted for 'the most original and subtle mind in the French army'. An able professor of military strategy, his famous saying was: 'Hard pressed on my right. My centre is yielding. Impossible to manoeuvre. Situation excellent. I attack.' Sacked after the Battle of the Somme he was later reinstated and went on to win the war. At the surrender, he refused to shake the hand of the German signatory.

9. Jean-Honoré Fragonard (1732-1806)

The son of a glove-maker and Court painter to Louis XV, Fragonard produced over 550 voluptuous and erotic paintings (not counting drawings and etchings). His daughter Rosalie was one of his favourite models. Later, he fell in love with his wife's 14-year-old sister. His career took a dive during the French revolution when the guillotine deprived him of most of his customers. Now feted as one of the all-time masters of French painting, he died in Paris in 1806 almost completely forgotten.

10. Anatole France (1844-1924)

The novelist Anatole France was born Jacques Anatole Thibault: he took his pseudonym from the name of his father's bookshop. He won the Nobel Prize for Literature in 1921, the year after the Vatican placed him on *The Index of Forbidden Books*. One of his mistresses, whom he had been cheating on for six years, died in 1910; a second one, whom he had deserted, killed herself in 1911, and his daughter Suzanne died in 1917. He also slept with his housekeeper, cheating on her too.

11. César Franck (1822-90)

Considered by many (including Franz Liszt) to be the greatest writer of organ music after J.S. Bach, Franck's first major public success as a composer did not come till he was 68 years old, the last year of his life. An innocent and absent-minded man, he scurried about Paris in an overcoat that was too large and trousers that were too short and died as a result of being run over by a bus. He lived most of his life in France but his mother was German and his father was a Belgian German.

THE F-UNNIES

'I'm not famine - I'm a supermodel.'

'I couldn't afford Bleak House.'

'I'm logged on to Imaginary Friends Reunited.'

'You've got to see someone about
your incontinence.'

85

Fragrance

by Kathy Phillips

Nothing is more memorable than a smell… or more difficult to describe.

As Diane Ackerman points out in her brilliant book *A Natural History of the Senses* (1990), most people, even if blindfolded, could instantly recognise the smell of a shoe shop, a church or a butcher's, but would be quite unable to describe the familiar aroma of a favourite chair or the inside of their own car. The vocabulary of smells is so small that we are forced to describe one in terms of another. Blood, it has been said, smells like dust and, according to Coleridge, a dead dog at a distance smells like elder flowers. But the fragrance of many things is completely unique: among them, penguins, which just smell… like penguins.

Essence of penguin has not (to my knowledge at least) ever been used in perfume but an amazing number of other things have. Not just the ones you might expect, like roses, jasmine, coconut or frangipani, but also baby powder, banana, butterscotch, cactus, coffee, dandelion, driftwood, grass, ginger, kiwi fruit, hazelnut, marshmallow, soil, spearmint and tomato. *Odeur 53* by Comme des Garçons has notes of oxygen, washing drying in the wind, nail polish, burnt rubber, tarmac and sand dunes. Tommy Hilfiger's *Tommy 10 For Men* cologne even claims to incorporate a whiff of Seattle rain.

include Christian Dior's *Dioressence* (1979), *Gucci No 1* (1972), Mary Quant's *Havoc* (1974) and *Monsieur Rochas* (1969).

Robert created *Calèche* in 1961 and for many years it was Hermès' best-selling women's fragrance (worn by, amongst others, Lady Mary Archer of 'fragrant' fame). He blended mandarin, orange blossom, jasmine,

© 2a for *Vogue China*

grass that smells of wet earth. It's used in many countries to control soil erosion. Ylang-ylang belongs to the magnolia family. Native to Indonesia and the Philippines and widely grown in the South Pacific, it is used as an aphrodisiac. It sounds like a created perfume in itself, with notes of rubber, custard, orange blossom and jasmine. Ylang-ylang is Malay for 'the flower of flowers' and Guerlain use so much of it that they have bought their own plantation on the Comoros Islands in the Indian Ocean.

For many centuries, there were just four key components of scent, none of them at all romantic. Musk is a red jelly found in deer-guts: it produces hormonal changes in any woman who smells it. Ambergris is a glutinous fluid found in the stomachs of sperm whales that protects them from the sharp beaks of the cuttlefish they swallow. It has a sweet, woody smell. Castoreum, a yellow secretion from the anal glands of mature beavers, has a whiff of leather. Civet is a honey-like goo exuded from the genitals of a nocturnal, fox-like, carnivorous, Ethiopian mongoose.

Nowadays, for under-standable reasons, these grisly concoctions are reproduced in the laboratory, along with *calone*, an artificial 'sea breeze' aroma, and *cashmeran*, which is said to evoke the fragrance of cashmere. *Ozonic* compounds mimic the smell of the air after a thunderstorm. *Coumarin* is extracted from lavender, sweetgrass or the tonka bean (a cheap vanilla substitute) but is banned in the US as a food additive and is also used to make rat poison. But there remains an enduring connection between bottoms and perfume. The organic chemical *indole* is widely used in the perfume industry. It smells floral in low doses (and is present in many flowers, such as jasmine and orange blossom), but at high concentrations it smells like shit. Indole is found in human faeces.

Perfumes are the feelings of flowers.

HEINRICH HEINE* (1797-1856)

Scientists say that smell was the first of the senses to evolve. When primitive jellyfish began to develop brains, these actually began as buds on their olfactory organs. We think, as Diane Ackerman puts it, because we smelled.

People who create perfumes are known in the trade as 'noses'. For example, Jacques Polge became the 'nose' of Chanel in 1978 and Loc Dong was the nose behind Vera Wang's *Bouquet* (2008). *Le nez* responsible for *Calèche* was Guy Robert, the former president of the French Society of Perfumers, whose other hits

lily of the valley, rose, gardenia, iris, sandalwood and cedar with bergamot, oakmoss, vetiver and ylang-ylang.

What are these last four mysterious ingredients? Bergamot is an inedible variety of bitter orange present in the distinctive flavour of Earl Grey tea. Oakmoss (the more poetic-sounding *mousse de chêne* in French) is a kind of lichen. When it grows on oak trees it has a sharp, woody, slightly sweet smell; on pines it smells like turps, which some perfumers like a drop of. Vetiver (also known as khus khus) is a

The fragrance always remains in the hand that gives the rose.
CHINESE PROVERB

MEN! SPLASH IT ALL OVER! GET THE EDGE WITH ESTÉE LAUDER'S **DONALD TRUMP, THE FRAGRANCE**, A MELANGE OF EXOTIC WOODS, BLACK BASIL, MINT AND CUCUMBER.

One thing eluded me.
I never managed to capture
the smell of honeysuckle.
FRANÇOIS COTY* (1874-1934)

Headspace Technology, the newest form of perfume extraction, allows the scent of a living plant, flower, fruit or herb to be captured without having to damage it. For the first time, fragrances such as lilac, gardenia, violet and lily (known as 'the perfumer's despair') can be collected without destroying the plants. A single bloom, still attached at the roots, is placed in a bell jar through which a neutral gas is passed, acquiring the flower's vapour. Analysis of this gas enables the perfumer, using organic and synthetic ingredients, to reconstitute the perfume exactly.

FRAGRANT FACTS

- Perfume smells strongest just before a storm.
- Cleopatra's ship had perfumed sails.
- Louis XIV decreed that a new perfume be invented for him every day.
- At the court of Louis XV, doves were drenched in different scents and released at banquets.
- The sweat of schizophrenics smells different to that of other people.
- Doctors use their noses to aid diagnosis. Typhus smells of mice, the plague of over-ripe apples and measles of freshly plucked feathers.
- 2 million Americans have *anosmia* - the inability to smell anything at all.
- A *factice* is a perfume bottle (sometimes giant size) made for display only: the contents aren't actually perfume.

Leather results from tanning, a disgusting and malodorous job that involves kneading animal skins with a mixture of human urine, dog dung and dissolved animal brains. Such foul odours inevitably lingered on the finished product. When Catherine de' Medici (1519-89) went to France at the age of 14 to marry the boy who would become King Henry II, she brought with her a whole host of ideas new to the French - including eating with a fork, corsets, ballet, high-heeled shoes and most importantly gloves scented with jasmine. These quickly became all the rage, to such an extent that the glove-making trade (huge in the 16th century) eventually transformed itself almost entirely into perfume manufacturing. Catherine's retinue included her personal perfumer, a sinister figure called René le Florentin. In his laboratory, connected to her quarters by a secret passage, he devised cunning new perfumes and medicines and he was also an expert in the use of poisons. His speciality was to send toxic gloves as gifts to the Queen's many enemies, including the pair said to have done for Jeanne d'Albret, mother of the future Henry IV.

*Heine was a poet and a German Jew; Coty was a Corsican fascist and newspaper baron (a well as a perfumer), born Joseph Spoturno. A shared passion for fragrance transcends both time and politics.

Fletcher Christian, THE BOUNTY MUTINEER

In 1789, Acting Lieutenant Fletcher Christian led a mutiny against Lieutenant William Bligh, aboard the *Bounty*, a ship sent to Tahiti to collect breadfruit trees for cultivation as cheap food for slaves in the West Indies. The story of the mutiny is well known, thanks to Hollywood films, and countless books. But this most famous of Fletchers deserves to be remembered for more than just his rebellion...

ADRIAN TEAL fecit

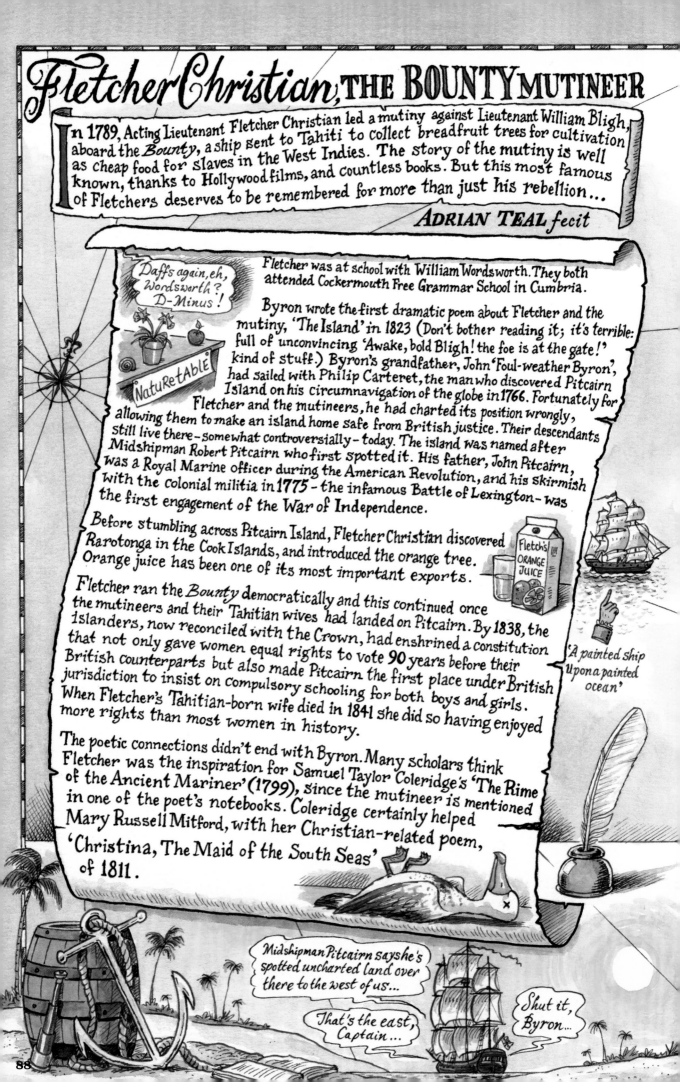

Daffs again, eh, Wordsworth? D-Minus!

NatuRe tAbLE

Fletcher was at school with William Wordsworth. They both attended Cockermouth Free Grammar School in Cumbria.

Byron wrote the first dramatic poem about Fletcher and the mutiny, 'The Island' in 1823 (Don't bother reading it; it's terrible: full of unconvincing 'Awake, bold Bligh! the foe is at the gate!' kind of stuff.) Byron's grandfather, John 'Foul-weather Byron', had sailed with Philip Carteret, the man who discovered Pitcairn Island on his circumnavigation of the globe in 1766. Fortunately for Fletcher and the mutineers, he had charted its position wrongly, allowing them to make an island home safe from British justice. Their descendants still live there – somewhat controversially – today. The island was named after Midshipman Robert Pitcairn who first spotted it. His father, John Pitcairn, was a Royal Marine officer during the American Revolution, and his skirmish with the colonial militia in 1775 – the infamous Battle of Lexington – was the first engagement of the War of Independence.

Before stumbling across Pitcairn Island, Fletcher Christian discovered Rarotonga in the Cook Islands, and introduced the orange tree. Orange juice has been one of its most important exports.

Fletch's ORANGE JUICE

Fletcher ran the *Bounty* democratically and this continued once the mutineers and their Tahitian wives had landed on Pitcairn. By 1838, the Islanders, now reconciled with the Crown, had enshrined a constitution that not only gave women equal rights to vote 90 years before their British counterparts but also made Pitcairn the first place under British jurisdiction to insist on compulsory schooling for both boys and girls. When Fletcher's Tahitian-born wife died in 1841 she did so having enjoyed more rights than most women in history.

'A painted ship upon a painted ocean'

The poetic connections didn't end with Byron. Many scholars think Fletcher was the inspiration for Samuel Taylor Coleridge's 'The Rime of the Ancient Mariner' (1799), since the mutineer is mentioned in one of the poet's notebooks. Coleridge certainly helped Mary Russell Mitford, with her Christian-related poem, 'Christina, The Maid of the South Seas' of 1811.

Midshipman Pitcairn says he's spotted uncharted land over there to the west of us...

That's the east, Captain...

Shut it, Byron...

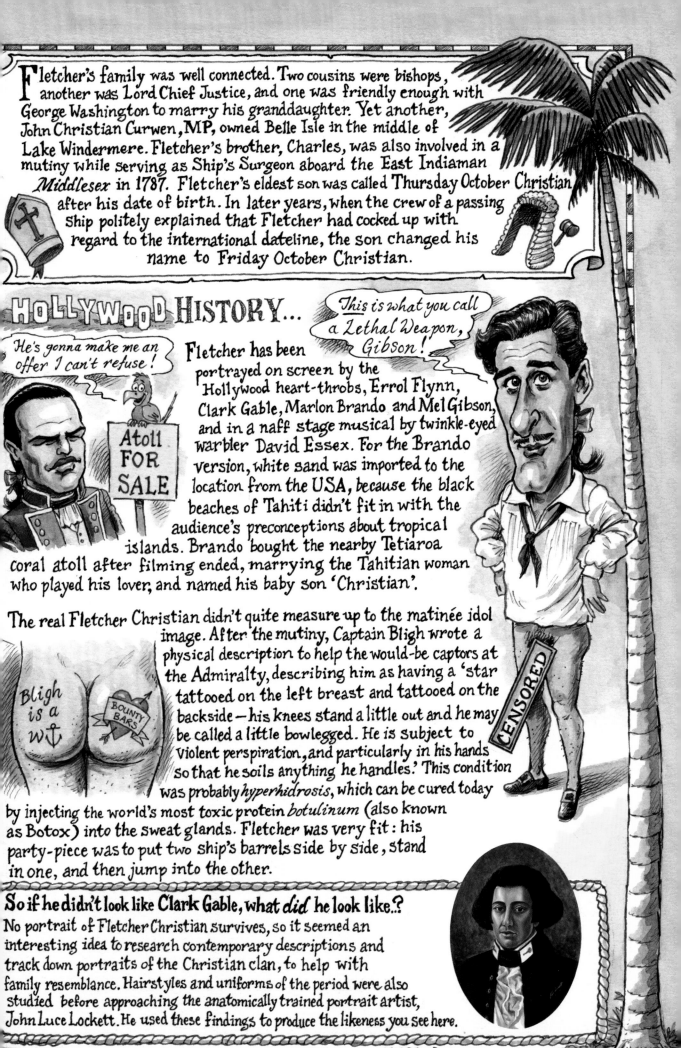

Fletcher's family was well connected. Two cousins were bishops, another was Lord Chief Justice, and one was friendly enough with George Washington to marry his granddaughter. Yet another, John Christian Curwen, MP, owned Belle Isle in the middle of Lake Windermere. Fletcher's brother, Charles, was also involved in a mutiny while serving as Ship's Surgeon aboard the East Indiaman *Middlesex* in 1787. Fletcher's eldest son was called Thursday October Christian after his date of birth. In later years, when the crew of a passing ship politely explained that Fletcher had cocked up with regard to the international dateline, the son changed his name to Friday October Christian.

HOLLYWOOD HISTORY...

Fletcher has been portrayed on screen by the Hollywood heart-throbs, Errol Flynn, Clark Gable, Marlon Brando and Mel Gibson, and in a naff stage musical by twinkle-eyed warbler David Essex. For the Brando version, white sand was imported to the location from the USA, because the black beaches of Tahiti didn't fit in with the audience's preconceptions about tropical islands. Brando bought the nearby Tetiaroa coral atoll after filming ended, marrying the Tahitian woman who played his lover, and named his baby son 'Christian'.

The real Fletcher Christian didn't quite measure up to the matinée idol image. After the mutiny, Captain Bligh wrote a physical description to help the would-be captors at the Admiralty, describing him as having a 'star tattooed on the left breast and tattooed on the backside — his knees stand a little out and he may be called a little bowlegged. He is subject to violent perspiration, and particularly in his hands so that he soils anything he handles.' This condition was probably *hyperhidrosis*, which can be cured today by injecting the world's most toxic protein *botulinum* (also known as Botox) into the sweat glands. Fletcher was very fit: his party-piece was to put two ship's barrels side by side, stand in one, and then jump into the other.

So if he didn't look like Clark Gable, what *did* he look like..?

No portrait of Fletcher Christian survives, so it seemed an interesting idea to research contemporary descriptions and track down portraits of the Christian clan, to help with family resemblance. Hairstyles and uniforms of the period were also studied before approaching the anatomically trained portrait artist, John Luce Lockett. He used these findings to produce the likeness you see here.

89

MAD FRANKIE FRASER

'ELLO READERS. MY NAME'S MAD FRANKIE FRASER, AN' I'VE SPENT 'ARF MY LIFE IN PRISON FOR VIOLENT CRIMES, SOME OF WHICH I NEVER DONE. LIKE PULLIN' OUT BENNY COULSTON'S TEEF WIV A PAIR OF PLIERS. THAT NEVER 'APPENED. HONEST

BUT THAT'S ALL 'ISTORY NAAH, COS I'VE GOT A NEW JOB... AS A QI CARTOON CHARACTER!

THIS 'ERE IS MY FISH BOWL FULL OF FASCINATING FACTS ALL ABAAHT FINGS WHAT BEGIN WIV THE LETTER EFF

YOU GET THE PICTURE?

SO, LET'S FISH ABAAHT A BIT, AN' SEE WHAT WE FIND

IT'S AN 'AZELNUT! AN' THE FASCINATING FING ABAAHT 'AZELNUTS IS THAT ANUVVAH NAME FOR AN 'AZELNUT IS... A FIRKIN....

I FINK

QI EDITOR'S VOICE → NO FRANK. IT'S A **FILBERT**

OH **FACK**! IT'S A FILBERT FRANKIE, NOT A FIRKIN. YOU DARFT **CAANT**!

CAN I START AGAIN?

IN YOUR OWN TIME FRANK

SORRY 'BAAHT THAT. OKAY. NEXT FING IS A **FISH FINGER**! THESE WAS INVENTED IN 1929, BY CAPTAIN BIRDSEYE

NO. IT'S **CLARENCE** BIRDSEYE, FRANK

FACK IT! THAT'S WHAT I MEANT... **CLARENCE** FACKIN' BIRDSEYE!

KER-SMASH!!!

YOU **SLAAAG**!

JUST CALM DOWN FRANK, AND TELL THE READERS ALL ABOUT CLARENCE BIRDSEYE!

RIGHT. OKAY. SORRY 'BAAHT THAT. ERM....WHILE WORKIN' FOR THE U.S. GOVER'MENT AS A NATURALIST IN THE CANADIAN ARCTIC, BIRDSEYE LEARNED OFF THE INUITS 'OW TO FREEZE FISH. AN' 'E FOUGHT TO 'IMSELF, 'ELLO. MIGHT BE AN EARNER IN THIS'

SO 'E LEGS IT BACK T'NOO YORK AN' 'E SETS UP A FIRM TO FLOG FROZEN NOSH. BUT THE 'ILLMAN 'UNTERS DON'T BITE, AN' IN 1924 BIRDSEYE'S BUSINESS GOES TITS UP.

THEN 'E COMES UP WIV A NEW MACHINE FOR FREEZIN' STUFF QUICKA, AN' BINGO! 'E'S 'IT THE FACKIN' JACKPOT! IN 1929 'E SELLS UP FOR A COOL $22 MILLION. NOT A BAD RESULT.

CLARENCE F. BIRDSEYE

AN' GUESS WHAT? 'IS MIDDLE NAME WAS FRANK. HONEST

'ERE! SOME **CAANT'S** FACKED ME FISH BOWL!

IF I GET MY 'ANDS ON THE **BARSTAD** WHAT DONE THAT...

CALM DOWN FRANKIE! JUST STICK TO THE SCRIPT. THE NEXT FACT WAS ABOUT THE HUMAN FACE, REMEMBER?

OH YEAH! THE 'UMAN FACE! THERE IS FORTY-FOUR MUSCLES IN THE 'UMAN FACE. THAT'S ENUFF T'MAKE ABAAHT TWO 'UNDRED AN' FIFTY FAAHSAND DIFF'RENT EXPRESSIONS!

LIKE THIS ONE, WHICH IS **FRETENIN'**

AN' THIS ONE, WHICH IS NOT FRETENIN' AT ALL.

BACK IN '56 WE REARRANGED JACK 'SPOT' COMER'S FACE FOR 'IM! THEY RECKON 'IT TOOK ABAAHT SIXTY STITCHES TO PUT HIS BOAT RACE BACK TOGEVAAH AGAIN!

FWITT!!

PUT THE KNIFE DOWN FRANKIE

MIND YOU, 'E DESERVED IT, COS 'E WAS A **WICKED**, EVIL, 'ORRIBLE FACKIN' **GRARSE**!

an' 'is FISH BOWL Full of Fascinating Facts abaaht fings what begin wiv F

JUST 'COS 'ARF A DAAZEN OF US BEAT 'IM VICIOUSLY WIV' STICKS, AN' CUT 'IS FACE T'RIBBONS, 'E WENT SQUEALIN' T'THE FILTH!!

THAT WAS **WELL** OUT OF ORDAAH!

HERE FRANKIE. CATCH!

OH YEAH! FOOTBALL! SORRY 'BAAHT THAT. I WAS MILES AWAY

HISSSS!

MY FASCINATIN' FACT ABAAHT FOOTBALL IS THAT MY GRANDSON, TOMMY FRASER, PLAYS MIDFIELD FOR BRIGHTON AN' 'OVE ALBION!

'E'S A GOOD BOY, MY TOMMY. 'E'S ONLY BIN SENT ORF WANCE SO FAR, AT BRISTOL CITY IN 2007, FOR STAMPIN' ON THE KEEPER.

BUT 'E NEVER DONE IT! 'E WAS FACKIN' INNOCENT. EVEN THE KEEPER SAID SO.

I'LL TELL YOU SUMFINK... THAT REFEREE... MIKE RILEY...'E'S A **FACKIN' WANKAAH!**

SINCERE ED'S VOICE

YOU CAN'T SAY THAT FRANKIE! I'D LIKE TO APOLOGISE, ON BEHALF OF EVERYONE AT QI, TO REFEREE MIKE RILEY

RIGHT! WHAT'S AFTER FOOTBALL? OH YEAH! THE NEXT EFF IS FOR **SHITE.** ...I MEAN FAECES.

ERM... WOMBATS... 'AVE SQUARE SHAPED TURDS. APPARENTLY.

FUNNILY ENAAFF, I ONCE FREW A BUCKET OF SHIT OVER THE GUVNOR'S 'EAD. IN WANDSWERF, ABAAHT 1947.

WELL, ON THAT RATHER DISAPPOINTING NOTE I THINK WE OUGHT TO CONCLUDE TODAY'S INSPECTION

YOU FACKIN' **BARSTAD!!**

YOU **SLAAG!**

COME ON FRASER. IT'S THE HOSPITAL WING FOR YOU... VIA THE PUNISHMENT CELL!

MIND, THAT BUCKET OF SHIT CAME BACK TO 'AUNT ME WHEN I WAS UP FOR TORTURE AT THE OLD BAILEY, IN 1967...

THE BEAK TURNS AAHT TO BE NUN UVVA THAN **JUDGE FREDERICK LAWTON,** 00'S FARVA I 'AD DOUSED IN EXCREMENT ALL THOSE YEARS AGO!

AH! MR FRASER. I BELIEVE YOU WERE AQUAINTED WITH MY FATHER

OH **FACK!**

'ERE! YOU 'AVE TO LARF ABAAHT IT THO', DON'T CHA!

HEH HEH HEH!

'E GIVE ME A TEN STRETCH FOR THE TORTURE. BUT LIKE I SAID, I NEVER USED NO PLIERS

FACKIN' 'ELL! IT'S **FREDDIE 'BRAAHN BREAD' FOREMAN!** WHAT ARE YOU DOIN' 'ERE?

I'VE BROUGHT YOU A LITTLE SURPRISE FRANKIE, BEGININ' WIV AN EFF

OH YEAH? WHAT'S THAT THEN?

MY FACKIN' **FIST!**

POP!

RIGHT! I'M LOOKIN' ARFTA THIS STRIP, AN' FROM NAAH ON **I'LL** BE SUPPLYIN' ALL THE FACTS ABAAHT FINGS WHAT BEGIN WIV AN EFF

STARTIN' OFF WIV FLYIN' FISH...

CD 8/08

FLYING FISH DON'T 'AVE FEVAAHS. THEY 'AVE FINS. THE FURVEST A FLYING FISH 'AS EVAAH FLOWN IS ABAAHT QUARTER OF A MILE. I RECKON.

A FLYIN' FISH

A FEVVAH

RELIEVED QI ED'S VOICE

I'M AFRAID THAT'S ALL WE'VE GOT TIME FOR, THANK YOU

THANK FUCK FOR THAT

READER'S VOICE

91

31. Dutch. It means 'lemon'. The Citroen were a Dutch Jewish émigré family, who added the diaresis (the two dots over the 'o') to their name to make it classier.

32. The five islands in the Netherlands/Dutch Antilles (Curaçao, Bonaire, Sint Eustatius, Saba and Sint Maarten), and Aruba, which separated from them in 1986, but remained within the Kingdom of the Netherlands. The Netherlands Antilles florin is usually called the guilder; since 1986, the Aruban currency is usually called the florin, but the two terms are interchangeable. 66% of the Aruban population speak Papiamento, a Spanish-Dutch-Portuguese-English dialect.

33. A thimble.

34. Fundy. The highest tides in the world occur near Wolfville, Nova Scotia in the Minas Basin in the Bay of Fundy between Nova Scotia and New Brunswick in Canada. The sea level can change as much as 16 m (45 ft) between high and low tide. At mid-tide, the amount of water travelling through the Minas Channel is equal to the combined flow of all the rivers and streams on Earth put together. The 14 cubic kilometres (14 billion tons) of seawater that flow into Minas Basin twice a day cause Nova Scotia to bend and tilt slightly under the strain.

35. FORFEIT: ANY PERCENTAGE EXCEPT 0
0% according to the UN Food and Agriculture Organisation. Guyana's rain forests have a similar level of biodiversity to those in the Amazon but, unlike Brazil's, they are not disappearing. Logging in Guyana is selective, with only 35 out of 1,000 tree species logged commercially. Because of Guyana's excellent record in forest management and conservation, the forests, ironically, are considered to have no value. Yet they seed rain that irrigates farmland as far away as the American Midwest, house thousands of species of plants and animals (including many rare ones) and store thousands of tons of carbon. The Iwokrama reserve in Guyana is 371,000 hectares in extent (roughly the size of Majorca). Trees are cut down at the rate of one per hectare per year and only from half of the reserve's total area. Iwokrama has recently signed a deal with British financiers Canopy Capital. They have 'valued' the forest at $20 per hectare. If this were a commercial proposition to store carbon, the deal would work out at $0.20 per ton. By comparison, BP is planning to spend $50-60 per ton pumping carbon into disused oilfields in the North Sea.

FLORILEGIUM✱

36. They were all cobblers. Stalin's and Hans Christian Andersen's mothers were both also washerwomen.

37. Teaching children to utter their first word.

38. FORFEIT: AMERICA/USA
The use of the word 'fall' or 'the fall' to mean autumn is commonly assumed to be an Americanism, but in fact it is found in the works of Elizabethan writers Michael Drayton (1563-1631), Thomas Middleton (1580-1627) and Sir Walter Raleigh (c 1554-1618). The expression was originally 'the fall of the leaf'. The earliest recorded use of 'fall' in this sense in English occurs in 1545 in *Toxophilus*, a treatise on archery by Roger Ascham (1515-68). Ascham's book was hugely popular, gaining him a royal pension of £10 a year. It was later taken as the model for *The Compleat Angler* by Izaak Walton.

39. The last Maltese falcon or Mediterranean peregrine (*Falco peregrinus brookei*). Gozo is the second largest island in the Maltese archipelago, after Malta itself.

40. The dragon that guards the treasure of the Nibelungen. It means 'Smith' in Norse, just as Cain, the first murderer, does in Hebrew.

✱ *Florilegium* means literally 'a collection of flowers' in Latin, hence, an anthology (a word which also literally means 'collection of flowers', but in Greek).

EFFING DIFFICULT ANSWERS

[See the Effing Difficult Quiz, p. 43]

F WORDS

1. 51 times. We've done the maths.
2. FORFEIT: PLANTS/ANIMALS
   The answer is neither: they have their own separate Kingdom – though they are thought to be more like animals than plants.
3. It has more chromosomes, 1,320, than any other living thing. Adder's Tongues are small strikingly inconspicuous plants less than 15 cm (6 in) tall. Each plant has just one smooth-edged, pointed, oval leaf. They look nothing like ferns and are easily mistaken for the seedling of a flower.
4. Fermentation.
5. The Old English name for the swastika.
6. Fulmars, also called tubenoses and stinkers, are large seabirds related to petrels. The name is from the Norse meaning 'foul gull'.
7. Pressed caviar.

FRUIT

8. Walnuts. (All nuts are fruit.) The taxonomic name for the walnut genus is *Juglans*, of the family *Juglandaceae*. It is Latin for 'walnut' but it literally means 'the head of God's penis'. *Juglans* is an abbreviation for *Jovis glans* ('the glans of Jove') - *Jove* (or *Jupiter*) being king of the gods, and *glans* being Latin for the head of the penis, from its original meaning 'acorn', which it closely resembles.
9. Vanilla. Vanilla is a kind of orchid. The English word 'vanilla' comes from the Spanish *vainilla*, the diminutive of *vaina*, a sheath or scabbard, hence pod, husk or shell. Vaina is from the Latin *vagina* of which the original meaning was also a sheath or scabbard. The word 'orchid' comes from the Greek *orchis*, meaning 'the testicles', plural of *orcheis*. Orchids are so called because of the shape of their roots.
10. FORFEIT: TOMATOES
    Walnuts. They were a fertility symbol and a rather painful form of confetti.
11. FORFEIT: HAWAII
    Thailand (11%), The Philippines (11%), Brazil (10%), China (10%), India (9%). Pineapple production varies from year to year, so any of these answers is acceptable. Hawaii, for many years the pineapple king, now produces less than 2% of the world's supply. Del Monte recently closed a factory there.
12. Strawberry. Strawberries are not fruit, they are 'false fruit' or pseudocarps. The actual fruit are the little white or brown specks that get stuck in your teeth.
13. FORFEIT: PRISONERS
    Monkeys, imported from Panama, were used to reduce labour costs. Each gang had a human foreman who set them loose in the orchards. They scampered up the trees, harvested all the plums as planned, and then ate the lot.
14. Lemon. 'Dribly' also has some lime in it.

FAITH

15. FORFEIT: ISLAM
    Mormonism. There are 5 times as many Mormons as there were in 1960.
16. Shinto. There are innumerable deities in Shinto, but the chief one is the sun goddess Amaterasu-o-mikami, 'the great shining goddess in the sky.'
17. The Jehovah's Witnesses: Jesus succeeded him. On taking command, he threw Satan and his wicked angels out of Heaven and down to earth. This is why things have become so unpleasant in the world since 1914.
18. Zoroastrianism. The swastika is an ancient and virtually universal symbol, which has been used all over the world from prehistoric times up to the present day, almost always representing prosperity and good fortune. It was a favourite sign on coinage in ancient Mesopotamia. In ancient Scandinavia, the left-handed swastika represented the hammer of the god Thor. In early Christian and Byzantine art it was called the *gammadion*, gammadion cross or crux *gammata* because it can be made from four Greek capital gammas (Γ). It occurred among the Maya in South and Central America, and in North America amongst the Navajo. In India, to this day, the swastika is the most widely used symbol of auspiciousness in Hinduism, Jainism and Buddhism.
19. To broadcast the powerful suggestion to the rest of us that telepathy does not exist.
20. Sitting.
21. Shakerism: her name was Ann Lee.
22. Once – or twice if you count the original declaration of papal infallibility in 1870. Pope Pius XII issued an infallible statement in 1950 regarding the Assumption of the Blessed Virgin Mary (ie that she was transported body and soul to heaven).

F FOLK

23. The romantic smuggling novel *Moonfleet* (1898).
24. Cuthbert.
25. Cyd Charisse. Cyd was a childhood nickname: her brother couldn't pronounce 'Sis'. She was married to Nico Charisse, a dancer.
26. C.S. Forester.
27. Jean Henri Fabre (1823-1915). He devoted his whole life to the study of insects, carefully and beautifully describing and illustrating them in book after book, but he was 84 years old before anyone noticed. A poverty-stricken schoolteacher in provincial France, Fabre was a gifted and self-taught amateur entomologist who, on the publication of his last book, *Souvenirs Entomologiques*, suddenly achieved both literary and scientific world-renown. Scientific societies in London, Brussels, Geneva and St Petersburg elected him to membership and the French government gave him an annual pension. All students of insect behaviour, of comparative psychology and of experimental biology are indebted to him.
28. The White Cliffs of Dover. *Foraminiferans* are a form of zooplankton (tiny marine creatures from the Greek for 'wandering animals'). They live in shells made of the same stuff as limestone, marble and chalk. They manufacture these themselves by drawing calcium carbonate from the surrounding seawater. The sticky protoplasm of the *foraminiferan* flows in and out of holes in the shell to catch food. The holes or pores are what give the animals their name – *Foramen* is Latin for a hole or orifice. As the animal outgrows its shell, it discards it and makes a new one.

THE F WORLD

29. He was neither Finnish nor a saint. He was English.
30. Only about 80% of it. Under French law, the French possessions of French Guiana in South America, Guadeloupe

·FIBONACCI·F·F·I·B·N·C·FB·

Flourish

führer

Fold

flash

FIZZ

F²o+m²ul=a

fife

fart

ORWARD F

FLIP

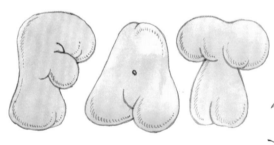

LYING FISH

farce

feuillemorte

FAR

~fluid~

AHRENHEIT

fetter

FLUCTUATE   foe

FRONT

FREUD

FONDL

BO·NN·CI·FOO·IBB·BCC·A

£1ood

fing@rprint

fez

F·8·I

FOOD

flora

Fancy

FLAT

FOUCAULT

flexible

FIRE

FINISTERRE

FAX

filibusterfilibusterfilibuster

FLY TRAP

fogey

FLOOD

Fossil

fault

Slummox

FADE

FLAINT

FELICID

95

Ye Daily Telegraph

MONDAY 18TH OCTOBER 1381
Free Advertisements of Sundry Kinds

Lord Mayor and Mercer to the King, Richard 'Dick' Whittington says *"I would probably still be sitting in a puddle of my own filth were it not for my MAGICAL CAT"*. Everybody knows it's impossible to improve yourself. No matter how hard you work or who you defer to the old phrase still holds true 'Once a peasant, always a peasant' - until now. Meet MAGICAL CAT. With MAGICAL CAT you can now aspire to better yourself in life. Imagine earning money and moving through society. Soon you'll be endowing grammar schools and leaving a SMALL FORTUNE to charity in the hope of preserving your greedy, mercenary soul from hell fire. And when you get back from a hard day counting money you'll be able to say *"Thanks MAGICAL CAT"*.

MAGICAL CAT – THERE'S NO OTHER EXPLANATION FOR IT!

PLEASE Rush me my MAGICAL CAT for the bargain price of TEN ENGLISH POUNDS. I am astonishingly gullible. Send money NOW to: The Richard Whittington Home for Stray Cats, Suthwerk, Nr London.

. . . .

END PLAGUE MISERY NOW

Are there times when you wonder if the pestilence will ever go away? Now you can say *'bye-bye buboes'* with our fabulous 'pomander'. Pomander is a revolutionary metal ball stuffed with leaves, sticks and other stuff probably proven to be effective against pestilence and **MUCH MORE**. Pomander is not only proof against all forms of miasmas and foul airs – it's also fun and fashionable. Pomander costs just 1 angel – is your family worth it?

. . . .

You Too Could Become a Writer – With the majority of the population *WHOLLY ILLITERATE* there's never been a better time to become a writer and with the new notion of 'printing', your words could literally reach hundreds. Writing everything from scurrilous pamphlets to pornographic chronicles can be exciting and rewarding and the SCRIVENING SCHOOL is with you all the way°. You will receive personalised tuition from a host of published authors (*G. Chaucer or W. de Worde*) and before long the farthings will come flooding in. *Full money-back guarantee if you can find us.*

"I just copied out a French fablieau and changed a few bits and now I'm considered the father of English literature – Brilliant!" G. Chaucer

Send a stamped addressed parchment for further details to: Wynkyn de Worde School of Scrivening, The Swan Tavern, St. Paul's Churchyard, London.

°up to, but not including, arrest, torture and execution.

▗▘ VACANCIES: ▗▘

Why not become an anchoress? Being walled up alive can be more rewarding than you might think. In return for simple prayers and advice your community will feed you for free (terms and conditions may apply) and, when necessary, bury you in the hole you have spent your life excavating in the floor of your cell. Become an anchoress and really dig your own grave! Apply Julian of Norwich.

VACANCY: King of Poland. Owing to the unexpected running away of the previous incumbent a vacancy now exists for the position of Polish Monarch. Poland is a vibrant and backward mediaeval state at the heart of a brutal theocratic Europe and the role of king requires an unusual combination of naivety and recklessness. With a history of unprovoked regicide, Poland will provide an exciting challenge for the successful applicant who, in return, can expect a handsome compensation package including a gloomy official residence and a full state funeral. *Previous applicants need not, and largely cannot, apply. Please fill in coupon for further details.*

YES PLEASE! I have what it takes to be the next King of Poland. I also have no next of kin.

Name:

Address:

Send to: "I want to be King", The Human Resources Manager, Kraków Castle, Kraków, Poland.

. . . .

THOUGHT ABOUT NECROMANCY?

WE SINCERELY HOPE NOT. THE NATION OF ENGLAND OFFERS NECROMANCERS A VARIETY OF PAINFUL DEATHS DEPENDING ON SOCIAL STATUS. MINOR CLERICS AND LOCAL BUMPKINS CAN EXPECT ALL THE PAGEANTRY OF BEING HANGED, DRAWN AND QUARTERED IN FRONT OF A LIVELY AND ENTHUSIASTIC CROWD. THOSE OF A HIGHER STATION IN LIFE CAN LOOK FORWARD TO ANYTHING FROM A 'MYSTERIOUS DISAPPEARANCE' TO BEING BANISHED FOR LIFE TO THE ISLE OF MAN.

. . . .

WANTED: Stale piss. Top prices paid by London fuller. Help keep the nobility smelling like a cess pit.

. . . .

LUXURY TOURING HOLIDAYS

For years the idea of walking slowly and painfully to Canterbury on unmade roads in the company of drunks was little more than a DREAM for most peasants. Now even the humblest turnip-eater can join in the magic. Walking parties leave from the Tavern in Suthwerk every Monday. Tour includes brigands, insults and the chance to be WHOLLY DEFRAUDED by the monks of Canterbury on arrival. So why not come to Canterbury and have your own tale to tell? *Apply G Chaucer, Customs House, Newgate.*

. . . .

LIMB LOSS?

Worried about unsightly limb loss? The Leper Hospital of St. Nicholas can help. Look years younger with one of our wooden legs, hand carved from old wood and, at a sufficient distance, almost indistinguishable from the real thing. Also just in – crutches!

Apply now for a free colour parchment to: The Hospital of St. Nicholas Beyond the Walls (actually quite a long way beyond the walls), York.

. . . .

AFTERLIFE INSURANCE: Only the Holy Catholic and Apostolic church offers genuine PURGATORY afterlife insurance. Endow a chantry chapel, build a cathedral or even just give bread to the poor to earn **Remission of Sins** in Purgatory. Remember the prayers of the poor can save YOU from hell. No other religion offers this simple and convenient way to avoid DAMNATION. Just leave us your money and we'll do the rest, leaving you to really *'rest in peace'*. And remember, the more you leave us, the shorter your torment.

The Catholic Church **is** Purgatory!

▗▘ DOMESTIC SITUATIONS ▗▘

Serf required for busy manor. Must be willing to work to outmoded feudal concepts. Apply The Abbot of St.Alban's, Dining Hall, St. Alban's Abbey.

Executioner – Reliable and imaginative executioner required by busy tyrant. Excellent rates of pay and exotic travel. Not for the squeamish. *Apply Tamerlane, Khan of the Timurids, Royal Palace, Samarkand.*

££££ EARN Groats as a Pardoner ££££
Why slave under feudal tenure when you could be earning up to a groat a day – every day? Pardoning is easy to learn and fun to do. Your bishop will provide you with all necessary materials – you just have to go out and sell a little bit of heaven!

▗▘ FOR SALE ▗▘

'The World Turned Upside Down' – read John Gower's explosive new manuscript *Vox Clamantis* on why modern life is rubbish. Available in all good scriptoria.

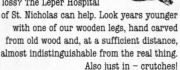

Sheep – one careful owner. Some superficial damage. All offers considered. *Apply Roger Lambkin.*

Magnificent moss-stuffed winkle-pickers. Note – may not comply with your local sumptuary laws. Check before buying. *Symond the Cobbler.*

Village full of peasants, available individually or as a lot. Owing to move into sheep farming no longer required for lives of meaningless servitude. Not allowed to drown them so will give them to any suitable or unsuitable home, provided they don't come back. *Apply Richard of Cotesford, Tusmore.*

Hilarious tabards – 'My Other Cart is a Cart', 'My Wife of Bath Went to Canterbury and All I Got Was This Lousy Tabard' and many, many more. Available in off-white only. As seen at the opening of Parliament. *Send for full details to 'Tabardtastic', Gropecunte Lane, London.*

▗▘ LONELY HEARTS ▗▘

FABULOUSLY UGLY YORKSHIRE HARRIDAN (probably a witch) wltm gentil parfait knight. **Apply Alison Gross**

Notts-based bandit seeks posh lass for fun in the forest. **Apply R. Loxley, Sherwood.**

GAY KING GSOH REQUIRES TEEN BRIDE FOR SAKE OF APPEARANCES. **APPLY TOWER OF LONDON.**

When Adam Delved and Eve Span, Who was then the Gentilman?
With a third of the population dead there's never been a better time to think about a career change. Ever wondered what it would be like to lord it over your very own peasants? Ever thought about dying in a different station in life to the one you were born into? Now you can with my simple Manor Invasion Programme. I'll show you in three easy steps how to (1) Destroy the manorial records that bind you to the land; (2) Seize untenanted property; (3) Bribe the local aristocracy to keep schtum. Or join me on Blackheath Common for our first seminar, featuring Wat Tyler and me, John Ball.

NOTE: *Written programme requires basic literacy.*

The *QI F Annual* was written, researched, illustrated and otherwise enhanced by Ronni Ancona, Clive Anderson, Rowan Atkinson, Jo Brand, Craig Brown, Derren Brown, Rob Brydon, Jimmy Carr, Tom Climpson, Stevyn Colgan, Mat Coward, Alan Davies, Cherry Denman, Ted Dewan, Chris Donald, Geoff Dunbar, Hunt Emerson, Stephen Fry, James Harkin, Tony Husband, Phill Jupitus, Roger Law, John Lloyd, Sean Lock, John Mitchinson, Ben Morris, Nick Newman, Molly Oldfield, Kathy Phillips, Justin Pollard, Anthony Pye-Jeary, David Stoten and Adrian Teal.

Designed by David Costa and Nadine Levy at Wherefore Art? Email david@whereforeart.com
Cover illustration: Adrian Teal

Editorial: Sarah Lloyd
Editorial Administrator: Liz Townsend

Picture research: Wherefore Art? with help from Mark Boutros, Will Elworthy, James Harkin, Caitlin Lloyd and Liz Townsend.

Photography: Jim Marks (www.marks.co.uk) for Rowan Atkinson's 'Furniture Masterclass' and the 'Foto Love Story'; Brian Ritchie (ritchiestills@btinternet.com) for the *QI* production photographs; Mark Boutros (markpaulboutros@hotmail.com) for 'Five Go Fact Finding on Formosa'; Harry Lloyd and David Costa for 'A Farrago of Fruit'; 2a for *Vogue* China, for 'Fragrance'.

The researchers for the *QI F Annual* were Mat Coward; James Harkin; John Lloyd; John Mitchinson; Molly Oldfield and Justin Pollard.

QI Logo design: Jules Bailey.

With thanks to Steve Colgan and Chris Hale for permission to adapt their 'Middenshire Chronicles' for 'Fakenham'; Sally Cooper for lashings of ginger beer and chocolate cake; Sarah Falk; The Groucho Club; Kate Kessling; Coco Lloyd; Ben Morris for the illustrations of Jimmy Carr; NASA; Oxfordshire County Council Museum Resource Centre at Standlake; Oscar Pye-Jeary; Jan 'Boris' Szymczuk; the *Daily Telegraph* for permission to use their logo, and all at Faber, especially Dave Watkins for his patience and support.

With special thanks to **HEAL'S** for permission to photograph Rowan Atkinson at their store in Tottenham Court Road, London.

Photo credits:
Bigstockphotos (www.bigstockphoto.com) for 'Form' and 'Fried Fish'
Corbis (www.corbis.com) for 'Fallacybuster' (figures); 'France' (man with onions); 'Effing Difficult Quiz'; 'A Farrago of Fruit' (blossom); 'Funambulism' (background image, woman on a wire)
DK Picture Library (www.dkimages.com) for 'Falcon vs Ferret' (Falcon)
Getty Images (www.gettyimages.com) for 'Fallacybuster' and 'Fours' and 'Fives'
Mary Evans Picture Library (www.maryevans.com) for 'France'(group of soldiers) and 'Fairly Famous F Frenchmen'
PA Photos (www.paphotos.com) for 'Funambulism' (Philippe Petit)
Punchstock Picture Library (www.punchstock.com) for 'Falcon vs Ferret' (Ferret)
Rex Features (www.rexfeatures.com) for 'Football in Mouth'
Topfoto (www.topfoto.co.uk) for 'Jo Brand's Fags of the World' (title image)
V&A Images Victoria and Albert Museum (www.vandaimages.com) for 'Funambulism' (lion)

The answer is 'Smith'. The list is the top twenty surnames today in Vancouver, capital of the province of British Columbia in Canada. Smith is the eighth commonest name in the city.

FIN

afafine n (Samoan) A boy raised as a girl. **fabaceous** a Bean-like. **fabal** a Of or belonging to a bean. **fabiform** a Bean-shaped. **fabulose** a Fond of gmas. **facetiae** n Bookseller's euphemism for pornography. **facety** a (Jamaican slang) Impudent, arrogant, rude; excessively bold or feisty. **faciale** n A e-cloth for a corpse. **faciendum** n Something that ought to be done. **facilize** v To make easy. **facinorous** a A very common 17th century word meaning remely wicked, grossly criminal, atrocious, infamous, vile. **facrere** n The art of make-believe. **factice** n Artificial rubber made from vegetable oil. totum n Someone who meddles with everything. **facula** n A bright spot on the surface of the sun. (An equivalent dark spot is called a macula.) **faculent** a ing forth light like a torch. **fadge** n A short, fat individual. **fado** n A melancholy Portuguese folk-song. **fagdom** n The condition of being a fag. **faggoteer** ne who makes faggots. **fagong** n A fireplace used on board a ship. **faham** n An orchid from Réunion or Mauritius, whose leaves are used by the French make tea. **fainéant** n Someone who does nothing. **fairess** n A female fairy. **fairney-cloots** n Horny substance above the hooves of sheep or goats. sandé a Affected, artificial, theatrical; 'spicy'. **faitour** n A criminal who shams illness or pretends to tell fortunes. **fakelore** n Fake folklore. **fala** n Dutch handkerchief. **falasha** n An Ethiopian Jew. **falcate** a Bent or curved like a sickle. **falciform** a Sickle-shaped. **falcon-gentle** n A female peregrine con. **faldage** n The right of a lord of the manor to set up pens in his fields and compel his tenants to put their sheep in them, the object being to get free nure. **faldetta** n A combined hood and cape, worn by women in Malta. **faldistory** n The seat or throne of a bishop within the chancel. **faldstool** n An nless chair used by bishops. **fallaciloquence** n Deceitful speech. **fallalish** a Slightly showy. **fam** v To feel or handle. **famble** v To speak clumsily. nble-crop n The first stomach in ruminating animals. **famelic** a Exciting hunger. **famicide** n A destroyer of one's reputation. **fample** v To put food into hild's mouth. **fanacle** n A small temple or shrine. **fanikin** n A small flag or banner. **farandine** n A kind of cloth used in the seventeenth century, made tly of silk and partly of hair. **farang** n The Thai term for a foreigner. **farcetta** n A short farce. **farger** n A false dice. **fario** n A half-grown salmon. merish a Somewhat resembling a farmer. **farol** n A bullfighting move in which the matador lures the bull by passing the cloak rapidly over his own ad. **farouche** a Sullen, shy and repellent in manner. **farsang** n A Persian measure of distance equal to about four miles. **fartlek** n A method of training middle- and long-distance running. **fascistoid** a Resembling a Fascist. **fattoush** n A middle-eastern salad. **faulx** n A wrestling trick where one grips small of an opponent's back. **faunology** n The study of the geographical distribution of animals. **favaginous** a Resembling a honeycomb. **favism** n A editary form of anæmia, brought on by contact with broad beans. **favonian** a Of or pertaining to the west wind; hence, favourable, gentle, propitious. vnguest n One who swindles another under the guise of friendship. **fazart** n A coward or dastard. **feaberry** n An unripe gooseberry. **feak** n A dangling l of hair. **fear-babe** n A thing fit only to frighten a baby. **featish** a Elegant, neat. **feaze** v To unravel a rope. **fec** n A definite interval in space or time: a ited distance, or fixed period. **fecifork** n The anal fork on which some larvæ carry their faeces. **feijoada** n National dish of Brazil containing black beans, k and sausages. **felicific** a Tending to produce happiness. **feliform** a Cat-shaped. **felo-de-se** n One who deliberately or accidentally kills himself while nmitting a crime. **fellmonger** n A dealer in sheep-skins. **femillet** n An ornamental clasp, buckle, or setting. **femocrat** n An influential female politician. estrate v To provide small holes in a bandage. **fenestriform** a Window-shaped. **feniculaceous** a Resembling fennel. **fenks** n The fibrous part of whale bber, which contains the oil. **fennish** a Belonging to, produced from, living in, or smelling of the fens. **feretory** n A portable shrine. **feria** n An ordinary ekday, as opposed to a special one like a festival. **ferly** a Wonderfully great; sudden, unexpected; terrible, frightful. **fernticle** n A freckle on the skin, embling a fern seed. **ferraunt** a Of a horse, iron-grey. **ferruginate** v To make something rust-coloured. **fermata** n A pause of unspecified length. **ferrific** a ducing iron. **fervefy** v To make boiling hot. **festoonery** n A group of objects arranged in festoons. **festucaceous** a Stalk-like. **festuceous** a Straw-like. tucine a Straw-coloured. **festucous** a Resembling straw. **fetch-light** n The spectral glow seen before a person's death, travelling from house to grave. hok n A polecat. **feuillemorte** a Coloured like a dead leaf. **fewter** n The rest or support for a lance attached to a knight's saddle. **fewter** v To pack men se together. **fianchetto** n In chess, to move a bishop one square. **fiants** n Badger dung. **fibulate** v To fiddle with one's buttons; to button and unbutton. iform a Fig-shaped. **fictile** a Suitable for making pottery. **fid** n A small but thick piece of anything. **field theory** n Any theory about fields. **fiendkin** n undersized sprite. **fiendly** a Hostile or unfriendly. **fig-boy** n A pickpocket. **figgum** n Juggler's tricks. **figling** n A little fig. **fikiness** n Taking a lot of uble over something. **fili** n A group of ancient Irish poets. **filiciform** a Fern-shaped. **filly-folly** n A ridiculous hobby. **filmiform** a In the form of a film. sella n A kind of stuff. **filsne** v To lurk. **fimbria** n The fringed end of the Fallopian tube. **fimbrilla** n A tiny fringe. **fipple** n 1. The plug at the mouth of vind instrument used to reduce its size. 2. A large, loose dangling lower lip in either men or animals. **fiqh** n The study of Islamic religious law. **firk** n A art sudden blow from a whip. **firn** n Snow above a glacier that has not yet turned to ice. **fisc** n The public treasury of Rome. **fissipede** a Having arated toes. **fiumara** n A flooded river or mountain torrent. **fix-fax** n The thick tendon found in the necks of cattle or sheep. **fizgig** n A light, frivolous man. **flaccescency** n The quality of becoming flaccid. **flamfloo** n A gaudily dressed woman. **flancard** n A piece of armour for the thigh. **flanconade** n ncing) A thrust in the flank or side. **flang** n A two-pointed pick used by miners. **flangeless** a Having no flange. **flap-sauce** n A glutton. **fleay** a Full of as. **flemensfirth** n The offence of entertaining a banished person. **fleshquake** n A tremor in the body. **flewsey** a Fluffy. **flexanimous** a Having the ver to bend or influence the mind. **flexicostate** a Having bent ribs. **flickermouse** n A bat. **flingee** n One at whom anything is flung. **flirtigig** n A giddy, hty girl from Yorkshire. **flix** n The down of a beaver. **floggee** n One who is flogged. **florey** n Blue pigment made from the scum that collects in a vat d in dyeing with woad or indigo. **florimania** n A rage or passion for flowers. **florisugent** a Sucking honey from flowers. **flounderkin** n An insulting rd to describe a Dutchman. **fode** n One who beguiles with fair words. **fogo** n A disagreeable smell. **föhn** n A warm dry south wind which blows down valleys on the north side of the Alps. **foilist** n One who fences with a foil. **folivore** n An animal that mainly eats leaves. **fonduk** n A North African pub. tful n As much as a font will hold. **fooker** n A financier. **foozle** n One who is behind the times. **foramen** n An opening or orifice; a hole or short passage the protrusion of an organ. **fordreamed** a Tired out by too much dreaming. **fore-backwardly** adv Beginning at the wrong end. **fore-buttock** n Ancient ular word for a woman's breasts. **fore-eatage** n A chance to get one's cattle to pasture before someone else's. **fore-gallant** n The chief performer in a rris dance. **forflitten** a Overwhelmed by unreasonable and out of proportion scolding. **forfrorn** a Stuck fast in the ice. **forfried** a Over-fried. **forglopned** verwhelmed with astonishment. **forgreme** v To forfeit by displeasing God. **forplaint** a Exhausted by complaining. **forpossed** a Pushed violently, tossed out. **forroast** v To torture by roasting. **forswat** a Covered with sweat. **forslug** v To neglect through laziness. **forswithe** v To torture by burning. swunk a Exhausted by overwork. **forwall** v To torture by boiling. **forwallowed** a Wearied with tossing about. **fossor** n A church officer charged with burial of the dead. **foulbrood** n A bacterial disease of bees. **foud** A governor of the Orkney, Shetland or Faroe Islands. **foudroyant** a Thundering, nning, noisy. **fou rire** n A fit of wild or uncontrollable laughter. **foy** n A last drink given by or to someone setting out on a journey. **fozy** a Spongy; loose-tured; fat-witted. **frabble** n Confused wrangling. **frag** v (US military slang) To throw a grenade at one's superior officer. **frail** n A rush basket for keeping sins in. **fraise** n A tool for enlarging a circular hole or for cutting the teeth on a wheel in a watch. **framboesia** n A chronic contagious disease racterised by raspberry-like excrescences. **framea** n An ancient German javelin. **frample** v To swallow or gobble up. **frampold** a In people, sour-npered and peevish; in horses, fiery and spirited. **franchemyle** n A sort of haggis. **franion** n A gay, reckless fellow. **frantling** n The noise made by acocks. **frass** n The excrement produced by boring insects. **fraunch** v To feed greedily. **frawn** n A popular Irish word for the bilberry. **frayne** n A mark streak on a horse. **frazil** n Ice formed at the bottom of a stream in Canada. **fream** n The noise made by an angry boar. **freemartin** n A hermaphroditic **freke** n Someone who is eager for a fight. **fremish** a Of an army, to waver in the ranks. **fremitus** n A dull roaring noise. **fremman** n Someone you're related to. **frescade** n A cool walk or shady alley. **fresher** n A young frog. **freshet** n A small freshwater stream. **fretter** n A branch that rubs. **friable** a sily crumbled. **fricatrice** n A lewd woman. **frigidarium** n The cooling-room in a Roman bath. **frill** v To scream like an eagle. **frillock** n A wanton young **frim** a Luxuriant, plump, full-fleshed, juicy, moist, melting easily. **froghood** n The quality of being a frog. **fructiform** a Fruit-shaped. **frumple** n A nkle. **frushy** a Fragile, easily broken. **fruz** n A collection of short frizzy branches. **fub** n A small, chubby person. **fuchsite** n A green mineral containing omium. **fucivorous** a Eating, or surviving on, seaweed. **fucoid** a Seaweed-like. **fud** n The buttocks or bottom. **fufu** n A kind of dough made from anas. **fugie** n A cock that will not fight. **fuk** n A type of sail. **fulgur** n A flash of lightning. **fulmen** n A thunderbolt. **fum** n The phoenix: a symbol of erial power in ancient China. **fumist** n One who cures smoky chimneys; a chimney-doctor. **funk-hole** n A place of safety into which one can retreat. fur n A bran-like sediment found in the urine. **furphy** n A false report or rumour; an absurd story. **fusiform** a Shaped like a cigar or spindle: tapering at n ends. **fuzzword** n A deliberately confusing piece of jargon, used more to impress than to inform. **fyrd** n The military strength of the whole of England ore the Norman Conquest.

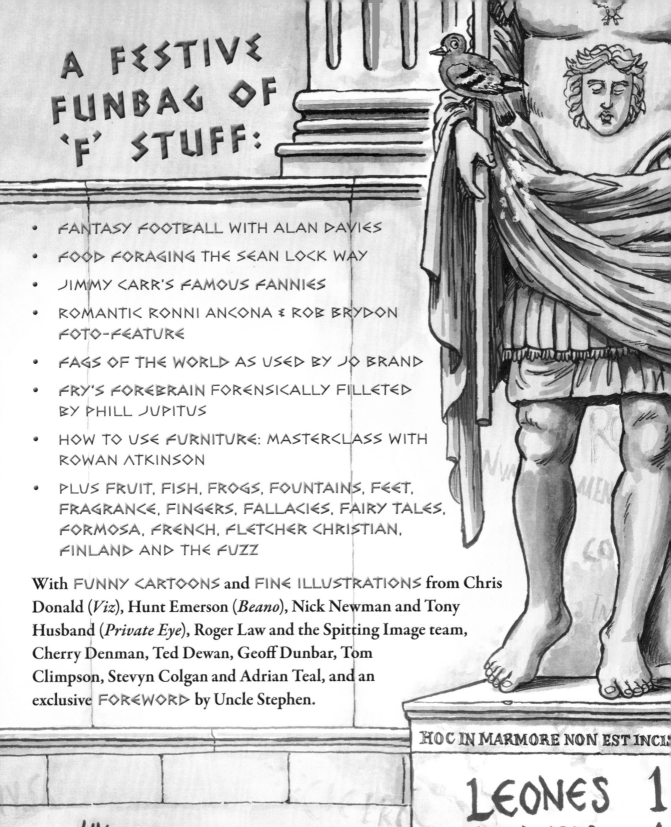

A FESTIVE FUNBAG OF 'F' STUFF:

- FANTASY FOOTBALL WITH ALAN DAVIES
- FOOD FORAGING THE SEAN LOCK WAY
- JIMMY CARR'S FAMOUS FANNIES
- ROMANTIC RONNI ANCONA & ROB BRYDON FOTO-FEATURE
- FAGS OF THE WORLD AS USED BY JO BRAND
- FRY'S FOREBRAIN FORENSICALLY FILLETED BY PHILL JUPITUS
- HOW TO USE FURNITURE: MASTERCLASS WITH ROWAN ATKINSON
- PLUS FRUIT, FISH, FROGS, FOUNTAINS, FEET, FRAGRANCE, FINGERS, FALLACIES, FAIRY TALES, FORMOSA, FRENCH, FLETCHER CHRISTIAN, FINLAND AND THE FUZZ

With FUNNY CARTOONS and FINE ILLUSTRATIONS from Chris Donald (*Viz*), Hunt Emerson (*Beano*), Nick Newman and Tony Husband (*Private Eye*), Roger Law and the Spitting Image team, Cherry Denman, Ted Dewan, Geoff Dunbar, Tom Climpson, Stevyn Colgan and Adrian Teal, and an exclusive FOREWORD by Uncle Stephen.

HOC IN MARMORE NON EST INCIS

LEONES 1
ALANVS -1

LINGVA SPECIEM INVOLVTAM PRÆBET, SED SAT CITO EAM COMPREHENDES

CALIGVLA
♥
EQVVS

THE Qi ANNUAL

From the team that brought you
THE BOOK OF GENERAL IGNORANCE

ff

GOOG10^100L
GALILEO
GILL
Grand Guignol
GAG Grail GCHQ
GRUMPY
GAIA GADARENE
Glabrous
GANDHI
GIFT ?uess GUM
GEISER la GANJA
GIACONDA
GRAVY TRAIN GAUL
GEN L ~string
gout
1 Gettysburg St,
Gettysburg,
Pennsylvania.
goofy
graffiti
GAS GIGOL

gabarage *n* That which Irish Goods are wrapped in. **gabbart** *n* A sailing vessel for inland navigation. **gabbock** (Scots) *n* A dog-fish. **gabel** *v* To mark a sheep on the ear. **gabelle** *n* A salt-tax imposed in France before the Revolution. **gaberlunzie** *n* (Scots) A strolling beggar. **gablet** *n* A little gable. **gablock** *n* An artificial metallic spur on a fighting cock. **gadi** *n* The cushioned throne of an Indian ruler. **gaduin** *n* A fatty substance found in cod-liver oil. **gagaku** *n* A type of Japanese music performed on ceremonial occasions. **gage d'amour** *n* a love-token. **gaggee** *n* One who is gagged. **gaijin** *n* A Japanese term for a foreigner. **gaita** *n* A Spanish musical instrument resembling bagpipes. **gaiterless** *a* Having no gaiters. **galapee** *n* A West Indian tree. **galeage** *n* Royalty paid for land in the Forest of Dean. **galimatias** *n* Confused, meaningless talk. **galiongee** *n* A Turkish sailor. **gallantissimo** *n* An exclamation meaning 'Most gallant sir!' **galler** *n* someone who irritates. **gallet** *n* A chip or splinter of stone. **gallicide** *n* (nonse-wd) A fox, i.e. a killer of chickens. **gallimaufry** *n* A dish made by hashing up odds and ends. **gallinipper** (U.S) *n* A large mosquito. **galliwasp** *n* A small lizard. **gallopade** *n* A lively dance of Hungarian origin. **gallows-bird** *n* Someone who deserves to be hanged. **galoot** *n* (slang) an awkward soldier. **galp** *v* To vomit. **galziekte** *n* An illness of the gall bladder. **gamahuche** *v* To practise fellatio or cunnilingus. **gamelyn** *n* A dainty Italian sauce. **gametangium** *n* A testicle or ovary; the organ in which gametes are produced. **gamin** *n* A neglected boy running the streets. **gammerstang** *n* A tall, awkward woman. **gamp** *v* To eat greedily. **gandy-dancer** *n* (US slang) A railway maintenance-worker. **gang-days** *n* The three days preceding Ascension-day. **gangliform** *a* Having the form of a ganglion. **gangrenescent** *a* Becoming gangrenous. **ganne** *v* To bark like a fox. **gansel** *n* A garlic sauce especially eaten with goose. **gapy** *a* Disposed to yawn. **garagist** *n* The owner of a commercial garage. **garbagey** *a* Resembling garbage. **garbanzo** *n* The chick-pea. **garbologist** *n* A binman. **garçonnière** *n* A bachelor's rooms or flat. **gardyloo** *n* A warning cry uttered in Edinburgh before throwing dirty water from a window. **gargilon** *n* The oesophagus of a deer. **garible** *n* A flourish in music. **garri** *n* Grated cassava. **garrisonize** *v* To furnish with a garrison. **garuda** *n* The eagle shown on the official seal of Indonesia. **garum** *n* A Roman sauce prepared from fermented fish. **garus** *n* A medicinal liqueur. **gaseosa** *n* An effervescing drink. **gaseyn** *n* Marshy ground. **gash-gabbit** (Scots) *a* Having a projecting chin. **gaspereau** *n* A canadian ale-wife. **gastræa** *n* A primitive sac-like animal. **gastromancy** *n* Divination by the belly. **gat** *n* An opening between sandbanks. **gaudeamus** *n* Merry-making of college-students. **gayal** *n* A domesticated ox of South Asia. **gazee** (nonse-wd) *n* One who is being stared at. **gazob** *n* In Australian slang, a fool or a blunderer. **gazogene** *n* A gas-producer. **gazon** *n* A sod or piece of turf, used in fortification. **geadephagous** *a* Pertaining to a tribe of predaceous beetles. **geckoid** *a* Resembling a gecko. **geebung** *n* Australian fruit. **geisteswissenschaftler** *n* One who studies the arts or humanities. **geitje** *n* A venomous African lizard. **gemelliparous** *a* Producing twins. **geminiflorous** *a* Having flowers in pairs. **gemmaceous** *a* Pertaining to the nature of leaf-buds. **gena** *n* The cheek; especially in insects. **genethliacon** *n* A birthday song. **genin** *n* A steroid found in toad venom. **genipap** *n* A west indian fruit resembling an orange. **genizah** *n* A store-room for damaged, discarded, or heretical books. **genoblast** *n* The bisexual nucleus of the impregnated ovum. **gentoo** *n* A non-Muslim inhabitant of Hindustan. **gentoo** *n* A kind of penguin. **genu** *n* A knee-like bend in various organs of the body. **geoduck** *n* A large edible clam. **geophyllous** *a* Having leaves of an earthy colour. **gewgaw** *n* A pretty thing of little value. **ghaffir** *n* A local Egyptian policeman. **ghanta** *n* A bell or gong, used as an instrument in Indian music. **ghazal** *n* A type of Oriental poetry, generally of an erotic nature. **ghazeeyeh** *n* An Egyptian dancing-girl. **gherao** *n* An Indian labour dispute whereby workers refuse to let bosses leave until their claims are granted. **ghurry** *n* A period of 24 minutes. **gillaroo** *n* A species of trout found in certain Irish rivers. **gilly-gaupus** (Scots) *n* A foolish or awkward person. **gingivostomatitis** *n* Gingivitis combined with stomatitis. **ginnle** *v* To tickle the gills of a fish. **gixy** *n* A wench. **gizz** *n* A scottish wig. **gjetost** *n* A Norwegian cheese made from goat's milk. **glabreity** *n* Baldness. **glairigenous** *a* Producing slime or mucus. **glandiform** *a* Acorn-shaped. **glarney** *n* A glass marble. **glene** *n* The eye socket. **glimflashy** *a* Angry. **glögg** *n* A Scandinavian winter drink. **gloppen** *v* To be distressed or downcast. **gloriette** *n* A highly decorated chamber in a castle. **gloriole** *n* A halo. **glost** *n* The lead glaze used for pottery. **glottochronology** *n* The application of statistics to vocabulary to determine the degree of relationship between languages. **glut-glut** *v* To swallow or gulp down. **gnátoo** *n* Bark of the Chinese paper mulberry tree used for clothing. **gobar** *n* Cow dung used as fuel in South Asia. **gobemouche** *n* Someone who credulously accepts any news, no matter how incredulous. **godling** *n* A little god. **gongoozler** *n* An idler who stares at length at things happening on a canal. **gonotocont** *n* Any cell that may undergo meiosis. **gony** *n* A booby. **goodwilly** (Scots) *n* A volunteer. **gopak** *n* A lively Ukrainian dance in 2/4 time. **gorbymania** *n* Excessive enthusiasm for Mikhail Gorbachev. **gowpenful** *n* A double handful. **graip** (Scots & North) *n* A three or four-pronged dung-fork. **granilla** *n* An inferior quality of cochineal made from small or half-grown beetles. **great-willy** *a* High-spirited or strong-willed. **greegree** *n* An African charm, amulet, or fetish. **greenie** *n* In surfing slang, a large wave before it breaks. **grège** *n* A colour between beige and grey. **gregicide** (nonse-wd) *a* The slaughter of the common people. **grex** *n* A phase of the life cycle of cellular slime moulds. **griceling** *n* A little pig. **griggles** *n pl.* Small apples left on the tree by the gatherer. **groupuscule** *n* A small political group. **grrrl** *n* A strong and aggressive young woman. **grucchild** *n* A female grumbler. **grume** *n* A clot of blood. **grysbok** *n* A small grey South African antelope. **guazu** *n* The South American marsh-deer. **guazuti** *n* The brown and white South American pampas deer. **guemal** *n* A small Andean deer. **gueuze** *n* A type of sour, fizzy, strong Belgian beer. **guffy** *n* A sailor's name for a soldier. **gumbo-limbo** *n* A gum-yielding tree. **gum-gum** *n* A hollow iron bowl used as a musical instrument. **gundy-gut** *n* A fat paunch. **gunyah** *n* A native Australian hut. **gurk** *n* A belch. **guttiform** *a* Drop-shaped. **gyniolatry** *n* Excessive devotion to women. **gyoza** *n* A Japanese crescent-shaped dumpling. **gyral** *a* Moving in a circle or spiral. **gyrovague** *n* A monk who wanders from monastery to monastery.

Other books from QI

The Book of General Ignorance
The Book of General Ignorance: The Noticeably Stouter Edition
The Book of Animal Ignorance
Advanced Banter: The QI Book of Quotations
The Sound of General Ignorance
The QI 'E' Annual
The QI 'F' Annual

First published in 2009 by Faber and Faber Ltd
Bloomsbury House, 74–77 Great Russell Street, London WC1B 3DA

Printed and bound in Great Britain by Butler Tanner & Dennis, Frome, Somerset
All rights reserved
© QI Ltd, 2009
The right of QI Ltd to be identified as author of this work has been asserted in accordance with Section 77
of the Copyright, Designs and Patents Act 1988
A CIP record for this book is available from the British Library

ISBN 978–0–571–25182–7
4 6 8 10 9 7 5 3

This book belongs to...

This book belongs to...

THE Qi ANNUAL

G

Editor: John 'Scissorhands' Lloyd

ART DIRECTOR: DAVID 'GUITAR DAVE' COSTA

ff

faber and faber

Another year passes.

Your home planet completes another cycle around your yellow sun taking you
further from the dawn of creation and nearer to the night of destruction that
you know must come. How puny, pitiful and futile seem to me to be the
ambitions of you tiny earth people. Your history is a history of impotence,
failure and madness. You build only to destroy. You slice potatoes, crinkle
them, freeze them and reheat them. They are poured onto a plate, salted and
stuffed into the wet holes in your faces, often to the accompaniment of a red
sugared acetic sauce. You shave ovine mammals, card and comb their fleeces
and transform this material into swathes of fabric with which you sheathe
your ~~gelatanous~~ gelatinous flesh.

Ever since I have come down and moved amongst you I have wavered between
pity, contempt and disgust at your ways.

But I was commanded by Pattathrax Sillywee the Elder to remain within your
oxygenated atmosphere and remain I have.

I have communicated messages from the High Council through the medium of QI.
Those of you with eyes to hear and ears to smell have understood the orders
hidden within the seemingly trivial factoid data-nodules that are the
apparent purpose of the programme. You will know **that the time to ~~strike is
soon~~ and ~~that our~~ victory will** be complete.

in the meantime here is the Seventh Volume of Commandments issued by Her
Serene Quibbock, Princess Tampula Widdlevest.

Learn the commands well, my little ones.
Burn them before committing them to memory.

Yunt, yunt.

The One They Call
Stephen Fry*

*c/o Doctor Jeremy Marshall, Devonhall Rehabilitation Centre, Bromsgrove.

CONTENTS

'I downsized from a gateau in the Black Forest.'

GALAXIES

SOMBRERO GALAXY

Objects moving away from us look slightly red - this is because the wavelength of the light is stretched. (Imagine the change in the 'nee-naw' of a speeding police car as it goes past, but with light instead of sound.) In 1912, Vesto Slipher found that the Sombrero Galaxy exhibited 'red-shift' and is moving away from us at 2.5 million mph (4 million kph). This led to the then astonishing idea that the universe is expanding.

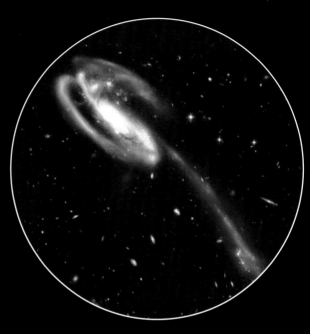

TADPOLE GALAXY

The little, blue 'eye' you can see in the top left corner of the Tadpole is actually another whole galaxy that has collided with it. The 'tail' is the result: the debris of stars and gas stretching out more than 280,000 light years. Because the universe is expanding, such collisions are rare: the Tadpole Galaxy gives us an idea of what the early universe was like, when collisions were more common.

SUNFLOWER GALAXY

The Sunflower Galaxy is an unusual galaxy in that it has many arms. The outer stars spin so fast that, theoretically, they should defy gravity and fly off into space. Something must be preventing this happening: a powerful additional force that we can't see. Because we have no idea what causes this force, it goes by the name 'dark matter'.

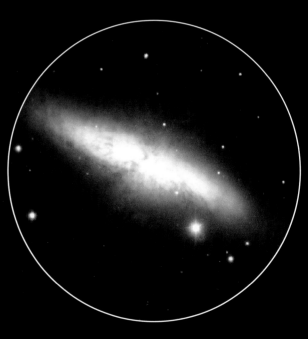

CIGAR GALAXY

The Cigar Galaxy is a 'starburst galaxy': one that generates an exceptionally large number of stars. It is 100 times brighter than the centre of the Milky Way. All stars give off charged particles called 'stellar wind', compressing gas to make even more stars. In the Cigar Galaxy, there are so many at work that their combined effect is called 'superwind'.

WHIRLPOOL GALAXY

The Whirlpool Galaxy was the first in which a spiral structure was discovered, in 1845, over 50 years after the object was first noticed. It is 'only' 30 million light years away and can actually be seen by anyone with a good pair of binoculars.

WHALE GALAXY

The Whale Galaxy is actually a spiral galaxy like many others. It only appears in the shape of a whale (or herring) because it is almost side-on to the earth. It is similar in size to the Milky Way but gives off an impressive halo of glowing x-rays, suggesting that it conceals a 'superbubble': a huge cavity of very, very hot gas.

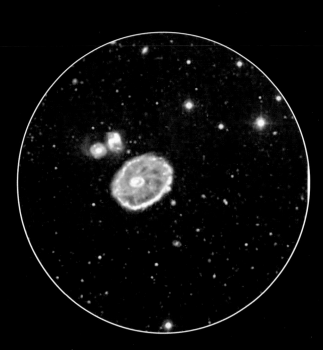

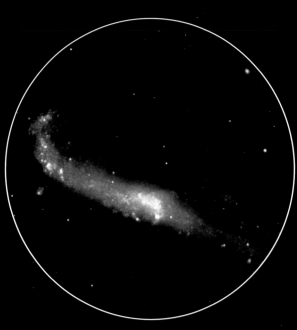

CARTWHEEL GALAXY

The Cartwheel is in fact two galaxies, one of which has punched a hole in the centre of the other, like dropping a stone into a pond. The ring that you see is a wave of energy containing newly formed, extremely bright, massive stars.

HOCKEY STICK GALAXY

The proximity of the Whale Galaxy has distorted this galaxy into the shape of a hockey stick (or a golf club, as some prefer). There is a 'bridge' of hydrogen gas connecting the two galaxies. William Herschel discovered the Hockey Stick Galaxy in 1787, six years after he discovered Uranus.

QI's A-TO-Z OF ALL THAT IS HOLY AND WORSHIPPED

OH MY GODS!

WORDS BY EMMET O'SHEA, DRAWINGS BY ROGER LAW

'MAY THE GODS FORGIVE US'

A IS FOR AAH

The Old Moon God of Egypt rules the 360-day moon calendar. The other five days were won from Aah in a dice game with Thoth, the God of Wisdom.

B IS FOR BES

Bes, another Egyptian God, is a rude, hairy dwarf with bowed legs who, among other household duties, is protector of children and women in labour. Only a mother could love him.

C IS FOR CALVA

Calva is the Roman Goddess of Bald Women. She rose to fame when she cut off her hair and donated it for bowstrings. 'Bald is beautiful.' She looked better bald than Britney.

D IS FOR DIONYSUS

Greek God of Luvvies, Sex, Wine and Intoxication. Dionysus was born after Zeus spent the night with Persephone…or was it Semele? Probably involving wine, intoxication and, frankly, careless sex.

E IS FOR EWAH

Ewah, a Native American Demon, is probably the loneliest God on our list. Just a quick glimpse of him can cause complete and utter madness, which is why we decided not to draw him.

F IS FOR FLYING HEAD

Another Native American God. A huge, winged flying head that devours livestock with his big fangs but he is forever hungry as he has no stomach to fill. The heavenly hot-head became a burnt offering when he gobbled up an entire barbecue, hot coals and all.

G IS FOR GAMA

Cheerful Japanese God of Longevity. He carries a scroll containing Secrets of the Ages but even if he gets saki-ed up and loses it no one will ever be able to read it as it is written in ludicrously small calligraphy. Like Hollywood stars he can change his skin and become young again.

9

H IS FOR HADES

Hades is God of the Greek Underworld which he owns along with a ridiculous three-headed dog. He can't have much clout as the underworld is overrun with Greek heroes creating havoc.

I IS FOR IAT

The Egyptian Goddess of Milk. The immortal milk monitor exists to keep the milk flowing so 'drink-a-pint-a-milk–a-deity'.

J IS FOR JARI

A primitive Oceanic Goddess with a bad track record in men. She married Snake Man who ate her mother. Then, whilst running for her life, she met Lizard Man who was in more trouble than she was. He had no backside or family jewels. So Jari made him some from fruit and nuts and, amazingly, Jari and the fruit and nut case went on to make plenty of babies together.

K IS FOR KALMA

Finnish Goddess of Death and Decay which is a perfect job for someone whose name means 'the stench of corpses'.

L IS FOR LAUFAKANAA

Laufakanaa, the Oceanic God of Wind and Bananas, works hard creating sea breezes to speed banana boats on their way. 'Dayo, dayo, daylight come and Laufakanaa wanna go home.'

M IS FOR MAMU

Australian Aboriginal Spirit Dingo who captures and eats the souls of children who stray from the camp. Possibly why dingos have such a bad press down under.

N IS FOR NGARU

Oceanic God of the surfboard Ngaru challenged the Great Shark to catch him on his new surfboard. After a week of spectacular surfing the Great Shark gave up and swam to Bondi Beach where he has recently enjoyed more success.

O IS FOR OGUN

African God Ogun erupted into the world from a volcano full of pent up anger and energy, always ready to explode. God of Iron and Truckers, not the politest of deities, he is associated with war and rum in the Caribbean where it is customary to offer him a tot when he shouts 'My balls are cold!' but voodoo you believe?

P IS FOR PAN

Pan, the Greek God of shepherds, sheep and fornication was himself born with the legs and horns of a goat. He enjoys frightening people walking through the forest at night – hence the word 'panic'. Pan also plays the pipes and has a fine voice (he could possibly pass as Welsh).

Q is for Qamaits

Native American Sky Goddess who knocks mountains into shape. Thankfully she rarely visits earth. When she does she causes mayhem, earthquakes, forest fires and, more recently, the swine flu epidemic.

R is for Ruadan

Celtic God of Spying. Licensed to kill. However, unlike James Bond, he was hopeless with weaponry. He met his end when an enemy demonstrated the correct use of the latest designer spear on the hapless Ruadan. Other Celts have enjoyed more success in the role of 007.

S is for Shojo

Gentle Japanese monkey-like Gods who live in the briny depths and spend their time making homemade wine and drinking heavily. Visitors to Davy Jones' Locker who lived a good life will find the wine heavenly. For those who were bad it will taste like Hungarian Riesling.

T is for Taiowa

The Native American God of Job Creation has the dubious distinction of being the laziest of all the deities. He created Sotuknang, another Creation God, to do all the work of making the universe.

U is for Unut

The Egyptian Hare Goddess. She was the Snake Goddess until she got herself a makeover and was mysteriously promoted to the Goddess in charge of information about magical mad March hares.

V is for Vari

A self-existent Oceanic God who lives at the bottom of a coconut shell, which is the universe… 'Cosmic coconut, far out man.'

W is for White-Bird

An Incan God and twin brother to the God of Lightning. Pigs might fly because this God changed his name from the rather lowly 'Piguerao' to the more majestic White-Bird.

X is for Xuan-Wenhua

Chinese God of Hair and Shampoo, 'He's there for you because you're worth it!'

Y is for Yalungur

Australian Aboriginal God of Transexuals. The Moon God, Gidja, castrated Yalungur thereby creating the first woman. Very like the story of Adam and Eve except of course Aboriginal Yalungur would have eaten the snake.

Z is for Zhang Fei

The Chinese God of Butchers - the Sweeny Todd of Gods. Very tall and volatile. He started by butchering animals, then moved on to humans. Eventually he was killed by his henchmen for exploding into bellowing fury every time an underling spoke.

11

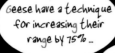

12

*Paralysis of the tongue. Not a problem with this lot, obviously.

GLAD ALL OVER

BEING A GLADIATOR IN ANCIENT ROME WAS A GREAT JOB (PROVIDED YOU DIDN'T MIND THE DYING AND THAT). HERE ARE SOME OF THE THINGS THAT MADE IT SO MUCH FUN ...

FREE MALE GROOMING PRODUCTS

As a gladiator, you could expect to be regularly rubbed down with onion juice by your trainer, to tone up your musculature. (Just how that might have worked no one seems to know, but many cultures have valued onions for their antiseptic and wound-healing properties.) Your owners would also provide you with special sports drinks made from bone ash, perhaps in the belief that you'd benefit from the body-building calcium and phosphate present in the bones. The medical facilities available to gladiators were second to none, especially in the crucial areas of amputations and skull wounds.

LAUGHS GALORE!

There is nothing funnier in the world than watching a bloke in a blindfold trying to kill another bloke in a blindfold. Or at least, there wasn't if you were a Roman. The *andabatae* weren't proper, trained gladiators. They were criminals under sentence of death, who provided the warm-up acts at gladiatorial shows. The subtle humour in their performances came from the fact that they wore helmets with no eye-holes. And that they fought to the death, of course. Pure comedy gold.

AVOID PREMATURE BURIAL NIGHTMARES

You were in very little danger as a gladiator of being incorrectly declared dead by an incompetent medic. To avoid suspicions of match-fixing, the apparently departed were first poked all over with red hot poles. Then, an attendant dressed as Charon, the Hades ferryman, would smash your head in with a double-headed hammer. Finally, when they got you backstage, they cut your throat. You're sorted.

GOOD WAY TO MEET GIRLS

Quite apart from the groupies, some of your co-workers were female. Not much is known about female gladiators – some historians say they were merely a novelty act, others maintain that they were serious fighters. We know they existed because they were eventually banned (by Emperor Septimus Severus in 200 AD). Earlier, in 19 AD, new laws had forbidden daughters, grand-daughters and great-granddaughters of senators from becoming gladiators. Which rather suggests that until then, they were queuing up to have a go.

HUNT EMERSON

PLAY ALL THE COOLEST VENUES

It's thought that the gladiatorial games had their origins in entertainments put on at funerals. Nice touch - even more tasteful than playing 'You'll Never Walk Alone' over the PA - but sadly it all got out of hand. The rich, especially if they happened to be standing for public office at the time, began to compete with each other for which of them could give their friends and relatives the showiest send-off. Truly elite funerals went on for days, and would feature 70 or more pairs of gladiators.

WORK AS PART OF A TIGHT, INTIMATE TEAM

After the Spartacus revolt of 73 BC, the Senate set a limit on the number of gladiators who could be assembled in any one place at a time. This put a right damper on Julius Caesar's electoral victory celebrations in 65 BC. He was forced to limit himself to a mere 320 pairs of gladiators in silver armour. Bloody local government killjoys, ruining everyone's fun!

PLENTY OF SPARE TIME

Professional gladiators were only expected to fight two or three times a year. If they survived for more than five years, they could buy their freedom. The biggest stars would by now be pretty well off, and the others might get jobs as trainers at gladiator schools, or as instructors in the army. Which would be something to look forward to, wouldn't it? Ever so slightly on the downside though, analysis of epitaphs and skeletons suggests that very few gladiators survived more than ten bouts, and that most died in their 20s.

MIX WITH TOP TOFFS

Several Roman emperors liked taking part in gladiatorial shows. Commodus (Emperor from 180-192 AD) fought 735 bouts, dressed as Hercules in a lion skin. He was undefeated in the ring throughout his career (gosh, what a surprise). He also enjoyed killing animals in the arena, including panthers, hippopotami, rhinoceroses, a giraffe - and a fearsome ostrich, which delighted the crowd by running around after he'd shot its head off with a special arrow. When he was bored with that, he staged fights between dwarfs and women. His own death was no less noteworthy: strangled in the bath by a professional wrestler named Narcissus.

WIN A SMART HEADSTONE

Each different genre of gladiatorial fighting had its own professional association, which could usually be relied on to provide a decent memorial to a fallen comrade. Trainers didn't like it when their men got killed - they would demand huge compensation from the fight's promoter. It might still be worth it for the promoter though, as it proved that he was running a classy show, unlike his downmarket rivals who couldn't afford to let anyone die. The death of a gladiator was considered a great act of generosity on the part of the promoter - to the crowd, that is, not the gladiator.

LEARN HOW TO DIE LIKE A MAN

As part of your training as a gladiator, you'd be taught how to die stoically, without crying out or flinching, perhaps even guiding the tip of your opponent's sword to the correct point on your throat, knowing that a noble death cancels out the shame of a lowly birth. This is always a useful skill to possess, and it's a pity that, due to the dumbing down of the educational system, it's largely missing from the modern curriculum.

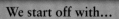

We start off with…

…the best of intentions.
But it's all too easy…

…to betray that tiny
flicker of excitement…

…or disappointment.

The skilled gambler is…

…inscrutable.

It's hard to tell
what he is thinking.

Or what the hell
he thinks he is doing.

The player who appears
bored…

…may be bluffing.

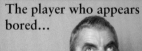
Intense concentration
may be a sign of weakness.

Or strength.

ADVANCED BLUFFING

There are many ways…

…of concealing your intentions.

Hats can help you bluff…

…or double bluff.

Dark reflective glasses…

…can hide your emotions.

But be careful that they aren't *too* dark…

…or too reflective.

Neatly stacked chips…

…indicate a somewhat effete personality.

You may want to bluff…

…about some of your cards.

But not about others.

The hedge-fund manager
with a double first in maths

The total arse

The 'shy, retiring' type

The 'victim'
who is really a 'twat'

The barrack-room lawyer

The one who pretends
to have forgotten the rules

The one who has never
seen a playing card in his life

The escaped axe-murderer

Your stepfather
from whom you stand to
inherit a gigantic fortune

MAJOR-GENERAL ORDE WINGATE (1903-44)

Orde Wingate was a Scottish general from a family of devout Plymouth Brethren. During the Second World War, with an irregular army mounted on camels and horses, he defeated Italian forces six times the size of his own in Abyssinia, and then harried the Japanese in Burma, where he was outnumbered 700-1. He dressed shabbily, ate raw onions, wore an alarm clock on his wrist, and often met visitors in the nude, rubbing his naked body with a rubber brush and claiming it was better than showering. He invented a method of guerrilla warfare called 'Long-Range Penetration', which involved manoeuvring deep in the enemy's rear. Killed in a plane crash before his only son was born, he never achieved his greatest ambition: to lead a Jewish army.

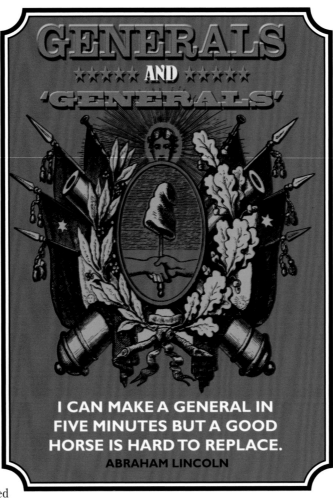

GENERALS AND 'GENERALS'

I CAN MAKE A GENERAL IN FIVE MINUTES BUT A GOOD HORSE IS HARD TO REPLACE.
ABRAHAM LINCOLN

the lung and was so seriously injured that his grave was dug. He only survived because a sergeant who came to rescue him was killed and his body protected Monty from the enemy's fire. His wife died after being bitten by an insect at Burnham-On-Sea in 1937. He named his pet spaniel Rommel, after his German arch-rival in North Africa. He believed homosexuality should be legal for Frenchmen but illegal for the English, who ought to know better.

GENERAL CHARLES DE GAULLE (1890-1970)

The full name of Charles de Gaulle, the general who spearheaded French resistance during the Second World War, was Charles André Joseph Marie De Gaulle. When he was taken prisoner during the First World War, his escape attempts all failed, mostly because he was 1.98 m (6 ft 5 in). Because of his height and his huge nose he was nicknamed 'Cyrano' and 'The Great Asparagus'. There were up to 30 attempts to assassinate him during his life, including one plan to shoot him with cyanide bullets from a gun disguised as a camera. Alexander Cadogan, a British diplomat, said of him 'He's got a head like a pineapple and hips like a woman.' He died playing Patience.

GENERAL BERNARD MONTGOMERY (1887-1976)

Montgomery was almost expelled from Sandhurst for setting fire to another cadet during a fight. His father was Bishop of Tasmania and was away most of the time, and his mother constantly beat him. He didn't go to her funeral, saying he was 'too busy'. At Mons, in 1914, he was shot in

'GENERAL' THOMAS COOK (1808–92)

Thomas Cook, the world's first travel agent, was originally a cabinet-maker's apprentice and travelling missionary. He arranged holidays for thousands of people all over Britain, but behaved so brusquely that the tourists called him 'The General'. He held wholesome picnics where revellers were fed on buns and ginger beer instead of liquor. In Italy, he harangued his customers on the evils of the demon drink, with the words, 'Gentlemen, do not invest your money in diarrhoea.' He once took a group of 350 walkers up Snowdon and led the first tour group ever to go round the world. He put these experiences to good use at the relief of the siege of Khartoum, transporting troops and supplies up the Nile. He founded the *Children's Temperance Magazine* and invented travellers' cheques, which he called 'circular notes'.

'GENERAL' FLORA DRUMMOND (1878–1949)

Flora Drummond became a suffragette mainly because, at 1.55 m (5 ft 1 in), she was just too short to be a postmistress. She was nicknamed 'the General' as she led feminist protests on horseback, wearing military garb. (She was also called 'Bluebell' and 'The Precocious Piglet'). She once hired a boat on the River Thames, sailed it up to the House of Commons, and shouted through a megaphone at

the MPs having tea on the terrace. She also chained herself to Downing Street's railings, found underground entrances to Parliament and danced a highland fling outside Holloway Prison. Another time, she dodged inside No. 10 Downing Street while her friend was busy being arrested for knocking on the door. She died after a stroke brought on by the effort of attempting single-handedly to build a new house on the Scottish coast.

FRIEDRICH ENGELS, 'THE GENERAL' (1820-95)

Engels, the co-founder of communism, kept a dog named Nameless, which he fuelled with alcohol and trained to bark at aristocrats. A big drinker himself, his son-in-law called him 'the great beheader of champagne bottles'. He often fought duels, and reacted to being called a 'bloody foreigner' by a man in a Manchester pub by hitting him over the head with an umbrella. He got so grumpy about the difficulties in printing *Das Kapital* that he called it 'this economy shit'. He married his wife only a few hours before she died. Karl Marx's family nicknamed him 'The General' because of his essays on military matters. He once filled in a personality quiz, writing: 'Favourite virtue: jollity'; 'Idea of happiness: Château Margaux 1848'; 'Motto: take it easy.'

T. H. HUXLEY, 'THE GENERAL' (1825-95)

Professor Thomas Henry Huxley, father of modern biology and President of the Royal Society, only went to school for two years (aged 8 to 10). He later taught himself German, Greek, Latin, theology and biology. Known to his students as 'The General', he coined the words 'agnostic' and 'missing link'. On reading Charles Darwin's *On The Origin of Species* he exclaimed: 'How stupid of me not to have thought of that!' and became such a passionate defender of the theory that he was nicknamed 'Darwin's Bulldog'. In 1858, he calculated that, if the offspring of two aphids survived ten generations, they would give rise to a biomass equal to the weight of 500 million 'stout men'. Despite being an agnostic, he insisted that miracles were possible and that given the right chemical processes, water could turn into wine.

'GENERAL' HARRIET TUBMAN (1822-1913)

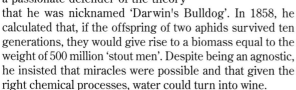

Harriet Tubman got the admiring nicknames 'General Tubman' and 'Moses' from the slaves she helped to liberate. An escaped slave herself, she returned to the American South twenty times, freeing over 300 slaves, threatening to personally shoot any of them who wanted to turn back or give up. She was the first woman to lead an armed raid in the Civil War, and was widely believed to be clairvoyant. (She had been hit on the head with an iron weight as a girl and suffered dreams and visions throughout her life as a result.) During the war she also acted as a scout, nurse, laundress and spy, but she was paid so little that she had to support herself by selling homemade pastries.

MAJOR-GENERAL SICKLES (1819-1914)

Just before the American Civil War, Congressman Daniel Edgar Sickles shot and killed the son of the composer of 'The Star Spangled Banner' for having an affair with his wife. He was acquitted with the first-ever use of the defence of temporary insanity. In 1863, serving as a Union general, he was hit in the leg by a Confederate cannonball. As he was carried away on a stretcher, he smoked a cigar. At the field hospital, he drank a shot of brandy before a doctor amputated his leg above the knee. Sickles then sent the limb to the Army Medical Museum, which had been founded the year before, with a note reading: 'With the compliments of Major General D.E.S.'

GENERAL BENJAMIN BUTLER (1818-93)

Butler was a Union general nicknamed 'The Beast of New Orleans'. The Confederate President, Jefferson Davis, declared him an outlaw and ordered his execution if he was caught. Butler created rules defining slaves as contraband of war (so he could keep them) and threatened to arrest as a prostitute any woman in New Orleans who was rude to any Union soldier. He was so hated in the South that, long after the war, chamber pots could be found with his face painted on the inside of the bottom of them. He was an extremely unsuccessful general, lost a huge number of battles for the Union, and was widely considered the ugliest general on either side of the war.

BONUS GENERAL FACTS

✳ *Gebhard Leberecht von Blücher (1742 -1819), the Prussian General whose intervention won the Battle of Waterloo, suffered from the paranoid delusion that he was about to give birth to an elephant.*

✳ *General Sir William Erskine (1770-1813), one of Wellington's senior commanders during the Peninsular War, was insane and committed suicide by jumping out of a window in 1813. Found dying on the ground, he asked bystanders 'Why on earth did I do that?'*

✳ *During the First World War, Lieutenant-General His Highness Farzand-i-Khas-Daulat-i-Inglishia, Maharajah of Patiala (1891-1938), spent £31,000 a year on trousers. On the day he died, he breakfasted on a 10-egg omelette.*

✳ *General Hajianestis, Commander in Chief of the Greek Army in the war against the Turks in the 1920s, claimed to be unable to get out of bed because his legs were made of sugar and would shatter if he stood on them, and often pretended to be dead if anyone tried to wake him up.*

The Mystery of the Missing
Garden Gnomes

Starring the late
Graham Greene

Gosh! That's queer, Uncle Graham. Ginger seems to have taken a fancy to one of your gnomes!

Yes, and I must say that I do not entirely approve

Would-be detective Will White and his cat Ginger had gone to spend the summer holidays with Will's uncle, the late novelist Graham Greene, who lived with Aunt Augusta in a quaint cottage in the Sussex village of Goldstone. But Graham Greene's suspicions were aroused when Ginger developed a sexual attraction to one of his ornamental garden gnomes.

That summer the village had suffered a spate of mysterious garden gnome thefts. Almost every morning another crime was discovered.

Help! Help! Police! My garden gnome has been stolen!

Goodness me, Ginger! Mrs Watkins is the latest victim!

GONE!

That tea-time all the talk was of the missing garden gnomes.

Uncle Graham used to be a _real_ spy, Ginger! How about we help him solve this mystery?

Prrrrrrrr! Dribble

I was merely an intelligence officer, Will. Not nearly as exciting as you think. And _must_ that cat of yours sit on the table?

Bright and early the next morning Will and his cat Ginger set out to investigate the mysterious gnome disappearances.

Come on Ginger. Let's look for clues... Crikey! What's that you've got?

Meeee-oww! Hiss!!

It looks like Ginger is onto something. The trail leads up this tree!

Good work Ginger! Wait for me. I'm right behind you

After a disappointing day's detective work Ginger fell asleep straight after tea, and soon Will was ready for his bed.

The following day was a Sunday, but when Will awoke there was no sign of his trusty cat companion. He dashed outside and found Uncle Graham busy in the garden.

Graham Greene and Aunt Augusta were regulars at the nearby Catholic church of St Gertrude the Great.

Throughout the service the late Graham Greene seemed to be paying particular attention to the priest's words.

...but deliver us from evil. For thine is the kingdom, the power and the glory. Forever and ever. Amen

No.2 704 1973

Right. We're gonna do a song... I mean *hymn*... next

As they were leaving, Uncle Graham stopped to speak to Father Raven.

Thank you Father. I found your service most enlightening

That's cool

Say, who's the kid? Wanna join the choir son?

This is Will, my young nephew. He is very interested in ecclesiastical architecture, and I was wondering if you might let him have a look around the belfry?

I am?

Oh God no! I mean... for *Health and Safety* reasons no. It's far too dangerous up there

In the interests of your own personal health and safety, I strongly advise that you do as I tell you, Father Raven

Corr!! Is that a real gun?

Now, if you'd be so kind, we'd like to see inside the bell tower

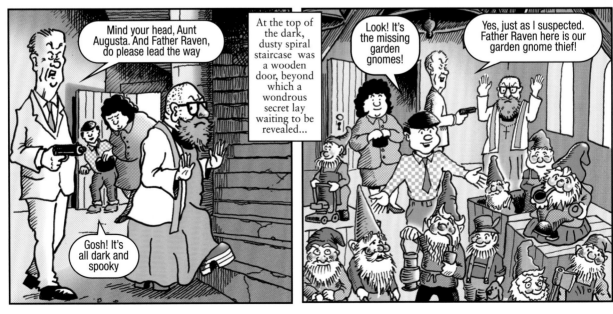

Mind your head, Aunt Augusta. And Father Raven, do please lead the way

At the top of the dark, dusty spiral staircase was a wooden door, beyond which a wondrous secret lay waiting to be revealed...

Look! It's the missing garden gnomes!

Yes, just as I suspected. Father Raven here is our garden gnome thief!

Gosh! It's all dark and spooky

You missed the first clue, Will. A bat's natural habitat is the church belfry, not the tree. Those bats Ginger found had been evicted from this belfry by Father Raven, to make room for his stolen garden gnomes. It is of course an offence to disturb a bat roost, for which the maximum penalty is a £5000 fine, or a six-year jail sentence

Ah! So Ginger was onto something!

The second clue was in the church service. Father Raven concluded the Lord's Prayer with the words 'For thine is the kingdom' etc. This exaltation, known technically as a doxology, was added during the reign of Elizabeth I in an attempt to rid the Church of England of any Catholic vestiges

Shit

Ooh!

It would not be used by a Catholic priest

So, Uncle Graham... if Father Raven isn't a priest, then who the devil is he?

I'm glad you asked, Will. I was about to introduce him

Behind this clever disguise 'Father Raven' is none other than...

SWIPE!

...Gary Glitter!

Oh crikey!

Using this hidden computer the evil pop fiend has been grooming garden gnomes for internet sex, using 'wi-fi'

From this vantage-point high above the village the sordid star had every garden gnome for miles around at his mercy

After handing Gary Glitter over to the church authorities the detectives headed home for a well-earned Sunday lunch.

What will happen to Gary Glitter now, Uncle Graham?

Well, that's for the Bishop to decide, Will

He's been a very bad man. He may even have to be moved to another parish

In memory of
STEVE
1958 - 2008

After lunch Will set about solving the one mystery that remained; *What had become of his missing cat Ginger?* Can you spot the clues hidden in the garden?

Ginger! Where are you?

Did you guess what happened to Ginger? You'll find the answer written below.

DÉCÉ 8/09

Answer: *The late Graham Greene drowned Ginger the cat in a bucket of water, and buried it in the garden using a spade.*

25

a gallery of GOONS and their goofy nicknames

year in a well aimed blow, Mayor La Guardia announced a ban on the sale, display and possession of artichokes. The former 'Artichoke King' died penniless after a massive stroke in 1938.

FRANK 'THE DASHER' ABBANDANDO (1910-1942, ELECTRIC CHAIR)

There is some disagreement over how 'The Dasher' got his nickname. Some put it down to his youthful display of baseball skills on the fields of Elmira reform school. Others attribute it to an early incident in Brooklyn when he was trying to shoot an adversary. Frank's gun jammed and his victim turned and gave chase. Speedy on his toes, Frank lost him, ran round the block and came up on him from behind, despatching him with a bullet to the head. 'The Dasher' went on to become a noted triggerman for Murder Inc, the guns-for-hire arm of The Syndicate.

VINCENT 'THE CHIN' GIGANTE (1928-2005, PRISON)

Vincent earned his nickname, not on account of his sizeable chin, but due to the childhood name of Cincenzo used by

his mother. Gigante is best known for keeping up the rigid pretence, while under close and constant FBI surveillance, of being mentally disabled from the late 1960s up until 2003. When finally brought to trial he pleaded guilty to obstruction of justice. Before that time, The Chin could often be seen shuffling around his Greenwich Village neighbourhood in a bathrobe and slippers, mumbling to himself. Such behaviour earned him the secondary nickname of 'The Oddfather'. From his ascent to the head of the Genovese crime family in the early 1980s, security had always been a primary concern and The Chin insisted that no business associates use his name or nickname in conversations. Instead they were instructed to point to their chin or form the letter 'C' with their fingers. After seven years of legal battles over his mental competency to stand trial, Vincent was sentenced to 12 years in 1997.

CIRO 'THE ARTICHOKE KING' TERRANOVA (1889-1938)

Terranova, at one time the boss of the Morello crime family earned his nickname when he decided to foray into the artichoke business. He created an effective monopoly by purchasing all the artichokes shipped to New York from California at $6 a crate and selling them on to dealers under threat of violence at a 30-40% profit. His reputation suffered in 1931 when as the getaway driver in one of the most significant murders in gangland history, that of Joe 'The Boss' Masseria, he nearly botched the job by failing to put the car in gear. A series of underground manoeuvres saw that by 1935, Ciro's only source of income was artichokes. However in December that

AL 'SCARFACE' CAPONE (1899-1947, ALCATRAZ)

This most famous of Mafioso got his nickname as a 17-year-old bouncer at a mob-owned bar in Coney Island. On remarking on the commendable rear of one of the female patrons, the fair lady's brother, a certain Frank Galluccio, took offence and in the resulting scuffle sliced Al's cheek three times. The grudge did not stick though and Frank was later put on Scarface's payroll as a bodyguard. By 25, Capone was King of the Chicago underworld with an empire built on bootleg booze and prostitution. He also revelled in his role as a public figure, billing himself as a modern-day Robin Hood, serving up meals to the jobless at makeshift soup kitchens.

Old Scarface was eventually brought down on charges of tax-evasion in 1931 and sentenced to 11 years, serving most of his time in Alcatraz. Both there and after his release, his health declined on account of the syphilis he contracted in his youth. All the while, his custom built bullet-proof Cadillac, seized after his trial, was being used to ferry around then President FDR.

CHARLES 'HANDSOME CHARLIE' WORKMAN (1908-UNKNOWN)

Charlie was openly admired by the top crime bosses as the most gifted killer in Murder Inc. In 1939 Charlie was tasked with killing his friend Tootsie Feinberg. Charlie obliged and when he later went to trial for the murder, Tootsie's wife, now maintained by the mob, spoke on his behalf, so

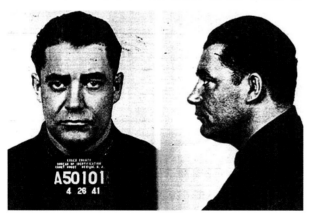

garnering the legend that when Handsome Charlie kills a man, the widow stands for him in court. Charlie was eventually sentenced to life imprisonment in 1941 for the murder of Dutch Schultz. Not long after, he volunteered his services to the US Navy for a suicide mission against Japan but was refused. He was paroled in 1964 and lived out the rest of his life quietly.

JOHN 'THE TEFLON DON' GOTTI (1940-2002, PRISON)

John Gotti rose to the head of the Gambino crime family after effecting the last known execution of a mob boss, Paul Castellano, in 1985. He earned the moniker of 'The Teflon Don' after beating a series of high-profile charges through the 1980s. No matter what the authorities threw at him, nothing stuck. He was also known in the press as 'The Dapper Don' for his style and self-promotion whereby he actively courted the press and public. Every 4th July he flouted New York's ban on fireworks with a huge display, while Andy Warhol painted his portrait for the front cover of *Time* magazine. In 1992 he finally became 'The Velcro Don' largely on account of his egotistical recklessness and the key testimony of his underboss Sammy Gravano. On being sent to jail he delivered his own obituary, 'I'll always be one of a kind. You'll never see another guy like me if you live to be 5000.' 10 years later, having died of cancer in a maximum

security state prison, thousands turned out to see his funeral procession through Queens.

IRVING 'BIG GANGY' COHEN (DATES UNKNOWN)

'Big Gangy', named for his hulking size, was one of the few members of Murder Inc. to successfully run away and disentangle himself from the mob. He quite literally ran for the trees immediately after fulfilling orders to kill his best friend Walter Sage in 1937. The mystery of Gangy's whereabouts was answered in 1939 when ex-colleagues Pretty Levine and Dukey Maffeotore went to see the film *Golden Boy* and spotted him as an extra in the film. Big Gangy had fled to Hollywood and taken up

bit-part acting under the name Jack Gordon. He would go on to appear as an extra in *It's a Wonderful Life*. Ironically, it was his portrayal of a cop on screen that got the attention of the New York authorities who hauled him back East to face trial for the murder of Sage. He was acquitted and lived out his days peacefully in Hollywood.

ARNOLD 'THE BRAIN' ROTHSTEIN (1882-1928, MURDERED)

Rothstein was the father of organised crime as we know it and the first thoroughly modern gangster. In his role as financier to the underworld he had many nicknames, 'Mr Big', 'The Man Uptown', 'The Big Bankroll', and among the younger Jewish mobsters 'Ph.G'(Pappa has gelt). Rothstein became a mentor to promising young guns such as Lucky Luciano, Meyer Lansky, Waxey Gordon and Frank Costello and by proxy fashioned the future business structure of the mob. Popular legend along with his immortalised representation as Meyer Wolfsheim in *The Great Gatsby* have cemented him as the man that fixed the

1919 World Series, though in reality it would seem he turned this proposal down. 'The Brain' was gunned down aged 46 for 'welching' on a bet he saw as fixed.

IRVING 'WAXEY GORDON' WEXLER (1888-1952, ALCATRAZ)

512x283 32kb

Wexler made his name as a pickpocket on the Lower East Side. His trick was to wax his fingers, and the name 'Waxey' stuck (Gordon was a preferred alias). It was Waxey who took the plan for large-scale bootlegging to Rothstein in 1920, and later controlled this lucrative racket across the East Coast, earning him around $2million a year. These figures didn't quite match his declared earnings of $8100 for 1930 and he was convicted for tax evasion in 1933. Once out, he tried to rebuild his empire on narcotics but was picked up in 1951 for trying to sell heroin to an undercover narcotics agent. On failing to bribe the agent he reportedly asked him to shoot him on the spot.

CHARLES 'LUCKY' LUCIANO (1897-1962)

'Lucky' was an apt nickname for Luciano, the only hood to survive being 'taken for a ride'. Caught up in The Castellammarese War, he was kidnapped by goons, beaten, stabbed and left for dead on a New York beach. But 'Lucky' wasn't dead and made sure that he emerged victorious in the war. In 1931 he became the first effective Capo di tutti Capi (boss of all bosses), presiding over a newly formed National Crime Syndicate that would represent the business interests of the Five Families of New York and other mob outfits throughout the country. This saw him listed in *Time* magazine's 100 'Builders and Titans' of the 20th Century. Luciano was sent down in 1936 for 30-50 years but after the 1942 sinking of the Normandie troop ship in New York harbour, 'Lucky' started

taking meetings in his cell with naval intelligence officers in a bid to use his muscle to guarantee the safety of the ports from enemy sabotage. He also offered invaluable contacts for espionage in Sicily and was even said to have a plan to 'whack' the Fuhrer. In 1946, in return for his wartime services, Luciano's sentence was commuted and he was exiled to Italy from where he continued to play a major part in organised crime across continents.

LLEWELYN MORRIS 'MURRAY THE CAMEL' HUMPHREYS (1899-1965)

A Chicago mobster of Welsh descent, Murray was named on account of the 'Hump' in his surname. 'The Camel' rose to become the chief political fixer and labour racketeer for the Chicago Outfit hugely respected by Capone and his successors. Murray was well connected in the political world and by his later years it was generally known that he had dined with presidents and kings across the world. 'The Camel' was also well liked among the FBI for his charm despite their constant surveillance. In bugged conversations he could often be heard to say, 'Good morning, gentlemen, and anyone listening. This is the nine o'clock meeting of the Chicago underworld.' Legend has it that on another occasion 'The Camel' having being tailed all day by FBI agents, stopped his driver and sent his car on before telling the Feds that there was no point them having two cars and that he'd ride with them.

GROWING PAINS

GRUESOME GOBBETS CONCERNING THE GHASTLY GOINGS-ON DURING PUBERTY

The DAYAK people pierce boys' penises at puberty and their grandfathers insert a PHALANG, a stud with a lump at each end, through the tip of the penis.

"GEORGE MICHAEL" is cockney rhyming slang for "MENSTRUAL CYCLE"

← OESTROGEN

menstrual cycle

TRADITIONALLY Malay boys were circumsized when they reached puberty, rather than at birth. Ouch....

PUBERTAL SPURT — contrary to what you might fear, the term actually describes the sudden surge in a boy's growth rate during his teenage years.

← TESTOSTERONE

SEX

THE WORD VIRGIN ORIGINALLY REFERRED TO A GIRL WHO HAD NEVER HAD SEX. GERMAN & FRENCH BOTH HAVE A WORD FOR A MALE VIRGIN — "JÜNGLING" IN GERMAN — "PUCEAU" IN FRENCH — BUT ENGLISH DOESN'T.

The first BRA was patented as the "backless brassiere" (from the French word for 'upper arm') in 1914, by New York socialite Mary Phelps Jacob

BREASTS COME IN ALL DIFFERENT SHAPES & SIZES

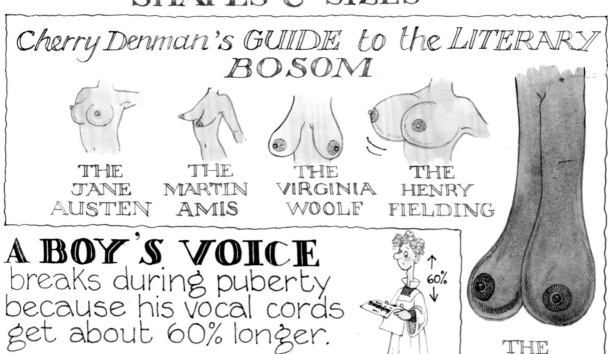

Cherry Denman's GUIDE to the LITERARY BOSOM

THE JANE AUSTEN

THE MARTIN AMIS

THE VIRGINIA WOOLF

THE HENRY FIELDING

THE MAYA ANGELOU

A BOY'S VOICE

breaks during puberty because his vocal cords get about 60% longer.

UP UNTIL THAT POINT, GIRL'S AND BOY'S VOCAL CORDS ARE THE SAME LENGTH.

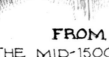

According to Captain Cook, Tahitians had their buttocks tattooed black after puberty.

PUBARCHE
The first appearance of pubic hair

There is an old Slavic custom of mothers slapping their daughters when they have their first period.

FROM THE MID-1500s TO THE LATE 1800s, BOYS WERE DRESS-ED IN GOWNS OR DRESSES UNTIL THE AGE OF FIVE TO SEVEN, WHEN THEY WERE 'BREECHED' OR PUT IN THEIR FIRST PAIR OF TROUSERS.

EVEN RAMESES II SUFFERED FROM ACNE

PUBESCENT = covered with soft, downy hair.

Five Go Gallivanting After Ghosts!

JULIAN would like to be an actuary or an exotic dancer.

GEORGINA likes to be called 'George' and is a bit of a tomboy.

ANNE likes the sort of things girls like, but not girls like George.

DICK: Likes cake – that's basically it.

...and not forgetting Timmy the Dog!!

Julian, Dick, Anne, George and Timmy have heard rumours that the Olde Manor House is haunted. Knowing about the Amityville[1] and Borely Rectory[2] hoaxes they have decided to investigate...

"Come on", says Julian, "Let's gain entry through this window. As it's open we won't need a gablock[3] and surprisingly, as we have no intention of stealing, we are not committing a crime, although we are trespassing - which is a tort[4]."

But what's this? They're not alone.

"I thought you said this place was empty?", gowls[5] Dick.

"Gosh! Even a perfect vacuum is not technically empty'", opines Julian, "Not at the Planck scale[6]"

"Hello Children", says Miss Elizabethe, the gothic[7] housekeeper. "Feel free to look round but I warn you, this place is haunted. If someone doesn't exorcise the ghost soon then the market value of this property will sink even further, just as the *Daily Mail* predicted"

n is suspicious.
"Hmmmm. According to the *QI Book of Supernatural -Gravy* Miss Elizabethe's 'My Chemical Romance' irt is more emo than goth. I wonder..."

ust then...

Wooooahhh!
Anne has heard a disembodied voice. "Perhaps it's a restless spirit trying to contact us from beyond the grave? After all the Chamba people of the Cameroon/Nigerian border hold that the incomprehensible babbling of infants and the old is the language of ghosts."

"Don't worry Anne", laughs Dick. "According to the x the voices are probably in your head and could be ptoms of psychosis or perhaps just cake deprivation."

"And you're not alone Anne", adds Julian. "You might be hearing things but Dick is seeing them. Look, the sunlight projecting through the window is creating an illusion similar to Pepper's Ghost[8] developed by Henry Dircks and John Henry Pepper and first demonstrated theatrically during a scene in Charles Dickens' *The Haunted Man* in 1863."

Timmy has found a tarot deck and pulled out 'death'.
"Bad luck Timmy", says George. "Using tarot for divination began in 1781 with Antoine Court de Gébelin's publication of *'Le Monde Primitif'*[10] which suggests the symbolism of Tarot cards represent a survival of arcane knowledge into the modern world. As such you're probably about to die."

Dick, Anne and George try guessing the future with the cards.
"Tarot, or Tarocchi to give them their original name, are just a different style of playing card popular from the mid-fifteenth century." counters Julian. "You're just as likely to be able to predict your future playing Happy Families or Snap."

" I don't think too many happy families have lived here" chortles Dick, "Look, a warning written in blood, the same medium used by the German Dr Faustus for making his pact with Mephistopheles[11]."

Look out Dick!

"Look what you've done Julian", groans George, "you've scorned the tarot and now we're all doomed. If only you weren't so cynical."
"Of course I'm not a true cynic in the Greek sense," rejoinders Julian, "although I do believe that the road to virtue is to free oneself from any influence such as wealth, fame, or power, which have no value in Nature."

"It is a cake," shrieks Dick, "But more like 'Gob', a type of chocolate cake associated with the Pennsylvanian Amish." Dick knows a lot about cake.

But just as the gang are about to make a grab for the gateau...

"IT'S THE GHOST!"
"It's a Ghoul, perhaps, as some cognitive neuroscientists now think, caused by the stimulation of the temporal lobes brought on by changes in the earth's geomagnetic field," cries Anne.

"No it's not", declaims the insufferably smug Julian. "It's Elizabethe, the emo housekeeper, hoping that reports of ghosts combined with the global recession would suppress the value of the house enough for her to buy it herself."

"But that's obtaining pecuniary advantage by deception," exclaims George, "an offence under the Theft Act of 1968. She's going to Gaol."

"As the American writer Lloyd Douglas once said," drones Julian, "If a man harbors any sort of fear, it makes him landlord to a ghost."

"Can anyone else hear a voice saying 'Kill Julian'" asks Anne.

NOTES 1: **Amityville** is in Suffolk County, New York, and features in the novel *The Amityville Horror*, based on a real-life multiple murder case and the subsequent alleged haunting crime scene at 112 Ocean Avenue. 2: **Borley Rectory** A Victorian mansion in the village of Borley, Essex, built in 1863. After unexplained 'events' in the late 1920s paranormal investigator and confidence trickster Harry Price claimed the site as 'The Most Haunted House in England'. It was destroyed by fire in 1939. 3: **Gablock** A dialect word for an iron crowbar. 4: **Tort** In English Law, the breach of a duty imposed by law, whereby some person acquires a right of action for damages. 5: **Gowl** To howl, yell, cry or whine (14th century). 6: **Planck Scale** The Planck length is around 1.616×10^{-35} metres. When describing time or gravity at this scale, normal physics stops working and the mysterious rules of quantum physics take over. 7: **Gothic** A genre of fiction characterised by suspenseful plots involving supernatural or macabre elements as in Horace Walpole's 1765 *The Castle of Otranto* which is subtitled 'A Gothic story'. 8: **Pepper's Ghost** An illusion used in magic tricks, using a plate glass and special lighting to make objects seem to appear or disappear. 9: A **non-Newtonian** substance whose molecules do not obey Isaac Newton's rules of motion e.g. quicksand and custard, both of which get thicker the more you mix them. 10: **Antoine Court de Gébelin** (1719-84) was a former Protestant pastor who initiated the interpretation of the Tarot as an arcane repository of hermetic knowledge (as opposed to being simply a set of playing cards) in an essay included in his *Le Monde primitif*, vol viii, 1781. 11: Christopher Marlowe's *Dr Faustus* sells his soul to the devil in return for power and knowledge.

Gee-Kwiz!

With one person as quizmaster, you can play this at home. Five rounds of 8 questions each; 2 points for a correct answer, but playing your joker before any one round doubles your score on that round.

Let's warm up with an easy one...

GEOGRAPHY!

1. What do they do at Lloyds of London when a ship is reported sunk anywhere in the world?
2. What do most Spaniards have after lunch?
3. Name a famous brand name of a German wine drunk in Germany.
4. Whose national flag is this?
5. What's the only part of mainland South America that is not an independent country?
6. Which country in the world is home to the ethnic groups the Bangi, the Binga, the Benga and the Banga?
7. What's quite interesting about the tides in the Mediterranean?
8. Which English county is Wigan in?

> A survey by Heinz in 2008 found that many British children don't like vegetables at all, with aubergines being the most hated. Amongst other things the survey discovered was that rather than eat vegetables, an astonishing seven out of 10 British children hide them around the house.

GARDENING!

1. Where do Welsh onions come from?
2. What do the American gooseberry, the Tahiti gooseberry, the Cape gooseberry, the Coromandel gooseberry, the Barbados gooseberry and the Chinese gooseberry have in common?
3. Which vegetable has the same number of chromosomes as a gorilla?
4. Where is the greatest and densest diversity of plant life on the planet to be found in a single place?
5. Approximately how many celery seeds weigh 1oz (28g)?
6. How many parsnips have won the Nobel Prize for Literature?
7. What did John Boyd Dunlop find in his garden that enabled him to become world famous?
8. What kind of fruit would you find in a plum pudding?

> QI's favourite G-Man is the great American columnist and sports writer Lewis Grizzard, who is an absolute mine of laconic pith. This for instance: 'I don't think I'll get married again. I think I'll just find a woman I don't like and give her a house.' Here are some other G-related Men.

G-MEN!

1. He had a biscuit named after him, and was born in a town after which a different biscuit is named. Name the biscuits.
2. What G connects all these men? Burhan Asaf Belge, Conrad Hilton, George Sanders, Herbert Hutner, Joshua S. Cosden, Jack Ryan, Michael O'Hara, Felipe de Alba, Frédéric Prinz von Anhalt and the inventor of the hologram?
3. Of which eponymous Oscar winner was it said 'he was everything the voting members of the Academy would like to have been - moral, tan and thin'?
4. How did the great Spanish pianist and composer Granados die?
5. Who famously described Ingrid Bergman as a 'nice woman who speaks five languages but can't act in any of them'?
6. Whom did Colonel Gaddafi claim wrote the Works of Shakespeare?
7. Which G-man was born in the same year as William Shakespeare, the year that Michelangelo died?
   This next one is seriously difficult: bonus points for anyone who gets it right.
8. According to James Joyce, the three greatest literary talents of the 19th century were Leo Tolstoy, Rudyard Kipling and ....
   (fill in the blank)

GREATNESS!

1. What was the first wife of Herod the Great called?
2. What familiar modern technology is named after King Canute the Great's grandfather?
3. What was the first building in the world to be taller than the Great Pyramid of Cheops at Giza?
4. What was the name of the father of the first and greatest Duke of Marlborough?
5. Who was Sophie Auguste Friederike von Anhalt-Zerbst?
6. What is the name of the storm twice as big as the earth that has been raging for 300 years?
7. The cathedral treasury at Aachen has a famous collection of sacred relics, among which are the tights of Jesus' father, St Joseph. Four of these sacred relics are known as *The Great Relics*. Two points for each one of them you can name.
8. George Graham (c.1674-1751) was the greatest instrument-maker of his age, the Master of the Clockmakers' Company and a Fellow of the Royal Society. He is buried in Westminster Abbey. He invented something that he might easily have called a Boyle, but he didn't. What did he call it?

> Baltasar Gracián y Morales (1601-1658) was a Spanish Jesuit and philosopher who influenced La Rochefoucauld, Voltaire, Nietzsche and, especially, Schopenhauer (who considered his Criticón one of the best books ever written). In The Art of Worldly Wisdom (1647), Gracián wrote: 'The greatest wisdom often consists in ignorance'. So, feel free to feel smug if you get all of these wrong.

GENERAL IGNORANCE!

1. How many possible pronunciations of the letter 'G' are there in English?
2. What is the largest moon in the Solar System?
3. How many galaxies are visible to the naked eye?
4. Who was President of the Olympic Games in 12 AD?
5. What contains enough steel to make 64 double decker buses or 16 Chieftain tanks but only costs £3.60 every time it is used?
6. What word beginning with 'G' was invented by the Dutch chemist van Helmont in about 1600 and is said to be the single most successful invention of a word whose author is actually known?
7. Penultimately, a question on G-forces. What travels well over twice as fast as the fastest jet fighter with its afterburners on, and almost twice as fast as the space shuttle on re-entry?
8. What is Spurius Carvilius Ruga's claim to fame?

Answers on p94

IN THE GARDEN

GODWOTTERY~ Affected, archaic, or excessively elaborate speech or writing concerning gardens. From T.E.Brown's poem "A GARDEN IS A LOVESOME THING, GOD WOT."

GNOME~ a dwarfish creature. .... ~a maxim or aphorism.

GRAMINACEOUS ~ Grassy

GLEY ~ a sticky waterlogged soil.

GNOMON the rod or pin on a sundial that shows the time by the position of its shadow.

GOWK .... a cuckoo

GINKO AN ornamental tree

GALLIMAUFRY a jumble or medley

GINGLMUS a hingelike joint ~a knee~

GERMINATION putting forth shoots

GUM BOOTS

GOWAN a daisy

HOW TO SEE GULLS

1. People are often surprised to see seagulls far inland.

'They're sea gulls!' they cry. 'They should be by the sea!' But there's something even more surprising about this: *seagulls don't exist.* Like the Cabbage White Butterfly, the Seagull is a name unknown to science. Ornithologists insist on the word 'gull', several varieties of which spend their whole lives miles from the sea.

2. You won't see gulls at Sellafield.

They're in the fridge. Any bird that lands at the accident-prone Cumbrian nuclear power plant – which a lot of gulls do – gets shot by snipers, to prevent it carrying radioactive contamination to neighbouring areas. The ever-growing mountain of avian corpses is classed both as 'low-level nuclear waste' and as 'putrescent waste', and therefore can't be tipped on a dump.

3. Keep your mouth shut where gulls are concerned.

Many local authorities in Britain spend fortunes on gull control, fearing that the birds can infect tourists with salmonella through their droppings. Experts pooh-pooh this. A leading gullologist writes: 'Only 2.7% of gulls are infected. For a human to get salmonella, he would have to walk around looking upwards with his mouth open. A rare infected bird would then have to defecate straight into his mouth and he would have to swallow it.'

4. And whose little chick are you, then, hmm?

In some gull species, parents don't recognise their own chicks until 5 - 7 days after hatching. Before the chicks are mobile, there's no need to know what they look like — only to remember where they are. Orphaned chicks often stowaway in a neighbouring nest. The evolutionary risk of the parents not feeding one of their own outweighs the cost of feeding an interloper — on the other hand, if they do happen to spot the intruder, they kill the scrounging little bastard.

5. The Seagull Diet.

Gull eggs can fetch four quid each in the restaurants of posh London clubs. And prices are rising, due to a disastrous decline in gull numbers over recent years. Nobody knows why the gulls are disappearing. It couldn't possibly be because fat toffs have scoffed all their eggs, could it?

6. Can you see what it is yet?

When birds cause aircraft to crash, investigators analyse the bits of beak, blood, guts and feathers adhering to the wreckage, to establish the particular species of bird involved (often gulls or geese). To gather this gunk, which scientists call 'snarge', they spray the piece of plane with water, and then wipe it down with paper towels, which are sent to the Feather Identification Lab in Washington, DC.

7. Big-eyed gulls.

"...HAVEN'T SLEPT FOR WEE THREEKS..."

The swallow-tailed gull of the Galapagos Islands is the only fully nocturnal seabird on earth. It has enormous eyes, the better to hunt squid as they rise to the surface of the sea at night in search of plankton.

8. The Seagull Effect.

FLAP FLAP

In 1963, the Father of Chaos Theory, Edward Lorenz (1917-2008), explained how tiny events can have large and unpredictable effects elsewhere. His example: the flap of a seagull's wings affecting the weather many miles away. Years later, he was due to present a paper at a conference, but hadn't come up with a title. It was sent to press using the heading *Predictability: Does the flap of a butterfly's wings in Brazil set off a tornado in Texas?* Boo! Join The QI Campaign to Reassert the Centrality of Gulls to Chaos Theory!

9. Gulls don't just eat chips and ice cream, you know!

Off the coast of Argentina, Kelp Gulls have taken to lunching on Southern Right Whales. They simply land on their backs and start eating them alive, pecking away at their skin and blubber. The whales are in real danger, not just from their huge wounds, but because they spend so much time evading gull attacks, disastrously disrupting their sleep cycles.

10. And now see what gulls have done!

They've only gone and led to yet ANOTHER new science! Ethology, the study of animal behaviour, was pioneered by Niko Tinbergen (1907-88). His understanding of 'pre-programming' – animals knowing how to behave as soon as they're born – came from studying the feeding

behaviour of herring gulls. When a chick pecks at the red spot on the adult's beak, the parent sicks up a gorgeous load of fish paste into the baby's gullet. Tinbergen found it's the spot, not the parent, that counts: chicks respond the same to a lump of wood with a red blob painted on it.

I must down to the seas again to the vagrant gypsy life,
To the gull's way and the whale's way where the wind's like a whetted knife.

JOHN MASEFIELD (1878-1967) 'Sea-Fever'

am I great?

'He's great'... 'That was great'... 'I had a great time.' Everything these days seems to be great. It's a word we use every day – but what does it mean to really be Great? Are you personally Great or just 'OK'? *Why not take our fun coffee-break quiz to find out...*

Q1: It's Friday afternoon, you've had a really hard week and you just want to go home and curl up with a book but your friends want you to go to the pub. **Do you:**

A: Tell them you're just not up to it and take a rain check for next week?
B: Agree to go along 'just for one'?
C: Single-handedly take on the might of the Persian Empire?

Q2: Your boss calls you in and tells you he's had a great team-building idea – a karaoke night for the whole office – and he wants you to arrange it. **Do you:**

A: Ask the girls in the office if they know a good karaoke pub you could go to – even if it's a disaster at least you can all have a drink?
B: Get on the phone to admin and demand they buy a karaoke machine – on expenses?
C: Develop a novel system of notation for devotional chant melodies inspired directly by the whisperings of the Holy Spirit?

Q3: You're halfway through a romantic dinner à deux with that dreamy guy from sales when, biting into a crusty roll – crunch! – you break a tooth. **Do you:**

A: Excuse yourself for a moment, rush to the loo and take a handful of aspirin for the pain – this chance may never come again and the dentist can wait for the morning?
B: Pretend you've had a call on your mobile summoning you home straight away, but not before you reschedule the date!
C: Take an extended tour of Europe to learn the modern science of dentistry, returning home in triumph to your backward nation to dazzle the peasantry with your newfound skills?

Q4: It's not easy dating when you've got young kids – it can scare the men off. So, you're having lunch with the new man in your life and he asks the fateful question: 'Have you got any kids?' **What do you say?**

A: Lie and say no. If the relationship goes any further AND he's really the one for you then he won't mind.
B: Ask if it would make any difference to him before answering.
C: Proudly boast of your 56 sons and 44 daughters.

Q5: You've hit a rough patch with your man – he just wants to watch football and play on the Xbox, neither of which activities were in your marriage vows as far as you can remember. Perhaps you can rekindle the flame – but how? **Do you:**

A: Take a bath and slip into that little black dress that used to drive him wild, before offering him a game that's not available on any Xbox!
B: Make the best of a bad deal. After all, isn't this how all men end up? Perhaps it's time to get a hobby… or a lover!
C: Arrange for his immediate removal by Imperial troops to a distant palace where your lover's brother can quietly strangle him?

Q6: You really need a loan but you're worried that your menial job title might look bad on the application form. **What do you put down?**

A: 'Secretary' – it's the truth and the bank will appreciate your honesty.
B: 'Executive Assistant' – it makes you sound like management and isn't a complete lie.
C: 'King of the world, great king, mighty king, King of Babylon, King of the land of Sumer and Akkad, King of the four quarters, son of Cambyses, King of Anshan, grandson of Cyrus, descendant of Teispes, progeny of an unending royal line, whose rule Bel and Nabu cherish, whose kingship they desire for their hearts' pleasures.'

Q7: The boss has requested you attend a posh reception for potential graduates. The booze is flowing freely BUT you've been explicitly told to set a good example and not get drunk. The waiter comes up and asks what you want to drink. **What do you say?**

A: Ask him to get you an orange juice with a double vodka in it – who's to know?
B: Take one glass of champagne and make it last – you want to look relaxed but you're keen to stay focused.
C: Tell the waiter that you only drink pure water from the river Ganga, for it is the Water of Immortality.

Q8: You're at a dinner party and a guy keeps going on about how much he does for charity. He then rudely asks you what you've done. **What's your response?**

A: Mumble something about always buying the Big Issue.
B: Tell him that you don't like to talk about your charity work – it's vulgar.
C: Crisply draw to his attention the 84,000 Buddhist monuments, shrines, temples and monastic residences you have built across Asia.

Q9: It's Halloween and you and some mates have stayed up drinking. The conversation has moved onto the spooky subject of what sort of funeral you'd all like. **So how do you want to go out?**

A: Just a simple cremation thanks. Forget the flowers and give the money to charity.
B: A big party. No crying. Just lots of music and lots of drink. I want you to celebrate my life.
C: Return my body to the Steppe. Should my cortege meet anyone or anything en route they must be instantly killed so that none know where I lie. When you bury me, divert a river over my grave so that I may enjoy eternal peace.

Q10: Your kingdom is being repeatedly over-run by marauding Vikings but no matter how much you pay them they just keep coming back for more. **Do you:**

A: Decide to call in sick and snuggle up in front of daytime TV with a cup of tea and a big box of chocolates?
B: Buy the Viking chief a Bacardi Breezer and suggest he makes contact with his 'inner woman'?
C: Completely re-arrange the administration and military organisation of your country to respond to multiple threats over extended time periods. Combine this with a radical overhaul of the educational system, a rewriting of the laws of the country and a unique defensive building programme which you hope will, in time, neutralise the threat.

So how did you do?

Mostly A:
Frankly you're more grating than great. It's time to take charge of your life and stop just saying what you think other people want to hear. Did Hitler bother about what people said about him? No – and neither should you.

Mostly B:
You might be great company but you're not 'Great' in the strictly historical sense that is meant here. Being a supreme being is rarely about having a laugh with your mates, it's about paranoid delusions, megalomania and Messianic self-belief. You need to work on these.

Mostly C:
You're Great!
You have the ambition of ALEXANDER THE GREAT (Q1); the dedication of ST GREGORY THE GREAT (Q2); the work ethic of TSAR PETER THE GREAT (Q3); the fruitful loins of RAMESES THE GREAT (Q4); the man-management flair of CATHERINE THE GREAT (Q5); the PR skills of CYRUS THE GREAT (Q6); the great taste of AKBAR THE GREAT (Q7); the generosity of ASHOKA THE GREAT (Q8); the forward-planning smarts of GHENGIS (THE GREAT) KHAN (Q9); and the legislative and supervisory can-do of ALFRED THE GREAT (Q10).

But you're probably short on friends.

41

QUITE INTERESTING
GOLF

The world's most challenging 9-hole golf course – designed by the QI Elves using real locations from all over the world ...and beyond.

HOLE 1: LOST CITY COURSE, SOUTH AFRICA
The first hole at the QI golf course also doubles as the par-3 thirteenth hole at the Lost City Course in the Pilanesberg Game Reserve, South Africa. The green, which is shaped like the continent of Africa, is protected by 9 bunkers and a crocodile pit that one must play directly over.

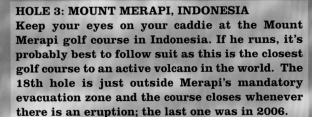

HOLE 2: LEGEND GOLF, SOUTH AFRICA
The second hole is only 50 miles or so south of hole one, and can be found at the Legend Golf and Safari Resort. This course's 19th hole is known as the million-dollar par 3. The tee is perched over 1,300 ft (396 m) up, at the top of Hanglip Mountain – access only by helicopter – with the putting green at the bottom of the vertical drop. A hole-in-one here and you will receive $1,000,000.

HOLE 3: MOUNT MERAPI, INDONESIA
Keep your eyes on your caddie at the Mount Merapi golf course in Indonesia. If he runs, it's probably best to follow suit as this is the closest golf course to an active volcano in the world. The 18th hole is just outside Merapi's mandatory evacuation zone and the course closes whenever there is an eruption; the last one was in 2006.

HOLE 4: THE ARIKIKAPAKAPA COURSE, NEW ZEALAND
Also troubled by volcanic activity is The Arikikapakapa Course on New Zealand's North Island. The course has a number of unusual hazards including bubbling mud pools, steam vents and strange sulphur mounds. Best to aim to the right of the 14th green as the left is guarded by a monster of a thermal crater.

HOLE 5: URBAN GOLF, HAMBURG

Urban Golf, that is golf played in a city centre rather than on a golf course, was the invention of German Torsten Schilling, a former TV set-designer who found himself playing in hotel corridors to pass the time. The game is played with a leather ball stuffed with goose feathers in order to prevent damage and is usually only played with two clubs so that proponents can quickly scarper if the police should take offence. Usually a bin is designated as the hole, while lamp-posts are trees and drains are bunkers.

HOLE 6: UUMMANNAQ, GREENLAND

In the 1890s, living in Vermont, Rudyard Kipling invented 'snow golf' a game involving red balls and tin cans for holes. His spirit is still alive with the World Ice Golf Championship that takes place at Santa Claus's home course of Uummannaq every New Year. Polar bears are not an inconsiderable hazard, and your card will warn of the risks of falling down seal breathing holes.

HOLE 7: CAMP BONIFAS, KOREA

Natural hazards are not the problem at the Republic of Korea's Army post, Camp Bonifas. It has a 'golf course' which consists of a single par-3 hole with an astroturf green that is surrounded on three sides by minefields. It is not unknown for a wayward drive to land out-of-bounds and set off one of the explosives.

HOLE 8: CLUB DE GOLF RIO LLUTA, CHILE

Club de Golf Rio Lluta is the driest golf course in the world as its position would suggest, in the Atacama desert, the driest desert in the world. Rain never stops play here, in fact, it has never rained in the history of the club, so there is not a single blade of grass anywhere to be seen. Make sure you hit the fairways that are marked with chalk lines and you might find the putting green which is created with oil and dirt.

HOLE 9: OUTER SPACE

Alan Shepard was the first man to hit a golf ball on the Moon, hitting a shot in 1971 that he claimed went 'miles and miles and miles'. It was later estimated that his shots had travelled only 200 to 300 yards. A more difficult hole is the elves' 9th hole which begins at the international space station; in 2006, Russian cosmonaut Mikhail Tyurin hit a shot from there which will have carried around a million miles, but will never have hit any green as the ball would have burned up in the atmosphere before reaching earth.

GROG,
GIN, GAS, GREEN PARK,
&
A GLOBE-TROTTING GOAT

by way of Pickled Cabbage, a Pickled Ear & the Portobello Road

SEAFARING AND BINGE DRINKING HAVE ALWAYS BEEN ESSENTIAL ELEMENTS OF
THE BRITISH CHARACTER, AND THEY HAVE HELPED TO SHAPE THE NATION'S
HISTORY IN SOME REMARKABLE AND UNEXPECTED WAYS

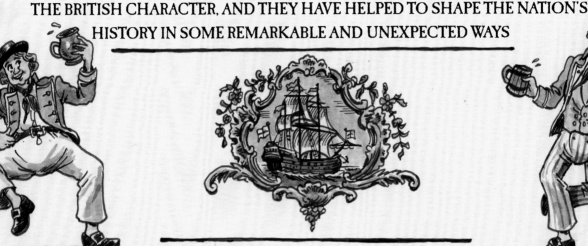

The naval drink known as GROG was named after Admiral Edward Vernon (1684–1757), whose nickname 'Old Grog', came from the grogram cloak he always wore. (Grogram, from the French *gros grain*, was a coarse cloth made of silk, mohair and wool, sometimes stiffened with gum.) Vernon was concerned about the effects of serving neat rum to ships' crews. So, at Port Royal, in August 1740, he issued an order from HMS *Burford*, to tackle the 'pernicious custom of the seamen drinking their allowance of rum in drams, and often at once, which is attended by many fatal effects to their morale as well as to their health.' Henceforth, their daily ration of half a pint of rum was to be mixed with a quart of water. The practice, soon adopted by the rest of the Fleet, lasted for over two centuries and, although by the end it had evaporated to just an eighth of a pint of rum (59 ml) diluted with a quarter of a pint (118 ml) of water, the Royal Navy only finally discontinued it in 1970.

Vernon was a remarkable man. The son of one of William III's Secretaries of State, he managed to find time to serve as an MP as well as a seaman and, in 1745, he was to prevent French reinforcements reaching Bonnie Prince Charlie's Jacobite rebels. He had earlier fought against the Spanish, and in November 1739 captured their colony Porto Bello (now in Panama) 'with six ships only'. This victory was hugely popular back in Blighty. In 1740, the same year he invented grog, Vernon received the Freedom of the City of London. The Portobello Road (as well as an area of Dublin and another in Edinburgh) was named after the battle; the song *Rule Britannia* was composed as part of the victory celebrations; and George Washington's older brother Lawrence, who had served under Vernon in the Caribbean as a Captain of Marines, returned home to Virginia and renamed the family plantation 'Mount Vernon' in his commander's honour. *

·PORTOBELLO ROAD·

The engagement at Porto Bello was part of the curiously named 'War of Jenkins's Ear'. In 1731, a Captain Robert Jenkins was transporting sugar from Jamaica to London in the ship *Rebecca* when he was stopped and boarded by the Spanish coast guard, who accused him of carrying contraband. To discover where he had stowed the treasure, they tied Jenkins's wrists and ran him up the rigging, yanking him around to get him to talk. Jenkins kept his mouth shut, so the Captain of the coastguard hacked off his ear with a sword and advised him to take it back to King George. Seven years later, Jenkins attended a parliamentary committee investigating disputes with Spain and took along what he claimed was his ear, which he had pickled in a jar of rum. The bottled ear was waved about and the mob bayed for revenge, forcing the PM, Robert Walpole, to declare war on Spain and its ally France.

*Four Royal Navy warships have also been named after Admiral Vernon, as well as the shorebase HMS *Vernon* in Portsmouth, which was operative from 1923 to 1986. Home of the Navy's Torpedo and Anti-Submarine Branch (TAS) and Diving School, for several years in the 1960s it was commanded by Captain H.L. 'Harpy' Lloyd CBE, DSC RN, father of John Lloyd, the editor of this Annual.

by ADRIAN TEAL, Efq; MMIX

The War of Jenkins's Ear soon expanded into the Europe-wide conflict known as the War of the Austrian Succession. When this finally ended in 1748, King George II decided to celebrate with a huge fireworks display at GREEN PARK in London. Six months of preparation went into the event, and the Italian firework maestros, the Ruggieri brothers, were hired for the occasion. It took place in April 1749 but, on the night, a big bust-up erupted between the Italian and English pyrotechnicians. A firework hit one of the pavilions – the Temple of Peace, ironically enough – setting off many thousands of fireworks inside, and three spectators were killed.

Anyway, back to the subject of grog. After his introduction of the grog ration, Vernon's men became noticeably healthier than other crews. The Admiral had ordered lemon juice to be added to the grog to disguise the taste of the stagnant water, and, though it wasn't known at the time, this prevented scurvy. Today, scurvy has a slightly comical ring to it like piles or leprosy, but in fact it's a hideous and degrading disease that destroys the immune system – and it killed far more seamen than cannonballs, grapeshot, fire or drowning ever did. Even during the Napoleonic wars, only 6 % of sailors were killed by enemy action, as compared to a staggering 84 % lost to disease. All sorts of mad cures were tried, from being buried up to the neck in sand to urine mouthwashes and bathing in the blood of animals, and it wasn't until 1747 that a young Scottish naval doctor, James Lind, proved conclusively that scurvy could be simply and quickly ended by eating oranges and lemons. His report, however, was stubbornly ignored by the authorities and Lind left the Navy the following year to pursue an academic career.

Scurvy continued to decimate the Navy until 1795, *almost half a century* after Lind's original experiments, when the First Sea Lord finally decreed that lemon juice was to be added to the diet of all ships' crews abroad. Within two years, a study at the Royal Naval Hospital at Haslar in Portsmouth, failed to locate a single case of scurvy. Lind himself had died in relative obscurity, unrecognised by the Admiralty, only the year before.

Scurvy is caused by a lack of vitamin C in the diet. Humans, other primates and guinea pigs are among the very few species that suffer from it because most animals synthesise their own vitamin C and don't need to get it from food. Though it was clear by the end of the 18th century that scurvy was caused by a dietary deficiency, it wasn't known exactly what that deficiency was until 1928, when vitamin C was finally isolated by the Hungarian biochemist Albert von Szent-Györgyi. For this, nine years later, he was awarded the Nobel Prize for Physiology or Medicine.

One of the reasons that lemon juice had taken so long to catch on as a cure for scurvy was that the great navigator Lieutenant (later Captain) James Cook recommended sauerkraut (sour pickled cabbage) instead. His men initially refused to eat it, so Cook used reverse psychology. He made sure the officers were always served conspicuously and exclusively with large portions of the stuff, and the men, who thought they were missing out, started to demand their share.

Cook's crews had a remarkable health record given that they had sailed to uncharted waters right round the world, but it wasn't the sauerkraut that did it. Nearly all the vitamin C had been boiled out during the preservation process: the lack of scurvy was almost certainly due to fresh fruit and vegetables taken aboard along the way. In his second voyage (1772-75), Cook lost only one man to scurvy, but by then he had switched to lemon juice. When the Admiralty finally followed suit in 1795, scurvy almost completely disappeared for a time. However, political pressure from British lime-growers in the West Indies resulted in a switch to lime-juice, which contains only about a quarter as much vitamin C as lemons, and the disease reasserted itself. This may be why the word 'limeys', originally 'lime-juicers', used by American seamen about their British counterparts, has such a disparaging tone – the British tars drank lime-juice – but many of them were toothless from scurvy. The use of the word *limey* by Americans, incidentally, is much more recent than you might think. It was first recorded in print in 1918.

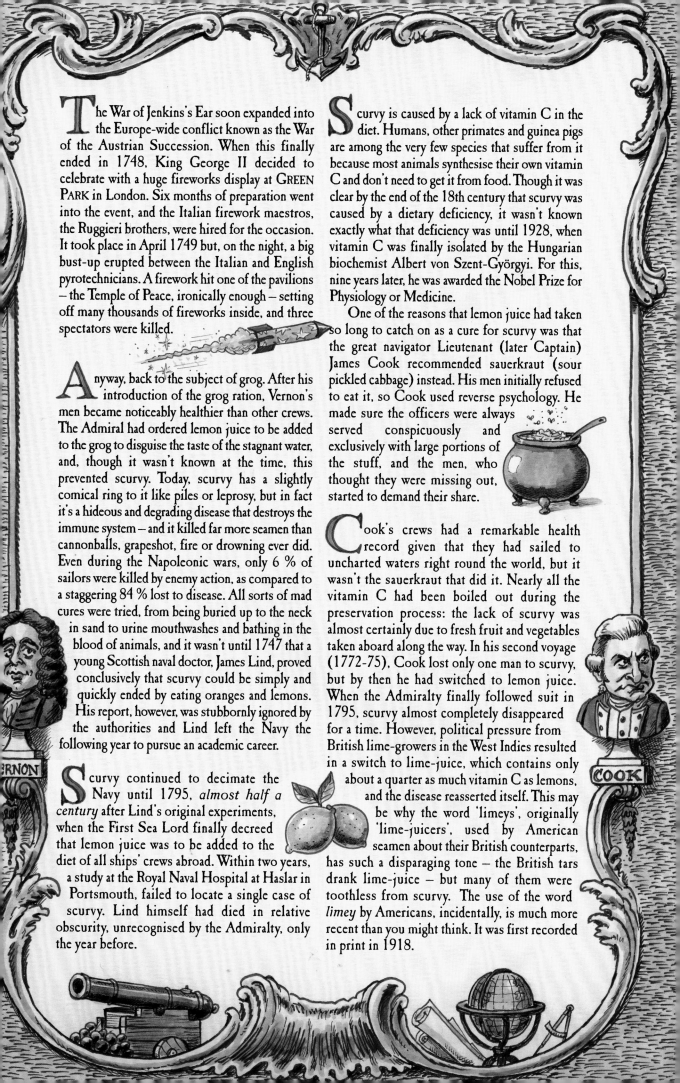

GROG, GIN, GAS, GREEN PARK…

It's perhaps slightly ironic that scurvy – the disease that caused such problems on the booze-soaked ships of the British fleet – also led to the foundation of the British soft-drinks industry. In the 19th century, Lauchlan Rose (1829–85) started a company to produce preserved lime-juice to prevent the condition, inventing Rose's Lime Juice Cordial in the process. Johann Jacob Schweppe (1749-1821) – the man who recognised that Joseph Priestley's invention of carbonated water was a commercial goer – manufactured it at his London-based firm. He then sold it on to one of Priestley's closest friends, the entrepreneur Matthew Boulton (1728-1809). The brand still exists today: owned by CadburySchweppes.

In his quest to improve shipboard nutrition, Cook also took a GOAT with him on his first round-the-world voyage (1768-71) to provide fresh milk. Before that, the goat in question had served in the West Indies for three years and was then taken around the world in the *Dolphin* (1766–68). So, when *Endeavour* returned to England in 1771, she had circumnavigated the globe twice. She 'never went dry', and was so valued that she was retired to 'a good English pasture for the rest of her life'. Dr Johnson wrote a letter about her to Cook's shipmate, Sir Joseph Banks (founder of Kew Gardens), including a Latin couplet:

PERPETUA AMBITA BIS TERRA PRAEMIA LACTIS,
HAEC HABET ALTRICI CAPRA SECUNDA JOVIS.

Johnson's biographer and friend, James Boswell, later translated this as:

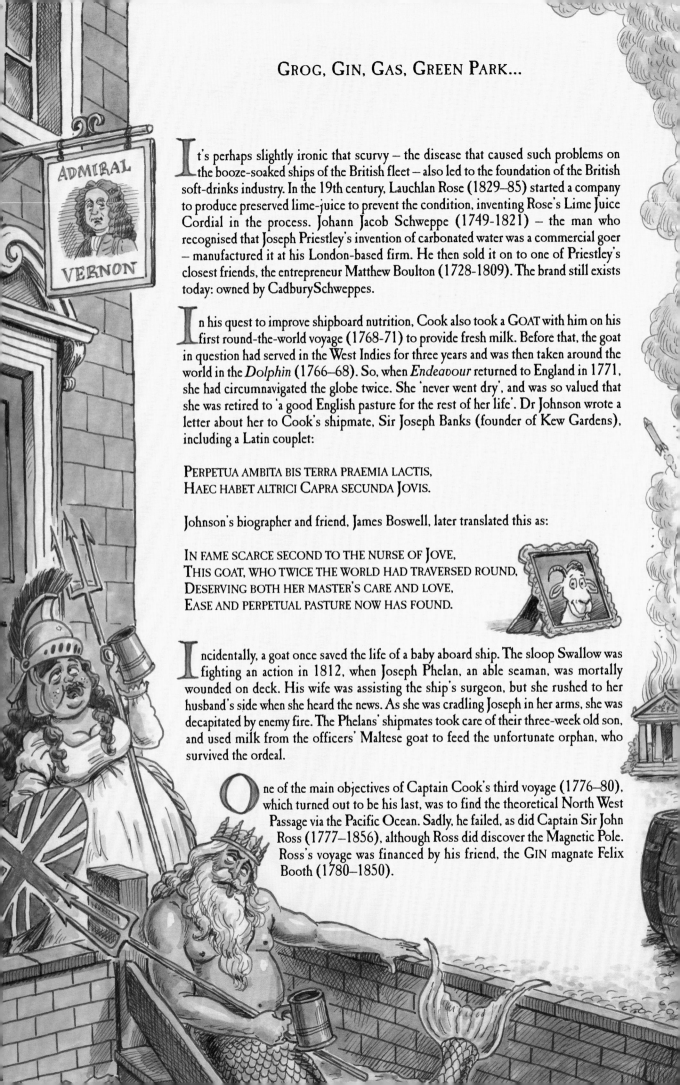

IN FAME SCARCE SECOND TO THE NURSE OF JOVE,
THIS GOAT, WHO TWICE THE WORLD HAD TRAVERSED ROUND,
DESERVING BOTH HER MASTER'S CARE AND LOVE,
EASE AND PERPETUAL PASTURE NOW HAS FOUND.

Incidentally, a goat once saved the life of a baby aboard ship. The sloop Swallow was fighting an action in 1812, when Joseph Phelan, an able seaman, was mortally wounded on deck. His wife was assisting the ship's surgeon, but she rushed to her husband's side when she heard the news. As she was cradling Joseph in her arms, she was decapitated by enemy fire. The Phelans' shipmates took care of their three-week old son, and used milk from the officers' Maltese goat to feed the unfortunate orphan, who survived the ordeal.

One of the main objectives of Captain Cook's third voyage (1776–80), which turned out to be his last, was to find the theoretical North West Passage via the Pacific Ocean. Sadly, he failed, as did Captain Sir John Ross (1777–1856), although Ross did discover the Magnetic Pole. Ross's voyage was financed by his friend, the GIN magnate Felix Booth (1780–1850).

As well as gin, Booth was one of the first to see the commercial possibilities of GAS, and built the Brentford Gas Company (of which he was chairman) next to his distillery, to light the road between Brentford and Kensington.

The word 'gas' was invented in about 1600 by the Flemish chemist and physician, Jan Baptista van Helmont (1580-1644), and is said to be the single most successful invention of a word by a known individual in history. Other, less generous, souls say that it was in fact just his Belgian mispronunciation (and spelling) of the Greek word 'chaos', which is what he actually meant to call it.

Gin is made from grass. More specifically it's made of wheat or rye, which is 'malted' (meaning melted or softened) and flavoured with juniper berries. It was originally a medicine, invented in the Netherlands in about 1650 by Franciscus de la Boe, a medical professor at the University of Leiden. He called himself 'Dr Sylvius' (the Latinisation of his surname de la Boe, meaning 'of the woods') and he intended gin to relieve stomach complaints. But British soldiers serving in Holland soon found another use for it. They called it 'Dutch courage'. By the early eighteenth century, gin was the heroin of its day, causing terrible social problems, drunkenness and riots. Excise revenues tell us that, in 1733, eleven million gallons were distilled in London. By 1742, the figure was twenty million. (1 gallon = 3.78 litres *Ed.*) The Gin Act, passed in 1736, sought to put 'Mother's Ruin' out of the reach of the poor, by prohibiting the sale of quantities smaller than two gallons. However, in the first two years of the Act, 12,000 people were convicted of offences against it. This was good news for informants, who were rewarded for snitching on illegal gin shops.

One such nark was Captain Dudley Bradstreet, who later switched sides and set up the world's first slot machine since the time of the ancient Greeks. In his autobiography, he tells us he erected the sign of a cat by his ground-floor window. Passers-by would put money in the cat's mouth, and whisper 'Puss, give twopence worth of gin.' A lead pipe with a funnel at the end then dispensed a measure to the expectant dipso. In his first month's trading, Bradstreet raked in £220, a massive sum at the time.

Between 1710 and 1750, thousands of people died as a result of London's 'Gin Craze'. This wasn't merely because they drank seven (3.3 litres) or eight pints of it at a time. As well as containing alcohol and innocent juniper berries, the gin was often adulterated with turpentine and sulphuric acid.

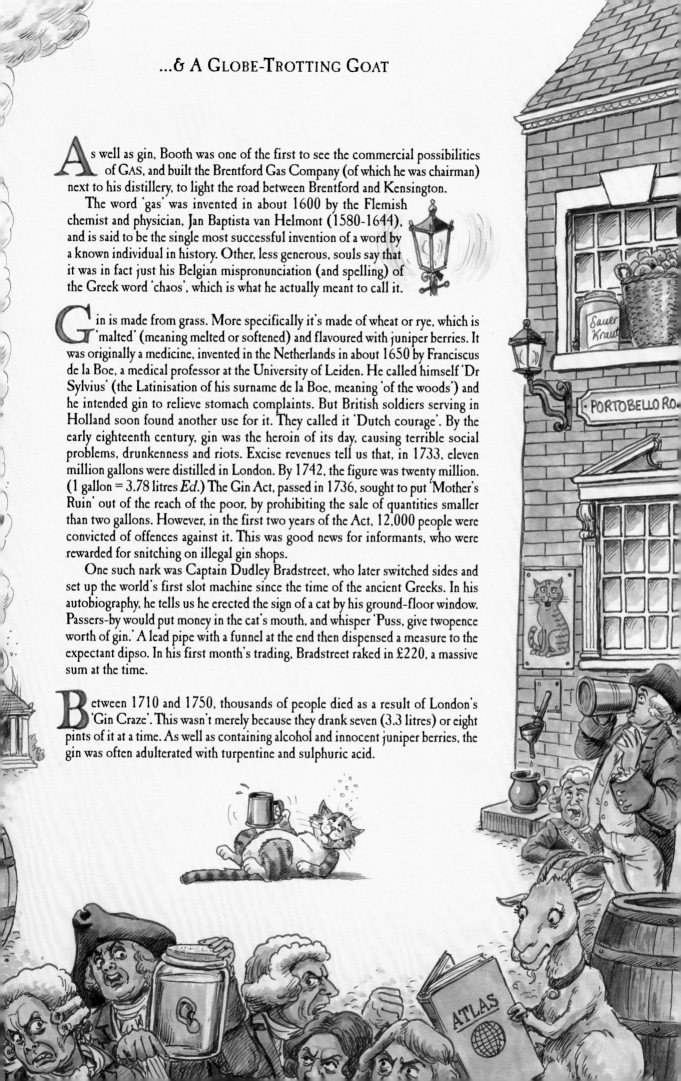

George Stephenson was born in 1781 at Wylam in Northumberland, the son of a colliery fireman. He had no education, could not read or write, and at the age of 10 he began work in the colliery as a coal picker, sorting coal by hand to remove rocks and debris. George had a way with all things mechanical and repaired clocks as a hobby. He was soon given more responsible jobs looking after colliery pumps and winding engines. At the time of his promotion to enginewright, George was living in a small cottage with his sister Nelly and his young son Robert. Robert's mother, Frances, had died of consumption in 1806.

George's reputation spread and he was retained as an engineer by several colliery companies. In his spare time he invented a miners' safety lamp to help reduce the risk of explosions in mines, and tested it himself by walking into a mine filled with gas. When the celebrated scientist and would-be poet Sir Humphry Davy came up with a similar lamp, The Sunderland Society for the Prevention of Accidents in the Mines controversially awarded Sir Humphry Davy a £2000 prize for his design...

It was eventually proven that Stephenson's Geordie Lamp had been demonstrated to work prior to Sir Humphry's Davy Lamp. George was awarded a consolation prize of £1000 by a group of his supporters in Newcastle.

50

George Stephenson surveyed, drew up the plans and oversaw the construction of the entire railway. And when the Stockton & Darlington opened in 1825 – the first public railway in the world – George was at the controls of Locomotion, one of several engines he built for the line. However Stephenson did not invent the steam railway locomotive. Richard Trevithick had done that 21 years earlier at Pen-y-Daren in Wales. Stephenson had observed several pioneering locomotives at work in Northumberland, analysed their various designs and then set about improving upon them.

In 1823 George opened the world's first purpose-built steam locomotive factory near where Newcastle railway station stands today. He named the business Robert Stephenson & Co and gave his son the job of managing it. But trade was very slow to begin with, due largely to the fact that there weren't any railways yet to build locomotives for.

It was Robert Stephenson who took charge of designing and building the new locomotive while his father oversaw the building of the railway. However it was Henry Booth, the secretary and treasurer of the Liverpool and Manchester Railway, who came up with Rocket's most significant design innovation. Booth suggested using a multi-tubular boiler containing a large number of narrow copper pipes. This radically increased the heat exchange between the furnace and the water, and was to become a standard feature on all future steam locomotives. (A French engineer, Marc Seguin, had applied to patent a similar boiler design two years earlier.)

In October 1829, five pioneering locomotives lined up to compete for the £500 prize plus a contract to build engines for the Liverpool and Manchester Railway. On the final day of the Rainhill Trials a crowd of ten thousand turned up and witnessed the Stephensons' locomotive Rocket steaming to a clear victory.

51

Jolly Giraffe, Gray Jolliffe and Jeffy Gorilla
An out-of-depth scrutiny of

GENIUS

'Having the originality, intellect and imagination to think in hitherto unexplored areas and thus give mankind something of unique value it wouldn't otherwise possess.'

Encyclopaedia Britannica

Ok you two. Let's get to the nub of this.

I'll start with Jung. Were it not for Jung's 'collective unconscious' my plane would still be on the tarmac. Passenger 'will power' alone got it in the air. Karl Jung was a genius. And the airlines agree.

Many people claim Freud was the genius.

Not in Jung's class! Jung could wipe the floor with Freud.

Whoa! Freud made a big comeback since neuroscientists proved him right about booze and cash having a direct effect on our emotions.

But neither Jung's analytical psychology nor Freud's psychoanalysis could help James Joyce's daughter Lucia.

Joyce says that was because she was jung and easily freudened.

J.G. Ballard asserts that for the first time in 500 years there are no living geniuses.

Ballard?

Sounds like a duck with a head cold. How about Wayne Rooney?

He's no genius.

You didn't see the Croatia match.

Hummm... Better wind this up. But first, who are your personal favourite geniuses?

Shakespeare. He produced all that stuff with a feather – clever or what?

Antony Worrall Thompson. If I could cook half that well I'd be one happy griller.

We only use one third of our brain.
British Medical Journal

What do we do with the other third?

Thousands of geniuses live and die undiscovered by others, but mainly by themselves.
Mark Twain

Your mother is here to see you Mr Darwin

Nobody in football should be called a genius. A genius is a guy like Norman Einstein.
Joe Theisman

Only two things are infinite; the universe and human stupidity, and I'm not sure about the universe.
Albert Einstein

"I think they're for 1 a.m"
Descartes (preparing petits fours for an all night party)

Our curiosity about a thing is always obstructed by our preconceived ideas. The genius can see through that veil.
Theodore Zeldin

It's how the rockets go up, not where they come down, that's not my department says Werner von Braun.
Tom Lehrer

Your unconscious brain outweighs the conscious by ten million to one. Your brain is much smarter than you are, but only a genius will consult it.
Michael Gelb

52

GENIUS in brief

ALBERT EINSTEIN was dyslexic, a womaniser and hated wearing socks. Even so, without him we would never have had the benefits of a curved universe, the atom bomb and nuclear power.

THOMAS EDISON invented the practical electric light. And for more than 70 years after his death he held the world record for the most patents. All this from someone who, aged 7, was expelled from school after only three months for being 'retarded'.

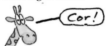

LEONARDO DA VINCI not only dreamed up the helicopter and the machine gun, but he was also handsome, a gifted musician and exceptionally strong. He could bend a horseshoe with his bare right hand.

ISAAC NEWTON is the most important scientist in history and his *Philosophiae Naturalis Principia Mathematica* the single most important work in the history of science ever. But he was a mean, angry religious zealot who had no friends and probably died a virgin.

RICHARD FEYNMAN was a brilliant scientist and mathematician. Noted for his sense of humour, his work at Caltech had mainly to do with quantum physics and other arcane stuff like whether or not photons had mass.

GENIUS in fiction

There are lots of geniuses in fiction. Captain Nemo and Sherlock Holmes are two. Douglas Adams' paranoid android, Marvin, had four billion times the intelligence of any human but was lumbered with menial tasks and depression.

In *Catch 22* Milo Minderbinder was a crazy genius conducting business between both sides in the Second World War. 'Frankly' he said, 'I'd like to see government getting out of war altogether and leaving the whole thing to private enterprise.'

When a true genius appears in this world you may know him by this sign, that the dunces are all in a confederacy against him.
Jonathan Swift

Although there have been many women who have made huge contributions to the sum of human knowledge and progress, not one has been hailed as a true genius. Historically this is because most were too busy giving birth to them.
In popular lists of geniuses, Dolly Parton is the only woman who appears consistently, but no one really knows why.

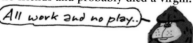

A national poll of 4,000 Britons, to find the 100 greatest living geniuses (conducted in 2007 by global consultancy firm Creators Synectics) included: Damien Hirst (15=), Rupert Murdoch (20=), Osama bin Laden (43=), Richard Branson (49=) and, of course, Dolly Parton (94=).

A genius is someone who has *two* great ideas.
J. Bronowski

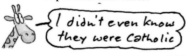

I-Spy GRAVEL

On your drive, on the path and, er, in the gravel pits – it's all around you and life just wouldn't be the same without it. Welcome to the world of **gravel**!

But how much do you really know about this geological wonder?

Gravel spotting is often the first step in a life-long interest in gravel. Finding and sketching gravel in situ is cheap, healthy and fun and will allow you ample time to consider whether to invest in the more time-consuming (and expensive!) hobby of gravel *collecting*.

A gravel collection

Let's start with the basics: Is it gravel at all? If it's made of stone and its largest dimension is over 2 mm but less than 64 mm (2½ in) then – congratulations! - you've found gravel. Any bigger and it's a 'cobble' any smaller and, well, that's sand. (The word gravel actually comes from the Old French *gravelle* meaning 'coarse sand', which is a typically confusing French approach to things).

Not gravel

Gravel

Not gravel

Types of gravel: Gravel comes in all shapes and sizes (within the limits defined above). So let's look at some of the many fascinating types.

Bench gravel is found on the side of a valley, indicating a former, higher level for the river. It is a type of 'plateau gravel'. The first proof that mankind was millions (not thousands) of years old came when Boucher de Perthes (1788-1868) discovered both flint tools and the bones of extinct animals in the same bench gravel beds in Abbeville, Northern France.

Creek rock is the name for the water-smoothed gravels dredged from rivers and streams, mainly for use in concrete. It was extensively studied by the geographer Stanley Beaver (1907–84), whose work was vital in locating gravel sources for the building of RAF airfields in the Second World War.

Crushed rock, also known as 'Fool's Gravel' is pretend gravel made by crushing rocks. Careful not to be taken in! In 1912, Charles Dawson (1864–1916) hoaxed the archaeological establishment when he presented the skull of the first known

'missing link' between apes and humans to the Geological Society of London. He claimed to have 'discovered' it at a (real) gravel pit near Piltdown in Sussex. Known as The Piltdown Man, the forgery was actually made of the jaw of an orang-utan and some chimpanzee teeth glued onto a human skull, but this was not finally accepted until 1953, more than 30 years after Dawson's death.

Crushed stone is another 'false gravel' (usually pulverised limestone) used in road surfaces. The only really collectable form of this is granite Dense Grade Aggregate (DGA). You may hear 'pro' gravel collectors refer to this as 'crusher run'. Worldwide, many

more roads are surfaced with gravel than concrete or tarmac. Russia alone has over 400,000 km (249,000 miles) of gravel roads. In Australia, 10 mm (0.39 in)-sized crushed stone is called 'blue metal' despite being neither blue nor made from metal.

Fine gravel, often preferred by the ladies, is defined as having a long axis no greater than 2 mm, leading to some enthusiasts claiming it is really coarse sand. When the fine gravel is removed from a sample what is left is known as 'lag gravel', often preferred by lags.

Pay gravel is perhaps the king of gravels and is the preserve of the wealthy gravel collector. It is gravel that is rich in precious metals, making it suitable for mining and particularly for gold panning. It's where the term 'hitting pay dirt' comes from.

Pea gravel is the ideal starting point for the new gravel collector. It consists of small rounded stones often used in garden paths and aquaria. Archaeologists can sometimes deduce the location of ancient buildings by the accumulation of pea gravel in an area. Sir Arthur Conan Doyle (1859–1930) modelled Sherlock Holmes on Joseph Bell, his mentor at Edinburgh University Medical School. Bell would impress his students with his study of the minutiae of evidence – such as gravel on the sole of a shoe, indicating the route a patient had taken to work.

Piedmont gravel is coarse gravel swept down by mountain torrents and deposited on plains. It is a type of 'river-run gravel' - that is, any gravel found in or near a river. Deep-sea diver William Walker (1869–1918) saved Winchester Cathedral from collapse between 1906 and 1911. The building, which rested on wooden foundations in a marsh, had began to sink. 235 holes were cut into the sodden ground, which rapidly filled with water. Wearing a full diving suit, Walker plunged into these holes to reach the solid river gravel, 8 metres (26 feet) below the surface. On the gravel he methodically placed 25,000 bags of cement, 115,000 concrete blocks and 900,000 bricks. Working in total darkness, he did this for 6 hours a day for 5 years. Every weekend, he cycled 240 km (150 miles) back home to see his family in Croydon.

Gravel is another name for bladder and kidney stones, the solid concretions formed in the body from minerals dissolved in the urine. In Wrexham, Wales on 7th August 1740, the poet Jane Brereton (1685–1740) died after a 5-week attack of 'the gravel.'

Grose Indecency

English has traditionally excelled as a FILTHY LANGUAGE. For centuries, Britons were RENOWNED for their inexhaustible ability to be rude in all sorts of colourful ways.

But in these days of POLITICAL CORRECTNESS GONE MAD, the rich traditions of British MUCK have been progressively watered-down. Thanks to NANNY-STATE DO-GOODERS and Brussels bureaucrats, only twelve insults or nicknames are now legal, and none of these are allowed on the BBC at all.

Come with us back to the Golden Age of Rudery, when the rumbustious fruitiness of our native tongue was still in full flood, when you only had to walk down the street to have some MUTTON-MONGERING LULLY TRIGGER call you a quiffing rantallion.

So don't be a gullgroper, put down your gaying instrument and let's teach the gotch-gutted grumbletonians that WE'VE HAD ENOUGH of their rum-gagging!

Captain Francis Grose (1730/1 1791)

As with many people in the 18th century, we don't know exactly when Francis Grose was born, but he was baptised on 11th June, 1731. The son of a wealthy Swiss jeweller who had moved to London, he started his working life as a teenage soldier, serving in Flanders, fighting smugglers in Kent and retiring from the army at 21. He was Richmond Herald of Arms in Ordinary from 1755 to 1763 – a position bought for him by his father – and was made a captain in the Surrey Militia in 1778. But Captain Grose wasn't cut out to be either a soldier or a herald; he was to flourish as an artist, satirist, historian and lexicographer. An amiable man of extraordinary diligence, he began writing at the age of 40, publishing torrents of his work in instalments. His popular *Antiquities of England and Wales* (1772-76) was followed by the satirical *Advice to Officers of the British Army* (1782), then *Antiquities of Scotland* (1788-91), *A Provincial Glossary, with a Collection of Local Proverbs, and Popular Superstitions* (1787) and *Rules for Drawing*

Caricatures: with an Essay on Comic Painting (1788). He had just begun *Antiquities of Ireland* when he died suddenly of an apoplectic fit. Grose liked to eat rich foods and to drink port. He also liked to tell stories. An enormously fat man, he took great pleasure in the pun linking his name to his size. One of his best friends was Robert Burns who wrote in his letters that he had 'never seen a man of more original observation, anecdote and remark'. Today, Grose is best known for *A Classical Dictionary of the Vulgar Tongue* (1785), a collection of street slang, much of it deliciously foul-mouthed. The book was compiled by Grose and his appropriately named assistant Tom Cocking on midnight walks through London, where they would pick up choice vocabulary in slums, drinking dens and dockyards, adding them to their 'knowledge-box'. Taken together, *A Classical Dictionary of the Vulgar Tongue* and *A Provincial Glossary* define some 9,000 words then in common usage – all of which Dr Johnson had managed to miss out of his more famous *Dictionary of the English Language* (1755).

6 *Bum brusher?* 9

6 *Ballocks!* 9

Are you a member of the teaching profession?

Indeed not, I am a clergyman.

BUM BRUSHER and FLAYBOTTOMIST were both slang words for a teacher, i.e. one who regularly caned bottoms. BALLOCKS: As well as its better known meaning, 'ballocks' is an old slang word for a parson. In 1977, this piece of obscure and apparently useless information came in rather handy for Mr Christopher Seale, manager of the Virgin Records store in Nottingham. He was arrested by a policewoman for displaying the album Never Mind the Bollocks, Here's the Sex Pistols in his window, and charged under the Indecent Advertising Act, 1899. (The display was 2.74 m/ 9 ft long and the word BOLLOCKS appeared in letters 10 cm/4 in high). At Nottingham Magistrate's Court, John Mortimer QC, defending, called as an expert witness the Reverend James Kingsley, Professor of English at Nottingham University and a former Anglican priest, who gave a comprehensive history of the word bollocks and its various uses, after which the magistrates, while wholeheartedly deploring the situation, acquitted the defendant of all charges.

Do you play the purser's pump, sir?

No, I'm a pricklouse.

I'm as queer as dick's hatband.

Do you play the bassoon, sir?

No, I'm a tailor.

I'm not feeling very well,
but I don't know why.

PURSER'S PUMP: The Purser was the Supply Officer on a naval ship: one of his jobs being to supervise the rum ration. The rum was drawn out of the cask by inserting a syphon into the bunghole in the top. This was known as a purser's pump because it wasn't a pump: pursers, in charge of all food and drink aboard, were derided as cheapskates. *Purser's logic* is 'false economy'; a *purser's dip* is an undersized candle; *a purser's grin* is a sneer; a *purser's loaf*, a ship's biscuit; a *purser's medal*, a food stain on clothing. The curved mouthpiece of a bassoon somewhat resembles a syphon. PRICKLOUSE: Contemptuous word for a tailor (one of many). Tailors, like pursers were deemed to be mean – and also effeminate. There was an old saying 'nine tailors make a man'. Grose reports that one London tailor, ordered to provide 'half a man' to the local militia, asked how that could possibly be done. He was told: 'by sending four journeymen and an apprentice'. Other insults for tailors were 'botch' (for obvious reasons) and 'woodcock' because of their 'long bills'. 'Pricklouse' is from the tailor's imagined pernickety assaults on individual vermin with his needle. Samuel Pepys records his wife angrily calling him a pricklouse in his diary. DICK'S HATBAND: Until recently this was a very common expression on both sides of the Atlantic. It appears in many forms – 'tight as Dick's hatband', 'twisted as Dick's hatband', 'crooked as Dick's hatband' etc – but no one really knows where it comes from. A popular story has it that the phrase commemorates Richard Cromwell who took over control of England when his father Oliver died, but was not really up to the job. The 'hatband' is a humorous reference to the 'crown' that sat so uncomfortably on 'Dick's' head. Known as Tumbledown Dick or Queen Dick for his indecisive character, he was deposed after less than nine months in 1659. If the derivation is true, it's odd that the first person to record it in print was Francis Grose himself, 126 years later.

I dine with Duke Humphrey!

Come polish a bone with me! My tits can spank us to town where I'll sluice your gob.

I'm too poor to eat.

Let me buy you dinner. My horses will take us
merrily into town where I'll buy you a drink.

DINING WITH DUKE HUMPHREY: This ancient phrase relates to Humphrey, Duke of Gloucester (1390-1447), fourth and youngest son of Henry IV. A generous man, known as 'the good Duke', he kept an open house where anyone was welcome to drop in for dinner. When he died, 'to dine with Duke Humphrey' meant to go dinnerless, his hospitality having ceased at his death. In the 18th century, people with insufficient funds to pay their way at a meal would excuse themselves by saying they were 'dining later with Duke Humphrey'. This was a jokey reference to an aisle in Old St Paul's Cathedral where beggars gathered, named 'Duke Humphrey's Walk' because it was supposed to be near to the tomb of the good Duke. In fact, as Francis Grose pointed out in another of his books, *A Provincial Glossary* (1787), the tomb in question was actually that of John of Gaunt. Duke Humphrey is in fact buried in St Alban's Abbey. TIT: Originally applied to any small animal or object as in tomtit or titmouse, then to a horse, small for its kind or not fully grown, thence to any horse at all.

'I'm a prigger of prancers and I've been polishing the king's iron with my eyebrows.'

'You've had a norway neckcloth too, I'll be bound, and you'll be scragged, ottomised and grin in a glass case.'

I'm a horse-thief and I've been in prison.

And in the pillory too, I imagine. You're going to end up being hanged, dissected and your skeleton exhibited at Surgeon's Hall.

POLISHING THE KING'S IRON WITH MY EYEBROWS: i.e. looking out of metal-barred windows, whilst detained at His Majesty's Pleasure. NORWAY NECKCLOTH: A pillory was a device for public humiliation and physical (sometimes lethal) abuse. It had hinged wooden boards with holes cut into them, into which the victim's head and hands were inserted, after which the boards were locked together. The timber for pillories often came from Norway spruce trees. SCRAGGED: To be scragged was to be hanged by the neck until dead. The scrag-end of lamb or veal is the thinner and scrawnier part of the neck.

'I popped a tatler in the urinal of the planets!'

'A busnapper seized my rammer and ramped my munster plums!'

'Are you a flaybottomist?'

'No, I'm a fartcatcher.'

I pawned my watch in Ireland!

A constable grabbed my arm and forcibly took away my potatoes!

Are you a teacher?

No, I'm a footman.

TATLER: A tatler or tattler was originally a striking watch, i.e. one that made a noise to mark the hour - and comes from the word tattle (1481) meaning 'to prattle'. Today, tattler is black American slang for an alarm clock. URINAL OF THE PLANETS: It rains a lot in Ireland. The equivalent insult for Scotland was 'Louse Land'. BUSNAPPER: To 'buzz' someone was to pick their pocket, so 'a buzz' is a pickpocket. To 'nap' or 'nab' is to catch, steal or seize, so a busnapper or buzz-nabber is someone who catches pickpockets, in other words a constable. FLAYBOTTOMIST and BUM BRUSHER, as we've indicated earlier, were both slang words for a teacher, i.e. one who regularly caned bottoms. FARTCATCHER: Footmen were known as 'fartcatchers' because they walked behind their master or mistress in the street.

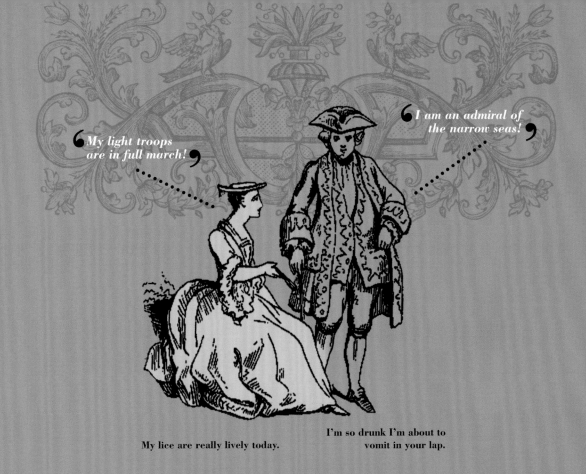

My light troops are in full march!

I am an admiral of the narrow seas!

My lice are really lively today.

I'm so drunk I'm about to vomit in your lap.

ADMIRAL OF THE NARROW SEAS: Whereas an 'admiral of the narrow seas' is a drunk whose vomit sails across the narrow gulf between his mouth and his neighbour's lap, a 'vice admiral of the narrow seas' is one who urinates into his companion's shoes under the table.

Rum ogles!

May I cock my organ?

Six cackling farts, please, strangle goose.

You're milking the pigeon – this is a nicknackatory!

Nice eyes.   Mind if I smoke my pipe?

Six eggs, please, my good poulterer.

You're attempting the impossible, madam – this is a toyshop.

RUM OGLES: 'Rum' was 16th century slang for 'fine' or 'excellent', it only came to mean 'strange' in the late 18th century. Ogles were eyes, from which we get the verb 'to ogle'. COCK MY ORGAN: The cock of a gun is the lever raised and brought down by the trigger. In old firearms, this brought a lit match into contact with the gunpowder in the flash pan, which then exploded firing the ball. To 'cock a gun' was to place a match into the appropriate part of a matchlock. Hence, 'to cock' a pipe was to light it. Pipes of the smoking kind were nicknamed organs as a pun on their pipes of the musical kind.

59

GIRAFFES

The Eleven Most Commonly Asked Questions (probably)

1. WHY DON'T GIRAFFES FAINT?

You might expect them to, when you see them raise their heads up from ground level - a distance of around 5.5 metres (18 feet) - in just a couple of seconds. Luckily, they have very high blood pressure, and are wise enough not to take tablets for it. Their legs are covered in tight skin that prevents blood pooling, and have strong muscles to pump it rapidly brainwards. It's long been thought that their jugulars contain a series of check valves to prevent sudden light-headedness. Latest research, however, suggests that the real key to the giraffe's anti-fainting mechanism is simply the massive size and power of its heart, which makes up 2.3 per cent of its body mass, compared to 0.5 per cent in humans.

2. DO GIRAFFES EVER FEEL FAINT, THOUGH?

Very probably. Mathematical models show that when a giraffe has its head at floor-level to drink, and then raises it suddenly in response to potential danger, it takes nearly ten seconds for normal blood-flow to be restored. In other words, say scientists, 'Giraffes feel faint when startled.'

3. WHY AREN'T GIRAFFES' NECKS LONGER?

Typically, a giraffe's neck accounts for half of the animal's total height. Even taller would be even better, perhaps - but the size of heart required to service it would, it is thought, be entirely unfeasible. The factors potentially affecting evolution are of course limitless ... but who'd have guessed that the avoidance of fainting was one of them?

> I know who I am. No one else knows who I am. If I was a giraffe and somebody said I was a snake, I'd think 'No, actually I am a giraffe.'
>
> **RICHARD GERE**

4. WHO WAS THE TALLEST GIRAFFE EVER, AND SHOULD I CARE?

George, an inmate of Chester Zoo in the 1960s, is said to be the tallest known captive giraffe, at just under 6 metres (20 feet). And you should care because even the dullest piece of trivia hides an interesting story.

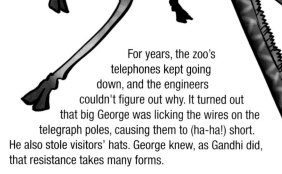

For years, the zoo's telephones kept going down, and the engineers couldn't figure out why. It turned out that big George was licking the wires on the telegraph poles, causing them to (ha-ha!) short. He also stole visitors' hats. George knew, as Gandhi did, that resistance takes many forms.

5. WHAT'S THE ONE THING EVERYONE KNOWS ABOUT GIRAFFES?

That they never lie down, other than to die. But of course, they do. Conservationists at Oakland Zoo, California, note that: 'They often lie down to sleep, with head and neck lying across the flanks, although these sleeping periods tend to be brief - one to twenty minutes.' That's a long way down, for 60 seconds of shut-eye.

6. WHAT DO GIRAFFES DO FOR FUN?

Same as you, my friend: they drink. In the wild, splaying their legs and lowering their heads to drink makes them vulnerable, and they avoid it: they can go without water for longer than camels can. But in captivity, when water is provided at a convenient height, they will drink and drink and drink ... not from necessity, but for pleasure.

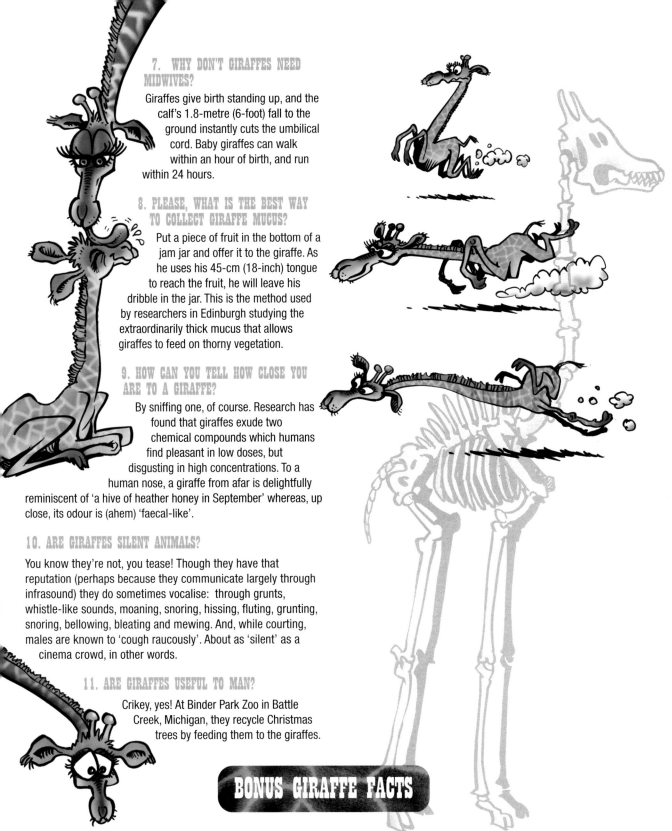

7. WHY DON'T GIRAFFES NEED MIDWIVES?

Giraffes give birth standing up, and the calf's 1.8-metre (6-foot) fall to the ground instantly cuts the umbilical cord. Baby giraffes can walk within an hour of birth, and run within 24 hours.

8. PLEASE, WHAT IS THE BEST WAY TO COLLECT GIRAFFE MUCUS?

Put a piece of fruit in the bottom of a jam jar and offer it to the giraffe. As he uses his 45-cm (18-inch) tongue to reach the fruit, he will leave his dribble in the jar. This is the method used by researchers in Edinburgh studying the extraordinarily thick mucus that allows giraffes to feed on thorny vegetation.

9. HOW CAN YOU TELL HOW CLOSE YOU ARE TO A GIRAFFE?

By sniffing one, of course. Research has found that giraffes exude two chemical compounds which humans find pleasant in low doses, but disgusting in high concentrations. To a human nose, a giraffe from afar is delightfully reminiscent of 'a hive of heather honey in September' whereas, up close, its odour is (ahem) 'faecal-like'.

10. ARE GIRAFFES SILENT ANIMALS?

You know they're not, you tease! Though they have that reputation (perhaps because they communicate largely through infrasound) they do sometimes vocalise: through grunts, whistle-like sounds, moaning, snoring, hissing, fluting, grunting, snoring, bellowing, bleating and mewing. And, while courting, males are known to 'cough raucously'. About as 'silent' as a cinema crowd, in other words.

11. ARE GIRAFFES USEFUL TO MAN?

Crikey, yes! At Binder Park Zoo in Battle Creek, Michigan, they recycle Christmas trees by feeding them to the giraffes.

BONUS GIRAFFE FACTS

A giraffe's heart is 2 feet (0.6 m) long and weighs about 25 pounds (11 kg).

A giraffe's tongue is 18 inches (45 cm) long and almost as dextrous as a hand. It's a purpley-grey, blue-black colour, supposedly to prevent sunburn.

A giraffe's neck, like that of almost all mammals, has only seven bones in it. A hummingbird's neck, like that of most birds, has 14.

Poachers kill giraffes for the metre-long tufts of hair on the end of their tails, which are cut off for making into bracelets. After the tail is removed, the dead giraffe is simply abandoned.

Some African tribes treat nosebleeds with the smoke from burning giraffe skin, whereas others have found that their leg-tendons make excellent bowstrings.

More than half of all giraffes do not live to be more than six months old.

Giraffes are notoriously accident-prone and unintentionally dangerous. Being tall they fail to see tents, tread on them, and then panic and start thrashing about.

Giraffe hooves are the size of soup-plates.

In 2002, anxious to examine its hooves for incriminating evidence, police pursued a giraffe suspected of murdering Father Karaffa, an American priest, by trampling him to death in a Kenyan game park. But, after an hour-long chase, the animal committed suicide by jumping off a cliff.

What Use is a Goose?

As 80s pop sensations *Frankie Goes to Hollywood* once remarked: 'War - What is it good for? Absolutely Nothing!' The same could be said about geese, except for the fact that they are... er... really very useful indeed.

BUT BEFORE YOU RUSH OUT AND BUY A FLOCK,

just exactly what can you do with geese?

HERE ARE 15 HELPFUL SUGGESTIONS:

1. EAT ONE

Roast goose is traditionally eaten in Germany on Martinmas (11th November) in memory of Saint Martin of Tours, who, according to legend, hid in a barn full of geese to avoid being made a bishop, until the geese gave him away with their honking. He is the patron saint of geese.

2. EAT ANOTHER ONE

Goose is also traditionally eaten in Britain at Michaelmas, the Feast of St Michael the Archangel, on 29th September. According to legend, this came about because Queen Elizabeth I was tucking into goose when she heard of the defeat of the Spanish Armada in 1588, and so ordered that goose be eaten on that day every year to commemorate the event. Sadly, this is nonsense. In 1588, the tradition was already at least 100 years old and, in any case, the Armada was defeated in August. According to Jane Austen, eating goose on Michaelmas Day ensures that you won't be short of money in the following year. She tried this just before the publication of the second edition of *Pride and Prejudice*. It worked for her.

3. GO ON, HAVE A THIRD, YOU KNOW YOU WANT TO

Goose has always been popular for Christmas dinner in Britain. It was Henry VIII who first came up with the idea of turkey instead. In Charles Dickens' *A Christmas Carol*, the Ghost of Christmas Present shows Scrooge a vision of the Cratchits eating goose for Christmas dinner but, after Scrooge has mended his ways, he orders a more fashionable turkey for them. Dickens doesn't say what happened to the Cratchit's goose. Lord Byron was in the habit of buying geese to fatten them up for Christmas but became so attached to them that he couldn't kill them. He ended up with four pet geese. Until the 19th century, Christmas geese were walked to London from East Anglia in flocks over 1,000 strong. With their feet dipped in tar and sand as makeshift walking boots, they managed a brisk nine miles a day.

4. STUFF THEM AND STUFF YOURSELF

The discerning goose gourmet will salivate at the mere thought of *pâté de foie gras* – made from the swollen livers of geese, force-fed with grain through a metal tube – although over 95 per cent of French *foie gras* is now made with duck liver instead. This is much kinder to the geese. You can now also get 'ethical' *foie gras* from Spain, where the geese are plumped up slowly and voluntarily and then only lightly killed. The wartime recipe of pig's liver and potato casserole was known as 'poor man's goose'.

5. SERVE THEM AS FISH

For centuries it was mistakenly thought that geese hatched from the barnacles washed ashore on driftwood - hence the names *barnacle geese* and *goose barnacles*. Because such geese were never seen in summer, it was assumed they bred underwater (rather than, as we now know, in the Arctic). As a result, some Catholic dioceses allowed them to be eaten during Lent because they were 'fish'. In 1215, Pope Innocent III banned this absurd practice as it was patently silly. About as ridiculous, in fact, as translating the Bible into French… which he also banned.

6. SLEEP WITH THEM

Goose is an old slang term for 'prostitute'. The prostitutes of medieval Southwark came under the protection of the local landowner, the Bishop of Winchester, and so were known as 'Winchester geese'. 'Goose' also became a common name for venereal disease. 'Gooseberry bush' is 19th century slang for pubic hair – which is why babies are found under it.

Right: Ménage à trois including Goose.

A GOOSE BETWEEN TWO FOXES.

7. PLAY A ROUND WITH THEM
Early golf balls were made of goose feathers enclosed in a leather ball and were known as 'featheries'. From 1848, these were superseded by latex 'gutties' made from the rubbery sap of the *gutta percha* tree.

8. DOODLE WITH THEM
Penna is Latin for 'feather', and is where we get the word 'pen' from. *Quink*, the world's top-selling ink, is also an old name for a Brent Goose. When writing with quill pens, right-handed people used feathers from the left wing of the goose, and vice-versa.

9. SWEEP CHIMNEYS WITH THEM
Geese were used by Irish chimney sweeps in the 19th century. Inserted into the fireplace, they'd try to fly up the chimney, beating their wings in a tremendous panic, dislodging soot as they went.

10. SWEEP ACROSS EUROPE WITH THEM
The goose step, called in German *Der Stechschritt* (or 'prick-step'), was an early 19th century Prussian invention, later adopted by the Imperial Russian Army. Contrary to what you imagine, the Nazis actually phased it out very early on in the Second World War: after 1940 it was no longer taught to new recruits. But it's still used today in the Russian Federation, North Korea, Cuba, Vietnam, Chile and Iran – and in China, where slow goose-stepping soldiers presented the Olympic flag at the 2008 Beijing Games.

Above: 'A first lesson in the Goose Step' by W. Heath Robinson

11. INSTALL THEM AS A BURGLAR ALARM
According to legend, in the 4th century BC, a flock of sacred geese famously saved Rome by squawking an alarm during a stealthy night attack by the Gauls. It's less well known that, since 1959, Ballantyne's Whisky warehouses on the Clyde have used a flock of 70 guard-geese known as 'the Scotch Watch' to protect their stock. Quite interestingly, geese don't get goose-bumps when they're frightened.

12. GET THEM TO DO THE WEEDING
Many farmers in the USA employ 'weeder geese' to keep orchards and fields clear of unwanted vegetation. For some reason, geese eat grass and weeds voraciously, but leave the valuable crops – strawberries, coffee, cotton, Christmas trees, onions, asparagus, tobacco – completely alone. Only geese do this. Working from dawn to dusk, they root out weeds that are inaccessible to tools or machinery, and which would otherwise have to be expensively hand-weeded or poisoned with noxious chemicals.

13. GET THEM TO HELP WITH THE COOKING
Geese make excellent kitchen skivvies – there are several 19th century accounts of them turning spits, using their powerful necks like an arm.

14. KEEP ONE NEXT TO THE FIRST AID KIT
Geese offer an organic alternative to Bonjela for treating mouth ulcers, as detailed in this account from 1881: '*A goose was brought to the little patient's side, and the bird's head was thrust into the child's open mouth, and held there for about five minutes, for nine successive mornings. By that time the inflammation of the mouth had disappeared.*' A goose-bill is also a type of forceps used for removing bullets.

15. WIPE YOUR BOTTOM WITH THEM
Geese make superb, fully-recyclable soft toilet paper* (especially if you've run out of puppies), as the great French Renaissance writer François Rabelais (1494-1553) records in *Gargantua* (1534):

'I have, by a long and curious experience, found out a means to wipe my bum, the most lordly, the most excellent, and the most convenient that ever was seen. I wiped my tail with a hen, with a cock, with a pullet, with a calf's skin, with a hare, with a pigeon, with a cormorant, with an attorney's bag, with a falconer's lure.

But of all torcheculs, arsewisps, bumfodders, tail-napkins, bunghole cleansers, and wipe-breeches, there is none in the world comparable to the neck of a goose that is well downed, if you hold her head betwixt your legs. For you will thereby feel in your nockhole a most wonderful pleasure, both in regard of the softness of the said down and of the temperate heat of the goose.'

*Toilet paper as we know it today was only invented in 1902, at the Northern Paper Mill at Green Bay, Wisconsin. However, it wasn't until 1935 that they were finally able to advertise it as 'splinter-free'.

65

GORDON IS A MORON was a one-hit wonder for Jilted John in 1978. My father's name was **Gordon**, and though the lyrics make it clear that the **Gordon** in the song has many impressive qualities (better looking, cooler and trendier than Jilted John, at any rate), in my family the repeated phrase *Gordon is a Moron*, caused us much amusement. The song includes the line 'I was so upset I cried all the way to the chip shop' - making it the second best British hit single to mention the classic British takeaway after Kirsty McColl's *There's A Guy Works Down The Chip Shop Swears He's Elvis*.

The expression (and the song) *Gordon is a Moron* have come back into vogue since **Gordon** Brown went from Greatest Chancellor Of All Time to Worst Prime Minister In Living Memory about as fast as it takes to get from No. 11 to No. 10 Downing Street. His first name is actually James but the use of his second name **Gordon** avoids confusion with James 'Sex Machine' Brown whose showbiz career began entertaining troops at Camp **Gordon** in Georgia. **Gordon** Brown's father was a Church of Scotland Minister, which makes **Gordon** a 'son of the manse'. Many Scottish politicians and public figures are sons of the manse, but where in England are the sons of the vicarage? **Gordon** Brown lost the sight of his left eye (and very nearly the right as well) in a school Rugby game.

Another one-eyed **Gordon** is **Gordon** Banks, OBE, England's greatest goalkeeper. He lost his right eye in a car accident in 1972, putting a stop to his sporting career. Gordon Banks played every game in the legendary 1966 World Cup, but his most memorable save was against Brazil in the 1970 World Cup in Mexico, when he kept out a header by Pele. His biggest *mistake* as a goalkeeper was to eat whatever it was that upset his stomach before the quarter-final game against West Germany in the same tournament. Peter Bonetti took his place and England lost 3-2. Things might have been different had Banks been between the posts. In fact, England might even have had a second World Cup victory to bang on about.

The classified football results on BBC Radio have, for 35 years, been graced by the voice of James Alexander **Gordon**. His clear delivery and subtly weighted emphasis give

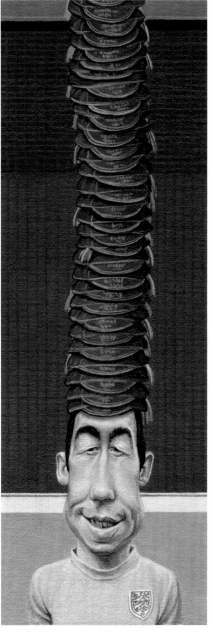

the simple list of names and numbers a familiar, comforting rhythm. His pronunciation is so admired in Sweden that tapes of his work are used to teach English to university students. One thing you can't tell from James Alexander **Gordon's** voice is that he contracted polio as a baby, was in and out of hospital until he was 15 years old and still walks with a limp. As a child, he had a serious speech defect but he overcame it by immense and prolonged effort. His mother said the only time she had ever seen her husband cry was the day his son did his first radio broadcast. 'The wee bugger's done it!' he exclaimed.

The most famous historical **Gordon** is **Gordon** of Khartoum. Like General Custer, King Harold or Admiral Nelson, General **Gordon** is doomed to be remembered for his last, lost battle, rather than his earlier exploits. In his lifetime he was known as Chinese **Gordon**, a war hero who led his 'Ever Victorious' army in China in the 1860s, returning loaded with honours from the Emperor. Visiting Brussels in the 1880s, **Gordon** so impressed the King of the Belgians that he gave him the job of running the Congo. Sadly, it was not to be. The British needed **Gordon** in the Sudan. Khartoum was under threat from a revolt led by the so-called 'Mad Mahdi', Mohammed Ahmed, and **Gordon's** job was to evacuate civilians to safety. This he did with great success, holding out against the Mahdi for more than a year before he was cornered, killed and beheaded, just two days before the British relief expedition reached the city to help him.

Gordon was a Christian evangelist who believed in reincarnation: he was looking forward to another life. He also believed that the Earth was surrounded by a sphere on which God's throne hovered directly above Jerusalem, with the Devil at the opposite point over Pitcairn Island in the Pacific.

'**Gordon** Bennett!' This useful euphemism, which sounds like a swearword but isn't, is thought to be named after James **Gordon** Bennett Jr, the American playboy son of James **Gordon** Bennett Sr. Gordon Bennett Sr was originally from Scotland, and left his son a fortune and the *New York Herald* newspaper. In his mid-20s **Gordon** Bennett Jr became engaged to the socialite Caroline May. At a grand New Year's party to celebrate the occasion in 1877, **Gordon** Bennett got so drunk he peed in the fireplace in front of his prospective parents-in-law.

His fiancée broke off the engagement and her brother gave **Gordon** Bennett a public horsewhipping.

Nowadays, perhaps, we should really cry out '**Gordon** Ramsay!' after the hugely talented chef who is as well known for his profanity as his profiteroles. **Gordon** Ramsay claims he was once on the books of Rangers Football Club. If only he had met Delia Smith early on, he could have been taught not to be so excitable while explaining cooking on telly, and played for Norwich City as well.

Gordon Ramsay advertises **Gordon**'s Gin, invented in Clerkenwell, London in 1769, by a Scot called Alexander **Gordon**. According to legend, his recipe is still used today: a secret formula known only to 12 people at any given time. Strangely, in these days of global branding, **Gordon**'s Gin is sold in green bottles in Britain but in clear glass bottles everywhere else in the world.

The amusingly titled Scottish dance 'The Gay **Gordons**' is named after the **Gordon** Highlanders, the tough regiment originally raised by the Duke of **Gordon** of Clan **Gordon** in 1794. The word gay had a rather different meaning when the **Gordons** were first called it. The word is probably a corruption of 'gey', an old Scottish term for hostile or ferocious. Or perhaps they just looked good in their kilts.

In the late 18th and early 19th century, Elizabeth **Gordon**, Countess of Sutherland, and her husband, the Marquis of Stanford, were the largest landowners in Britain. A Countess in her own right, Lady **Gordon** is chiefly remembered for the dreadful clearances of the Highlanders from her Sutherland estates in 1807-21.

Oddly enough, **Gordon** County, Georgia – though a long way from Camp **Gordon** where James Brown learned to dance – roughly corresponds to the last stronghold of the Cherokees before they were forced out of their traditional hunting lands in 1850.

g-g-g-gags
NICK NEWMAN

'We think he's going to be a ventriloquist.'

'Death, War, meet Global Warming.'

'Genesis? I don't Adam and Eve it!'

'I advertise golf sales, but it's my day off.'

'It was either this or teaching.'

'I'm going to conserve energy and not vote.'

'Oh no! Gypsies!'

'Do we have to have giraffes?'

'Sorry to have kept you waiting – now what seems to be the problem?'

69

*A girl should be two things:
classy and fabulous.*

COCO CHANEL

The whisper
of a pretty girl
can be heard
further off than
the roar of a lion.

ARABIAN PROVERB

Girls

BY JACQUELINE BISSET

*It's the good girls who keep diaries:
the bad girls never have the time.*

TALULLAH BANKHEAD

I never cared
for fashion much, amusing little
seams and witty little pleats:
it was the girls I liked.

DAVID BAILEY

Put your hand on a hot stove for a minute and it seems like an hour. Sit with a pretty girl for an hour and it seems like a minute. That's relativity.
ALBERT EINSTEIN

Even today, well brought up English girls are taught by their mothers to boil all veggies for at least a month and a half, just in case one of the dinner guests turns up without his teeth.
CALVIN TRILLIN

I never expected to see the day when girls would get sunburned in the places they do now.
WILL ROGERS

As soon as she can stand, a girl searches out what is hidden. ALGERIAN PROVERB

There is no such thing as an ugly girl; there is, however, such a thing as not enough vodka. RUSSIAN PROVERB

71

ARE YOU A GUINEA GENIUS?

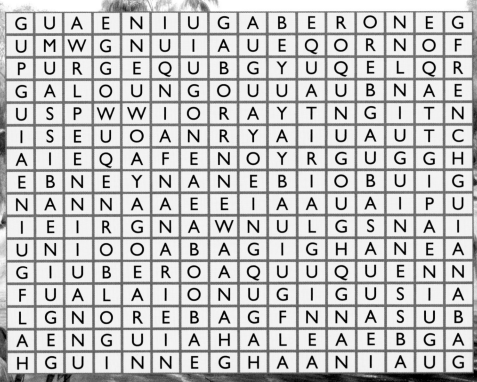

G	U	A	E	N	I	U	G	A	B	E	R	O	N	E	G
U	M	W	G	N	U	I	A	U	E	Q	O	R	N	O	F
P	U	R	G	E	Q	U	B	G	Y	U	Q	E	L	Q	R
G	A	L	O	U	N	G	O	U	U	A	U	B	N	A	E
U	S	P	W	W	I	O	R	A	Y	T	N	G	I	T	N
I	S	E	U	O	A	N	R	Y	A	I	U	A	U	T	C
A	I	E	Q	A	F	E	N	O	Y	R	G	U	G	G	H
E	B	N	E	Y	N	A	N	E	B	I	O	B	U	I	G
N	A	N	N	A	A	E	E	I	A	A	U	A	I	P	U
I	E	I	R	G	N	A	W	N	U	L	G	S	N	A	I
U	N	I	O	O	A	B	A	G	I	G	H	A	N	E	A
G	I	U	B	E	R	O	A	Q	U	U	Q	U	E	N	N
F	U	A	L	A	I	O	N	U	G	I	G	U	S	I	A
L	G	N	O	R	E	B	A	G	F	N	N	A	S	U	B
A	E	N	G	U	I	A	H	A	L	E	A	E	B	G	A
H	G	U	I	N	N	E	G	H	A	A	N	I	A	U	G

1: PURE GUINEAS WORDSEARCH

WORDS TO FIND: GUINEA – PAPUA NEW GUINEA – EQUATORIAL GUINEA – GUINEA-BISSAU
GUINEA PIG – GUINEA FOWL – GUINEA WORM – GUINNESS – HALF-GUINEA – GHANA – GUYANA
FRENCH GUIANA – GABON – GABORONE – GOLBORNE

2: RIDDLE-ME-RE

*My first is in Guinea, but not in Bissau
My second's in Guinea and in Guinea fowl*

*My third is in Guinea and isn't in Ghana
My fourth is in Guinea and also Guyana*

*My fifth is in Guinea and also in Guinea
It's also in Guinea, and Guinea and Guinea*

*My last is in Guinea but isn't in pig
If you can't get the answer then you're a bit thick.*

3: HOW WELL DO YOU KNOW YOUR GUINEAS?

1. This country contains half the world's bauxite
2. This is the only Portuguese-speaking country in the world with a Muslim majority
3. This is the world's third most aid-dependent country
4. Around a tenth of this country's population are refugees from neighbouring countries
5. This country has more recorded orchid species than any other country in the world
6. This country has more languages than any other in the world
7. This country has the fastest growing GDP on Earth
8. This is the only Spanish speaking country in Africa

4: MATCH THE COUNTRY TO THE FLAG

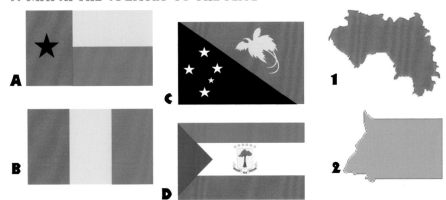

THE SUDO-N'KO

The official language of the ten million people of the Republic of Guinea in West Africa is French, but each of the 24 ethnic groups in the country also has its own language. These are known as the Mandé group of languages, from Maan-Den meaning 'Children of the Kings'. In the 1940s, Solomana Kante (1922-87), a Guinean nut merchant, became annoyed that his countrymen were seen as 'cultureless' because all their languages were oral and had no written alphabets. This was an ancient difficulty, first recognised more than 700 years earlier at a conference summoned by Sunjata, Emperor of Mali, in 1236. For seven years, Kante wrestled with the problem, experimenting for four years with an Arabic script and three years with a Latin one, before deciding that neither would do. According to legend, the solution came to him after a night of deep meditation and, on 14th April 1949, he unveiled his unique N'ko script to the world. N'ko – also known as The Clear Language – means 'I say' in all Mandé languages and is now used by 27 million people around West Africa.

THE QI SUDO-N'KO IS LIKE A NORMAL SUDOKU, BUT YOU MUST COMPLETE THE GRID SUCH THAT EACH ROW, EACH COLUMN AND EACH 3x3 BOX CONTAINS THE DIGITS 1-9 IN THE N'KO ALPHABET:

╏	╏	╏	╏	╏	╏	╏	╏	╏
9	8	7	6	5	4	3	2	1

For solution to QI Sudo-N'Ko please visit www.qi.com

RIDDLE-ME-RE ANSWER: Guine

HOW WELL DO YOU KNOW YOUR GUINEAS? ANSWERS
1. Guinea 2. Guinea-Bissau 3. Guinea-Bissau 4. Guinea 5. Papua New Guinea 6. Papua New Guinea 7. Equatorial Guinea 8. Equatorial Guinea

MATCH THE COUNTRY TO THE FLAG ANSWERS:
1=B (Guinea), 2=D (Equatorial Guinea), 3=A (Guinea-Bissau), 4=C (Papua New Guinea)

g-g-g-gags

Newm.

'Where do you stand on gay priests, God?'

'So much for omniscience'

'I suppose we'd better put an announcement in The Bible'

73

A dodgy cartoon of Graham *Norton* presents *(with Les Dennis' hair)*

GOLDEN GRAHAMS

(Nothing to do with the popular breakfast cereal of the same name)

A garrulous gander at some of my more notable namesakes

Hey baby I'm your telephone man?

Probably the most famous Graham in the history of the world is Alexander 'Graham' Bell (1847-1922), but he wasn't a proper Graham. As a child he was christened plain Alexander Bell. For some reason, unlike his two brothers - one older, one younger – his parents had neglected to give him a middle name. As a child he went on and on about this so, on his 11th birthday, his father allowed him to adopt Graham as his middle name... though everybody went on calling him Alec.

No, it's not a 3-D pool table...

....it's an orrery!

George Graham (c.1674-1751) was the Master of the Clockmakers' Company and a fellow of the Royal Society. Born into a poor farming family in Cumberland, Graham was to become the greatest instrument maker of his age, and partner of the famous watchmaker Thomas Tompion. Graham provided John Harrison with advice and a loan which enabled him to build his first marine chronometer, and many claim that (with Tompion) Graham built the world's first orrery - a mechanical model of the solar system - commissioned by (and named after) Charles Boyle, 4th Earl of Orrery. He also used precision clocks to measure the exact shape of the earth.

Brothers' Oporto port package did not portend well

Ehhm... Excuse me! I think this looks more like Paul Daniels than me!

W. & J. Graham, makers of the world famous Graham's Port, only got into the wine trade by accident. In 1820 two brothers, Albert and John Graham, working for the family textile business, were sent to open an office in Oporto, Portugal. While there they accepted 27 pipes (3,105 gallons) of port wine in settlement of a bad debt and shipped it back to their head office in Glasgow. Initially reprimanded for not sending cash, Graham's port quickly proved more popular than Graham's textiles, and W. & J. Graham have never looked back.

Graham's Crackers

Graham is the 30th most common surname in Scotland. Given a choice, however, Jocks tend to leave it well alone. In 2008 it failed to make the Top 100 boys' first names, trailing behind perennial Scottish favourites like Aaron (7th), Kayden and Muhammad (joint 82nd) and Noah (88th). The name originates from Grantham, in Lincolnshire, which is referred to in the *Domesday Book* as Graham. It means either 'grey home', 'gravel area' or 'Snarler's village'.

MASTICATION NOT MASTURBATION!

Feeling a tad frisky today? Fancy a bit of rough-age? Then get your teeth into this!

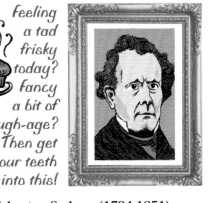

Sylvester Graham (1794-1851) was a dietary reformer who invented the Graham Cracker in 1829, and laid the foundation for modern-day breakfast cereals. A Presbyterian preacher, fanatical teetotaller and vegetarian, he recommended hard mattresses, cold showers and a diet of fruit, vegetables and home-baked bread made from unsifted, coarse-ground wheat. A bit of a cracker biscuit himself, he believed that an unhealthy diet containing meat and factory-baked bread would lead to alcoholism and excessive sexual urges. Graham's views caused some controversy, and during a visit to Boston in 1837 he was almost attacked by an angry mob of butchers and bakers.

Graham's Crackers

TV evangelist William Franklin 'Billy' Graham was a regular golf partner of Presidents Eisenhower, Johnson and Nixon. (Not all at once, though.) By 2008 he had preached to an estimated 2.2 billion people.

George Rex Graham (1813-94) was the American publisher who founded *Graham's Magazine* in 1841. The magazine's first editor was Edgar Allan Poe, and it was in *Graham's Magazine* that Poe's short story *The Murders in the Rue Morgue* was first published. This is widely (although not universally) claimed to be the first ever work of detective fiction. Poe's successor as editor of *Graham's* was his staunch critic and bitter rival, Rufus Wilmot Griswold,

Boo! Hiss! Rufus sounds like a barrel of laughs, doesn't he?

74

'What knight lives in that castle over there?'

Am I a gnome or a leprechaun? Or Alan Shearer?

I beg your pardon...

Graham Stuart Thomas (1909-2003) was perhaps the most influential rosarian of the 20th Century. His books, beginning in 1956 with THE OLD SHRUB ROSES, helped restore the then wilting popularity of England's national flower. In 1975 Thomas received the OBE for his work as gardens advisor to the National Trust, and the yellow rose 'Graham Thomas' is named after him.

Comedy legend Graham Chapman died in 1989, one day before Monty Python celebrated its 20th anniversary. Chapman was cremated and his ashes kept by his lover David Sherlock until the Millennium, at which point they were scattered over Wales as part of a firework display.

Graham's Crackers

American choreographer Martha Graham (1894-1991) taught Kirk Douglas, Bette Davis, Liza Minnelli, Gregory Peck and Madonna how to dance. In 1998, *Time* magazine named her 'Dancer of the Century'. (Just ahead of the BBC's John Sergeant.)

This Graham's NOT so Golden...

More **gunky** I'd say!

Stop there, it's getting too silly!

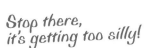

Graham Bond (1937-74) sold fridges and encyclopedias for a living before becoming a musician. His band The Graham Bond Organisation featured the impressive rhythm section of Jack Bruce (bass) and Ginger Baker (drums), both of whom went on to form Cream with Eric Clapton. Bond, who was born illegitimately and adopted as a child, was convinced that Aleister Crowley was his real father.

Optometrist Robert Klark Graham (1906-97) became a millionaire after inventing plastic eye-glass lenses. But he is perhaps best remembered for his achievements in the field of bespoke wank banking. In 1980 he set up the Repository for Germinal Choice, a sperm bank for clever tossers. Graham believed that not enough brainboxes were having babies. His solution was to travel around the world asking Nobel Laureates and male geniuses if they fancied a quick five-knuckle-shuffle. He died in 1997 after falling in his hotel bathroom during one such mess-collecting mission. His pioneering sperm bank closed soon afterwards.

Slow down! You're putting the wind up me!

Kenneth Grahame (1859-1932) was Company Secretary at the Bank of England when his first book was published in 1895. *The Golden Years* was a collection of short stories about a family of orphaned children. Grahame invented the character Toad while making up bedtime stories for his son, Alastair. However *The Wind in the Willows* was not well received by publishers or critics, most of whom seemed to want more stories about orphans. In 1920 Grahame's son Alastair was found dead on a railway line at Oxford. After his son's death Grahame wrote no more stories.

Graham's Crackers

James Graham (1878-1954), 6th Duke of Montrose, invented the aircraft carrier. Well, sort of.

Bette Nesmith Graham (1924-1980) invented typewriter correction fluid. Born Bette McMurray, she married a Nesmith and was the mother of Monkee Mike. Fortunately for me, in 1969 she re-married a Graham. In 1979 she sold her Liquid Paper business to the Gillette Corporation for a whopping $47.5 million.

Thomas Graham (1805-69) invented the word 'gel'. He also discovered dialysis, founded the Chemical Society of London, and formulated the law of diffusion of gases, known as Graham's Law.

Graham Bartram is the only living Graham deemed worthy of a mention on my page! He is a vexillologist and vexillographer (he researches and designs flags). A Fellow of the Flag Institute (yes, there is one), he is also the author of *British Flags and Emblems*, and flag consultant to the British Government.

Crambs! That's all we've got room for!

GNUS OF THE WORLD.

Gnus are a kind of antelope also known as wildebeest. There are two types of gnu: the White-tailed Gnu (Black Wildebeest) and the Brindled Gnu (Blue Wildebeest). White-tailed gnus are extremely rare and live in South Africa. They are extinct in the wild and only exist in game reserves.

Brindled gnus live in East Africa and aren't rare at all, outnumbering all the elephants, warthogs, giraffes, gazelles, zebras, impalas, lions and hyenas in the region put together. Once a year, over a million of them travel 3000 km from the Serengeti in Tanzania to Kenya's Masai Mara and back again. Every day they eat 7,000 tonnes of grass and drink enough water to fill five swimming pools.

GNUS FLASH

BLACK DAY FOR WILDEBEEST In June 2009, a baby black wildebeest was born at Newquay Zoo in Cornwall: the first white-tailed gnu to be born in the UK in decades. Sadly, he died of a stomach complaint after only 29 days.

Hummmmmmmmmmm

I heard you the first time.

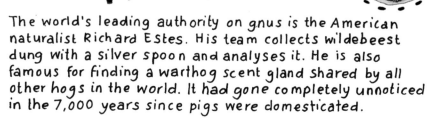

HELLO GNU FANS

GURU OF GNUS

The world's leading authority on gnus is the American naturalist Richard Estes. His team collects wildebeest dung with a silver spoon and analyses it. He is also famous for finding a warthog scent gland shared by all other hogs in the world. It had gone completely unnoticed in the 7,000 years since pigs were domesticated.

Most of the year, male gnus bellow 'ga-noo' but, at the first full moon after the rainy season, they also start to hum - and this turns female gnus on. The Guru of Gnus describes it as "a basso profundo mating chorus" - a cross between lowing cattle and giant bullfrogs - that "rumbles like waves against a headland."
Hmmmm

The Guru of Gnu is trying to prove that it is this humming that causes all female gnus to become sexually receptive at the same time. Eight months later 500,000 calves are born within 3 weeks of each other. Predators have a field day - but can't eat as many as they would if the births were spread out. Gnuborn babies can stand within as little as 3 minutes and run with the herd from 2 hours after birth. In large herds, 80% of newborns survive the first month.

HAVE I GOT GUNS FOR YOU

RUBBISH

CLUCK CLUCK

Before guns came along, the sensible gnu hunter would put an ostrich's head on a stick and tuck some ostrich feathers into his loincloth. Gnus and ostriches often graze together & the disguise allowed hunters to approach to within spear range.

Matt's Gravity

LAST GRAVITATIONAL PULL FOR 238,000 miles

GRAVITY
ON
OFF

SIR ISAAC NEWTON DISCOVERS THE PRACTICAL JOKE

'I'm not overweight, I just suffer from overactive gravity'

MATT

Bill Bailey's Air Guitar Masterclass

STEP 1: First select your air plectrum.*

You are now ready to air guitar.

LET'S ROCK!

*This could be an imaginary Jim Dunlop 0.73mm, or a 1.0mm for maximum rockage. Or a piece of stale naan bread. Or a tiddlywink.

STEP 2:
Try not to drop it.

STEP 3:
Place a lit cigarette upright in the headstock, preferably non-filter Gaulois etc. for bonus cool. Extreme caution advised (note the pinky raised in concentration).

STEP 4:
Warm up with some limp indie noodling. Don't go mental just yet, light strumming, and a gloomy demeanour.

STEP 5:
Bit more oomph now with some basic plucking. Here I'm demonstrating the classic Bert Weedon 'education can be fun' look.

Chord Positions

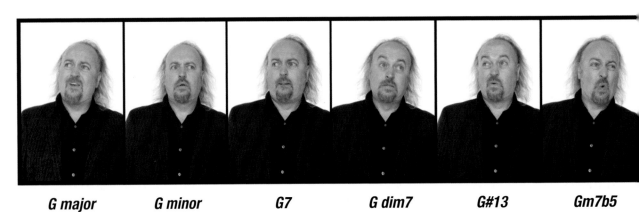

| G major | G minor | G7 | G dim7 | G#13 | Gm7b5 |

Photography by Andy Hollingworth

STEP 6:
Now try a few rock leaps –
are you nimble enough for the
Hair-Metal Scissor?

STEP 7:
The Amp-Smash. Recreate the classic
by Kurt Cobain at Reading in '92.

STEP 8:
Rawwk! Screwed up eyes and screwed down
hairdo - like some cat from Japan!

You have now completed Basic Air Guitar!

1. THE CLASSIC.
This is the twiddly
middle bit from the
classic riff (and air
guitar standard)

Free's 'Alright Now'
(or any riff at any
time since guitars
were invented).

2. THE HAMMER.
This involves
banging the strings
onto the fretboard,
or 'hammering on'.

This technique is
often used by
guitarists when they
can't remember what
song they're playing.

3. THE CRAB.
Thumb and
forefinger remain
clamped to the
neck, while the

three others (the
Crab's Legs) can
scuttle freely –
good for jazz.

4. THE LEMMY.

5. THE VULCAN.
(Spock's Delight).

6. THE CROCODILE.
This was pioneered
by Chic guitarist Nile
Rogers. Due to his
classic see-through

guitar, he was able
to perform shadow
puppetry during Le
Freak to the delight
of the crowds.

Classical
Spanish Styles

1. Rondo (Andrés Segovia).

2. Fandango (Paco de Lucia).

3. Hombre Con Gigante
Molinillo de Pimienta
(Carlos el Camerero)*

Broaden your range of silences
with these other air instruments

1. Air Triangle.

2. Air Flute.

4. Adjusting an Air Amp.
(This one is a 1969
Marshall Master
Lead Combo).

3. Air Sitar.

*Man With Giant Pepper-Grinder (Carlos the Waiter)

82

PHIL JUPITUS radio ④ idea machine

HELLO CHUMS... HAVE YOU EVER WANTED TO SUBMIT IDEAS FOR SHOWS TO RADIO FOUR? IT'S EASY! ALL YOU HAVE TO DO IS WHAT I DO! JUST TAKE THE EXISTING SCHEDULE AND ADD THE LETTER G... THESE SHOWS WILL MAKE THEMSELVES!

"THE GNUS QUIZ"

SANDI TOKSVIG ENTERS A WORLD OF TOPICAL WHIMSY WITH 4 WILDEBEEST...

"FEEDBAG"

ROGER BOLTON IS FORCE FED A LARGE BAG OF OATS...

"GROSSING CONTINENTS"

VARIOUS BBC FOREIGN CORRESPONDENTS TRY TO FEED PEOPLE BRITISH FOOD AROUND THE WORLD...

"SHIPPING GORECAST"

LEADING SURGEONS DESCRIBE OPERATIONS AS THEY PERFORM THEM TO NAUSEOUS SAILORS...

"THE ARGHERS"

A SIMPLE TALE OF COUNTRY FOLK WHO SCREAM AT EACH OTHER FOR NO REASON...

"THE GEEK IN WESTMINSTER"

AN I.T. CONSULTANT AND DUNGEONS AND DRAGONS FAN IS FORCED TO DO AN INTERVIEW WITH POLITICIANS

"DEAD GINGERS"

A PROGRAMME FEATURING VARIOUS DECEASED "STRAWBERRY BLONDES"...

"G.M."

EDDIE MAIR'S DNA IS MANIPULATED EVERY NIGHT AT FIVE O'CLOCK...

"GO 4 IG"

EVERY WEEK A YOUNG LISTENER IS ENCOURAGED TO ATTACK IGGY POP THEY ARE INTERVIEWED IN HOSPITAL.

"LOOGE ENDS"

CLIVE ANDERSON IS TAKEN UP THE ALPS AND STRAPPED TO A TEA TRAY TO CONDUCT CELEBRITY INTERVIEWS AT SPEED...

"THE MORAL GAZE"

BASICALLY A NUN HYPNOTISM SHOW.

"QUST A MINUTE"

NICHOLAS PARSONS IS TAKEN INTO A WIND TUNNEL FOR HALF AN HOUR

"MUGGY BOX"

PAUL LEWIS IS NAILED INSIDE AN UNVENTILLATED CRATE AND FLOWN TO MUMBAI IN THE SUMMER

"GIN OUR TIME"

MELVYN BRAGG AND HIS PANEL OF GUESTS DRINK A CASE OF GIN AND HAVE A MASSIVE FIGHT...

"LAG IN ACTION"

EX-CONVICTS GATHER IN THE STUDIO AND MOAN ABOUT THEIR CRAPPY LAWYERS...

"ANY ANGERS?"

JUST 'ANY ANSWERS' WITH A NEW NAME...

"GOO AND YOURS"

ENTIRE FAMILIES ARE COVERED IN CUSTARD FOR NO REASON...

"THE GOOD PROGRAMME"

ENOUGH SAID...

"FROM OUR GOWN CORRESPONDENT"

KATE ADIE FORCES BBC JOURNALISTS TO WEAR DRESSES...

I'M SOGGY & HAVEN'T A CLUE
FOOOSH
BARRY CRYER, TIM BROOKE TAYLOR & GRAEME GARDEN ARE HOSED DOWN FOR 30 MINUTES...

gremlins: little known facts

The word 'gremlin' was first recorded in 1923.
It may come from the Irish gruaimin, 'a bad-tempered little fellow'.
The word 'fact' was first recorded in 1539. It originally meant 'an evil deed'.

A dietician writes:
The staple diet of the
Gremlin is Hot Snot
and Bogey Pie.

Roald Dahl reputedly
popularised the Gremlin legend
during the Second World War,
when gremlins were blamed for
inexplicable mechanical failures
in fighter aircraft. But their
reputation lives on and they have
recently been held responsible for
the sub-prime crisis and for MP's
expenses. 'That's correct',
said a reliable source.

FYI:
Sir Dahl lived in
a shed and wrote
popular stories
for children.
His father was an
Indian take-away
dish and his
mother couldn't
spell Ronald*.

Gremlins are very
keen on staring
competitions and
will stare at you for
many days, possibly
even weeks, on end.

* Spelling mistake copyright Peter Spence, 1979

84

A baby Gremlin is called a 'heggessey'. The collective noun for Gremlins is a 'lorimer'.

A Gremlin will steal your braces at the most embarrassing time.

I dub thee, Sir Willie.

Gremlins at play.

Stephen Spielberg made a movie about Gremlins. 'It was hard work', one of Sir Spielberg's associates told our correspondent. 'They were pesky little creatures who kept breaking down the whole time. We used to blame them.'

Walt Disney first brought Gremlins to the cinema in the 1940s. Sir Disney originally dubbed his creations Michael and Donald Gremlin.

Is this true? – Ed.

Gremlin mashing potatoes.

Female Gremlin making off with a pizza cutter.

> Greetings, globe fans! Glanville Glibbthorpe here, with a gleeful glimpse into the glamorous world of GLOBES!

The GLOBAL GLEANINGS of GLANVILLE GLIBBTHORPE

Straight through the globe in 42 minutes and 12 seconds flat!

> If I dug a tunnel here, I could go through the earth in about twelve seconds...

> ...then for the other forty-two minutes I'd be here waiting for my luggage.

The biggest globe in the World is … the World!

And since the dawn of time Man has dreamed of digging a tunnel straight through the World and seeing where he comes out (go on, you know you have). So what's stopping him? Well, 40 miles[1] of rock for starters, followed by 8,000 miles[2] of white-hot magma for the main course, and then another 40 miles[1] of rock for pud.

It's easy to imagine that you might run over budget on a project like that.

But a man can have a dream, can't he? Here's mine: we've dug a tunnel from London to Sydney. We've built a frictionless train to run through the tunnel. For good measure, we've pumped all the air out of the tunnel so there's no wind resistance. Now all we need to know is: how long will it take us to get to Australia?

And here's the weird part: we know the answer, and we know it *exactly*, because it was worked out by Isaac Newton and his pen-pal Robert Hooke, 350 years ago. Here's what they figured: once your gravity train starts down the tunnel it'll fall like a jet-propelled stone. You'll pass the centre of the Earth doing 17,670mph[3], but then you'll start to slow down, until you reach the other end of the tunnel – where you'll stop, and then go all the way back again to where you came from, like a ball thrown into the air and falling back to earth. And those two old brain-boxes calculated how long each one-way trip would take: you'd go clear though the planet in 42 minutes and 12 seconds – exactly.

But suppose your tunnel didn't go right through the middle of the Earth? Suppose it went to New York, or Beijing, or Buenos Aires or somewhere. What then? This is the even weirder part: which-ever two points on the surface of the Earth you tunnelled between, the trip would take exactly the same time: 42 minutes and 12 seconds.

Realistically, it's not going to happen – there's just too much white-hot gunk in the way and, frankly, you may as well go by plane. **BUT:** on the *Moon*, it might be a different story. There's no molten core, no atmosphere, and no damn nimbys to tell you to go build your tunnel someplace else. So maybe the gravity train will be viable for real there one day. If so, here's another bit of weirdness. The Moon is only 2,000 miles[4] across, a quarter of the diameter of the Earth – but the trip would actually take longer there: 53 minutes, in fact. **Put *that* in your pipe and smoke it!**

Illustration: Ted Dewan

A Global Perspective from the Inside

Here's a problem with any Globe you care to name: whatever you do, you can't see more than half of it at a time. Or can you? An MP and geographer named James Wyld hit upon the answer in 1851, when he built a 60-foot[5] tall scale model of the Earth in London's Leicester Square – which could be looked at *from the inside*. All the land- masses and mountains and rivers were modelled in plaster of Paris on the inside surface of the sphere, lit by gas and viewed by Victorian visitors from platforms in the middle of the display. It was a popular attraction for eleven years. Sadly, in 1862, the lease on the land expired and it had to be demolished.

Apparently, everyone who visited Wyld's Globe loved the way it gave a truly accurate impression of the whole world all at once, simply by turning it outside-in. Curiously enough, you can make a mathematical model of the entire Universe inverted in this way: if we were living on the inside of a globe then the Sun would be 2.5[6] metres in diameter and every other star would be contained within a radius of 1mm[7] of the centre.

Now, much as I'd like to, I don't claim that we actually are living on the inside of the globe – but there have been people who really did think so. In the 1890s, Dr Cyrus Teed of New York convinced a substantial number of followers that they were doing just that – with the Sun, Moon and stars all floating in the middle of this huge sphere. Dr Teed built a device called a 'Rectilineator' to measure the curvature of the surface of the sea, and concluded that it was, sure enough, concave – which proved that he had been right all along!

Souvenir of WYLD'S GLOBE

The Globe Theatre

The Shakespearean theatre on the south bank of the Thames in London isn't globe-shaped and never was.

The modern version is a twenty-sided polygon, but it isn't a replica of the Elizabethan structure, as nobody knows quite what that was like. In fact, it's known to differ in a number of respects: the location is different for one thing. For another, in Elizabethan times the timbers would have been whitewashed – the dark timbers that we associate with Tudor buildings nowadays would appear distinctly odd to a Tudor time-traveller.

The original Globe burnt down on June 29th 1613 when a cannon being used on stage set the thatched roof alight. Only one person was hurt: a man whose britches were set on fire. He sorted himself out by pouring his ale on them.

A Globe of Salford

The globally respected presenter of the popular QI TV show once told a funny story about a man who went into a shop and said he wanted to buy a globe. They offered him a range of globes of the Earth, but he said he wanted a globe of Salford. Cue much laughter in QI-land. but it turns out that the laugh is on them, because 'Globes of Salford' really do exist; they are collectible old bottles with a globe logo on them, made by Groves and Whitnall of Salford. Wrong again, clever-clogs so-called QI Gnomes!

Well, that's the end of this glimpse into the glorious globe-tastic world of globes. Keep it global!

Your pal, Glanville Glibbthope

Glossoplegia

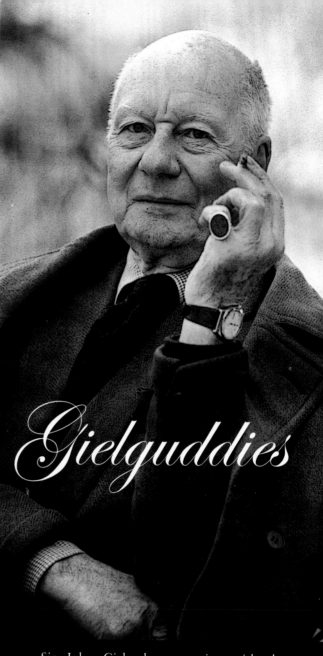

Gielguddies

Sir John Gielgud was eating with the playwright Edward Knoblock when an acquaintance walked past their table. '*Thank God he didn't stop,*' said Gielgud. '*He's a bigger bore than Eddie Knoblock… of course I don't mean you, Eddie.*'

Gielgud once remarked to Elizabeth Taylor: '*I don't know what's happened to Richard Burton. I think he married some terrible film star and had to live abroad.*'

Gielgud went to see Richard Burton in his first performance of *Hamlet* at the Old Vic and afterwards went backstage to take him out to dinner. The dressing room was packed, so Sir John shouted over the crowd: '*I'll go ahead, Richard. Come along when you're better – I mean, when you're ready.*'

Lunching with the theatre critic Kenneth Tynan who'd just seen a new play called *The Joint*, Gielgud asked what it was about. Tynan said: '*It's about a masochistic convict who keeps getting imprisoned because he likes being fucked by sadistic negro murderers.*' '*Well,*' said Sir John, '*You can't quarrel with that!*'

What is a pachyderm packing in its pants?

If they did wear underpants, African bull elephants would surely struggle to find any large enough to house their humungous happy lamp. For between their legs they maintain the largest love lighthouse of any land animal, with a penis measuring a metre or more in length. Their jumbo testes are located internally, as a pair of dangling bollocks weighing around 2 kilos (4lb 6oz) each would have an adverse effect on even the most agile elephant's gait. Each nad has a cubic capacity equivalent to that of a large football. A cow elephant's vagina measures 70 to 90 centimetres in length, and her clitoris a whopping 40 cm. Scientists believe that, because of their tusks, elephants don't do oral.

Genital Knowledge Quiz Question:

How do you MASTURBATE an elephant?

As tugging away at their cocks would be both dangerous and unproductive, when mammologists need to collect elephant sperm for insemination, one unfortunate individual has to shove their arm right up the animal's bottom and vigorously stimulate its prostate gland, while a colleague positions himself strategically... with a bucket.

Fuck a duck!

Most birds don't have dongs, but the Argentine lake duck definitely does have! For the drake is blessed with what genital experts are calling 'the Swiss army knife of knobs'. The duck's retractable multi-purpose corkscrew-style cock extends to a full-length of half-a-metre (17 inches). Duck cock experts speculate that these wondrous wangs act like a lasso for apprehending reluctant partners, and that their soft, brush-like bell ends might be used as a 'womb broom' to remove a competitor's sperm from the female's oviduct prior to ejaculation.

The human equivalent in terms of body length to penis size ratio would be a man with a six-foot chopper!

Let's look at... GIANT GENITALS

A focus on the fascinating world of very big reproductive organs

Words **Charlie Cheaplaugh**
Pictures **Tom Tracing-Paper**

Monsters of the deep

The largest testicles known to man are those of the right whale (also known as the Greenland whale, great whale or black whale) each knacker weighing in at 500kg (or 1,100lb). That's equivalent to the combined weight of Sir Elton John, at his least trim, playing a Steinway model D concert grand piano. But any underwater explorers hoping to catch a glimpse of these colossal conkers will be disappointed. Because like all other cetaceans, the whale keeps the family jewels tucked safely away inside.

Sir Elton John and barnacle's cock not drawn to scale

The unlikely king of the underwater cocks is the barnacle. In gentle waters barnacles develop long, flexible fun truncheons for greater reach. Those living in rougher water have shorter schlongs. A barnacle's John Bobbitt can grow up to eight times its body length, the longest trouser snake - relative to body size - of any animal.

Privates on parade

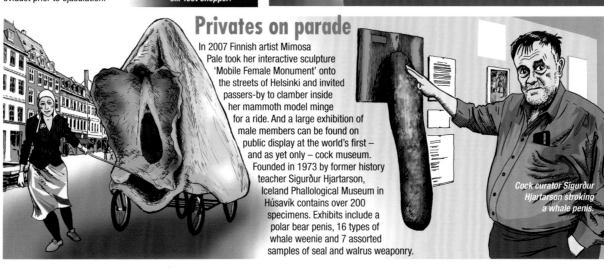

In 2007 Finnish artist Mimosa Pale took her interactive sculpture 'Mobile Female Monument' onto the streets of Helsinki and invited passers-by to clamber inside her mammoth model minge for a ride. And a large exhibition of male members can be found on public display at the world's first – and as yet only – cock museum. Founded in 1973 by former history teacher Sigurður Hjartarson, Iceland Phallological Museum in Húsavík contains over 200 specimens. Exhibits include a polar bear penis, 16 types of whale weenie and 7 assorted samples of seal and walrus weaponry.

Cock curator Sigurður Hjartarson stroking a whale penis.

How big was King Kong's dong?

It's the question which has been baffling cinema audiences ever since the original King Kong movie was released in 1933. And at last we have a definitive answer. Throughout the movie Kong's height varies, from 18 feet when he is discovered on Skull Island, to 60 feet during some scenes in New York. Kong's creator Merian C. Cooper, who wrote the original story, envisaged Kong being '40 to 50 feet tall'. But his fluctuating size on screen was due to animator Willis O'Brien and his crew who manipulated the giant ape's height by varying the scale of the miniatures and altering camera angles during the filming of special effect sequences.

A full-size bust of Kong used during the filming had been built in scale with a 40 foot ape, while RKO Pictures' promotional materials listed Kong's official height as 50 feet. Based on that official figure we can reveal that King Kong's dong would have measured a rather disappointing 13.7 inches – *on the bonk*. And his testicles would have weighed less than two cricket balls.

Real gorillas grow to about 5 feet 8 inches tall (1.7 metres) yet achieve an erection length of less than 2 inches! Their testes together weigh only 30 to 35 grams.

Giant's beanstalk

The Cerne Abbas Giant, carved into a hillside near Dorchester in Dorset, stands 180 feet tall and has a giant beanstalk measuring 30 feet from the tip of its bell end down to its biffin bridge. Local tradition has it that a giant was slain on the hillside and that the villagers of Cerne Abbot drew around his body to create the giant outline. That, with all due respect, is another big load of bollocks. The figure may represent the god Hercules and be of Iron Age or early Roman origin. But more recent research suggests that the giant carving, cut in the form of narrow trenches in the turf in order to expose the chalk below, may date from the 15th Century and be the work of an irreverent local land owner. Lord Denzil Holles, who owned the site between 1642 and 1666, was a fierce critic of Oliver Cromwell and the chalk man may have been designed to satirise Cromwell's puritanical ideals.

Giant toss-up between biggest cocks

Fish experts cannot say with any certainty which whale has the world's largest whanger. Both the right whale and blue whale are estimated to have 3 metre (10 foot) whalehoods. So it's a massive toss up for first prize. Three metres might seem impressive to a passing dolphin, but taking into account the blue whales' overall size – they can grow to a length of 30 metres (98 feet) and tip the scales at 180 tonnes – their 3 metre member is the equivalent of a human wielding a 10 centimetre pork sword.

How a big dick compares

MASSIVE · BIG · QUITE BIG · SMALL · TINY

UNITS OF WHALE COCK MEASUREMENT

At 1.85 metres in height Cristiano Ronaldo (right) is dwarfed by a blue whale's whanger.

Dino rods shrouded in mystery

Despite having museums stuffed full of dinosaur bones, paleontologists haven't got a clue how big their prehistoric boners used to be. However, the chances are they had a small vent tucked beneath their tail – a cloaca, like those of modern birds and reptiles – and whatever wedding tackle they did have at their disposal would be kept in there. On a more positive note, paleontologists can tell us that the world's oldest surviving penis is the 425-million-year-old fossilised member of an ocean-dwelling ostracode crustacean discovered in England during 2003 by scientists from Leicester University. They named it *Colymbosathon ecplecticosis*. Translated from Latin this means 'amazing swimmer with a large penis'.

'Oh yeah, baby!' No matter how big their tools were, dinosaurs (left) certainly knew how to use them.

Nigel's cock was too big

The biggest cock ever recorded measured an incredible 64 feet in length! But it didn't belong to a whale, a dinosaur or a giant monster from the movies. It was a massive metal monstrosity created by Sir Nigel Gresley, Chief Mechanical Engineer of the the London and North Eastern Railway. Gresley's gargantuan, powerful, rigid-bodied P2 class steam locomotive *Cock o'the North* was designed to *pound* up the steep gradients, *pump* its way around the shapely curves and *plunge* its streamlined front end deep into the moist, steamy tunnels of the Edinburgh to Aberdeen railway line. Built at Doncaster in 1934, *Cock o'the North* weighed 167 tons and had eight massive driving wheels, each measuring over 6 feet in diameter. Unfortunately due to track damage caused by its weight, over-heated *big ends*, hot *boxes* and the fact that some platforms were simply not big enough to accommodate the *Cock's* massive *load*, the engine was withdrawn in 1943 and rebuilt as a more manageable A2 class locomotive.

Sir Nigel Gresley, whose monstrous (if not somewhat tenuously defined) 'cock' was far too big.

GILFS
Goats I'd Like to Farm

BY SEAN LOCK, RETIRED GOATHERD

Although I am now a national celebrity and multi-millionaire*, I have always been a simple goatherd at heart. Here's my tribute to my beloved former colleagues from those happy days of my youth in Creuse, France

1: Goat Basics: When goat-herding there are really only two things you need to bear in mind:

1. There is nothing wrong with going to bed with someone of your own sex. People should be very free with sex, but they should draw the line at goats. SIR ELTON JOHN

2. By candlelight, a goat looks like a lady. FRENCH PROVERB

2: Goat Identification:

This is definitely a goat.

This looks quite like a goat, but isn't.

3: Goat Facts:

Ω There are about 480 million domestic goats in the world.

Ω China has far more goats than anywhere else: approximately 197 million of them. French gentlemen travelling to the Orient who are not of Sir Elton's persuasion should remember to carry a powerful torch.

Ω Goat soup is the national soup of Liberia. It is served at all important state functions.

Ω The ancient Greek word 'tragomaskalos' means 'with armpits smelling like a he-goat'. In Japan, you can get goat's milk and goat's meat-flavoured ice cream.**

Ω George Orwell had a pet goat called Muriel. She appears as a character in 'Animal Farm' – as the only animal that can read.

Ω A python can open its mouth wide enough to swallow a goat whole, but this is not good for either of them. The goats don't enjoy it at all and the pythons often die from the strain.

Ω The Mau Mau terrorists of Kenya in the 1950s initiated their guerrillas by making them have sex with goats. Or so they say. Kenyan rebel strongholds in the 1950s were very dimly lit. It could have been an honest mistake.

This is an artist's impression of me, in my herding uniform. For dramatic licence, the mountains behind are actually in Kazakhstan. The scenery in Creuse is very different – rolling farmland, lush wooded valleys and goats, goats, goats.

FAMOUS PEOPLE WHO BEGAN AS GOATHERDS: Genghis Khan, Pope Clement IX, George Orwell, Me, Kaldi, the legendary Ethiopian boy whose goats first discovered coffee.***

Without my morning coffee I'm just like a dried up piece of roast goat.

J.S. BACH (1685-1750) The Coffee Cantata

* Oh yes, ha bloody ha. ** Ben & Jerry's once made a rose-flavoured ice cream. It was tested before going on sale but abandoned almost immediately after one person who tried it remarked 'This tastes like my grandmother's armpit.' *** Google it! I don't see why I should do all the work here…

92

Goat-related puzzles

Goats are highly intelligent and enjoy problem solving – which ledge to stand on, where to go for lunch and so forth. I've never actually seen one do a crossword, but there's a first time for everything (as the bishop said to the goat!!!!).

5: Goatdoku

Place goats so that every square below has a goat on it.

4: Goatword

DOWN
1: A goat (1, 4)
2: (and 4 across) A cashmere goat (11)
3: Horned ruminant (4)

ACROSS
1: Not a goat (6)
3: Toga (anag.)
(Answers on page 98)

'She's doing porridge'.

'Oh no! Someone's invented gridlock!'

Gee-Kwiz!

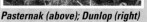

The Answers

GEOGRAPHY! *(Lots of forfeits in this round...)*

1. They don't ring The Lutine Bell (or 'a bell'). (MINUS 2)
The Lutine bell developed a crack and the practice of ringing news of lost ships has now ended. The last time the bell was used to announce the loss of a ship was in 1979 and the last time it rang a safe return was in 1989.

2. They don't have a siesta. (MINUS 2)
Less than half of Spaniards have a snooze in the afternoon. A study published in 2005 found Spaniards got an average of 40 minutes less sleep than the European average. Spanish men spend more time working or studying than their compatriots in Britain, Germany, Sweden and seven other northern European countries, a survey found.

3. It's not Liebfraumilch. (MINUS 2)
Liebfraumilch is made entirely for export. Most Germans have never even heard of it.

4. Hungary. (PLUS 2) **Not Italy.** (MINUS 2)

5. French Guiana or Guyane. (PLUS 2)
Guyane, a *Département* (DOM) of France, sends 2 deputies to the French National Assembly. One of them represents the largest constituency by land area in the French Republic.

6. Gabon. (PLUS 2)

7. There aren't any. (MINUS 2)
Uniquely, the Gulf of Gabes off the coast of Tunisia has an 8ft (2.4m) rise and fall.

8. The Metropolitan County of Greater Manchester. (PLUS 2) **Lancashire.** (MINUS 2)
Wigan has been part of the Metropolitan County of Greater Manchester since the Local Government Act, 1972.

The Lutine Bell

GARDENING!

1. Not Wales. (MINUS 2) **Asia.** (PLUS 2)
Welsh onions aren't native to Wales and have never been grown there to speak of. The word 'Welsh' is a corruption of Old English *welisc* and German *welsche* meaning 'foreign'. 'Welsh' onions originated in Asia: Chinese, Japanese and Korean all have their own words for them.

2. None of them are gooseberries. (PLUS 2)
They're all different kinds of shrub that resemble gooseberries or gooseberry bushes in some way. Chinese gooseberries are otherwise known as kiwi fruit.

3. A potato, which has 48, 2 more than humans. (PLUS 2)

4. Kew Gardens. (PLUS 2)
According to *Country Life* magazine.

5. 70,000. They're awfully small. (PLUS 2)

6. One. First name Boris. Pasternak is Russian for parsnip. (PLUS 2)

7. Garden hose, which he used to devise the first pneumatic tyre for his son's bicycle. (PLUS 2)

8. Not plums. (MINUS 2)
Dried grapes or raisins; sultanas, currants, almonds, figs, cherries, lemons, figs (2 POINTS FOR ANY OF THESE).

Pasternak (above); Dunlop (right)

G-MEN!

1. Garibaldi, Nice. (PLUS 2)
Garibaldi, the liberator of Italy, was born in what is now part of France. In those days, Nice belonged to the Duchy of Savoy, and was known as Nizza.

2. Gabor. (PLUS 2)
The nine husbands of Zsa Zsa Gabor (7 divorces, 1 annulment, I survivor) and Gábor Dénes aka Dennis Gabor, the British Hungarian inventor of the hologram and, incidentally, the flat screen TV in 1958, 30 years before Clive Sinclair. (His patent ran out in 1968 before it could be manufactured.)

3. Gandhi. (PLUS 2)
Quote is from Joe Morgenstern in the *Los Angeles Herald Examiner* (1983).

4. He was torpedoed (or drowned). (PLUS 2)
Pantaléon Enrique Granados y Campina (1867-1916) sailed to the US in 1916 to oversee the premiere of his masterpiece *Goyescas* at the New York Met. A White House summons to play for President Woodrow Wilson meant he missed his boat and, on his eventual way home to Spain, he and his wife were torpedoed and drowned.

5. Sir John Gielgud. (PLUS 2)
'I've dropped enough bricks to build another Great Wall of China.' *For more Gielguddies, turn to page 89.*

6. The distinguished Arab playwright, Sheik Zubair. (PLUS 2) Actually it was a joke (and quite a good one), originally made in a speech in 1988, but it was printed in *Playboy* as if he'd meant it and widely reported as such in the British press.

7. Galileo Galilei. (PLUS 2) The year was 1564.

8. Gabriele D'Annunzio (1863-1938). (PLUS 5)
D'Annunzio was an Italian nationalist playwright, poet and novelist. In 1919, with a small volunteer force, he occupied the town of Fiume, where he remained as dictator till 1921.

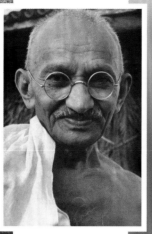

Galileo (left); Gandhi (centre) and the amazing hummingbird (above). Below, Jupiter's Great Red Spot.

GREATNESS!

1. Doris. (PLUS 2)

2. Bluetooth. (PLUS 2)

Gorm the Old began the Danish ruling dynasty. His son Harald Bluetooth succeeded him and completed the conquest of Denmark. Bluetooth's son was Sweyn Forkbeard and one of his grandsons, Canute the Great (1018-35) became a memorable King of England. The name Bluetooth was chosen to suggest Scandinavian unity.

3. Lincoln Cathedral. (PLUS 2)

For almost 300 years, from 1280 to 1549, Lincoln Cathedral was the tallest building in the world, its 525 ft/160 m tall spire overtaking the Great Pyramid. Though this collapsed due to bad weather in 1549, the cathedral kept the title till 1884 when the Washington Monument (555 ft 5⅛ in or about 169 m) was built.

4. Sir Winston Churchill. (PLUS TWO)

His son, John Churchill, the famous general, was created Duke of Marlborough by Queen Anne in 1702 – oddly enough before the victories for which he is remembered. His wife was a favourite of the Queen, but John had already been made Earl of Marlborough in 1689 by King William III.

5. Catherine the Great. (PLUS 2)

Like her grandmother-in-law Catherine I (a Lithuanian peasant christened Marta) she wasn't called Catherine and she wasn't Russian. She was Saxon. Zsa Zsa Gabor's present husband comes from the same family.

6. The Great Red Spot on Jupiter. (PLUS 2)

7. The swaddling clothes that wrapped the baby Jesus in the manger; the loincloth Christ wore at the Crucifixion; the Virgin Mary's cloak; the cloth that John the Baptist's head was wrapped in after he was decapitated. (PLUS 2 FOR EACH ONE)

8. The orrery. (PLUS 2)

A mechanical model of the Solar System. Commissioned by and named after Charles Boyle, 4th Earl of Orrery.

GENERAL IGNORANCE!

1. Five, including a silent one. (PLUS 2)

All can be seen in the phrase 'mighty rough garage gin'.

2. Ganymede, one of the moons of Jupiter. (PLUS 2)

Larger in diameter than the planet Mercury, it has only half its mass. It has the highest mass of all planetary satellites – twice that of the Earth's moon. Ganymede's discovery is credited to Galileo Galilei, who observed it in 1610.

3. Five. (PLUS 2)

The Milky Way, Andromeda, The Large & Small Magellanic Clouds and the Triangulum. They're not all visible from both hemispheres at once, and you need pretty good eyesight for a couple of them.

4. Herod the Great. (PLUS 2)

5. The Gateshead Millennium Bridge. (PLUS 2)

Linking Gateshead and Newcastle across the Tyne, it's the world's first, most energy efficient and (so far) only tilting bridge. It sits on 19,000 tonnes of concrete and cost £22 million to build.

6. Gas. (PLUS 2)

Van Helmont also invented the word 'blas' (meaning astral radiation) but it didn't catch on. Unlike gas. Even George W. Bush knows what that means: 'Natural gas is hemispheric. I like to call it hemispheric in nature because it is a product that we can find in our neighbourhoods.'

7. A hummingbird. (PLUS 2)

For its size that is, measured in body lengths per second (bps). They do this amazing dive when courting. Jet fighter: 150 bps; Peregrine falcon: 200 bps; Space shuttle: 207 bps; Hummingbird: 385 bps.

8. He invented the letter 'G'. (PLUS 2)

In around 200 BC, according to Plutarch. Latin originally had no letter G at all: the hard 'C', 'K' and 'G' sounds were all represented by 'C'. Ruga was also the first man in recorded history to open a private elementary school.

GUESS THE GEOFF

1. This Geoffrey was the most prolifically talented comedy producer of his generation and the nicest man you could possibly meet. Sadly missed by us all at QI.

2. This Geoffrey nearly died aged eight when he fell onto some iron spikes. He once famously said: 'I'm glad two sides of the cherry have been put forward.'

3. This Geoffrey is the only footballer in the world to have scored a hat trick in a World Cup Final – one goal with each foot and one with his head.

4. Known as 'the Geoffrey Boycott of gardening', this Geoffrey described rosemary as 'the bowler, batsman, slip fielder and captain of the herbal cricketing world'.

5. This Geoffrey is the only actor to have appeared in all top three of the BFI's 100 Greatest British TV Programmes: Fawlty Towers, Cathy Come Home and Dr Who.

6. This Geoffrey turned down offers to play the first two Doctor Whos, became famous as Catweazle, and later became the oldest Doctor Who ever.

7. This Geoffrey wrote some of the best-loved TV ads. The first British copywriter to earn £100K per year, his surname is advertising industry slang for a six-figure salary.

8. This Geoffrey began climbing rooftops while at Cambridge University. Despite having a leg amputated in the First World War, he went on to scale the Matterhorn in 1928.

9. This Geoffrey is one of only 20 people in the world to have won an Oscar, a Tony and an Emmy - the so-called 'Triple Crown' of show business.

10. This Geoffrey was a diplomat, scrap metal merchant, philosopher, spy, civil servant, courtier, prisoner of war, customs official, Member of Parliament and poet.

11. This Geoffrey once lectured Africans in Swahili, urging loyalty to 'Bwana Kingy George'. Being attacked by him was said to be 'like being savaged by a dead sheep'.

12. This Geoffrey drew all the other Geoffreys. He has been quoted as saying 'Single stick-figures can be just as exciting as 500 flopsy bunnies' and 'A large one, please.'

G's the fifth note in the scale of C major;
GG is a beast, on which you can wager.
GB is our land - and next former Prime Minister;
GM food is abundant, but frankly quite sinister.
GC marks great courage (not always in battle);
GLC was the place where bores went to prattle.
GBH rearranges your face into Gollum's;
GSOH is a must in personal columns.
GI Joes are all trained to follow instructions;
GBP's worth a dollar (after deductions).
GDP tells economists what we can afford;
GNP is the same – plus our earnings abroad.
GDR was a country, decidedly creepy;
GCSEs must never be tackled when sleepy.
GCHQ is in charge of tracking down spies;
GSR may be found when your worst enemy dies.
GWR is a railway (alas great no more);
G20's a forum (Sorry! No poor!).
GTA's not your game if violence offends
GPS has a woman who drives you round bends
GESTAPO were very unlike Sergeant Dixon;
G-strings aren't much better than having no knicks on.
GIB is a rock that's the home of some monkeys;
GQ readers believe that they're what a real hunk is.
GBS won an Oscar for writing 'Pygmalion';
Gina G sang for Britain but's really Australian.
G Spot marks a treasure that's deep in a cavity;
G Force is acceleration, relative to gravity.
G-Plan's retro furniture – not my style, I'll admit;
G&T is quite fizzy (unlike Gin and It);
GSK are the makers of Lucozade and pills;
GTIs are the cars that go faster up hills.
G Whizz! is a cry of surprise or delight;
GMT just keeps going all day and all night.
And let's not forget GATT, GEC, GMC -
But for now,
I must rush,
Toodle-pip,
GTG!

GB Great Britain, Gordon Brown; **GM** Genetically Modified; **GC** George Cross (the highest civilian award for gallantry); **GLC** Greater London Council (the capital's former local government body); **GBH** Grievous Bodily Harm; **GSOH** Good Sense Of Humour; **GI** Galvanised Iron*; **GBP** Great Britain Pound (Sterling); **GDP** Gross Domestic Product; **GNP** Gross National Product; **GDR** German Democratic Republic (the communist former East Germany); **GCSE** General Certificate of Secondary Education; **GCHQ** Government Communications Headquarters; **GSR** Gun Shot Residue; **GWR** Great Western Railway; **G20** Group (of finance ministers and heads of national banks of the world's) 20 (richest economies); **GTA** Grand Theft Auto; **GPS** Global Positioning System; **GESTAPO GE**heime **STA**ats **PO**lizei (Secret State Police); **GQ** Gentlemen's Quarterly; **GBS** George Bernard Shaw; **G Spot** Gräfenberg spot**; **GSK** GlaxoSmithKline; **GTI** Gran Turismo Injection; **GMT** Greenwich Mean Time; **GATT** General Agreement on Tariffs and Trade (UN agency); **GEC** General Electric Company; **GMC** General Medical Council; **GTG** Got To Go.

*GI (meaning a private soldier in the US army) is sometimes incorrectly said to stand for 'General Infantry', but in fact it has never meant that. The initials were originally used on government inventories to signify equipment made of galvanized iron. This was assumed (again incorrectly) to mean 'Government Issue', and thus applied to anything to do with the army. This stuck and was then adopted officially. So 'Government Issue' is another possible meaning of GI.

**The supposed (and possibly mythical) erogenous zone is named after German gynaecologist Ernst Gräfenberg (1881-1957), who theorised its existence in 1950.

The QI Annual was researched, written, illustrated, photographed and otherwise enhanced by Clive Anderson, Rowan Atkinson, Bill Bailey, Jacqueline Bisset, Craig Brown, Stevyn Colgan, Mat Coward, Jonathan Cusick, Cherry Denman, Ted Dewan, Chris Donald, Geoff Dunbar, Hunt Emerson, Arron Ferster, Piers Fletcher, Nadia Flower, Stephen Fry, James Harkin, Andy Hollingworth, Tony Husband, Gray Jolliffe, Phill Jupitus, Roger Law, John Lloyd, Sean Lock, Laura Maddison, Jim Marks, Andy Murray, Nick Newman, Graham Norton, Molly Oldfield, Justin Pollard, Matt Pritchett, Brian Ritchie, Katie Scott, Adrian Teal and Robert Thompson.

The QI Annual features Stephen Fry, Alan Davies and the guest panellists from the QI TV 'G' series: Ronni Ancona, Clive Anderson, Bill Bailey, Danny Baker, Jo Brand, Rob Brydon, Jimmy Carr, Jeremy Clarkson, Jack Dee, Hugh Dennis, Rich Hall, Andy Hamilton, Barry Humphries, Phill Jupitus, Sean Lock, Lee Mack, David Mitchell, Graham Norton, Dara O'Briain, Sue Perkins, Jan Ravens, Liza Tarbuck, David Tennant, Sandi Toksvig and Johnny Vegas.

Designed by David Costa (david@whereforeart.com)
Cover illustration: Jonathan Cusick (www.jonathancusick.com)

Editorial: Sarah Lloyd.
Editorial Administrator: Liz Townsend.

Picture Research: Liz Townsend and David Costa.

Photography by: Andy Hollingworth (andyhollingworth@me.com) with assistant Matthew Evered for 'The Gambler'; Andy Hollingworth with Moira Chapman as stylist for 'Bill Bailey's Air Guitar Masterclass'; Jim Marks (www.marks.co.uk) for 'Five Go Gallivanting After Ghosts'; Brian Ritchie (brian@brianjritchie.com) for the QI production photographs; photographs of the guinea pig in 'Are You A Guinea Genius' and 'Glee' taken by Kate Kessling (www.contrarypress.com)

The QI researchers and writers were: Mat Coward; Arron Ferster; Piers Fletcher; James Harkin; John Lloyd; Laura Maddison; John Mitchinson; Andy Murray; Molly Oldfield and Justin Pollard.

QI Logo design: Jules Bailey

With special thanks to Nicholas Johnston and Jo Jakemen of the Great Tew Estate for allowing us access to Tew Park; Caitlin Lloyd for the loan of 'Guin'; and Dinah Howland for the loan of her Tarot collection.

PHOTO CREDITS: Bigstockphotos (www.bigstockphoto.com) for bullet holes in 'Gallery of Goons'; 'Goatherd', except Mr Mountain Goat image from 'The Mountain and the Molehill', Normalsville Books, provided courtesy of Frank Newman and Pursuit Publishing (NZ) Ltd (www.pursuit.co.nz); silhouette background in 'Golf' and 'I Spy Gravel' pictures, except Justin Pollard for 'Gravel Collection'; Michael Davis, Clearwater, Florida, USA for pay dirt; bybee.com for Sisyphus; Mediscan for kidney stone, and Piedmont Gravel and Bench Gravel which were reproduced by permission of the British Geological Survey © NERC. All rights reserved. IPR/117-46CT. Mary Evans Picture Library for title page images; backgrounds 'Gee-Kwiz' and 'Gee-Kwiz Answers' and featured Gooseberry and Orrery; 'Geese' except feather & inkwell and white goose, courtesy of Getty Images. Getty Images for giraffe skin in 'Giraffes'; 'Gee-Kwiz Answers' and 'Guinea Genius', 'Gielguddies'; and the featured photos in 'Golf' except Arikikapakapa, courtesy of Paul Fowler (www.paulfowler.co.nz). NASA for 'Galaxies'.

THE ANSWER TO THE QI SUDO–N'KO IS AVAILABLE FROM WWW.QI.COM

ANSWERS TO 'GUESS THE GEOFF' (P96):
1. *Geoffrey Perkins (1953-2008)*
2. *Geoffrey Boycott, OBE (1940-)*
3. *Sir Geoffrey 'Geoff' Hurst, MBE (1941-)*
4. *Geoffrey Smith (1928-2009)*
5. *Geoffrey Palmer, OBE (1927-)*
6. *Geoffrey Bayldon (1924-)*
7. *Geoffrey Seymour (1947-2008)*
8. *Geoffrey Winthrop-Young (1876 -1958)*
9. *Geoffrey Rush (1951-)*
10. *Geoffrey Chaucer (1343-1400)*
11. *The Rt Hon. The Lord (Geoffrey) Howe of Aberavon, CH, PC, QC (1926-)*
12. *Geoffrey 'Geoff' Dunbar (1944-)*

ANSWERS TO 'GOATWORD' (P93)

Waiting for Mrs Godot

GIBBOUS Gecko geek
GBH Grandiflora
Girandole GRINLING
GWHIZZ GIBBONS
GERONIMO
GUT GROPE
O Glasnost
gothic Galvanise
greenhouse effect
Grin
GUEVARA
GOO
GASTROPOD
galactagogue
GAOⅢ
GIIZEBOI Googly

a Ginormous
Glut of G-ness
from
Galaxies, Gods
and Gravity,
to
Gin, Gnus and Gravel

Goose facts!
Giraffe tips!
air Guitar tutoria

plus!!!

everything you
never wanted to
know about
Grahams!

Gravel